Women of Faith

Women of Faith

The Chicago Sisters of Mercy and the Evolution of a Religious Community

Mary Beth Fraser Connolly

Fordham University Press | New York 2014

Fordham University Press has no responsibility for the persistence or accuracy of URLs for external or third-party Internet websites referred to in this publication and does not guarantee that any content on such websites is, or will remain, accurate or appropriate.

Fordham University Press also publishes its books in a variety of electronic formats. Some content that appears in print may not be available in electronic books.

Library of Congress Cataloging-in-Publication Data is available from the publisher.

Printed in the United States of America
16 15 14   5 4 3 2 1
First edition

For Michael

Contents

Illustrations

Acknowledgments

Over the past six years, I have accumulated a long list of people to thank for their help and support as I worked on this book. I only hope that I have found the right words to express my gratitude. What follows is my feeble attempt to thank the many colleagues, friends, and family who have buoyed me along the way.

After the Sisters of Mercy Chicago Regional Community decided to join other regional communities within the Sisters of Mercy of the Americas and form the West Midwest, they chose to hire a professional historian to write their long history. They formed a committee of five Sisters of Mercy and two outside scholars to act as a collaborative and supportive body for me as I researched and wrote this book. This project would be nowhere without their constant presence. I wish to thank Dominic Pacyga; Malachy McCarthy; Mary Ruth Broz, RSM; Nancy Houlihan, RSM; Margaret Mary Knittel, RSM; Joy Clough, RSM; and Joella Cunnane, RSM. I am grateful for their time, their reading (and more reading) of the drafts of the manuscript, and, more important, for the Sisters of Mercy on the committee, their trust that I would respect their community and their history. I will miss our conversations and debates as I tested out the structure of the book and hashed out content of the chapters. I am particularly grateful to Sister Joella; as archivist, she welcomed me into the Sisters of Mercy's history and guided me through the many boxes of records. She also graciously introduced me to the members of the Chicago Regional Community.

I also wish to thank Betty Smith, RSM; Sheila Megley, RSM; Sharon Kerrigan, RSM; and Lois Graver, RSM. They, along with Sister Mary Ruth Broz as the Administrative Team of the Chicago Regional Community, supported this project from its conception. I am particularly grateful to Sister Sheila Megley, who with the rest of the West Midwest Community Leadership Team continued to champion this history. For much of the time during which I conducted my research in the archives at the

Chicago Regional Community Center (now Mercy Meeting Place), I had the good fortune to inhabit an office with the regional community Administrative Team and the sisters and laywomen who staffed this building. I learned as much, if not more, about Mercy charism by joining in breaks and lunches with the women who worked in this building (and those who dropped in for a visit) than from the archival records. I am grateful to Mary Jo Valenti; Nancy Pepper; Carol Miller; Delmis Cruz-Menjivar; Mary Golden, RSM; Patricia M. Murphy, RSM; JoAnn Persch, RSM; Kathleen McClelland, RSM; Marie Shawn Grassberger, RSM; Margaret Johnson, RSM; and Dolores Zurek, RSM, for their hospitality and kindness.

The list of Sisters of Mercy to whom I owe thanks is long. I am especially grateful to the women who agreed to speak with me about their ministerial, spiritual, and community life as a Sister of Mercy. Catherine McAuley's spirit is alive and well in these women.

When I was not trolling the archives, I pestered the librarians at Purdue University North Central. During the research and initial writing phase of this project, I was aided by K. R. Johnson, Librarian; April Milam, Public Services Library Assistant; and Susan Anderson, Library Assistant. Ms. Milam and Ms. Anderson, in particular, helped me find much needed primary sources. I am particularly grateful for their patience when I kept an interlibrary loan book (or two) a little past the due date. Furthermore, I want to thank the faculty of the Social Sciences Department of Purdue North Central, who expressed interest in my work, and offered friendship along the way.

The editors and staff at Fordham University Press, particularly Fred Nachbaur, Katie Sweeney, Eric Newman, and Nancy Rapoport, showed me much patience as I eagerly sought to revise this manuscript for publication.

I am grateful to my colleagues at the Lilly Fellows Program in Humanities and the Arts. Over the last two and a half years, Kathy Sutherland, Program Coordinator, and Joe Creech, Program Director, have listened as I rambled on about chapter revisions and made space for me to finish this book. I want to thank the Postdoctoral fellows who listened patiently as I impressed upon them the importance of the Sisters of Mercy and women religious in general. I am grateful to fellows, both former and current, with whom I worked: Jen Miller, Linn Tonstad, Jason Crawford, Mina Suk, Piotr Malysz, Katherine Calloway Sueda, Robert Elder, Charles Strauss, Anna Stewart, and George David Clark. The community of Linwood House at Valparaiso University, the home of the Lilly Fellows Program, has sustained me over the last few years.

The community of scholars who engage in the history of women religious has grown over the last decades, but it has not lost its closeness and cooperative nature. I am grateful particularly to the participants of the Conference on the History of Women Religious, where I have found my intellectual home. I am grateful to Carmen Mangion, Margaret Susan Thompson, and Kathleen Sprows Cummings, among others who have, over the years, become valued colleagues and friends. Their scholarship, along with that of the many participants of the HWR Conferences, has inspired and challenged me to be a better historian. I want to thank especially those who have read and commented on early drafts and papers that went into the final project. I am particularly grateful to Margaret McGuinness, Elizabeth Smyth, and Suellen Hoy who read and gave suggestions on parts or all of the manuscript.

I am also blessed with the long-time friendship of Jeremy Bonner. Our friendship forged in graduate school at The Catholic University of America has persisted over the years, and I continue to rely on his advice and input in my scholarship. Another source of constant support and friendship has been Dolores Liptak, RSM, whom I came to know first through her scholarship, and then through her guidance of my work as a historian of women religious. I am grateful to Beth Leimbach Zambone for her friendship, and I value her keen mind and excellent editing skills. Beth graciously offered to help edit parts of this manuscript as I pushed to finish.

I owe the biggest debt of gratitude to those closest to me. My family has been patient, dutifully curious, and constant in their support. They have listened to me as I detailed exciting finds in the archives and talked through chapter ideas. I am grateful to Michael and Dianne Connolly, my in-laws and second parents, for their love and support. I am thankful that my brother-in-law, Pete Bernhard, let me bounce ideas off of him and gave me encouragement. My brother, Tom Fraser, (lovingly) pestered me as only an older brother can, asking if I was done yet. I am particularly thankful for the women of faith in my family. I am grateful for the free theology advice of my sister-in-law, Diane Michutka Fraser, who helped me navigate the nuances of post–Vatican II Catholic theology; for my mother, Mary Fraser, who has her own connection with the Mercys as teachers and as health care professionals, who willingly talked for hours and hours about growing up Catholic in America; and for my sister, Christine Fraser Bernhard, who read parts of this book, who is my touchstone, and who helps me speak with a clear and steady voice.

Last, I thank my long-suffering husband, Michael J. Connolly. One may argue there are negative consequences to two historians' marrying, not the least of which is the danger that our house will collapse under the weight of all the books, papers, and clutter. The reality is that I have a constant companion who understands my shorthand, who gets my long hours, who is always eager to read and help me with my work, and who reminds me to have a sense of humor. I dedicate this book to him.

Women of Faith

Introduction: "One Solid Comfort"

We have one solid comfort amidst this little tripping about: our hearts can al-
ways be in the same place, centered in God—for whom alone we go forward—or
stay back. Oh may He look on us with love and pity, and then we shall be able
to do anything He wishes us to do—no matter how difficult to accomplish—or
painful to our feelings. If He looks on us with approbation for one instant each
day—it will be sufficient to bring us joyfully on to the end of our journey. Let us
implore Him to do so at this season of love and Mercy.[1]

On December 20, 1840, Catherine McAuley, the foundress of the Sisters
of Mercy in Ireland, wrote Sister Mary de Sales White at the Bermondsey convent in London, England, saying, "I think sometimes our passage
through this dear sweet world is something like the Dance called 'right and
left.'" She continued with a description of the dance, incorporating the locations of various Mercy convents in Ireland and England with each turn
on the dance floor. McAuley used a metaphor of a dance to stress to Sister
Mary de Sales the temporality of the Sisters of Mercy in the world. She
wrote, "You and I have crossed over, changed places; your set is finished—
for a little time you'll dance no more—but I have now to go through the
figure." Each Sister of Mercy had her part to play in the dance, but no
single sister was more important than the whole movement; as one Sister
of Mercy remains behind, another goes forward into the world. Mother
Catherine continued her letter in a more pointed tone and described her
community's evolving life and movement throughout the world as "this
little tripping about" where only with God's help and will did they act.
When she wrote this letter in late 1840, McAuley did not know how her
community would grow and flourish throughout the world; she could only
rely on one essential component to all the works of mercy she and other
members of her community did: Wherever they went, their hearts were
"centered in God."[2]

McAuley's writings stand as her legacy to the generations of women
religious who came after her.[3] As Mary C. Sullivan, RSM, has shown,

McAuley was a tireless correspondent, writing to the various mother-houses founded from the original convent on Baggot Street in Dublin. By McAuley's design, when a new Mercy foundation or convent was established in a different location, it became separate from its parent house. Yet McAuley continued to communicate with and care about the sisters within these new convents, maintaining spiritual and emotional ties to them even though she was no longer their superior. When the Sisters of Mercy lost their foundress in 1841, stories of Mother Catherine passed on from one generation of sisters to the next. Her letters and spiritual writings and the congregation's Rule and Constitutions became her legacy. All religious congregations have Rules and Constitutions, which provide the governing structure and direct daily life.[4] As foundational documents, the Rule and Constitutions also embody the spirit of their authors. In this way, McAuley's Rule and Constitutions, along with her spiritual writings and correspondence, communicate the Mercys' founding charism. Each generation of Sisters of Mercy who came after her took these words and her spirit with them as they established new communities or foundations. McAuley established the original Sisters of Mercy and instructed and guided her sisters in the charism, or spiritual foundation, of the community. Mercys look to this charism to inspire and guide each other and those with whom they work, regardless of location, institution, or ministry.[5]

Raised by a wealthy, non-Catholic aunt and uncle in late-eighteenth-century Ireland, McAuley had money, education, and social status. However, instead of marriage, motherhood, an entrée into the growing middle-class Catholic society in Dublin, and a potential life as an influential and benevolent patron, she chose a vowed religious life in a religious institute of her own design, where she used her talents and gifts to alleviate the suffering of those around her. Her Catholic faith informed her choice, and countless other women made similar choices.

McAuley's choices were her own, though she did not make them in isolation. The Sisters of Mercy's foundress fits within a larger movement of women and men who sought to revive the Catholic Church in Ireland during the late eighteenth and early nineteenth centuries. Religious communities of women that developed as early as the mid-eighteenth century played a pivotal role in the cultural and religious revival of this period, as did the small middle class,[6] of which McAuley was a part, that emerged by the early nineteenth century. McAuley sought an active expression of her faith, as did other foundresses of religious communities for women, such as Honora Nagle (the Presentation Sisters, 1775) and Mary Aikenhead (the

Religious Sisters of Charity, 1815). She possessed a desire to work with the poor of Ireland, but not simply as a benevolent "lady bountiful."[7] By 1823, McAuley had inherited enough money to support her charitable work, but she wished for a deeper commitment to the poor than she believed her contemporary wealthy laywomen possessed. What she desired was a committed religious life to serve God and to be with the suffering poor. Voluntary poverty was an essential element of McAuley's conception of this life. She saw it not as a "requirement of religious life," but rather as "a necessity if they [the Sisters of Mercy] wished to live in credible solidarity with the impoverished people among whom they served, the 'have nots' of their world." Her dedication to the poor reflected a desire to follow the example of Jesus Christ on earth.[8]

Other women shared McAuley's vision for an active religious life, and the Sisters of Mercy grew from a small group of women in Dublin into an international community. Each new foundation developed within the context of its own society as it adapted to local needs, church officials, and personalities. Yet the spirit of the founding institute and the Rule and Constitutions provided instruction in how to live as Religious Sisters of Mercy. The growth and expansion of the Sisters of Mercy meant establishing schools, hospitals, and Houses of Mercy, the community's homes and shelters for working women, as well as staffing parish schools and providing orphan care. It meant creating and administrating institutions that were symbols of the Catholic Church in Ireland, England, and beyond. In the United States, by the mid–twentieth century, the Sisters of Mercy became identified with many of these institutions. They, along with other women religious, built the American Catholic Church infrastructure, which educated and cared for the laity for well over a century.

Catherine McAuley's Legacy in America

This study is a history of the Chicago Regional Community of the Sisters of Mercy,[9] but it is more than the story of the institutions that defined the territory and ministries of the women of this Midwestern region. This is a history of the women, the Sisters of Mercy, who made this regional community, whether as the foundresses of individual communities in Wisconsin, Iowa, and Illinois in the nineteenth and early twentieth centuries or as the teachers, nurses, and pastoral ministers who cared for and educated generations of Midwestern American Catholics. Although they had no immediate connection with McAuley, these women inherited her spirit and vision for religious life. Countless women in Illinois, Iowa, and Wisconsin discerned that they were called or were meant to enter a religious congregation, and they chose the Sisters of Mercy. They did not universally do this because they had a specific connection to McAuley; rather, they were drawn to the spirit and the life to which she gave birth in early nineteenth century Ireland.

The Sisters of Mercy of the Chicago Regional Community are just one facet of Catherine McAuley's legacy in America. They, like other regional Mercy communities, began as separate and independent foundations or convents in the nineteenth century. Just as the Catholic Church of 1830s Ireland needed women like McAuley to care for and educate countless impoverished (both materially and spiritually) Catholics, so did the church in the United States require McAuley's sisters to tend to a predominantly Irish immigrant population in America. While Catherine McAuley uses the phrase "tripping about" to characterize the impermanence of her travels through the world, in another way these words conjure images of effortless or easy "journeys out" from Ireland and across America to provide comfort and support to immigrant Catholics. In reality, arduous and lengthy travels confronted women religious who used ships, wagons, and eventually trains in the nineteenth century as they crossed the Atlantic Ocean and traversed rugged terrain in small groups or in some cases alone to conduct their missions.[10]

Mother Frances Xavier Warde, one of founding Sisters of Mercy in Ireland, brought the Irish Community to America in 1843. She and six young women, not all of whom were fully professed, made the first foundation in the United States in Pittsburgh, Pennsylvania. Three years after coming to Pittsburgh, she set out with five young women for Chicago, establishing the first religious community in that city. Over the next 162 years, the presence of the Sisters of Mercy expanded in the Midwest, and by the early twentieth century, eight independent Mercy communities developed throughout northern Illinois, Iowa, and Wisconsin that would make up the Chicago Regional Community. In the nineteenth and early twentieth centuries, whenever a group of Sisters of Mercy established a new foundation, it became an independent community, answering to a local religious authority. Yet, the common spirit rooted in their foundress, Catherine McAuley, tied sisters from disparate motherhouses together. While independent foundations, the Chicago South Side, Chicago West Side, Ottawa, Aurora, Davenport, Iowa City, Janesville, and Milwaukee motherhouses each shared in the same Mercy spirit, or charism, handed down to them from Catherine McAuley as they led vowed lives dedicated to God, each other, and the institutional Church. The Mercys shared religious identity, regardless of local differences and nuances, which makes the history of the Chicago Regional Community unique and compelling.[11]

That unity of spirit became instrumental as the Sisters of Mercy evolved and grew throughout the twentieth century. First in 1929, then in 1991, Mercy communities merged to create first the Sisters of Mercy of the Union, then Institute. These were new, unified, and centralized forms of religious government and affiliation, which united previously independent motherhouses into one larger province. The first merger, known as the amalgamation, brought the eight foundations of this study into one Chicago Province. The second merger in 1991, which created the Institute of the Sisters of Mercy of the Americas, did not alter the configuration of the Chicago Province. Rather, it gave it a new name, the Sisters of Mercy of the Chicago Regional Community, and expanded the identity of the sisters within this territory. They were at this point members of the larger Sisters of Mercy of the Americas. With a new name, but with the same Mercy spirit, they found unity in the charism of their religious institute, the spirit of Catherine McAuley.

Women of Faith

How did these changes affect how the Chicago Mercys understood their religious life and identity as sisters? Women's historians and historians of religion have commented on and brought to light the important relationship between faith and women's identities. Religious faith—a specific belief in God and participation in a church—was fundamental to how many women constructed their lives, related to their families, and moved through society. The extent of their devotion to a particular theology or doctrine inspired women to care about their own salvation as well as the condition of their husband's and children's souls. It might also have compelled them to care about their neighbor's salvation and the condition of the poor in their society, leading them to a life of public activism for a myriad of causes, from temperance to the rescuing of prostitutes. In fact, these activities led some women to demand political equality in the United States. Religion or church participation as a pathway to political activism in the nineteenth century is one of the established narratives of women's history. For example, antebellum Protestant benevolent reformers, like Elizabeth Cady Stanton, championed both moral reform and the vote for women. Faith inspired countless women to organize and fight against the sale and consumption of alcohol, which resulted in a national movement by the twentieth century and a full embrace of women's right to vote. In other times, women's faith bolstered their strength to resist oppression, as in the case of enslaved women in the antebellum American South.[12] Religious devotion empowered women to persevere and to move beyond the limitations placed upon them.[13]

These are clear-cut examples of the positive impact that religious belief and church affiliation had upon women's lives. The relevance of faith and the nature of women's identity and worldview become murky when we contemplate the less obvious connections to belief and action. In one sense, according to this traditional narrative, religious belief inspires women to embrace public activism and women's rights. Once moved into this public sphere, involvement in political and social causes and advancement in employment and education become the important story, and women's faith becomes a less significant part, albeit an interesting curiosity, of women's history. Faithful women who did not embark upon this journey to liberation, who chose to remain and support a church that did not make room for their total equality, confound and challenge this understanding of the past. In reality, women of faith did not compartmentalize their lives as well as historians have done it for them. The lives of women religious, like the Sisters of Mercy, provide rich examples of how faith cannot be separated from identity.

A closer look at a community of Catholic women religious is, in one sense, almost too obvious a challenge for this narrative. As Catholic sisters, faith was at the forefront of their identities. Yet this affiliation and identification as women religious has had the negative consequence of boxing women into a limited conception of who they were. They are often seen by their contemporaries and historians as the "good sisters," but this pejorative moniker robs these women of their rich and complex history and conflates their identities with the institutions they owned and staffed, making them nearly indistinguishable as people at best and treating them as interchangeable parts or tools within the larger institutional Catholic Church at worst.

Knowing more about Catherine McAuley and *why* she inspired generations of Sisters of Mercy is one means of bringing the history and identities of the Sisters of Mercy into better focus. Understanding *how* religious life called and sustained women in the nineteenth and twentieth centuries opens up a new view of how sisters conceptualized their spiritual lives, community, and ministries. The Sisters of Mercy from Ireland did not arrive in America and remain unchanged. Expansion and incorporation of new members over time, both Irish and American-born and of diverse ethnic origins, altered the organization's composition. Movement into new regions, whether emerging cities such as Chicago or rural towns in Iowa, required creativity and adaptability. All these variables factored into these women's choices, but their faith and relationship with their Church also enriches our understanding of their past.

McAuley sought an active expression of her faith, and she found it in the establishment of a religious institute, the Sisters of Mercy. From 1831 onward, other Catholic women have found a similar manifestation of their desire to serve God by becoming Sisters of Mercy. All of what went into who they were at various points in history contributed to their individual choices to enter a Mercy community, whether in Ireland or the United States. This study examines the history of women who chose this life in the Sisters of Mercy Chicago Regional Community. At the center of this decision, as McAuley articulated it, were God and their faith in what God intended for them. Motivated by faith and by a desire to be a part of a larger religious community of women, they bound their lives to the Sisters of Mercy.

Over the past ten to fifteen years, growing numbers of historians of women and religion have turned their attention to Catholic women religious. These subdisciplines of history had once only viewed sisters in discrete categories like the "good sisters" and the shadowy figures behind convent walls. They were considered women of little consequence to the advancement of women in society and in churches. Now, more historians incorporate questions about women who lived vowed lives into their narratives and seek out the study of religious communities like the Sisters of Mercy. Historians such as Carol Coburn and Martha Smith, CSJ, have examined religious communities over time and fit women religious within the larger context of American and Catholic history. With their 1999 study of the Sisters of St. Joseph of Carondelet, *Spirited Lives: How Nuns Shaped Catholic Culture and American Life, 1836–1920,* Coburn and Smith set the new standard for community history. Historians have enlivened the field by asking questions about gender, race, and faith in the identity of women religious, as Amy L. Koehlinger did in her 2007 study *The New Nuns: Racial Justice and Religious Reform in the 1960s*. At the heart of these studies and subsequent explorations of Catholic women (lay and religious) is seeing them as they were, not as living saints-on-earth, long-suffering martyrs for the salvation of men and children, or dupes of patriarchal authority. Both Mary J. Henold and Kathleen Sprows Cummings have provided excellent examples of where the study of religious women should go. Henold's 2008 study, *Catholic and Feminist: The Surprising History of the American Catholic Feminist Movement*, shows how women embraced feminism and grappled with their faith, carving out their own space in this late twentieth-century women's movement. In her 2009 study, *New Women of the Old Faith: Gender and American Catholicism in the Progressive Era*, Cummings goes to the heart of the question of how women could be loyal churchwomen and faithful supporters of women's advancement. These works are only some of the new scholarship that has helped our collective understanding of women religious. Asking new questions about the choices women made based upon their faith, like Catherine McAuley and the Chicago Regional Community's sisters did, enriches our understanding of the past, whether speaking of all women, Roman Catholic women, or all of society.[14]

"This season of love and Mercy"

The history of the Chicago Regional Community is complex and rich, encompassing over a century and a half of foundation and institution building. The community cast a wide net of influence over schools, hospitals, and social welfare institutions throughout Illinois, Iowa, and Wisconsin from the 1846 Chicago founding to the 2008 merger of the Chicago Regional Community with other Mercy regional communities to form the West Midwest Regional Community. This study, however, focuses on how the Chicago Mercys formed a community, lived their spiritual lives, and served within the institutional Catholic Church. This three-part perspective addresses community, spirituality, and ministry, providing a means by which we can trace the evolution of these women of faith as the world around them changed.

The first part of this study focuses on the origins of the Sisters of Mercy in the Midwest from the founding of the Chicago South Side community in 1846 through the amalgamation and creation of the Chicago Province in 1929. When the Mercys arrived in the Midwest, they established communities and navigated the expectations for Catholic women in general and sisters specifically as they helped build the American Catholic Church. The arrival of five young Sisters of Mercy escorted by Mother Frances Warde in 1846 began a period of growth and expansion of Mercys throughout the Midwest, with schools, hospitals, and shelters for women and orphans. Sisters faced impoverished conditions and few resources, but slow and growing support from the burgeoning Catholic population throughout Illinois, Iowa, and Wisconsin sustained their endeavors. These women provided an early social safety net for the Catholic immigrant population, but they also represented a complex and significant set of choices for women wanting a religious life. Just as McAuley was a real woman living within the context of her age, the Mercys in the nineteenth century were also authentic individuals, a reality that sometimes gets lost in the histories of nuns and sisters during this period.

The second part of this study examines how the Mercys came together as one province through the changes of Vatican II from 1929 to the 1980s. Throughout this period, the Chicago Mercys adapted to increased restrictions upon religious life as the Vatican imposed upon them (and all women religious) a more monastic style of religious life. The Chicago Mercys also dealt with the ever-increasing demands for personnel to staff expanding parish schools and their growing health-care institutions. As religious life became more structured, the pressure to maintain one, single image of the good sister came to the foreground. This false image, however, obscured the reality and lively religious life that lay under the surface. By the mid–twentieth century, the Mercys embraced movements designed to fully educate and form sisters, such as the Sister Formation Conference. With this push to prepare sisters for their ministries, congregations of women religious like the Sisters of Mercy sought to give members of their communities time to earn college degrees before they took up apostolic assignments. Changes like these, plus the ongoing conversation about what the role of women religious should be in the world and in the church, prepared the Sisters of Mercy in part for the changes of Vatican II in the mid-1960s.

As religious life erupted with the changes of Vatican II renewal in the 1960s, the heterogeneous identities of the Sisters of Mercy, long obscured by stifling norms and by the religious habits they wore, came to the surface. New life and new ministries expanded as Mercys broke through artificial barriers and monastic structures that had defined them for so long. Sisters shed their habits and engaged in new apostolates, or ministries. By the 1980s, they had also lost many of their members. Women were leaving the community in search of another manifestation of religious life and at the same time, fewer people were seeking out a life in a religious congregation. This change did not alter the Mercys' connection to their foundress's guiding spirit or their dedication to community needs, however. The renewal process enabled the Mercys to reexamine in depth McAuley's intention for the Sisters of Mercy and the gift of her charism.

The third part of this study examines life after the dramatic change of Vatican II in the 1990s and 2000s. Communities of women religious understood the need for shared resources as their numbers declined faster than new applicants could replenish them. In 2008, the Chicago Regional Community combined its resources with those of five other groups—Auburn and Burlingame, California; Cedar Rapids, Iowa; Omaha, Nebraska;

and Detroit, Michigan—to create a new regional community, the Sisters of Mercy West Midwest. The Chicago Mercys faced an identity crisis similar to the one that their sisters weathered seventy-nine years earlier when they formed the Union. In both the 1920s and the 1990s, however, the autonomous communities understood that to merge meant the preservation of their Mercy identity. The Chicago Regional Community ended in 2008, and the new West Midwest community has changed how sisters from Illinois, Iowa, and Wisconsin identify themselves to those outside the Sisters of Mercys and to each other. Their Mercy spirit, however, continues.

"Charity Embraces Those Who Abound"

The Spirit of Mercy Comes to America, 1846–1929

Figure 1. Irish-born biological sisters, Sisters Mary Monica, Mary Leo, Mary Catherine, and Mary Gabriel Fanning, who entered the Sisters of Mercy in Iowa City in the 1910s and 1920s.

Charity embraces those who abound, as well as those who are in need; but mercy finds exercise only in proportion to the necessity of its objects. In this spirit our Institute has been raised up and blessed by God, and propagated in no ordinary way to "devote" its members to the "service of the poor, sick, and ignorant." Hence, by our profession, we become for life the vowed and consecrated servants, not of the affluent, but of the "poor, sick and ignorant."[1]

Important Dates in the History of the Early Sisters of Mercy

1846: Sisters of Mercy arrive in Chicago, open Saint Xavier Academy.

1848: Galena, Illinois mission is established.

1852: Mercy Hospital, Chicago opens.

1854: Agatha O'Brien, first superior of Chicago's South Side, dies from cholera.

1859: Ottawa, Illinois foundation is established.

1863: Six Sisters of Mercy serve on Union hospital ships in the Civil War; Ottawa becomes an independent house of Chicago Motherhouse.

1867: DeWitt/Davenport, Iowa foundation begins.

1868: Mercy Hospital, Davenport is established.

1870: Janesville, Wisconsin foundation is established from Sterling, Illinois.

1871: Chicago Fire.

1873: Mercy Hospital, Iowa City opens.

1874: St. Xavier Academy for girls in Ottawa is established.

1876: Mother Agatha Looby brings sisters from Janesville to Fond du Lac, Wisconsin.

1883: Sisters from Nashville, led by Sister Catharine Feehan, arrive in Chicago, establish Chicago West Side, and open St. Patrick Academy and Motherhouse.

1885: Mother Mary Evangelist Holcomb and two sisters establish Milwaukee foundation from Fond du Lac, and some Sisters of Mercy return to Janesville.

1894: Mercy Home for Women (St. Catherine Residence) and Our Lady of Mercy Academy in Milwaukee are established.

1907: Mercy Hospital, Janesville is established.

1910: Aurora, Illinois foundation from Council Bluffs, Iowa is established.

1911: St. Joseph Mercy Hospital, Aurora opens.

1912: Saint Xavier College is officially incorporated as a college in the state of Illinois.

1921: Misericordia South in Chicago, a maternity home for women, opens.

1924: Mercy High School Chicago opens on Chicago's South Side.

1926: Our Lady of Mercy Academy becomes Mercy High School, Milwaukee, Illinois.

1927: Iowa City foundation votes to join with the Davenport Sisters of Mercy becoming one community.

1929: Amalgamation: Creation of the Sisters of Mercy of the Union. The Chicago Province is formed from Chicago's South Side and West Side, Ottawa, Davenport, Janesville, and Milwaukee.

1937: Aurora joins the Chicago Province and Union.

1   "The spirit of our Institute is mercy, as its name denotes"
The Nature of Mercy in Nineteenth-Century America

The spirit of mercy, then, should guide and govern all our actions; all our hope of happiness must depend not only on the love of Jesus Christ but likewise on His mercy. In our intercourse with mankind let us be mindful for it is the principal path pointed out by Jesus Christ to who are desirous of following Him.[1]

According to a nineteenth-century *Directory for Novices*,[2] any "hope of happiness" for Sisters of Mercy came from the love of Jesus Christ and "His mercy" bestowed upon them. Images of Sisters of Mercy from the nineteenth century often do not show this joy, but they do convey directly that they were religious women. They committed their lives fully to God; they cloaked themselves in their belief, and they *lived* their religion. Posed photographs of women religious, or sisters, reveal serene countenances, though their faces often possessed serious and determined expressions. Their religious garb, or habit, envelops and conceals their feminine frames. If the voluminous garments and veil did not speak plainly to their identity, then large crucifixes or rosaries provided further evidence to their commitment. If pictures show sisters' hands, they are usually folded holding prayer books.[3]

A portrait of Mary Ann and Catherine McGirr, two biological sisters who became Sisters Mary Vincent and Mary Francis Xavier in the Chicago South Side community, exemplifies this image of women religious (see Figure 2). The photograph of the McGirr sisters shows two Mercys with similar countenances (the family resemblance is apparent), staring intently forward as they held their pose for the camera, their hands folded in a prayerful clasp. Their faces reveal little of their personality or the breadth of their religious life. Who were these women, sisters both by blood and in religion? Posed together in their religious habits, little distinguishes the two. The photograph does not divulge that Sister Mary Vincent, standing on the right, was one of the first pioneers to Chicago in 1846, nor that

Figure 2. Biological sisters, Sisters Mary Francis Xavier McGirr, founder of the Ottawa Community, 1859, and Mary Vincent McGirr, one of the original five sisters to begin the Chicago Foundation and the first Superior and Administrator of Mercy Hospital, Chicago.

she was a musician who took on the operation of an orphanage in 1849, followed by the first Mercy Hospital in 1852. It does not show that she was the Mother Superior of the Chicago community in 1855. The portrait, furthermore, does not disclose any information about Sister Mary Francis Xavier, on the left, who led the group that established a foundation in Ottawa, Illinois, in 1859, which launched schools for both boys and girls.[4]

For antebellum America, images like these of nuns and sisters were foreign and mysterious sights. For many Protestants, debate over Catholic women's choice of and commitment to religious congregations centered on the belief that they were forcibly held captives by priests, thanks to the escaped-nun stories like that of Maria Monk, who claimed to have escaped captivity within a French Canadian convent in Montreal. Her story of sexual exploitation and the horrors of convent life were published in the book *Awful Disclosures of Maria Monk, or, The Hidden Secrets of a Nun's Life in a Convent Exposed*, in 1836. This book joined the 1835 publication of Rebecca Reed's *Six Months in a Convent*, which was published on the heels of the Charleston, Massachusetts Ursuline Convent burning in 1834. Many Protestant Americans, already convinced that Catholicism was antithetical to the U.S. political system, quickly believed that dangers lay behind convent walls for naïve young women.[5]

The early American Catholic Church, however, did not question the motives of women religious in the first congregations established in the United States, like the Sister of Charity, Sisters of St. Joseph of Carondelet, Sisters of Loretto, and Ursulines. Church hierarchy saw nuns and sisters as sources of education, health care, and welfare for the minority Catholic population. These women, while pious and devoted "Brides of Christ," were often free labor and a means of building and strengthening devout Catholics in defense against the Protestant threat. When the Sisters of Mercy arrived in antebellum America in 1843, Catholic women religious were still strange and exotic sights. By 1840, there were only a little more than 900 sisters and nuns in the United States, and the Irish Sisters of Mercy were a welcome arrival for the fledgling American clergy, who hoped they would expand the Catholic faith of the growing immigrant population. The laity, for its part, saw the sisters as an opportunity to preserve culture.[6]

Neither photographs of sisters and nuns nor lurid (and false) tales of convent life provide a complete and accurate picture of religious life. Why did women like the McGirr sisters want to enter religious life? What led these young women specifically to the Sisters of Mercy? Before Mother Frances Xavier Warde and the other Sisters of Mercy established a congregation at Pittsburgh, women could choose from only twelve religious congregations that existed in the United States. The establishment of an Irish community dedicated to serving the poor not only fit with the agenda of the larger Catholic hierarchy, which was faced with an increasing number of impoverished Irish immigrants, but also provided an opportunity for young women inspired by their faith to make a life-long commitment to serving God and those in need.[7]

The McGirr sisters were born in Youngstown, Pennsylvania, in the mid-1820s. They came from an Irish immigrant family, but one with a degree of financial stability. Their father, Patrick McGirr, was a physician, as was their brother, John. Both young women waited until they were twenty to enter religious life. Sister Mary Vincent entered first in 1845 at Pittsburgh, which made it possible to join the group that came to Chicago in 1846. She arrived in Chicago a novice and made her first profession of vows in December 1847. Her younger sister by two years, Sister Francis Xavier, chose to follow her sister to Chicago when she entered the congregation two years later, making her first profession in December 1850.[8]

The McGirrs' story begins before the large wave of Irish immigrants during the Great Famine. The McGirrs were an upwardly mobile family, with daughters entering religious life and a son following his father into the medical profession. Women like the McGirrs who helped establish religious communities in antebellum America, like their Irish counterparts, often came from middling or merchant classes. They had sufficient education, including religious training, to develop, expand, and administer congregations' schools, hospitals, and other institutions. The future of their ministerial work provided the foundation for generations of Catholics and inspired vocations among countless young women. Sisters Mary Vincent and Mary Francis Xavier, furthermore, entered the Sisters of Mercy during a period of increased Irish immigration, a period when anti-Catholic and anti-immigration sentiments by the native-born population along the East Coast were heightened. They chose a new Irish community devoted to alleviating the burdens of poverty, who were invited to the United States to serve an Irish immigrant population. This was also a period of increased religious piety regardless of denomination. While evangelical Protestant revivalism gripped much of the East Coast, Catholic clergy pushed to foster religious sentiments among the laity through devotional or spiritual activities, such as parish missions and sodalities, which placed the parish at the center of their religious life. During this dramatic confluence of religious and cultural events, the McGirrs and thousands of other young women entered religious life.[9]

The Sisters of Mercy throughout the nineteenth and early twentieth centuries offered young women an opportunity to devote their lives to God and to lead a religious life guided by both the works of mercy and deep spiritual foundation. By joining a religious congregation, women like Sisters Mary Vincent and Mary Francis Xavier also found community with others who had the same faith and purpose. These sisters did not have to enter religious life. As daughters of a professional, they had the potential for marriage and family. They could have emulated their Protestant neighbors and participated in benevolent societies to aid immigrants and the poor. Instead, they chose a life-long commitment as Sisters of Mercy. What did this life offer that they could not find as Catholic laywomen in the nineteenth century? To answer this question, we must look at the expectations for Catholic women during this period and examine the nature of religious life in a congregation like the Sisters of Mercy.

Catholic Womanhood

In the nineteenth century, Catholic women had few acceptable options or roles: marriage, religious life, or remaining single and caring for aging parents, unmarried brothers, or other relatives. Furthermore, during most of the nineteenth century, many Catholics had not reached a level of economic stability comparable to that of middle-class Protestants. Employment in and out of the home occupied Catholic women's daily lives and left little time for non-paid volunteerism. Meanwhile, the religious fervor of the Second Great Awakening had inspired many Protestant single and married middle-class women as early as the 1840s to engage in various reform efforts, including rescuing "fallen women" of the streets into Protestant institutions. Even under the guise of religious faith and church affiliation, women's public role in reform jarred many observers, male and female alike, particularly when their activities crossed over into the political realm. Despite inroads into public action, middle-class Protestant women rarely engaged in full-time, life-long careers outside of their homes, except possibly as wives of ministers or missionaries. Catholic laywomen faced similar obstacles, but vowed religious women did not.[10]

For those who opted for life in a religious congregation, faith plus a desire to put that belief toward public service was a central rationale for embracing life as a sister or nun. This choice was also attractive because it offered an alternative to marriage and motherhood, which, while not an end to social engagement, did prevent women from pursuing life-long careers. A life committed to service—to doing good—should not be glossed over as a motive for seeking out religious life, but antebellum women religious, as Joseph Mannard has described them, "were de facto career women. Though their work was a by-product of their primary religious calling—a means to an end rather than an end in itself—nuns nevertheless served as some of the earliest examples of women professionals."[11]

Most nineteenth-century women, whether Protestant or Catholic, conformed to the gender expectations of their time. For Catholic women in America, this meant complying with the roles prescribed by the specific cultural or ethnic identity of an immigrant group. For much of the nineteenth century, an Irish or Irish-American standard of femininity informed the dominant Catholic culture. At the same time, Irish-style Catholicism dominated the so-called "American" Catholicism. This was especially true as Irish Americans came to control the church hierarchy and religious communities. Despite German and German-American efforts to challenge the Irish Americans' hold on positions of authority within the Church, by the late nineteenth century, the latter held sway. Young women such as the McGirr sisters would have recognized the limited roles Irish-American girls could fill in the mid-1840s when they chose life in a religious congregation such as the Sisters of Mercy.[12]

In contrast to Protestant American roles for women, there was more than one valued path for Catholic womanhood. Protestant Christianity emphasized the home and the family as a center of religious life, and prescriptive literature touted the goals of marriage and motherhood for young women. Within this domestic sphere, they were supposed to exert their cultural and religious influence. According to the pages of popular women's magazines such as *Godey's Lady's Book*, Protestant women could only find fulfillment in this role. Catholicism, conversely, placed the parish at the center of religious life, despite the importance of home devotions. Home altars, family prayer, and spiritual readings supplemented and bolstered Catholic faith, but these devotions focused Catholics toward the parish church and the reception of the sacraments. As the nineteenth century progressed, Catholic mothers, much like Protestant mothers, increasingly had a duty to impart religious devotions to their children, but they modeled themselves and their families upon the Blessed Virgin Mary, the Holy Family, and Catholic saints. Nineteenth-century Catholic literature directed at women provided instruction on how they could accomplish this.[13]

The model of middle-class family life espoused by mid-century Protestants elevated a woman's role and influence in her husband's and children's salvation, but only within the home. This "cult of domesticity" resonated in Catholic homes, particularly concerning the emphasis on female self-sacrifice for the good of male relatives. Daughters within Irish immigrant households in this period understood that their brothers' needs came first, even if they worked just as hard or harder. Catholic diocesan newspapers and national magazines that published articles or entire sections for women often contained stories of mothers' near martyrdom for their children or their husbands. The larger message was sacrifice for God's will and their salvation. A Catholic family only had to point to Mary as mother of Jesus Christ and her sacrifices for the salvation of the world to understand what girls and women could accomplish. Mary, however, was not the only woman to emulate. The lives of female saints, particularly those who consecrated themselves to Jesus as Brides of Christ, or nuns and sisters, also served as examples. Catholic women also had the near example upon which to model themselves of aunts, sisters, and cousins who entered religious life. As the Catholic parish school system developed, sister teachers were a daily reminder of the religious possibilities for young girls.

A vowed religious life, for the nineteenth century and much of the twentieth century, elevated laywomen to a higher plane. While committing oneself to a life of service, poverty, and chastity, women appeared to step out of the world, leaving its base confines. The reality, of course, was that women who "left the world" entered and embraced it in a different way than wives and mothers. The "otherworldly" status of active or apostolic women religious and their religious habit enabled them to go where Catholic laywomen could not acceptably go. Not until the late nineteenth and early twentieth centuries did Catholic laywomen venture into the fields of the benevolent volunteer and the social welfare worker with women religious, although this had more to do with increasing levels of education and entrance into the middle class than with any conception of appropriate public spaces for Catholic laywomen.[14]

Catholic prescriptive literature of the nineteenth century in many ways mirrored its Protestant contemporary. As Colleen McDannell and others have shown, Catholic literature for women in the mid–nineteenth century tended more toward instruction for young women and girls on how to act as good, moral Catholic women. Articles in magazines, diocesan papers, and journals, as well as advice manuals, guided women on how to live, dress, work, and conduct themselves in a Protestant American society. This type of literature evolved over time to become more romantic and less instructive, but at its heart was the ideal of Catholic womanhood, which manifested in all manners of life, whether as a wife, mother, daughter, or woman religious.[15]

One early publication by Paulist Father George Deshon, *Guide for Catholic Young Women, Especially for Those Who Earn Their Own Living,* published in 1860, directly addressed working class Catholic women, especially those employed in Protestant homes as domestic servants. Deshon, as parish priest of the Paulist church in New York City, encountered working class Irish immigrant women who struggled with balancing their faith and the need to earn wages to help their families in America and Ireland. He offered solutions to encounters with Protestants, and advice on apparel, the benefits of daily prayer, and the types of books and articles one should read. He stressed the importance of the Sacraments, and how and why young women should avoid positions hostile to their faith. Deshon's first chapter, however, sets the tone and attitude young women needed in life. The chapter, "A Good Girl Has Reason to be Satisfied with Her Condition in Life," stresses the need to accept one's position, or lack of status, and not strive for material wealth. Rather, a working class girl should be content with her life as it was as she strove for spiritual wealth and closeness to God. Following this message are Deshon's chapters that stress the benefits of hard labor, humility, and subjection. The meek and lowly servant came closer to emulating Jesus Christ than the wealthy. Deshon offers the fourth century Saint Isidora of the Convent of Tabenna in Egypt as an example for young women. Also known as the Fool for Christ, she embraced an extreme sense of humility and "courted every way and opportunity of abasing herself." Acting the fool, or insane, Isidora performed the "hardest and lowest work, as if she had been the vilest slave, and no one ever saw her idle a moment."[16]

While Deshon did not necessarily advocate that Irish immigrant women debase themselves in the same manner as St. Isidora, he did touch upon an important theme for Catholics in general and women in particular in the nineteenth century. The humble found reward in Heaven. Often, Catholics (as a largely immigrant population for much of the nineteenth century) were excluded from higher status because of a lack of education and employment opportunities, particularly Irish immigrants. Young women did have to struggle and work long hours at menial positions as domestic servants, factory workers, and in shops. This same attitude, which stressed becoming the Fool for Christ and accepting joyfully the lesser place, was echoed in messages for wives and mothers who sacrificed for their husbands and children. Publications exhorted women to use their influence to "soften and subdue" the "hardest" souls, and devote themselves to the salvation of their husbands and children's souls. Furthermore, lovingly embracing self-sacrifice resonated with women religious in the nineteenth century. This was particularly true for members within congregations dedicated to serving poor immigrants.[17]

As with most prescriptive literature, it is difficult to determine who read it and, in terms of George Deshon, we cannot know if prospective candidates to congregations such as the Sisters of Mercy possessed copies of his volume. Deshon's instructions for young women possess a style and tone that was similar to handbooks or manuals such as the *Customs and Guide* or *Book of Customs* and spiritual writings for women religious.[18] Catholic priest-writers such as Deshon presented rules, duties, and modes of dress and comportment for young laywomen. They stressed devotion, piety, and attention to one's Catholic faith whether as a single working woman or as a dedicated wife and mother. Every moment or action in daily life provided an opportunity for prayer or contemplation of God's love. The humble working girl should pair washing her face, dressing for work, and preparing for the day, according to Deshon, with brief prayers, in much the same way as a woman religious undertakes daily prayers. *Customs and Guide*, lectures for novices, and volumes such as *Familiar Instructions of Rev. Mother McAuley* not only acquainted Sisters of Mercy with how they should focus their lives on God and their ministry but provided a rationale for embracing the vows of their congregation.[19]

Deshon's instructions to working women are often simple and direct, which fits with the perception that Irish immigrant Catholics needed basic lessons in their faith. He was not alone in his work; Deshon as a Paulist priest was part of a larger missionary effort in America to build the American Church, specifically parish life, and to increase devotional practices among the laity. In this way, he represents a larger movement in nineteenth-century America, which played a part in inspiring faith and, in many instances, vocations. Young women who entered religious life came from a tradition of everyday spiritual practices, which included attending Mass and domestic devotions. Yet advice manuals and lessons for laywomen were not the same as the formation process for young novices. Once entering religious life, young novices undertook a process that broke with the previous conceptions of secular life, intellectually and spiritually acclimating them to demands of Mercy life.[20]

Answering the Call from God

The McGirr sisters left their home and "answered the call" to become women religious. While other religious traditions speak of vocations, or a "call from God," in the context of the nineteenth century, Catholics believed that God chose individuals for religious life. This honored selection should have inspired gratitude from the individual religious and her family. Unfortunately, the nature of record keeping and history means that we lack personal accounts or manuscript records for the average woman religious in America, which prevents a clear understanding of the motivations of the individual sister during this discernment process. Most nineteenth-century sisters did not leave behind personal papers, such as letters and diaries, that provide clues or insights into motivations and faith life before and after they entered a religious congregation. Caches of letters written to and from superiors, or possibly retreat notes, may exist. Until recently, religious communities did not write histories of individual members unless they were foundresses or significant superiors. We know about Catherine McAuley's spiritual formation and development of a religious institute because members of her community preserved her papers and wrote about her life, and because of the larger impact of her congregation. For thousands of nineteenth-century Sisters of Mercy, their motivations and events of their lives, however, remain unknown. We can come to understand better if we consider the records and histories preserved in new ways.

Taking a closer look at the stories of a handful of Sisters of Mercy provides some insight into the religious foundation and subsequent vocation of many young women of the nineteenth century. Catholic women who entered the Sisters of Mercy in the nineteenth century were more likely to be Irish or Irish American. As the nineteenth century progressed, more recruits were American-born, but the number originating from Ireland was persistently high. Much like Catherine McAuley, the candidates' personal faith inspired and influenced their choices, but faith alone did not drive them. They also perceived opportunities outside of marriage and family in the Sisters of Mercy. All of these things influenced women like Mary Monholland, Annie and Bridget O'Brien, Catherine Fitzsimmons, and Mary Fanning.

Mary Monholland, the future Sister Mary Francis de Sales, was neither a typical applicant to the Sisters of Mercy nor unique. In many respects, she possessed similar characteristics to the McGirr sisters. She was also from an Irish immigrant family. While the McGirrs were born in Pennsylvania, Monholland came from Ireland and immigrated with her father and younger brothers to New York City as a young girl. Her father became a relatively successful grocer and Mary came to the Mercys with an education. Like Sister Mary Francis Xavier McGirr, Monholland's religious vocation took her west to enter in Chicago rather than a congregation closer to home. While Sister Francis Xavier followed her biological sister, Mary Monholland was inspired by the invitation of her former confessor, Bishop William Quarter, to enter a newly established Irish community.[21]

In many ways, Sister Mary Francis de Sales's life prior to and within the Sisters of Mercy reflects experiences of other Mercys and the history of nineteenth-century women religious. As a young Irish immigrant woman living in New York City, Mary Monholland assumed the role of obedient and supportive daughter. Despite expressing a vocation to a religious life to her father, she remained with her family because he wished it. Nineteenth-century single women in Ireland and America, particularly after the Famine, proved valuable sources of financial support. They emigrated from Ireland to find opportunities in America and sent their wages back to their families or contributed to family economies in the United States. Monholland's family depended upon her labor not only in her father's grocery business, but within their home. Monholland's mother died when she was a girl and even though her father remarried, he relied upon her to take care of the household and her younger siblings. While Patrick Monholland did not wish to lose a valuable laborer within his household, he may have also feared losing his daughter.[22]

In contrast, the McGirr sisters' family appears to have followed them west. Sisters Francis Xavier and Vincent's brother John graduated from Rush Medical College in Chicago in 1848, and he later became a member of the staff of the Illinois General Hospital of the Lake, which became Mercy Hospital in 1852. John was instrumental in Sister Mary Vincent's appointment as head of the hospital. The sisters' mother followed her daughters west as well, and she is buried in the same cemetery in Ottawa as their brother John. Other Sisters of Mercy maintained ties with family through correspondence or in the community itself as young women followed sisters, cousins, and aunts into religious life. Yet not all families could count on a close proximity to their daughters and sisters if they joined religious communities. Parents sometimes stood in the way of their daughters' vocations, as Patrick Monholland initially did. Mary, however, did not give up the desire to become a sister and her father relented; when she heard of the Irish Sisters of Mercy's new foundation in Chicago, she decided to go west.[23]

Mary Monholland's biographer, Isidore O'Connor, RSM, was also a member of her congregation. Sister Isidore entered the Sisters of Mercy in Chicago about a decade after Sister Mary Francis de Sales. Like Monholland, O'Connor was born in Ireland and came to Chicago directly from her family in New York City, and she eventually moved further west to

Iowa as a Sister of Mercy. Sister Isidore's clear affection for Sister Mary Francis de Sales is apparent in her 1894 biography, which fits within a particular genre of religious biography. *The Life of Mary Monholland* is both instructive and inspirational to Catholic laity; Sister Mary Frances de Sales's life and struggles are equal parts Irish immigrant story, tale of American triumph over adversity, and triumphant Catholic ascendancy. Sister Isidore depicts the young Mary as a plucky, strong-willed girl who was dedicated to Ireland and Catholicism from a young age. Her independent spirit helped her remain faithful to her spiritual devotions at home. In addition, like many religious biographies, the young Mary discerned her vocation to the religious life at an early age and remained true to it, despite opportunities for marriage. According to Sister Isidore, the lessons Mary learned working in her father's business and the economic upheavals of the antebellum America taught her that the pursuit of money was inconsequential when compared to the quest for God. While we may read Sister Isidore O'Connor's account of the life of Mary Monholland with a critical eye, we cannot ignore its message for the late-nineteenth-century American Catholic world. The story of Monholland's faithful dedication to her vocation, despite family objection and hardships, stood to inspire other young women to the religious life. Her continual sacrifice and suffering as well as strong leadership as a Sister of Mercy, also stood as an example for other women religious to emulate. Ultimately, the basic facts of Monholland's life remain: She was an Irish immigrant, brought up in New York City within the Catholic tradition, and she sought a religious life.

Mary Monholland initially wanted to enter the Sisters of Charity in New York City because she admired a friend and teacher in that community. When she finally was free to join a congregation, other personal inclinations or motivations inspired her to go west, an arduous journey for the times. According to Sister Isidore O'Connor, Monholland's father, Patrick, was an ardent Irish nationalist and implied that his political views forced the family's immigration to New York City in the 1820s. Did Monholland choose an Irish community in a newly developing city in the Midwest because she wanted to help Irish immigrants? By the 1840s, the number of religious communities for women in the United States increased and Monholland had other choices besides the Chicago Mercys. If she wished to enter a strictly Irish community, the Pittsburgh Mercys were within reach. Chicago, in contrast to New York and Pittsburgh, was on the frontier and while a growing and expanding city, it still had rudimentary streets of mud. The Chicago diocese, only established in 1843, three years before Mary Monholland arrived as an aspiring applicant, had no other communities of women religious besides the Sisters of Mercy. It did have Bishop William Quarter, who was elevated to his office when the diocese was established. He came to this position from St. Mary's Church in New York City, the Monholland family's parish. Mary Monholland, already in her early thirties, opted to go to Chicago in 1846.[24]

While the American Catholic Church in the expanding west needed women like Mary Monholland to teach Catholic children in parish schools and select academies such as those established by the Sisters of Mercy, the American West lured candidates for religious life. In colonial and early-nineteenth-century America, European communities desirous of missionary work among Native Americans established congregations intent on converting Indians. The Sisters of St. Joseph of Carondelet ventured from France to establish a school for deaf children in the newly formed diocese of St. Louis, and hoped to work among Native Americans for this purpose; the American Church, however, had other plans for them. They established schools and a hospital for European immigrant Catholics. The American west and all its financial, political, and social possibilities drew families, entrepreneurs, miners, and farmers as the United States expanded westward. Catholic immigrants went west as manual laborers who dug canal trenches and laid railroad tracks. They went in search of farmland or sought employment as miners, seamstresses, laundresses, domestic servants, and postulants in religious communities.[25] They journeyed by wagon, canal, and train as families and alone, as Mary Monholland did. As they moved west, the Catholic Church sought to provide an infrastructure to protect their faith.[26]

While Mary Monholland rejected marriage proposals and went west for a religious life, other women came directly from Ireland in order to join religious communities such as the Sisters of Mercy. While single Irish women immigrated to the United States throughout the nineteenth and twentieth century to find economic opportunities not available in Ireland, they also sought out life-long commitments to religious congregations. In the case of the Sister of Mercy foundations in Iowa, nearly half of all entrants in the second half of the nineteenth century up through amalgamation in 1929 emigrated from Ireland. Furthermore, family connections, much like the American-born Sisters Vincent and Francis Xavier McGirr, informed choices of biological sisters from Ireland as some women either came with their blood relatives, or followed each other to the same congregations. Irish-born Annie (Sister Alphonse) O'Brien was one such woman; she immigrated to the United States, traveling directly to the Motherhouse in DeWitt, Iowa in 1868, and ultimately professing vows in the Independence branch house. Her younger sister Bridget (Sister Aloysia) joined the community one year later, but took her final vows on her deathbed in the Davenport motherhouse on December 7, 1872.[27]

Sisters Alphonse and Aloysia O'Brien entered an American community instead of remaining in Ireland. The growth of religious congregations like the Sisters of Mercy in Ireland increasingly drew young women inspired by their faith to follow a vocation. While the number of convents and religious communities also grew at home, many women had better luck with convents abroad. American communities, with an ever-growing missionary field of immigrant and second-generation Catholics, needed more sisters to teach in parish schools and keep the expanding Catholic social welfare institutions running and congregations like the Sisters of Mercy actively recruited young women from Ireland. They also often required smaller dowries or waived them all together. Traditionally, when a woman entered a religious community, she brought with her a dowry, just like a bride did upon marriage. Congregations in Ireland and the United States required dowries to help cover the cost of sisters' lives and to support the community. Apostolic congregations like the Sisters of Mercy often provided their services for free or very little remuneration and they depended upon charitable donations to continue their work. By the mid–nineteenth century in Ireland, the average dowry for the Sisters of Mercy was £500, but they could also be as low as £50. Often congregations waved the dowry if the young woman had "qualifications for teaching or nursing." In some American communities, dowries could be moveable goods or sums of money, such as ten to twenty dollars. For these reasons, in connection with a religious vocation, young Irish women found opportunities for education, advancement, and a life-long commitment to a supportive community of women. Most American congregations, however, ended the practice of a dowry by the end of the nineteenth century.[28]

As Irish women looked to American communities, superiors of the Sisters of Mercy in the United States gazed back to Ireland to find more recruits. While Irish superiors, such as Mother Mary Josephine (Sarah) Warde of St. Maries of the Isle in Cork, sent young women to convents established by her biological sister and American foundress, Mother Frances Xavier Warde, other American superiors returned to familiar regions and in some cases to their own families for candidates for the Sisters of Mercy in places like Iowa City, which maintained a strong Irish identity well into the twentieth century. Between 1867 and amalgamation in 1929, twenty-eight of its entrants came from Ireland. Some, like Sister Dolores (Catherine) Fitzsimmons, left Ireland in 1886 with the intent of entering the Mercys in Iowa City. At the time of her entrance into the community in Iowa City, she had a minimal education and little money. According to the Register of Entrants, she "brought no property in money or otherwise but was sent in June $150.00." Twenty-five years later, she returned to Ireland to bring new postulants to the Iowa City Mercy community. In 1911, she recruited Mary Fanning, the oldest of four daughters who had little more than a sixth grade education and no money for a dowry, whose background was similar to Sister Dolores' own history. (See Figure 1.) The account of Mary Fanning's entrance made no mention of property or money, despite the recording of sums for other women at the same time.[29]

Mary Fanning, who became Sister Catherine in 1914, continued the recruitment legacy by returning to Ireland to bring her three younger sisters to the same novitiate: Sister Monica (Kathleen) in 1915, Sister Gabriel (Helena) in 1921, and Sister Leo (Annie) in 1923. Iowa City was not the only Mercy community seeking Irish missionaries. Traveling with young Helena Fanning in 1921 on the S.S. Albania were four other women, two Sisters of Mercy and two postulants like herself. These women were bound, not for Iowa City, but for Omaha, Nebraska. Sisters Gerard Killikelly and Stanislaus Morgan escorted Bridget Buckley and Mary Ellen Healy for the same purpose. Buckley, Healy, and Fanning were all listed as "postulants" on the passenger listing.[30]

Whether to find a new life in America or the west, to live a life devoted to God, to alleviate the sufferings of the poor, or all of these things, young women found a meaningful purpose as members of the Sisters of Mercy. Sisters Mary Francis de Sales, Alphonse, Aloysia, and Catherine are just a few examples of the type of Irish women who entered the Sisters of Mercy in the nineteenth and early twentieth centuries. Thousands of other women joined them throughout this period. Before the Civil War, the majority of entrants were not born in the United States, with nearly 100 percent of these coming from Ireland. Throughout the nineteenth century, as the numbers of entrants rose (more than seventy in the 1870s to over 200 by the 1900s), the percentage of those born in the United States also increased significantly.[31]

For those who came from a distance in the early years to join the Sisters of Mercy in Chicago, then later in Iowa and Wisconsin, the journey was not an easy one. (Certainly an ocean voyage could be difficult.) Progress in land transportation made that trip easier as rail lines spread west and replaced stage coach and canal boats, connecting various towns and cities, but whatever form, travel was often arduous. We can think of the path taken by a young woman who left home, family, and all she knew to enter a religious congregation as symbolic of what was to come. Ahead of the young applicant lay years of formation. When the future Sister Mary Francis de Sales Monholland set out for Chicago in 1846, rail lines did not connect from eastern cities to Chicago directly, and crossing over land along the Great Lakes and completing her journey on a ship across Lake Michigan had all the characteristics of a religious pilgrimage. According to community legend, as she was nearing the end of her voyage, a storm over Lake Michigan capsized Sister Mary Francis's ship with the port at Milwaukee in sight but her life was saved by the first mayor of Chicago, W. B. Ogden. From one perspective, her formidable trip may have tested her dedication to her vocation. The true test of her commitment and that of all applicants to the Sisters of Mercy did not occur before they entered, but afterword in the years of the novitiate.[32]

"To our own advancement of perfection"

This chapter begins with a quote from a mid-nineteenth-century directory, or guide, for novices and is from the section entitled "Of the Spirit of the Institute."[33] This quote is taken from a larger passage that explains the chapter of the *Rule and Constitutions* covering the aims of the Sisters of Mercy. This particular copy of the directory is a transcription of another volume of uncertain origin. Directories for novices typically provided expanded discussions of the congregations' vows, purpose of their ministries, and the order and actions of the day. In this respect, directories were like the various editions of *Customs and Guide*. These volumes also broke down the elements of religious life and provided commentary, often with selections from constitutions. The various foundations of Sisters of Mercy, which later formed the Chicago Regional Community, possessed these types of readings for their novices and professed sisters. The directories and *Rule and Constitutions* provided the starting points and touchstones for women at all levels of formation and state of profession. They communicated the "spirit of [their] Institute," the spiritual center of the Sisters of Mercy.

When candidates such as Mary Monholland, Catherine and Mary Ann McGirr, and Mary Fanning entered one of the Sisters of Mercy novitiates, they received instruction from these volumes. They had arrived with a fundamental education in their Catholic faith, steeped in all the cultural and social expectations of women of their society, much like those expressed in the pages of Catholic prescriptive literature. They were young women of their age, but entered into a longer tradition of vowed religious life. Although the Sisters of Mercy as a congregation was relatively young, each new establishment or foundation possessed fervent desire to preserve the spirit of Catherine McAuley. As Mercy foundations developed in the United States, some sisters, like Mother Agatha O'Brien, the first superior of the new Chicago foundation, expressed concern that variations would occur and consequently distort the original intent of their foundress, Catherine McAuley. Women like Sister Mary Francis de Sales Monholland entered the Sisters of Mercy in Chicago only a little over a decade after the congregation was established in Ireland and only five to six years after their foundress had died; yet even in the few years since the establishment of the Chicago Mercys, changes had occurred in the everyday religious life and practices. In one letter to a Pittsburgh Sister of Mercy, the first superior of the first Chicago foundation, Mother Agatha O'Brien, noted that by 1851 differences existed between Ireland, New York City, and Pittsburgh. Sisters in New York, for example, did not receive Holy Communion throughout the week as often as the Chicago Mercys, nor did they share the same summer street dress. Mother Agatha's blood sister in Ireland, also a Mercy, reported that they said the "Office" in Latin, instead of English as they did in Chicago. In Pittsburgh, on recreation days, the sisters spoke after dinner. Mother Agatha assured her correspondent, Sister Elizabeth Strange, that "there [had] been no change in the smallest degree [and] every thing [was] done just as it was when [she] was in Pitts."[34]

While Mother Agatha assured Sister Elizabeth that her community had stayed true to the rule established by Catherine McAuley, it is more significant that despite the occurrence of some changes, Mercy congregations were concerned about preserving the spirit of their foundress. This desire to maintain Catherine McAuley's founding charism is a constant goal of the leaders of the various congregations throughout the nineteenth and early twentieth centuries. Consequently, although the congregation that Mary Fanning, the future Sister Catherine, entered in 1911 may have been in a different location (Iowa City) and she may have begun her novitiate training sixty-five years after Sister Mary Francis de Sales Monholland did in 1846, this vital spirit of Catherine McAuley and the first Sisters of Mercy still remained.

Change or adaptation, however, had occurred to fit the congregations' specific environments. New foundations, often separated by distances that did not allow for constant communication and observation, had to adapt to their surroundings. Despite her own concerns to the contrary, Mother Agatha knew this would happen. In the same letter to Sister Elizabeth Strange, she lamented the lack of a central motherhouse for all Sisters of Mercy. If the various foundations had this, she felt they would have the assurance that all the sisters would have the same religious formation. Mother Agatha faced the possibility of change when she sent a group to establish a branch house in Galena, Illinois in 1848. While this house closed a decade later, other new foundations followed and thrived, including the branch house in Ottawa, Illinois. From the late 1860s to the 1890s, more branch houses and foundations developed and flourished throughout Iowa and Wisconsin. In 1883, a new independent Sisters of Mercy community came to the west side of Chicago from Nashville, Tennessee. As the Sisters of Mercy expanded throughout this territory and their numbers grew, adaptation of the Rule was bound to happen. Mother Agatha O'Brien understood this in her 1851 letter and as she transcribed a copy of the *Book of Customs for the Sisters of Our Lady of Mercy* in 1852. As she wrote, she understood that circumstances and "particular cases" sometimes called for an individual superior to "[dispense] with the usual customs & observances as necessity may require." Yet Mother Agatha also knew that every effort must be made to "maintain the observance of our holy Rule, to be guided by its Spirit, to fulfil [sic] the purposes for which it was instituted, [which] has ever been the most ardent desire of [their] different communities."[35]

Despite adaptations, however small, the common elements for all women who entered the Sisters of Mercy, whether in Janesville, Wisconsin; Davenport, Iowa; or Ottawa, Illinois during this period were the documents and the professed members of the community. Both conveyed the purpose of the Sisters of Mercy and showed how to conduct spiritual life by providing models for aspiring women religious. Women like Sister Catherine Fanning, who entered in the early twentieth century in Iowa City, had a greater distance from Catherine McAuley, but the foundress's spirit and legacy remained in documents like the *Directory for Novices*. Both Sister Mary Francis de Sales Monholland and Sister Catherine Fanning, however, clearly understood the purpose of their life as Sisters of Mercy: "besides attending particularly to their own perfection which is the principal end of all religious orders [they] should also have in view what is peculiarly characteristic of this Institute, that is a most serious application to the instruction of poor girls, visitation of the sick, and protection of distressed women of good character."[36]

The ministries that were "peculiarly characteristic" to the Sisters of Mercy—education, caring for the sick, and the shelter of single women—were the basis of all employments of the Sisters of Mercy, but they were grounded, or supported, by the language that begins this passage: "attending to their own perfection." Catherine McAuley established the Sisters of Mercy so that the members of her congregation would attend to both their "own salvation and to promote the salvation of others." Education, health care, and the care of "distressed women of good character" went a long way toward others' salvation, as did strengthening their Catholic faith. Catherine McAuley intended that her sisters both conduct apostolic works of mercy and possess a spiritual life. According to the foundress,

> These two works are so linked together by our rule and observances that they reciprocally help each other. We should often reflect that our progress in spiritual life consists in the faithful discharge of the duties belonging to our state, as regards both ourselves and our neighbour, and we must consider the time and exertion which we employ for the relief and instruction of the poor and ignorant—as most conducive to our own advancement of perfection, and the time given to prayer and all other pious exercises—we must consider as employed to obtain the grace, strength, and animation—which alone could enable us to persevere in the meritorious obligation of our state, and if we were to neglect these means of obtaining Divine support we would deserve that God should stop the course of His graces, to make us sensible that all our efforts would be fruitless, except we were continually renewed and replenished with His Divine Spirit. God speaking to us by His inspired Apostle says—Attend to thyself.[37]

There is a double message in this text, which many of the *Customs* and other documents of the Sisters of Mercy echoed: to lead a "mixed life" dedicated to the "perfect combination of the duties of Martha and Mary." Catherine McAuley intended service and prayer life to be equally important aspects of the Mercys' religious life. One should not detract from the other, but should be mutually supportive. Sisters of Mercy, whether in Ireland, Illinois, Iowa, or Wisconsin, often had long, arduous days of work in classrooms, hospitals, and homes for women. Going out into the streets to assist the poor or visit the sick meant that they faced poverty, disease, and the suffering and misery that went along with them. A strong spiritual or religious foundation, consequently, was necessary and a part of all aspects of their ministries. Without one, the other might suffer. This dual and complementary dedication to the salvation of others and themselves underlies the works that the Mercys conducted throughout Illinois, Iowa, and Wisconsin in this (and subsequent) period.[38]

Catherine McAuley's concept for her religious community was based upon her experiences in 1820s and 1830s Dublin. She and the other women who joined her in her work before forming a religious congregation wanted to alleviate the sufferings of the poor. They wished to provide a safe home for working women. When Catherine McAuley started to construct the congregation that became the Sisters of Mercy, she went through the formation process of the Sisters of the Presentation and later used this congregation's Rule to shape her own. As Mary C. Sullivan, RSM, has shown, McAuley took the Presentation Rule and adapted it to her own vision of religious life for her new community. The fundamental differences between the two Rules were that McAuley added the special devotion to the women and children in the first chapter of the Rule, "Of the Object of the Institute," and she insisted that the sisters were not to be bound by enclosure. This last point was something new. Many religious communities prior to Catherine McAuley's time observed the rule of enclosure, or cloister, which barred women religious from going out into the world and actively engaging in the much-needed ministries, such as visiting the sick. Cloistered religious communities took solemn vows and had strict separation from the world, often physically blocked or protected by walls or gates. Convents of active congregations, who took simple vows, such as the Sisters of Mercy, tended to have spaces where the laity, even family members, were prevented from entering. Catherine McAuley specifically wrote her community's Rule without the restrictions of enclosure precisely because it ran counter to the purpose for her religious congregation.[39]

A further essential aspect of Catherine McAuley's construction of the Sisters of Mercy was the emphasis she placed on mutual respect and affection among sisters within the congregation. In particular, the chapter of the constitution on "Union and Charity," which McAuley modeled on the Presentation Sisters' rule, stresses the importance of a "union of mind and heart in a religious community." Love and affection for each other and their neighbors was grounded in Jesus Christ's message: "Love one another, as I have loved you." Emulating Jesus Christ, or striving to, placed charity and mutual love as central virtues for Sisters of Mercy.[40]

Catherine McAuley and the other first Sisters of Mercy in Ireland built their religious congregation upon this spirit and structured their religious life with the Rule and Constitutions. When branch houses developed and sisters spread the Mercy spirit to other parts of Ireland, England, and elsewhere, they brought this structure and spirit to forge new foundations. Frances Warde carried this with her when she brought sisters to Pittsburgh and to other parts of the United States, and each new foundation began the process of educating the next generation of Sisters of Mercy. That education began in many different places because each new or independent foundation had its own novitiate. Mary Monholland began her religious formation at the Convent of Mercy in Chicago in late 1846, while Mary Fanning commenced her religious life in 1911 at St. Xavier Convent of Mercy in Iowa City. By the early twentieth century, young women began their formation in different locations, including Saint Joseph Novitiate in Ottawa, Saint Patrick Academy on Chicago's West Side, the Convent of Mercy in Davenport, and Our Lady of Mercy in Milwaukee. To add further complexity, some women entered the congregation in branch houses, such as the short-lived Galena and Bourbonnais, Illinois, and Fond du Lac, Wisconsin. When the Mercys established branch houses, they drew interest and applicants. Shortly after the arrival of the Sisters of Mercy in Galena, eighteen-year-old Anne Drum, a native of the city, became Sister Mary Scholastica and remained in Galena until 1855. In another decade, she became the superior of the Convent of Mercy in Chicago, a position she held for ten years (1863–73). Mary Berry, born in Ireland in 1834, entered in 1851 and became Sister Louise. Her life in religion did not end in Galena, but continued in Chicago as well, and she served as a nurse during the Civil War on a hospital ship. Toward the end of her life, she became the superior of the Ottawa motherhouse from 1892 to 1898. Sisters Mary Scholastica and Louise entered the Galena branch house (which closed in1858) but had a significant impact on the direction of not only the Chicago South Side community but also the Ottawa motherhouse. These women helped knit together the religious life of Sisters of Mercy. Their experiences—as teachers, nurses, and superiors—combined spiritual and apostolic aspects of the Mercy community.[41]

While minor deviations occurred due to specific environments and circumstances of a foundation, the essence of Catherine McAuley's message passed from one generation to the next. While formation evolved over time into the twentieth century, its purpose remained the same: to shape the novice into a member of the Sisters of Mercy. The process was designed not to destroy individual will, but to mold it to the larger will of the community. Formation of postulants and novices infused the spirit of the Institute into the young women through the process of instruction of the total person. A lecture found in the handwritten *1849 Novice Guide of St. Xavier Convent* in Chicago declared that

> Sisters should frequently call to mind the end they have in view in quitting the world, which is to unite their hearts perfectly to God, by dying to themselves and to the world; so as to apply all the power of their souls to the service of their heavenly Spouse, by a spirit of evangelical poverty,

entirely divested of all inordinate attachments; by the purest chastity & by
an unlimited obedience, grounded on self denial, and an entire surrender
of their own will.[42]

The lecture continues to stress the importance of Christ's suffering and
the need for sisters to keep their religious purpose at the forefront of
their hearts and minds. Sisters needed to "surrender . . . their will" and
"crucify their senses, imaginations, & caprices, for the love of their Divine
Master."[43]

The language of this lecture is dramatic and the imagery is violent. By
these words, young women aggressively suppressed their ambitions and
desires to place God's will first. How much did this challenge the average
young woman who entered the Sisters of Mercy in the nineteenth and
early twentieth centuries? Most women who entered one of the Sister of
Mercy foundations in Illinois, Iowa, and Wisconsin were twenty-two or
twenty-three; however, women as young as sixteen and as old as thirty-
three entered prior to the amalgamation.[44] During this period, an applicant
had to be at least sixteen. In addition to age, a chief concern was the health
and soundness of mind of the applicant, as well as her moral character.
The Sisters of Mercy needed women healthy in both mind and body. If
an applicant had "forsaken [her] moral character," was married and her
husband was still living, or was burdened by debt, the community rejected
her application. A young woman must come to the community freely, not
pressured into a vocation. The life of the average Sister of Mercy was not
easy and superiors of the various foundations did not want anyone escaping worldly problems. On the other hand, a superior might reject an applicant, despite sound mind, good health, and moral character, if her family
did not approve of her choice or if she was the sole or an important means
of support of them.[45]

Once the Sisters of Mercy accepted an applicant, a woman typically
entered as a postulant for a six-month period. At the end of this time, the
professed sisters, upon the recommendation of the Mistress of Novices,
voted to receive or dismiss the postulant. If received, she became a novice
for up to two years before temporary profession, or making her first profession of vows. Then final profession or vows taken for life came after
the completion of another two to three years. At the end of this period
of temporary profession, a woman made the choice to continue, taking
her vows for life, or to leave, returning to secular life. The choice to leave
was available throughout novitiate training, and considering the religious
and physical rigors of formation, we can see the level of commitment ap-

plicants must have possessed to become women religious. They believed that they followed God's plan for their lives and once professed sisters, they put the spirit or object of the Institute of Sister of Mercy first. In the nineteenth and early twentieth centuries prior to amalgamation, most sisters followed this pattern, although the early pioneer days of the Sisters of Mercy often allowed for variation, with women entering at different times of the year and their time in the novitiate fluctuating.[46]

The process by which Sister Mary Francis de Sales Monholland became a fully professed sister, however, does not reflect the typical process for most women religious in the nineteenth century. In contrast, Sister Mary Francis de Sales arrived in Chicago and entered the Sisters of Mercy in November 1846, and by April 1847, she was a professed sister. The speed with which she moved through the novitiate indicates not only the need the young community had for women like Mary Monholland, but it also suggests that the future Mother Mary Francis de Sales had valuable skills, talents, and dedication to her vocation. Furthermore, she rose quickly to leadership, possibly because she had more experience and skills than other novices and sisters. This was also a period truly marked by frontier or pioneer life and Sister Mary Francis de Sales quickly became an integral member of the Chicago community. She assisted Agatha O'Brien in leadership as Bursar and served as Assistant to Mother Superior. Four years after Mother Agatha died in 1854, she served as Mother Superior. During the Civil War, she led a group of sisters and lay nurses to Missouri and provided medical care to an Irish brigade of Northern troops. In 1867, she joined the Iowa missions at DeWitt and Independence, Iowa, eventually becoming the local superior of Independence and Mother Superior of the Davenport foundation in 1881. She died in 1889 and is buried in Davenport Sacred Heart Cemetery.[47]

The pioneer days of the Sisters of Mercy in Illinois, Iowa, and Wisconsin occasionally resulted in atypical novitiate experiences such as Sister Mary de Sales'. Most women who entered the Sisters of Mercy in the nineteenth and early twentieth centuries followed the normal formation process, particularly once a community had the opportunity to establish itself with a degree of stability. Yet the missionary nature of the nineteenth century periodically led to non-traditional novitiate training and occasionally accelerated formation, as in the case of Sister Mary de Sales Monholland. When Mother Agatha O'Brien entered in 1843 as a lay postulant in Ireland, after she joined the original group that went to Pittsburgh, superiors quickly diverted her from the normal path. There, two years after her reception as a novice, she made her final profession as a choir sister[48] and became Mother Superior of the new community at twenty-four. Other sisters who helped establish the Chicago Mercys in 1846 experienced similarly quick-paced formations. Sister Gertrude McGuire, who entered at Pittsburgh in 1845, was a fully professed sister and the local superior (at the age of twenty-two) of the first branch house of the Chicago community by 1848. Tragically, she died three months after leading this new mission to Galena.[49]

While the very real threats to physical well-being and continued good health persisted in this period, financial support could result in instability. We can see this in the early years the Sisters of Mercy spent at Janesville, Wisconsin, beginning in 1870. While attracting novices and building this foundation, the lack of financial support from the local parish forced the sisters to relocate to Fond du Lac in 1876. By the mid-1880s, some Sisters of Mercy returned from Fond du Lac to Janesville to reestablish a convent when a new priest asked the community to return with promises of financial support. Meanwhile, Fond du Lac continued and eventually expanded to Milwaukee. Instability of place and growth could lend itself to an uneven formation process as novices began their education in one location, and continued it in another. Sister Mary Ignatius Kennedy was one woman who began her novitiate in one place and made her final profession in another. She entered the Janesville Convent of Our Lady of Mercy in 1872 and professed her final vows four years later in Fond du Lac. This type of uncertainty dissipated as the Mercys put into place an infrastructure, and religious life for the Sisters of Mercy began to normalize. Young women who entered the Mercys—whether in Chicago, or later in the nineteenth century in one of the Illinois, Iowa, or Wisconsin houses—followed a more traditional path from postulant to final vows.[50]

In the more structured or normalized religious formation, once a community accepted a young woman's application for admittance, her education as a religious began. The entire process was designed to help shape the young woman's identity to the spirit of the Institute. One cannot overlook the central importance of the larger community and how the individual fit within it. Whereas one might be born into a family, a woman chose to enter religious life in a community. The novitiate, according to the *Directory for Novices*, was "a time of spiritual infancy." Those who entered religious life held "the view of sanctifying [themselves] and of learning all that [was] necessary for becoming good and perfect religious." Just as Jesus had instructed and shaped his Apostles for their ministry, so too would the Mistress of Novices shape the novices. While this life and education was strict, it was essential "to subdue passion, overcome tempers, destroy bad

habits, renounce useless visits, and frivolous occupations in orders to ef-
face from remembrance the trace of sin, and the taunt of worldly ideas."[51]

The horarium, or daily schedule, determined the daily life of both novices and professed sisters.[52] For novices, the average day revolved around
prayers, duties, and study. Fully professed sisters' days were similar, with
more time for ministry and fewer hours of study. From waking to retiring each day, a novice was to focus her mind and heart on her purpose
and prayer. According to the *Directory for Novices*, the first thoughts of a
novice upon rising "were the first fruits of the day which should be wholly
consecrated to God." With the sound of the bell, the young novice was
to awaken and respond to the call and proceed to prepare for the day.
These preparations included dressing in her habit while saying specific
prayers related to each item of clothing. This prayerful state continued as
the novices proceeded to chapel to perform their devotions to the Blessed
Sacrament, "offering every thought, word, action, every pain, labor fatigue
and suffering of mind and body during the day in union with His." After
saying the Angelus, sitting in meditation, and saying the Office, novices
attended morning Mass. All this occurred before breakfast.[53]

The rest of the novice's day was dotted with both manual duties and
periods for study. Even these, such as arranging cells (space for sleep) and
domestic duties had a larger religious purpose. The novices' cells were to
contain only the items allowed by the Rule: a "bed, clothes press, chair,
crucifix, water pitcher, basin, mug, soap plate, lamp, match box, large and
small brush, dust pan and duster." Professed sisters' rooms had similar
items, but also contained their framed vows. While the cells were uniform
and all sisters possessed the same type of items, the *Directory for Novices*
stressed the importance of respecting the individual sister's space, and
that no one should remove another sister's things. Embedded in the listing
of items and stress on the sparseness of the cell was a lesson on the vow of
poverty and the need to focus oneself on the religious life and "to imitate
[their] Divine Lord more perfectly every day."[54]

Along with sparse living quarters, novices needed also to understand
that their personal inclinations or preferences should not take precedence
over the needs of the larger community. In matters both large and small,
Mistresses of Novices and the Novice Directories instructed young women
on how to accomplish this and in all things to avoid singularity. They
cautioned sisters to do nothing that would draw attention to themselves,
whether by deviating from the common order, or by seeking praise for
their accomplishments. To avoid praise, novices needed to embrace the
spirit of humility, placing themselves last and showing other sisters defer-

ence. Even simple conversation among other novices and sisters "should carefully [be] avoid[ed]" and regulated. If they must speak "then in as few words as possible." Dissuading novices from idle conversation was not simply a tool for avoiding singularity, but it was also connected to developing the interior spiritual perfection of novices. Silence, according to the Rule, was the "faithful guardian of interior recollection," and without it, "there can be no regularity or order in the beauty of God's house; that there can be no true obedience, no charity and union, no recollection and prayer, where silence is neglected." The Mistress of Novices' directives on comportment and means of achieving religious perfection were intended to shape young sisters to place the needs of the community, the Catholic Church, and their neighbor before their own. In reality, young Catholic women began this lesson before they entered religious life. They came from a culture and society that stressed women's sublimation of individual desires for the betterment of their family in a manner suggested by Catholic writers and commentators mentioned previously. When Catherine McAuley, in her *Familiar Instructions*, stressed humility, modesty, and "holy poverty" to the members of her congregation, novices and sisters understood the fundamental context of these ideas. The novitiate, however, reinforced and developed them in a deeper spiritual way.[55]

While regulations that focused on seemingly minor things, such as mode of dress, reading in the refectory, letter writing, and the contents of a sister's cell, seem extreme, they were part of the larger process and life of a religious. Rules and regulations by which to govern their lives, while strict and possibly illogical to the outside observer, had the purpose of forming a single identity as a Sister of Mercy; they all related to the vows and how sisters lived them. One had to learn the meaning of true religious obedience, poverty, and chastity. Obedience to one's superior meant more than blindly following the orders of Mother Superior. Ridding oneself of personal property was not the sole purpose of the vow of poverty, nor was abstinence from sexual activity the chief aim of the vow of chastity. Foregoing marriage and motherhood was a consequence of choosing something else. The purpose of the Rule and the vows of the Sisters of Mercy was to emulate the life of Jesus Christ. Obedience to God's will, desiring to be as poor as Jesus Christ, and denying the individual desires were all a part of the spirituality of the religious. The works or ministries of the community were an outgrowth of this spiritual desire to be Christ-like.[56]

To reinforce these lessons, novices studied the various aspects of religious life, including prayer, catechism, the Rule of the Institute, and how to comport oneself as a good religious. Time was devoted each day to reading such texts as *Imitation of Christ, Poor Man's Catechism, Reeve's History of the Bible, Lives of the Saints, Spiritual Combat,* and *The Sufferings of Christ.* An important element of the novice's study was the *Directory for Novices,* or a novice guide. All of these readings were central to the overall preparation of the postulant for reception into the community after the first six months and the novice for profession of their temporary and then final vows. One month prior to their reception ceremony, postulants intensified their study of certain volumes, such as selected chapters from *Imitation of Christ,* and meditated upon entries from the *Spiritual Retreat Book.* A similar process began two months before sisters made their profession of their first vows. In this case, novices examined their motives and their desire to become Sisters of Mercy. They understood the vows and the direction of the Institute and once again meditated on selections from the *Imitation of Christ,* as well as chapters from the New Testament. These last two months were an intensive period of preparation, where novices restricted their communication with family and friends outside of the community. The *Novice Guide* reiterates the choice a young woman made at this point to unite with God, the "Divine Spouse." Novices made this decision after two years of study following reception, and the Mistress of Novices assisted them in this choice.[57]

While the intensity of the formation process subsided after final profession, sisters maintained and refreshed their spiritual life with continued meditation on spiritual readings and daily lectures, or addresses. Furthermore, a one to two-week retreat complemented this more frequent, albeit less intensive, daily study. Whereas novice retreats were meant to enhance formation, professed sisters' retreats were intended to help them rededicate themselves to their vocation. These retreats often lasted over a week and involved daily lectures and conferences given by a priest and superiors, who often spoke on different aspects of religious life. Retreat lectures (reflections addressed to the sisters by the retreat director) often reflected the times in which they were given and connected the spiritual to the temporal. In the case of the mid–nineteenth century, concerns about preserving Catholic religious life in the midst of a Protestant nation abound in retreat instructions. Lectures on obedience or humility, qualities on which all women religious needed to meditate, could also draw from the social and cultural challenges of a Protestant American environment. One lecture on obedience given at an August 1857 retreat in Chicago criticized the "spirit of independence" that existed in America. The priest-lecturer cautioned sisters to avoid this "spirit" in favor of religious obedience because the former negatively affected religious communities in the United States, apparently "more than others in the world"; it was a spirit "of disobedience." This spirit of independence created discord, and disobedience grew within communities, between religious and their superiors, and priests and bishops. According to the lecturer, in "all the social relations of America . . . the independent liberty of the disobedient is universally agreed with. And this atmosphere . . . tainted religious houses in this country." The spirit of independence, which the priest cautioned sisters to avoid, had the potential to influence or tempt sisters to do "things that [they] would not for the world do at first, [but] come to do afterwards without remorse—[they] trifle with the vow."[58]

The root problem was this spirit of independence, or individualism. For the American Church hierarchy and religious superiors, the novices had to understand the nature of their obedience, despite the air of individualism or independent spirit that was an element of American culture. These ideas ran counter to the ideal of Catholic religious life. Women religious in the nineteenth century, however, provide numerous examples that contradict this image of religious obedience. Sister Mary Francis de Sales Monholland, with a plucky independent spirit, boarded a train and numerous coaches, and undertook a dangerous lake crossing to commit herself to God. The young Margaret O'Brien volunteered to join the group that established the Pittsburgh community, and later as Mother Agatha, willingly walked among contagious cholera patients. Sister Josephine Donnellan, who entered religious life in 1873 and was among those who established the Milwaukee Mercy community, traveled frequently with a companion to various Mercy convents outside her region in Milwaukee, gathering information on the history of her congregation in the United States. Monholland, O'Brien, Donnellan, and hundreds of Sisters of Mercy made similar individual choices, but under the guise of religious vocation, their independent spirit manifested itself as the "good sister," obedient to God's will.[59]

Women like Mother Agatha O'Brien literally gave their lives to their vocation. Despite the risk to their health, women who entered the Sisters of Mercy chose a religious life for what it offered. When considering dramatic stories like Mother Agatha's and others (three others died in the same cholera epidemic in 1854), how can we evaluate the less dramatic, or romantic stories of sisters whose history is less known? Women like the irrepressible Sister Mary Francis de Sales made choices for their religious life based upon their faith and believed that by "giving up the world," they received something better in return. In reality, sisters in the nineteenth and early twentieth centuries did not live separate from the world; they lived in it, in a way different from laywomen. As an apostolic community that was not enclosed, their ministries took them *into* the world. Sister Mary Francis de Sales left her father's home and business in New York City and made her treacherous journey to Chicago to commit her life to God. She did not retire from the world, but marched through it. She did this when she led a group of sister nurses headed for hospital ships during the Civil War. Inspired by her faith and her commitment to the spirit of her religious congregation, she, and many other sisters, visited the sick in their homes and in asylums as well as the imprisoned.[60] Sister Mary Catherine Fanning for her part crossed an ocean and several states to join the Iowa City community. She, too, stayed in the world as a religious as she worked in Mercy Hospital, Iowa City as a nurse and pharmacist, earning bachelor's and master's degrees in nursing and pharmacy. She eventually directed the pharmacy and X-ray departments at the hospital. Furthermore, lay people—Catholics and non-Catholics alike—came into the sisters' places of work, including schools, hospitals, and homes for women, which doubled as their convents. Sisters' vocation to religious life and the vows that they took set them apart in terms of purpose and patterning of their lives.[61]

The diversity of experiences among the various Mercy congregations in Illinois, Iowa, Wisconsin, and throughout the United States caused some concern for members of the Catholic Church hierarchy. By the end of the nineteenth century, all congregations of women religious faced questions and criticisms from Church authorities in the Vatican who wanted to impose more uniformity and structure on religious life. In particular, apostolic or active communities like the Sisters of Mercy had too much diversity of practice for Church authorities. Up until the early twentieth century, apostolic religious congregations operated, as described by historian Margaret Susan Thompson, in a "state of canonical limbo." Since the mid-eighteenth century, the Vatican distinguished between religious institutes that professed solemn and simple vows. The former were interpreted as maintaining a more traditional and "more perfect" religious life because they adhered closely to the rules of cloister or enclosure. Catherine McAuley founded the Sisters of Mercy without such restrictions and with simple vows. The Vatican made room or tolerated active religious institutes like the Mercys (and gave them papal approbation or approval) but the many variations of religious life resulted in restrictions that altered religious life for much of the twentieth century.[62]

In 1918, the Vatican directed religious communities to revise their Rules and Constitutions to conform to the revisions to the 1917 Code of Canon Law. A central point of this new Code was the implementation of a centralized government that ran counter to the traditional practice of the Mercys. A branch house could and often did separate from its original parent or motherhouse, as was the case in Ireland when the Sisters of Mercy first began to expand beyond Dublin. The Vatican wanted the Sisters of Mercy to restructure and create a uniform religious life, in keeping with the larger movement to provide more controls on communities of women religious. Individual communities and their superiors accepted the Holy See's directive and formed the Sisters of Mercy of the Union in 1929. They obeyed and amalgamated, but they also desired to act on their own terms. While not all Sisters of Mercy desired this shift toward union, the leaders of the various foundations came to advocate for amalgamation in part because they wanted to be faithful members of the Catholic Church, but also to protect the legacy of Catherine McAuley and to move the Sisters of Mercy into the future.[63]

Uppermost in the minds of the leaders who planned for amalgamation throughout the 1920s was the preservation of the spirit of Mercy and fidelity to the legacy of the first pioneers of their foundations. Some of these women had literally given their lives to plant the seeds of the Sisters of Mercy in American soil. They had traveled hundreds of miles to build schools, hospitals, orphanages, and Houses of Mercy because they believed not only in the Sisters of Mercy's mission, but that God had called them to this purpose. Amalgamation, the superiors realized, would be a step toward preserving that heritage. They hoped that a generalate system, creating a larger province merging Chicago South Side and Chicago West Side, Ottawa, Davenport, Iowa City, Janesville, and Milwaukee would strengthen their position within the region, combining personnel and financial resources to better serve parish priests, the laity, and each other. The Aurora motherhouse opted not to amalgamate until 1937.[64]

From the mid-1840s to the 1930s, the Sisters of Mercy expanded their presence in northern Illinois, Iowa, and Wisconsin. They staffed parish schools in both rural and growing urban centers. They built female academies and established a women's college. They built hospitals and homes for women. They visited the sick in their homes and brought comfort to those suffering from poverty and injustice. They followed their charism articulated in documents like their *Directory of Novices* and "[t]he spirit of mercy . . . guid[ed] and govern[ed] all [their] actions; all [their] hope of happiness . . . depend[ed] not only on the love of Jesus Christ but likewise

on His mercy." Whatever the challenges and changes throughout this pio-
neering period, with the spirit of Catherine McAuley, the Sisters of Mercy
conducted the works of their institute in the American Midwest. Their
ministries or their active life "not bound by the rules of enclosure" took
them into the streets and into a public world not experienced by most
American women in this era. The Sisters of Mercy kept their desire to follow Jesus Christ at the center of their spiritual life and, grounded in this
faith in their community and Catherine McAuley's founding spirit, they
shaped their apostolic life.[65]

2

"Not Bound by Enclosure"
The Sisters of Mercy Respond: 1846–1929

It is essential to our Institute that its members be not bound to enclosure, as it would preclude the exercise of these offices for which they [sic] congregation was established . . . It is essential to this Institute that its members seek their perfection not in Contemplation alone but in the union of the active and contemplative life as practised by our Redeemer on earth.[1]

The Sisters of Mercy in the nineteenth century acquired the name the "Walking Sisters" because they often traveled from their convents on foot in pairs. Sisters throughout Illinois, Iowa, and Wisconsin moved in and out of streets, classrooms, and sick rooms. They journeyed from convents into schools, hospitals, orphan asylums, and homes for women. They entered businesses and shops, and waded through crowded streets to conduct their works of mercy. They climbed into carriages and boarded streetcars with Catholic and non-Catholic men, women, and children, with little dividing them from the laity besides their religious habit. While walking was the primary means of transportation for the relatively short distances from convent to school or hospital (in many cases sisters lived upstairs from these ministries), Sisters of Mercy utilized all modes of transportation and joined in the tumult of movement west throughout the mid to late nineteenth century. They took wagons and carriages to new locations in western Illinois, Iowa, and Wisconsin as their ministries expanded and spread to new towns and cities. They climbed aboard the growing railroad system and covered larger distances between motherhouses and branch houses to keep in contact with parent congregations, exchange news, replenish resources, and respond when they saw a need.

The railroad was an essential element to Chicago's development in the nineteenth century and trains in many ways made the city. The train, the major technological innovation of the nineteenth century, shrank space and made previously insurmountable distances between cities less difficult to travel, as treks taking days became hours. By the 1860s, trains dominated the means of transporting goods to market in Chicago, and by

1869, the city became a hub, or the collection point, for west coast products and Pacific goods transported to the markets in the east. Businessmen and farmers took advantage of this technology for economic reasons. The Sisters of Mercy, however, used the train for religious reasons to respond to the needs of the laity.[2]

All this movement among and connection with the laity would not have been possible if the Sisters of Mercy had to obey the rule of enclosure. When Catherine McAuley established the Sisters of Mercy in Ireland, she insisted that members of her new congregation needed the freedom to move and act in society, and they must not be "bound by enclosure." This was an essential part of the Sisters of Mercy from its conception and the constraints of enclosure ran counter to her purpose. Catherine McAuley had created a religious community with an apostolic mission and the Sisters of Mercy, like similar communities emerging in Ireland at the same time, did not remain within their convent walls and did not devote their lives solely to prayer. Prayer fed their ministerial life, which brought them into the streets of Dublin, into classrooms, into the homes of the sick, and enabled them to open their doors to those in need. The generations of Sisters of Mercy who came from the first community in Dublin, including the Sisters of Mercy of Chicago, Ottawa, Davenport, Iowa City, Janesville, Milwaukee, and Aurora, held to this essential element.

The reality of women religious's lives prior to Catherine McAuley and her contemporaries was the model of nun within the cloister. Catholic life in Ireland and later the United States, however, required the presence of women and men to address the needs of the poor, sick, and uneducated. Catherine McAuley and the generations of Sisters of Mercy to follow identified the need to educate, nurse, and attempt to relieve the economic and physical burdens of their neighbors. Enclosure, or rules that governed and barred women religious from close association and contact with secular society either by going out of the convent or by inviting the laity into any but a few defined areas of the convent, stood as a potential barrier to Catherine McAuley's vision for her religious congregation. Nineteenth-century Irish and American Catholic life was chaotic, dynamic, and in need of the support provided by religious communities like the Sisters of Mercy. Catholic Ireland contended with the aftereffects of the Penal Laws, which prohibited Catholic affiliation. In America, the small native-born and the growing immigrant Catholic population faced opposition from Protestant Americans and the struggle of the immigrant experience.[3]

As we have seen, the lack of enclosure was a necessary and controversial element of religious life for sisters and nuns when Catherine McAuley established the Sisters of Mercy. When we consider the object of the Sisters of Mercy, we cannot see any other way. The purpose of the Sisters of Mercy throughout this period (and in later periods) was the "instruction of Poor Girls, the Visitation of the Sick, and the Protection of Distressed Women of good character." The Mercys could not do this if a cloister and rules of enclosure constricted their movements. Furthermore, beginning with Catherine McAuley, the women who made up the Sisters of Mercy did not wish this type of religious life. As we have seen, they put their faith in God and the example of Jesus Christ as the central guide of their religious life. God had called them to this religious life, and the sisters had proof of the glaring need in the nineteenth and early twentieth centuries for parish schools, female academies, hospitals, and homes for young women.[4]

Mother Agatha O'Brien, the young superior of the South Side Chicago foundation, understood the importance of maintaining the integrity of Catherine McAuley's original intent regarding life without enclosure. In 1852, as she transcribed a copy of the *Book of Customs for the Sisters of Our Lady of Mercy* for the members for her community, the opening reminded her and subsequent readers that "the death of [their] venerated Foundress [had] deprived [them] of a living rule for their interpretation." While local superiors had the right to adapt the Rule to their specific environment, maintaining its core purpose was essential to the Institute. In the 1840s and 1850s in Chicago when contact with other Mercy communities, particularly those who had a direct connection to Catherine McAuley, was difficult (although not impossible), documents such as this transcribed *Customs and Guide*, as we have seen, were a means of preserving the spirit of the Institute for the next generation.[5]

The spirit worth preserving meant, in part, that the Sisters of Mercy's faith in God and each other led them in many directions and into the world, despite potential threats to their safety. Mother Agatha O'Brien's faith in her purpose as a Sister of Mercy inspired her to lead her community in its early, pioneer days in Chicago. Her faith also helped her understand that patients needed her in the fledgling Mercy Hospital during a cholera epidemic in the summer of 1854. In the midst of that crisis, she walked into a hospital ward to provide care and comfort to sick and dying patients, despite the risk to her health. She died during the epidemic, as did three other sisters from her congregation, and her community had to continue with the mission of the Institute without her. The Sisters of Mercy persevered in Chicago and sent new missions to various parts of Illinois, Iowa, and Wisconsin to create new foundations, which carried on under their own authority separate from the Chicago Convent of Mercy. With each new foundation, the spirit of Catherine McAuley and the Institute was re-created around the *Holy Rule, Customs and Guide*, a handful of other documents, and the collected experiences of the sisters who traveled by wagon or train to their new foundation. Throughout the nineteenth and early twentieth century, these women continued a religious life steeped in the vows of poverty, chastity, and obedience, with a special dedication to serve the poor, sick, and uneducated of their regions. While striving to serve the laity, each other, and God, they carved out space within the larger American Catholic Church and created a template for how women religious existed in a modern world.

This chapter examines how the Sisters of Mercy lived their religion and sought "perfection" through the "union of [their] active and contemplative life" in their works of mercy throughout the nineteenth and early twentieth centuries. As the Mercys spread throughout Illinois, Iowa, and Wisconsin performing similar but not identical ministries, they built a network of parish schools, academies, hospitals, homes for women, orphanages, and other ministries that sprang from a common foundress, spirit, and purpose. By the early twentieth century, Mercys from Chicago South, Chicago West, Aurora, Ottawa, Milwaukee, Janesville, Davenport, and Iowa City, faced with changes to religious life directed by the Vatican and conscious of the need of their local foundations and communities, engaged in the discussion of consolidation of the disparate locations into one Province and by the end of the 1920s, the separate, but united, foundations merged into one.[6]

The nineteenth-century American Catholic Church required women religious to possess the ability to adapt to their surroundings and to provide services, whether health care, social welfare, or education. Circumstances of the antebellum American Catholic Church compelled them to be administrators, inventors, entrepreneurs, and pioneers as well as the silent workers within desperately needed institutions. Superiors and bishops called upon community members to adapt their rules and lifestyles to serve the needs of lay Catholics and others in various cities and rural areas throughout the nineteenth century. The Sisters of Mercy were no different in that respect. The first eighty-three years of the Sisters of Mercy in what would become the Chicago Regional Community are replete with dramatic stories of perseverance against terrible odds and struggles with disagreeable clergy.[7]

As we have seen, Catholic women religious in the mid–nineteenth century had more opportunities to act in ways that laywomen could not and they did this not necessarily to prove or obtain their equality in an androcentric society. While elite Protestant American women like Elizabeth Cady Stanton championed women's rights at Seneca Falls, New York in July 1848, the Sisters of Mercy struggled to provide valuable education and other material assistance, which bolstered Catholics in various locations such as Chicago and Ottawa, and later Iowa and Wisconsin. They provided basic education, one of the tools for the Catholic laity's success. The lack of outward interest in the nineteenth century women's rights movement suggests that Catholic women religious did not desire equality, because their Catholicism and Church frowned on it. In reality, women like the Sisters of Mercy came to issues like women's rights from a different perspective. They saw the inequity and injustices of their society, but sought to alleviate or mediate them by walking with the poor, sick, and uneducated women and girls.[8]

In the United States, part of how the Sisters of Mercy understood inequality had much to do with their own Irish identity, and their Irishness factored into how they related to immigrant Catholics and their Protestant neighbors. Throughout the nineteenth century, Sisters of Mercy in Illinois, Iowa, and Wisconsin were overwhelmingly Irish, and bishops and priests requested sisters from this congregation to come to their cities and towns to work among Irish immigrants. In contrast to Protestant benevolent reformers who sought to aid immigrants in the nineteenth century, women religious like the Sisters of Mercy had more in common and more sympathy with the people they sought to help. The crucial way that they could help was through affordable education, reliable health care, and when necessary, shelter for single women.[9]

Irish ethnic dominance waned in the twentieth century, but for the period prior to amalgamation in 1929, a large majority of sisters were born in Ireland, or one or both of their parents were. For women like Mother Agatha O'Brien and Sister Mary Francis Monholland, their Irish identity was linked to their Catholic faith. In a letter to her brother, Charles O'Brien, who had left home as well, Mother Agatha condemned the English government for its efforts to destroy the Irish people, compelling them to leave home for better opportunities. While she "abominate[d] the British Government" particularly for its efforts to "pass an awful bill against Convents," in Chicago Mother Agatha had to work with Protestants. In a letter to Sister Elizabeth Strange in Pittsburgh, O'Brien took an amused perspective on Protestants and other "worldlings" who observed the sisters carefully, and she commented on "how easily [they were] disedified." She begged "the Lord preserve [the sisters] from them," but found that in Chicago, she was "often afraid [she had] so much to do with protestants." Mother Agatha knew that they needed the acceptance of the Protestant population of Chi-cago, and she made efforts to build alliances with Protestant neighbors, such as opening a select school for girls, which apparently worked, as the sisters had "some very warm friends amongst them." Mother Agatha con-fessed in her letter that "almost all the children" at Saint Xavier Academy were Protestants. This did not prevent her from writing the next sentence asking Sister Elizabeth to entreat the "Lord to preserve & protect from all evil."[10]

It was not unusual for Mother Agatha and other Catholic women reli-gious to be wary of Protestant America. Other religious communities had experienced anti-Catholicism and nativist violence in the United States. Women like Mother Agatha also came from a nation that in its recent history outlawed Catholicism. Furthermore, in America, Roman Catholics fought for acceptance in a hostile environment. In the early part of the nineteenth century, the Catholic Church faced opposition from native-born Americans within largely mainline Protestant Churches, who believed Catholics were un-American. An increase in immigration from Ireland and Germany in the 1840s and 1850s aggravated negative opinions of Catholics. Convent burnings, such as in Charleston, Massachusetts in the 1830s, and attacks on churches and immigrant Catholics as in Philadelphia in the mid-1840s deeply concerned Catholics, both lay and religious alike. These same sentiments caused women religious such as Frances Warde to travel with her charges to Chicago dressed in secular garb. These views also inspired Catholic Church hierarchy to construct throughout the nine-teenth century an infrastructure, which enabled Catholics to coexist with Protestants, but preserved Catholicism. This was evident in the movement for each parish to have its own school, and the creation of diocesan and religious Catholic secondary schools and colleges. Alongside education, Catholic hospitals and orphanages, as well as welfare services that became the basis of Catholic Charities in the twentieth century, strengthened Cath-olics' position within American society. Women religious like the Sisters of Mercy participated in this movement and helped create the foundation of modern American Catholic culture.[11]

Education: "accept of all the labor and fatigue of it"

The image of the sister in the classroom or standing next to her charges for a posed photograph comes quickly to mind when we think of women religious in the nineteenth and early twentieth centuries (see Figure 3). This view of the nineteenth-century sister-teacher is only seconded by her mid-twentieth-century parochial school teacher counterpart. The various

Figure 3. Sister Mary Xavier Ryan, St. Joseph School, Janesville, Wisconsin, 1871–72.

editions published of the *Constitutions of the Sisters of the Mercy* in the nineteenth and early twentieth centuries describe the manner in which sisters appointed to this duty should undertake this work of the Institute. Along with embodying charity and humility, the sisters also needed to possess "purity of intention, and confidence in God, and—mindful of their vocation, and of the glorious recompense attached to the faithful discharge of this duty—shall cheerfully accept of all the labor and fatigue of it." Before sisters entered classrooms, they were to pray to God and to Mary to protect their charges and to instill in them devotion to Jesus Christ, his "Immaculate Mother," and the Roman Catholic Church, as well as provide the basics of education.[12]

In this context, we can easily imagine that sisters throughout this period took on "all the labor and fatigue" of their work. We can envision that Sister Mary Xavier Ryan, pictured with her class in 1871 or 1872, sent her prayers to "God and the Queen of Heaven, recommending [herself] and the children to their care and protection." She and other teachers from Chicago to Davenport to Milwaukee in parish schools, female academies, and the developing Saint Xavier College in the early twentieth century had reason to expect tiredness, or fatigue. Yet their labor was an essential and integral part of the growth of American Catholics, both lay and religious. For the Sisters of Mercy, education was a fundamental part of their congregation's identity. Sister Evangelist, who was born Lydia Holcomb in Batavia, New York in 1853, and migrated with her family to Fond du Lac, Wisconsin, spent her life in the Sisters of Mercy as an educator, in Fond du Lac and Milwaukee. For the American Church, sister-teachers' acceptance of "all the labor and fatigue" was a crucial component of the institution's efforts to build its foundation and ensure its stability and success for generations. A system of parish schools was one of the most effective means of passing on Catholic faith and culture in the United States. By 1929, the Sisters of Mercy staffed or administered sixty-six parish or elementary schools in Illinois, Iowa, and Wisconsin. They established or staffed twenty-three academies and high schools. Not all of these schools persisted into the post-amalgamation period, or emerged from the nineteenth century with Sisters of Mercy at the helm, but the record of the congregations' presence indicates a strong commitment to the education of Catholic children.[13]

According to the *Rule and Constitutions*, Sisters of Mercy instructed their students "how to direct all their thoughts, words, and actions to God's glory, implore His grace to know and love Him, and fulfill His commandments; how to examine their conscience, and respect parents and superiors." This covered broadly the intent of Catholic education, which also incorporated an education in the Catholic Mass, the various sacraments, including Confession, reception of the Eucharist (or Holy Communion), and Confirmation. Catholic elementary education, while hardly uniform and omnipresent in the mid–nineteenth century, steadily developed over the next several decades as the safe (and moral) alternative to public (and Protestant) education. An essential component to this education was instruction in the Catholic faith complemented by a Catholic-informed perspective of secular subjects, like history. Public school education, from the Catholic hierarchy's perspective, was riddled with Protestantism, namely in the form of the King James Bible. They also believed that instructors and curriculum taught the basic subjects laced with an anti-Catholic bias. Catholic parish schools provided an alternative, and after the Third Plenary Council in 1884, the American bishops required each parish priest to establish a school. They furthermore urged parents to send children to the Catholic parish school versus the public one, despite the public school's lack of fees. The Sisters of Mercy participated in this process, especially in growing urban areas such as Chicago where the Catholic parish school system was larger than the public school system by the early twentieth century.[14]

Catechism and instruction in the Catholic faith, however, was not the sum of Mercy education (or any other Catholic school) throughout this period. Parish schools, normally kindergarten through eighth grade, instructed students in basic subjects, such as mathematics, reading, writing, and history. Schools staffed by the Sisters of Mercy participated in a network of free or low-cost education for Catholic families. While the Mercys tended to populate schools attached to Irish American parishes, religious-based education of this kind provided a cultural bulwark for all ethnic Catholic faithful in the nineteenth and early twentieth centuries (and arguably up through World War II). When the Sisters of Mercy arrived in Chicago in 1846, one of their first objectives was to establish free schools for girls and boys, with St. Mary Free School for girls and then St. Joseph Free School for boys both associated with St. Mary Church. At the same time, they provided religious instruction to children from the largely Irish parish, St. Patrick Church.[15]

Beginning in 1846 and up until the first successful branch house foundation in Ottawa in 1859, the Sisters of Mercy established and staffed eight parish schools. Their tenure with some of these schools, like the two free schools in Galena, were short-lived. They added more schools as the 1860s and 1870s progressed, specifically in Chicago itself, St. John School for girls at 18th and Clark Streets, and by the early 1880s, St. Gabriel School at 45th Street and Lowe Avenue. While some schools closed, or shifted to the direction of another religious community, a close association or history developed with others. In the case of St. James Church, the Mercys staffed the parish school before it had a permanent building and continued until 2004. In this case, the then bishop of the Diocese of Chicago, Anthony O'Regan, established the parish in 1855 to serve the growing Irish immigrant population in this neighborhood, known as Carville. In this way, the Sisters of Mercy, the only religious community of women in Chicago until 1856, provided much needed free education to a working-class Irish immigrant population in this neighborhood.[16]

As the Sisters of Mercy grew and expanded, so did their presence in Catholic parish schools, particularly in areas where their efforts were needed most. When the community established a branch house in Galena in 1848, it did this in response to a request by Bishop William Quarter to serve the growing Irish Catholic population in this western Illinois town. The railroad had expanded west and Galena appeared poised to be an important center for commerce along the train line. The Irish population they came to serve included railroad workers as well as families able to afford a female academy education. After an arduous week-long journey by stagecoach to Galena, the five sisters appointed to the new Galena mission established a female academy, St. Joseph's Academy, and the two free schools, St. Mary Free School for girls, and St. Joseph Free School for boys in 1848. The decision to expand their ministries to an outpost over 160 miles from Chicago was a risk. Galena, at the far western point of Illinois and only connected to Chicago by wagons, pulled at the limits of the Mercys' resources. Yet when Bishop Quarter asked Mother Agatha O'Brien to send sisters to this mining community to serve the needs of Irish immigrants, she did. Bishop Quarter's request for Catholic education in Galena fit with the growing push to protect Catholic children from a secular or Protestant influence in public schools. Furthermore, the presence of an Irish community of women religious reinforced cultural Catholic ties. Despite the heavy Irish pull of Galena, the mission resulted in the addition of one the Chicago South Side Mercy's more influential superiors, the French Canadian Sophia Granger, the future Mother Genevieve, who entered the community from Bourbonnais, Illinois, but completed her novitiate training in Galena.[17]

The Sisters of Mercy remained in Galena, staffing their schools until 1857 when the community withdrew from this location. By this point, they had suffered the loss of several members of this branch house, including their first superior, Sister Mary Gertrude McGuire, who died of tuberculosis within three months of the congregation's arrival. Sister Mary Gertrude was one of the first Sisters of Mercy to come from Pittsburgh to Chicago in 1846. She was not the only sister to succumb to sickness while in Galena. Sister Mary Veronica Schmidt, not yet a fully professed sister, died in 1849 from typhoid fever. The entire Galena mission, despite its success at St. Joseph's Academy for girls, two free schools for boys and girls, and the care of orphans, had a cloud of failure in part because of the deaths, but also because the community did not flourish. Galena, set to become a center of commerce at the beginning of the mission, declined after the railroad lines went in different directions.[18]

Despite the failure of Galena and the possible risk of sending more sisters from Chicago, when an Irish priest from Ottawa requested sisters for his parish in 1859, Mother Mary Francis de Sales Monholland (superior at the time) agreed. Although it was a city about 80 miles from Chicago, Ottawa was another gamble.[19] Would sending a new mission to Ottawa result in the same difficulties as Galena? Despite the threat, Mother Mary Francis de Sales complied because it came from a familiar source. One of the reasons that the Sisters of Mercy spread throughout western Illinois and eventually into Iowa and Wisconsin was the established relationships between themselves and clergy, as in the case of Bishop Quarter's request for Galena. The request from an Irish parish priest for Irish sisters was also a compelling reason for Mother Superiors such as Mother Mary Francis Monholland. In July 1859, Reverend Patrick Terry, the pastor of St. Columba Church in Ottawa, traveled to Chicago to apply for sisters personally from Mercy Convent for his parish. St. Columba, established in 1838, served a largely Irish and Irish American population. On August 20, six sisters traveled to Ottawa by the Rock Island train.[20]

In contrast to Galena, this new mission in Illinois succeeded, becoming an independent foundation by 1866. Once established in Ottawa, the sisters opened St. Xavier Academy for girls and St. Joseph School for boys, both of which they continued to operate until 1892. At this time, the Holy Cross Fathers provided for the education of boys at St. Columba School, and the girls continued their education at St. Xavier Academy. Once they established a foothold in this region of Illinois, the Ottawa Mercys provided education in smaller regions, such as Streator, Mendota, Lacon, and Ivesdale in Illinois by the mid-1880s. In the case of a place like Streator, mining interests drew migration of European immigrants, including Germans and Irish warranting the presence of Catholic women religious. The Sisters of Mercy staffed a parish school, St. Mary, from 1880 until 1971.[21]

When we consider the development of parish or parochial elementary schools staffed by the Sisters of Mercy throughout the Midwest, we continue to see this pattern of call and response. We can trace groups of sisters' movements as they followed Catholic communities (often predominantly Irish) from one settlement to the next. The motherhouse of the first Chicago congregation of Sisters of Mercy continued through the 1870s and 1880s to be a source of personnel for new schools. When the Irish priest, James Scallon established a school at his parish, St. Joseph Church in De-Witt, Iowa, he turned to the community with which he had a connection and personal relationship. His cousin, Sister Mary Borromeo Johnson was there, and she and her cousins, Sisters Mary Baptist and Mary Evangelist Martin, made up three of the six sisters who responded in 1867. The Mercys' desire to respond to repeated applications for more sisters combined the spiritual foundation of the congregation with the urgent needs of the expanding Catholic population in the Midwest.[22]

The congregation's participation in the development of parish schools in places like DeWitt, Davenport, Burlington, and Mt. Pleasant, Iowa further underscores the community's investment in education. From the 1840s to the 1880s, the Catholic Church in the Midwest consisted of some major pockets of settlement, like Chicago, but also sparsely populated clusters in areas like Iowa. As the Catholic Church spread west, it acquired land and built churches for the Irish and German immigrants who moved into this territory. The process of creating a Catholic infrastructure in places like the Dubuque Diocese went a long way toward supporting the nascent Catholic community. Established in 1839 with about 800 Catholics, the diocese had little more than two churches in Dubuque and Davenport. By the 1860s, the number of Catholics had risen to over 59,000. The Sisters of Mercy's Irishness, furthermore, contributed to the reason priests such as Scallon in DeWitt and the Irish bishops that dominated the episcopacy in the diocese sought out this community. When the Sisters of Mercy arrived in DeWitt in 1867, and when they assumed the running of schools like Holy Family in Davenport in the 1890s, they participated in the establishment of a strong foundation of the Catholic Church in Iowa, while developing the faith of the Catholic laity.[23]

As in Iowa, Wisconsin parish priests needed to create and staff schools based upon the larger movement or pressure of the American Catholic hierarchy. While the first parish school in Janesville, Wisconsin in 1870 came before the Third Plenary Council's mandate for parochial education in 1884, the push to provide would-be sanctuaries of Catholic education in a Protestant society was evident in the continued pattern of requests by parish priests for sister-teachers. The pastor of St. Patrick Church, James Murdock Doyle, applied to the Chicago motherhouse, and eventually secured the relocation of a group of Sisters of Mercy from Sterling, Illinois. Unfortunately, Doyle's plans for a school could not be supported due to insufficient funds and the Mercy Sisters relocated to Fond du Lac. This relocation inspired further expansion to Milwaukee by 1885.[24]

The theme of call and response is again repeated here. We see that the Sisters of Mercy did not go where they were not invited and they responded when they were able because they recognized the need for quality religious education. Furthermore, the Catholic clergy's demands mounted. St. Patrick Church in Janesville repeated its call to the Fond du Lac motherhouse for sisters to return, which they did in 1876. By 1885, the Fond du Lac motherhouse extended itself to Milwaukee and St. Patrick School. A year later, requests came to staff another parish school in the city, Immaculate Conception. Although Milwaukee already had numerous parish schools staffed by other religious congregations, the needs or demands of the Irish Catholic laity required more from women religious like the Sisters of Mercy. By the early 1910s, the Mercys added more schools to their rosters in both Iowa and Wisconsin, stretching to St. Alphonsus in Mt. Pleasant, Iowa and St. Matthews in Shullsburg, Wisconsin.

The Sisters of Mercy instructed and helped form more children through their network of parish schools than in any other of their education ministries throughout the nineteenth and twentieth century. In comparison, fewer numbers graced the classrooms of their female academies and girls high schools, but this connection was also an important aspect of their duties as Sisters of Mercy. When Catherine McAuley and her sisters in Dublin began their work, their focus had been on poor girls and young women, with a particular attention to those who might work as servants or who would have to support themselves. The early institute had few plans to provide education for middle class or elite young girls. The chapter of the Constitutions, "Of the Schools," however, does not provide details or instruction on the manner or form education should take, and foundations in Ireland and America, even those dedicated to serving the poor and providing free schools, found pension schools, or female academies, both economically helpful to the support of their larger work, and socially and spiritually beneficial to Catholic and (very often) Protestant students. While "Of the Schools" pays much more attention to assisting poor children, and it includes discussion of "instruction of women" regardless of "the station they are destined to fill," the Sisters of Mercy believed the proper education of a girl or young woman would have a positive impact on society. The Mercys believed "their example and advice will always possess influence, and wherever a religious woman presides peace and good order are generally found" especially in female education.[25]

Catherine McAuley believed that young women, regardless of class, benefited from a solid Christian or Catholic education. If we consider the impact of the education of one of the female academies established by the Sisters of Mercy in Chicago, we can see a broader interpretation and application of Catherine McAuley's intentions for the "instruction of women." The Mercys in Chicago and elsewhere who ran female academies were not alone in conducting these types of schools. Such academies provided excellent female education in a protected, convent environment, which Catholic and many Protestant parents and guardians found appealing for their daughters. For aspiring and middle class Catholic parents, convent or female academies offered an opportunity similar to Protestant academies for young women, but also provided the security of a Catholic environment. As with parish schools, the need to create alternatives to Protestant education to protect the faith of Catholic children, in this case, young women and future Catholic mothers, became a concern for the American hierarchy. Catholic pension schools, like those established by the Sisters of Mercy, offered this alternative. By the 1880s and 1890s, parish schools established with greater frequency girls high schools, which competed with these types of academies, and many chose to expand their curriculums to include higher education. Female academies such as Saint Xavier Academy in Chicago created a college in 1912 that coexisted with the girls' pension school.[26]

One of the first things that the first Sisters of Mercy who arrived in Chicago did was establish a female pension school, Saint Francis Xavier Academy. Sisters repeated this process in Chicago and other locations, such as St. Xavier Academy in Ottawa. The South Side Chicago congregation founded Saint Agatha Academy in 1854, and later the West Side Sisters of Mercy also established St. Patrick Academy when they arrived in the city in 1883. St. Patrick's Academy, near St. Malachy Parish, was not the only high school operated by this west side Mercy foundation, and they developed Siena High School in 1925 from the former St. Catherine of Siena Academy established in 1895. In the late nineteenth century, the Milwaukee Mercys established Our Lady of Mercy, which transitioned into Mercy High School by 1925. Like other congregations of women religious at this time, the Mercys found that their academy schools provided a rewarding dual opportunity to live their religious Rule. The fees from the academy schools provided financial support, and they created chances to have a positive impact on both Catholic and Protestant young women.[27]

As Mother Agatha O'Brien attested, the congregation came in contact with Protestants frequently, including the many who attended schools such as Saint Xavier Academy, and these positive connections with Catholic women religious forged alliances with wealthy Protestant families. Alumnae of Catholic female academies, both Protestant and Catholic, proved to be valuable allies in the future and sources of fundraising. A notable exception to positive relationships stemming from select schools, however, was the concern that the sisters would seek to convert Protestant students to Catholicism. The occasional conversion or appearance of conversion did not help alleviate this fear. In one instance in 1851, a girl appeared near a conversion, but her father removed her from the school when he suspected her attraction to Catholicism. Four years later in 1855, a young woman attempted to sue Saint Xavier Academy, arguing that the Sisters of Mercy held her at the school against her will. While the case appeared in the newspapers, no mob formed at the gates of the school to search for imprisoned young girls or to burn it down as in Charlestown, Massachusetts. Newspaper accounts supported the Sisters of Mercy in this instance and insinuated that the young woman, Mary Parker, was wild. The case was dropped and Parker remained a student.[28]

In reality, the sisters of convent or academy schools understood aggressive evangelization of Protestant students would have negative consequences. Saint Xavier Academy promotional materials in the nineteenth century reminded prospective Protestant parents that "no undue influence [was] exercised over the religious opinions of non-Catholic pupils" and "only for the sake of order" were all students "required to conform to the external discipline of the Institution." Ultimately, Saint Xavier Academy and other Mercy pension and high schools are remembered more for the quality of education within a proper feminine environment than for potential scandals like the one involving Mary Parker or (near) conversions of its Protestant student body. The faculty of these schools provided instruction in refined subjects such as music, art, and foreign languages, and awarded students for "good conduct," "penmanship," "mending and darning," and "excellent deportment." They also instructed students in mathematics, including algebra and geometry; rhetoric; literature; grammar; the sciences, including botany, chemistry, and zoology; and more practical subjects such as bookkeeping. An essential element of this education was also Christian Doctrine and Bible history. A graduate of Saint Xavier Academy, and other schools like it, would emerge from her school years armed with a sound Catholic education and prepared to enter the world, whether as a wife, mother, or teacher, or a future Sister of Mercy.[29]

Saint Xavier Academy grew and matured throughout the nineteenth century. The fire that ripped through Chicago in 1871 forced its relocation south to 29th and Wabash Avenue. By 1901, it moved south again to 49th and Evans. Eleven years after this move, the Sisters of Mercy incorporated Saint Xavier College while maintaining its original academy. The Sisters of Mercy recognized that the future of female education lay in the total preparation of young women, which included college degrees. Catholic women attended high school and then college in growing numbers by the end of the nineteenth century. Female academies such as Mount Holyoke had already started the transition to accredited four-year colleges. Fear that Catholic girls would seek higher education in Protestant, or worse, secular state institutions inspired Catholic bishops to urge women religious to establish more high schools and, later, colleges. The Chicago Archdiocese was no different. The Sisters of Mercy, with Saint Xavier Academy, however, already had a system in place long before the Archdiocese began to actively recruit religious congregations to open boys and girls high schools. The South Side Chicago Mercys added to the growing number of Catholic high schools in 1925 with Mercy High School to serve Catholic girls on the south side of the city, and the west side Mercys began construction on Siena High School the same year.

Mercy High School in Chicago and many other Catholic secondary schools in the early twentieth century emerged at a period of strong institutional Church presence in American society. In Chicago, Cardinal George Mundelein urged the development of regional campuses or schools like Mercy High, which drew from area parish grammar schools and consolidated smaller parish high schools. In part, schools like Mercy High, as well as Siena and Saint Xavier Academy, flourished for decades because of the strength of the parish school system, which directed graduates to their schools. The language and content of the education provided by schools such as Saint Xavier, Siena, and Mercy High Schools changed or adapted with the times, but they continued to act in the tradition of Catherine McAuley, preparing young women to be productive members of society, imbued with Catholic principles of proper womanhood.[30]

Care of Women: "Of the Admission of Distressed Women"
In contrast to the young women who emerged from Mercy female academies, high schools, and college, unmarried women, alone in cities, who sought employment as domestic servants, factory workers, and shop girls

or sales clerks in the nineteenth century faced different challenges. Catherine McAuley's original *Rule and Constitution* identified young women in poor economic situations as a population her congregation had a particular interest in assisting. The inclusion of "the Admission of Distressed Women" as the object of the Sisters of Mercy is significant and points to a larger dedication to specific potential suffering of women in the nineteenth century. Catherine McAuley saw first-hand the consequences of women alone and unprotected in cities. When she established the House of Mercy in Dublin, Catherine McAuley intended to provide a safe haven and way station for working women and to help propel them to a better life.[31]

The use of the term "distressed women" persisted in Mercy constitutions up into the early twentieth century. The constitutions, furthermore, stressed that the Sisters of Mercy's Homes for Women admitted women of good character, however "distressed" they may be. These were nineteenth (and early twentieth) century code words for women who had not slipped into prostitution or lives of vice and depravity. This is not to suggest that the Sisters of Mercy shunned helping such "fallen" women; rather, as Catherine McAuley indicated, providing assistance to women of good character who were also distressed might prevent them from falling into vice.[32]

Guidelines for womanhood in the nineteenth and early twentieth centuries, including specific manners and modes of behavior, limited women's actions and employments. Yet single women immigrated to the United States and migrated from rural town to city, sometimes in family groups, but often alone.[33] The unpredictability of migration compounded by the consistently low wages women earned had the potential to thrust young women into morally dangerous positions. Often, employers did not believe female workers needed living wages as they believed girls and women were dependents, working only for pocket money or contributing to a larger family economy. As a result, women had minimal financial reserves to find a respectable residence as well as provide for their food and clothing, and possibly send part of their wages home to family. When we then consider the double standard of female morality confronting women in the nineteenth and early twentieth centuries, it is easy to imagine that once a woman "fell" or lost her reputation, she had little recourse toward rehabilitation.[34]

The lack of decent and affordable housing for young working women who flocked to American cities in the nineteenth century prompted the creation of the Young Women's Christian Association and other organizations to create safe-havens for "women of good character," meaning women who lived free of sin. In the second half of the nineteenth century, American urban centers such as Chicago and to a lesser extent Milwaukee drew women in search of work and a better life. The advances in transportation that enabled Sisters of Mercy to move from one area to the next and expand their works of mercy also affected single women. By the 1880s and 1890s, many found employment in greater numbers in factories, shops, and department stores, and in offices as clerks, stenographers, and secretaries. By the early twentieth century, domestic service, traditionally a draw of immigrant women, drew African American migrants from the South. As young women became increasingly mobile in the nineteenth century, migrating from farms to cities for better wages and a new life, they found homes in boarding houses and tenements. Out from under the protective arm of family, single women faced the potential immorality of the city. Women alone, or "adrift," in urban areas increased from 2.6 million to 10.8 million between 1890 and 1930.[35]

By the early twentieth century, the shift in women's education and labor created a new, modern American woman. Often referred to as the New Woman, this modern young woman was educated, independent, and employed. Women migrated to urban centers like Chicago and Milwaukee to attend women's colleges and universities, or to work in offices. Marriage continued to be the goal of the vast majority of Catholic women, but education and employment in white collar jobs, or as nurses and teachers, did not run counter to the expectations of Catholic womanhood. The Sisters of Mercy, armed with their religious rule and the inspiration of Catherine McAuley and the original House of Mercy, established homes for working girls as early as 1859 in Chicago. Initially known as the House of Providence, the House of Mercy offered shelter and lodging to young women alone in the city. The West Side Chicago congregation did the same but not until 1930, founding the Patricia Club for business women.[36]

Similarly inspired by their foundress, Catherine McAuley, the Sisters of Mercy in Milwaukee established two homes for working women: the Mercy Home for Working Girls in 1894, later renamed St. Catherine's Residence, and St. Clara's Home in 1915. For hundreds of women in the late nineteenth and early twentieth centuries who left smaller communities in Wisconsin for better employment in Milwaukee, these homes for working women provided a safe and clearly Catholic environment.[37]

The goal of homes like St. Catherine Residence and St. Clara Home was to provide a true home to the young women who lived there for a limited time, whether as students or as office workers. St. Catherine's Residence, for example, afforded its residents a chapel, parlors to entertain visitors, a billiard room, gymnasium, laundry, and a large dining room to accommo-date the nearly 200 women living there in the early 1910s. Young women paid a modest rent, which included meals. Despite their popularity, homes like St. Catherine's and St. Clara's struggled for financial support, as re-ported in the local Milwaukee press. The sisters relied in part upon the support of ladies auxiliaries, sometimes comprised of former residents, now married. While the Sisters of Mercy provided support, structure, and safe and affordable housing, laywomen's organization such as the St. Cath-erine's Council sought to provide recreations, lectures, and social clubs suitable for young women, while offering a model of married Catholic womanhood.[38]

Health Care: "comfort the sick and dying poor"

The object of the Institute of the Religious Sisters of Mercy was to edu-cate, provide protection for young women, and visit the sick. These three objects potentially covered all segments of the American Catholic and non-Catholic society. While their participation in the burgeoning Catholic parochial and academy school systems primarily involved children, and Houses of Mercy limited their focus to young single women, visiting the sick whether in private homes or in hospitals as nurses and other hospital personnel (namely hospital administrators and pharmacists) brought the Sisters of Mercy into contact with people of varying ages, religions, and ethnic origins. Consequently, the Mercys joined other congregations of women religious, acting as ambassadors for the Catholic Church in Amer-ica, who directly educated Protestants ignorant and potentially distrusting of Catholicism.

Sisters who voluntarily entered hospital wards during cholera epidem-ics and other self-sacrificing actions did not go unnoticed. Nursing sisters had some of the best opportunities to persuade Protestants that Catholi-cism did not pose a threat to American society. Their efforts as war nurses, during the American Civil War and Spanish American War at the end of the nineteenth century, further persuaded those unused to Catholic sisters in full habits that these women (and their Church) did not wish harm or have designs to evangelize Protestants. Catholic hospitals in the nine-teenth century, like schools and other institutions, began as an alterna-tive for Catholics who could not afford adequate medical care and faced not only further risk of disease in alms houses and other asylums, but also Protestant evangelization. The American hierarchy, when possible, championed the efforts of hospital sisters, or as in the case of the Sisters of Mercy, apostolic congregations who developed their call to visit and minister to the sick as a venue to expand Catholic health care. Once established for this purpose, Catholic hospitals operated on the principle that all were welcome and did not turn away non-Catholics, and self-consciously assured patients their personal faith was safe.[39]

In the nineteenth century, when quality health care eluded the vast majority of the population, women religious like the Sisters of Mercy developed much needed hospitals. Within three years of their arrival in Chicago, the Sisters of Mercy were thrust into the middle of a cholera epidemic, which revisited the city each summer until the city reformed its sanitation system. The Mercy constitution does not have a chapter on hospitals, nor does it provide detailed direction on their development or that of schools of nursing. It states simply that those who wish to emulate Jesus Christ and follow the path of mercy should "instruct and comfort the sick and dying poor." The remainder of this section of the Constitutions is devoted to describing the manner in which sisters should visit the sick (in pairs) and how they should direct their hearts and minds to this work.[40]

Despite the lack of direction from their Constitutions the Sisters of Mercy in Chicago, Davenport, Iowa City, Janesville, and other locations established hospitals, administered them, staffed wards, and created schools of nursing. When the Chicago sisters responded to the cholera crises in 1849 and 1850, the make-shift hospital at Illinois General Hospital of the Lakes came under their control, incorporated by the congregation as Mercy Hospital and Orphan Asylum in 1852. Over the next seventeen years, the Sisters of Mercy developed a reputation for health care, which inspired other locations to request their expertise and services. A closer look at the Sisters of Mercy's experiences in Iowa, specifically Davenport, shows the clear connection between spiritual motivations and the impetus to respond to the need for health care, whether Catholic or non-Catholic.[41]

The Mercy community's reputation as hospital sisters and the individual Sisters of Mercy's observation of the need for adequate health care led to the foundation of the Davenport and Iowa City Mercy Hospitals. In 1869, two years after arriving in DeWitt, Mother Borromeo Johnson and several sisters established a hospital in Davenport because they became aware of the state of mental health care in the city. Prior to the establishment of Mercy Hospital in Davenport, mentally ill patients received inadequate care at the Scott County asylum or poor farm. While one of the Mercys' original intent in Iowa was to expand their female academy in DeWitt, under the direction of Mother Borromeo, they resolved to relocate to Davenport and take over the care of mentally ill patients and to build a hospital.[42]

In the second half of the nineteenth century, Mercy Hospital, Davenport began as a cooperative of general patient and mental patient hospitals. Throughout the nineteenth century, care of mentally ill or psychiatric patients was sporadic and uneven. Often unsanitary and crowded, a lack of understanding of mental illness resulted in unsafe and chaotic hospitals. Efforts to reform the institutions for the mentally ill, often characterized as insane or incurably insane, developed from the larger reform movements of the mid–nineteenth century. Female reformers determined to extend their domestic moral authority to the public, addressed issues like sanitary conditions and mental illness. Reformers such as Dorothea Dix began a campaign to establish adequate mental institutions prior to the Civil War. In this respect, Mother Borromeo participated in a large movement to provide respectful and professional care for those suffering from mental illness. Motivated by their religious vocation and spiritual formation to care for the sick as Jesus Christ exhorted them, Mother Borromeo and her sisters in religion built and administered this institution.[43]

By 1871, Mercy Hospital, Davenport, housed in a former girls' academy run by the Sisters of Charity BVM, expanded to include a new and separate building, St. Elizabeth for the Insane, which provided more space for general care patients in the original building. The community added another building in 1884 for men, St. John, which enabled St. Elizabeth to serve only a female population. With the inclusion of St. John, Mercy Hospital, Davenport had space for mentally ill men and women, and a separate facility strictly for general care patients, which had been constructed by the late 1870s. The growth and expansion of the types of hospital care enabled the Davenport Mercy community to thrive, despite losing their founding superior in 1874 when Mother Borromeo Johnson died of cancer at forty-two. The sisters carried on under the leadership of Mother Borromeo's cousin, Mary Baptist Martin. By this time, Sister Mary Francis de Sales Monholland had joined the Davenport Mercys, and in 1882, the community elected her Mother Superior, a position she held until her death in 1888. While Mercy Hospital grew and provided more facilities to care for the mentally ill and general care patients, the Sisters of Mercy established the Mercy School of Nursing in 1895 at the hospital.[44]

Building upon their reputation and experience, the Sisters of Mercy developed hospital care throughout the Midwest. The Mercy Sisters' early successes in Davenport inspired the request made by the University of Iowa's Medical School to develop a hospital in Iowa City in 1873. The Mercys worked in cooperation with the University for over two decades. By the end of the nineteenth century, Mercy Hospital, Iowa City emerged as an independent and financially secure facility. Hospital care in Iowa spread to other areas, such as Marshalltown, Iowa, established in 1903, continuing to 1969. Throughout the nineteenth and early twentieth centuries, the Sisters of Mercy's presence provided the only option for residents in cases like Marshalltown or Mercy Hospital in Janesville, Wisconsin.[45]

Amalgamation: "to go on with the great work"

By the end of the nineteenth and into the early twentieth centuries, the Catholic immigrant population which the Sisters of Mercy, and other religious communities, served had evolved into a complex population of immigrant and second generation faithful, and the Mercys strove to keep up with the emerging modern American society of the twentieth century. The demands for sisters to staff schools and provide social services like health care continued to rise and throughout Illinois, Iowa, and Wisconsin requests went out to respective motherhouses for personnel. As dioceses expanded and built new parishes, bishops and archbishops sought to consolidate their control over the religious communities within their territories to fill needs not just in schools, but in hospitals, and charitable organizations. The episcopal consolidation process posed a potential threat to women's religious congregations. At the same time, Sisters of Mercy throughout the United States faced consolidation pressures of their own from the Holy See, who desired the restructuring of their government and religious life under the guidelines of the revised Code of Canon Law of 1917.

By the early twentieth century, American bishops and Vatican authorities alike expressed concern about the multiplication and the apparent diversity of religious life, which had developed in the nineteenth century. On the one hand, Church authorities believed consolidation of independent congregations like the Mercys would unify and normalize religious life. On the other hand, however, American bishops wished to direct the activities of the independent communities like the Sisters of Mercy within their territories. At the same time, the Sacred Congregation expressed concern that independent Mercy foundations had developed without proper guidance and oversight by the Holy See. One solution attractive to Rome, but not always to local bishops in the United States, was to combine all independent foundations under one religious governance, or a generalate system. This would create a large religious institute with provinces. Each province would have a mother provincial and councilors acting as the governance within their territory. Each convent, maintaining a local superior, would answer to the provincial, who in turn reported to the mother general and her generalate councilors. This model of religious government, however, was not the original intent of Catherine McAuley. The Sisters of Mercy expanded and established new religious houses, becoming independent, but they did not sever their spiritual ties with the foundress.

This new form of highly structured religious government with centralized authority, however, fit with what the Holy See wanted to see for all religious congregations by the early twentieth century, not simply the Sisters of Mercy. The diversity and seemingly independent movement of women religious in America and elsewhere troubled Church authorities, resulting in suggestions like the 1905 letter from the cardinal prefect of the Sacred d Congregation, Diomede Falconi to the American hierarchy advising that "all the Sisters of Mercy" in the United States unite "under a general superioress, dividing the Institute into separate provinces."[46]

The Mercys for their part did not want unification and a generalate government in 1905. While they were united by the spirit of their foundress and shared a common character and purpose, they did not see the necessity of this organizational change. Uniting under a generalate system could mean the independent community might lose the ability to direct its religious life and ministries, having to request permission from a provincial and then general council. Furthermore, Mercys worried how a generalate would impact where they conducted their religious lives. Would the new system require them to leave the local community into which they entered? They were also concerned with how a generalate religious government would impact their local relationships with bishops and clergy and with the laity. Would they be free to work in ministries, responding to real need? From their founding, the Mercys were not diocesan congregations; rather, they had papal approbation, meaning they answered to Rome. They, however, customarily were under the authority of the local bishop. If unification ran counter to the wishes of the local bishop (which in some cases it did), how would sisters obey both the local bishop and the Vatican? Conversely, there were potential positives for the Mercys to a generalate government. Union might honor the unity of history and purpose the Mercy congregation had with one another. Amalgamation also acknowledged the papal nature of the congregation and might empower the religious community in the face of encroaching local bishop authority. Religious communities of women throughout the nineteenth century had negotiated relationships with overbearing priests and bishops by arguing they had to confer with a mother superior in another location or with Rome itself. When the issue of merger was raised in the 1900s, Mercy foundations that did not wish to consolidate could not be compelled to do it.[47]

The debate among Mercys and local bishops over whether the independent groups should consolidate changed and gained momentum when the pope directed religious communities to revise their Rules and Constitutions in 1918. An essential part of this directive was that revised constitutions had to include a centralized government. The pope wanted the sisters to restructure and create a uniform religious life, thereby providing more structure and controls on communities of women religious. Individual Mercy communities and their superiors accepted the pope's directive, but they also desired to act on their own terms. The superiors who wanted amalgamation desired it to protect the legacy of Catherine McAuley and to move the Sisters of Mercy into the future.[48]

Faced with pressures to conform to the needs of local bishops and the Vatican, Mercys across the nation considered forming a central government. In Chicago, Ottawa, Milwaukee, Janesville, Iowa City, Davenport, and Aurora (and well beyond), Reverend Mothers and their assistants contemplated the benefits of amalgamation. Some had the support of their bishops, like Sebastian Messmer of Milwaukee and Henry P. Rohlman of Davenport. Bishop Rohlman had helped facilitate the unification of the Iowa City Mercys with the Davenport foundation in 1927, which made the latter location the motherhouse. The two Chicago superiors, however, did not have the approval of Cardinal George Mundelein. Despite this development, the Chicago superiors continued to work for amalgamation and looked for creative ways to champion their cause. In one case, they prepared to board trains to Milwaukee to plan in secret the merger of the American foundations of Sisters of Mercy into one congregation with a centralized generalate government, which would be known as the Sisters of Mercy of the Union.[49]

According to community lore, one rail line in particular played an important role in furthering the mission of the Mercys. The Milwaukee Road connected Chicago to Milwaukee and points west, and Sisters of Mercy used this train prior to amalgamation and after the Union to visit and maintain connections with other houses. The Milwaukee Road lines enabled sisters from Chicago to get to both Janesville and Milwaukee easily and when the Sisters of Mercy throughout the United States responded to the directive from the Holy See to revise their rules and constitutions in the early 1920s and moved toward amalgamating the various communities, superiors from Chicago and Milwaukee met on the train to discuss plans for a union.[50] Cardinal George Mundelein of Chicago, who opposed a nation-wide unification of Mercys, forbade the Mercys within the Archdiocese from discussing the matter. Despite the Cardinal's decree, the superiors from both West Side and South Side Chicago motherhouses supported the endeavor and sought ways to proceed. According to the legend, meetings occurred between the Chicago South superior, Sophia Mitchell, and the Milwaukee superior, Bernardine Clancy, on the train because technically, the Milwaukee Road was not within the archdiocese. The sisters managed to skirt the Cardinal's authority, without directly disobeying him.

No record, either written or oral exists to substantiate this story, but the sentiments behind it represent the larger spirit of the leadership and community of the Sisters of Mercy throughout the nineteenth and early twentieth centuries. As with most American communities of women religious, spirited women like the nineteenth-century Sisters of Mercy forged new foundations in otherwise uncharted territories of urban and rural United States. Venturing to America from Ireland, establishing new foundations as Frances Warde did in Pittsburgh and then later Chicago, the Mercys answered the call to serve Catholics and anyone in need. Often their efforts had the support of the clergy and laymen and women, but occasionally they faced opposition from members of the clergy who disagreed with their actions and direction as a female religious community. In the case of amalgamation, Mother Sophia Mitchell believed that a union of the various foundations of Sisters of Mercy would be in the best interest of her community on the South Side of Chicago, not simply an opportunity to thwart a troublesome Cardinal. Amalgamation meant to Mother Sophia that the Mercys would preserve the spirit and original intent of their foundress, Catherine McAuley, and their religious life would continue into the future. This was a sentiment that the other superiors who worked for the merger also shared. The changes that the Holy See required of religious communities pushed women religious to act in positive ways to ensure the integrity of their religious lives.[51]

Yet clerics like Cardinal Mundelein interfered as early as 1923 in the efforts toward a union. That same year, Mother Mary Margaret Murphy, superior of the west side Chicago foundation, communicated her community's support for a general religious government. Mother Sophia Mitchell of the South Side Chicago community, also aware of Cardinal Mundelein's objections, did not falter in showing her support for the efforts toward amalgamation. The Chicago South superior directed Sister Gregory Finnegan to take the train to Milwaukee to meet with Mother Bernardine Clancy and convey to her that Chicago South was interested in proceeding with a union of the various motherhouses. Knowing the Milwaukee Mercys had the support of their bishop, Archbishop Messmer, and that Mother Bernar-

dine would travel to Washington, DC to meet with Mother Carmelita Hartman, the superior of the Baltimore community, Mother Sophia wanted her
best wishes and support to travel there as well.[52]

Several years into the effort to create a union, Mother Sophia wrote to
Mother Carmelita in December 1927.

> Nothing great was ever accomplished without [obstacles] and this work
> [for amalgamation] is great—the greatest ever done by the Sisters of
> Mercy. So go on with the great work and you will soon have the gratifica-
> tion of knowing how many hundreds are with you. What a boon to the
> Mercies to shake off the chains that are being drawn tightly year by year
> by the Ecclesiastics of our country. How all our hearts will leap with joy of
> new life in our newfound spiritual freedom.[53]

Mitchell wrote this letter in the midst of the effort to achieve an amalgamation of sixty communities of the Sisters of Mercy throughout the United
States.[54] At this point, the superiors and other sisters who supported this
merger were uncertain if their efforts would be successful, despite the
support of the Holy See, primarily because of the power of some "Ecclesi-
astics" like Cardinal Mundelein, who stood in the way of amalgamation.
On June 6, 1928, Mother Sophia wrote another letter to Mother Carmelita
to give her continued support:

> With these lines go my heart and soul to the great movement about to
> commence. Would that I could be there in person. Please God we will
> some day be with you. Although the Cardinal showed disapproval yester-
> day when I took up the subject with him, I do not lose hope. I still see a
> light ahead.[55]

Mother Sophia believed in amalgamation and the good that it would
do for the Sisters of Mercy within her own community on the South Side
of Chicago as well as other Sisters of Mercy throughout the United States.
She and other superiors, such as Bernardine Clancy of Milwaukee, worked
throughout the 1920s to create the Union. This new form of government
would institute a uniform structure of religious life across the country and
a centralized government with Provinces answering to a General Council.
After decades of operating like diocesan communities, the Sisters of Mercy
would function in a manner more in keeping with what they were: a papal
community exercising considerable authority over their own affairs, while
subject to the authority of the Vatican.

Despite obstacles like Cardinal Mundelein, twenty-seven independent foundations voted to unite and become the Sisters of Mercy of the Union. By 1929, with the approval of the Holy See, nearly 1,000 Sisters of Mercy amalgamated, including the Mercys from both West Side and South Side Chicago, Ottawa, Davenport, Janesville, and Milwaukee. The Aurora community decided not to join the new Union in 1929, but became a part of the Chicago Province when they took another vote in 1937. The motherhouses that came together in 1929 to form the Chicago Province were spread throughout northern Illinois, Iowa, and Wisconsin, and separated by miles. Conscious of their shared origins and history, the independent motherhouses worked to unite based upon their common commitment to education, health care, concern for young women, and the desire to preserve their religion's congregation within the tradition of the Catholic Church.[56]

From 1846, with the first establishment of a community in Chicago, the Sisters of Mercy had expanded throughout northern Illinois and parts of Iowa and Wisconsin—the territory that became known as the Chicago Province. Each new mission, such as the expansion to Ottawa in 1859, Davenport in 1867, Janesville in 1870, Iowa City in 1873, a new foundation in Chicago West in 1883, Milwaukee in 1885, and finally Aurora in 1910, added to the complexity of the new Chicago Province. Throughout this roughly four-decade history, the communities of the Sisters of Mercy adapted to the needs of their society and age, while serving God, the Catholic Church, the laity, and each other. Along the way, they faced "obstacles" to their mission, but as in the case of the struggle for amalgamation, they sought always to remain faithful to their purpose as Sisters of Mercy. The formerly independent Iowa City, Davenport, Janesville, Milwaukee, Ottawa, Aurora, and Chicago South and West side foundations became one province when these separate communities voted to become one, subject to a generalate. Unity and a shared identity, however, were not guaranteed, as the preceding eighty-three years of history had created distinct identities for each foundation. Despite their diversity, each foundation held dear the memory of Mother Catherine and her spirit was infused throughout the sisters' work, which became the centering point around which their new identity had to evolve.

The ensuing decades after amalgamation would determine if this consolidation truly worked and a new Chicago Mercy identity could be forged. As the Chicago Province, the Sisters of Mercy continued to expand in numbers and institutions, while remaining faithful to the original vision of their foundress. The question remained as to how the revised constitutions and the new generalate government would change the daily religious lives of the Chicago Province members. Preserving the founding charism of Catherine McAuley through such a turbulent period with Episcopal and Vatican pressures, increasing demands of an ever-growing Catholic population, and the evolving modern society prepared them for the challenges ahead. The next chapter will examine how the Mercys engaged in this process of forming their members in a new and more structured religious life. In the midst of increased structural demands, they had to prepare members for professional ministries while striving to respond to staffing needs of an ever-expanding Catholic population.

II

"This Mutual Love and Union"

From Amalgamation to a Post-Vatican II World, 1929–1980s

Figure 4. Saint Xavier Academy school bus, Sister M. Innocentia Powers, and school children, 1945–50.

This mutual love and union should eminently characterize religious souls by dis-
tinguishing them from others as true spouses and servants of Jesus Christ. The
Sisters of this pious Institute, founded and built on charity, should make this
their favorite virtue, and they should study to maintain and cherish it among
themselves so that it may be said that there is in them but one heart and one
soul in God. This mutual love should be such as to emulate the love and union
which reigns among the blessed in Heaven.[1]

Important Dates from Amalgamation to 1980

1929: Amalgamation: Creation of the Sisters of Mercy of the Union. The Chicago Province is formed from Chicago South, Chicago West, Ottawa, Davenport, Janesville, and Milwaukee.

1929: St. Catherine Academy renames St. Patrick Academy in Des Plaines, Illinois. The Chicago Province locates its Novitiate to a wing of St. Patrick Academy.

1931: New St. Joseph Hospital opens in Aurora.

1935: Mercy Hospital, Chicago and Saint Xavier College establish the first baccalaureate nursing program in Illinois.

1937: Aurora joins the Chicago Province and the Union.

1945: Mercyville Hospital in Aurora opens a School of Psychiatric Nursing.

1954: Mercy Hospital, Chicago announces a plan for a new building and relocation north of Chicago in Skokie, Illinois, leaving the South Side of Chicago.

1954: Misericordia Maternity Hospital becomes a home for children with developmental and physical disabilities.

1956: Saint Xavier Academy is renamed Mother McAuley Liberal Arts High School and relocates to the south with Saint Xavier College and the Provincial House from 49th and Cottage Grove to Central Park Avenue between 99th and 103rd Streets.

1959: Mercy Hospital, Chicago announces plan to remain in its South Side location and make improvements to the existing structure there.

1961: Sisters of Mercy begin a mission in Sicuani, Peru.

1962–65: Second Vatican Council.

1966: Sisters of Mercy adopt a modified habit.

1967: The newly constructed Mercy Hospital building in Chicago is dedicated.

1968: St. Catherine Residence and St. Clara Club in Milwaukee merge and move to an East Knapp Street location.

1971: St. Joseph Hospital and Mercyville merge and become Mercy Center for Health Care Services.

1971: Mercy Manor for retired Sisters of Mercy opens in Aurora.

1975: Sale of Mercy Hospital, Janesville to the city.

1976: Misericordia North in Chicago opens.

3   New Community, Same Spirit

As idleness, according to the teaching of the Holy Ghost, is a great evil and we must render an exact account in judgment of our precious time, the Sisters shall be careful never to indulge in idleness. Whatever time they have to spare from the functions of the Institute they shall diligently employ in prayer, study, manual work, or other such occupations. They shall not run giddily through the convent, but shall preserve in their deportment that gravity becoming religious persons. They shall follow the horarium suited to the circumstances of the place and the duties of the Institute, as approved by the Mother Provincial and her Council.[1]

The preceding passage, an excerpt from the *Constitutions* of the Sisters of Mercy, describes the good and sober sisters, the "handmaidens" of the Church, who avoided idleness in favor of diligent and unquestioning service to God. It conveys a seriousness of purpose, with little room for humor. It reminded sisters of the gravity of a religious vocation, as it urged them to be always at the work of the Institute. Instructions such as this one combined with images of large groups of sisters in prayer, like the photograph of sisters in the chapel at Saint Xavier Academy and College in Chicago (see Figure 5), prompt us to see only one side of American sisters. While this view of the past is in part true, it obscures the human story beneath a nostalgic veneer. The American Catholic Church may have been strong, well-established, and thoroughly American by the mid–twentieth century with a network of schools, hospitals, and social welfare institutions, but Catholic sisters and nuns were hardly an interchangeable cadre of dutiful workers. If we look past the persistent stereotypical images of women religious as anonymous sisters in traditional habit, often a romanticized symbol of a Catholic Church, we will find the reality was far more complex.[2]

By the 1930s, the Catholic Church had become a strong and independent presence and gained wide acceptance within American society. "Brick-and-mortar" Episcopal leaders, such as Cardinal George Mundelein in Chicago, had literally built symbols of Catholic strength with each

Figure 5. Saint Xavier Academy/Sisters of Mercy Novitiate Chapel, 49th and Cottage Grove, Chicago.

new parish added to the urban and increasingly suburban landscapes. The laity in places like Chicago, Milwaukee, and Davenport had become less predominantly immigrant working class and more characteristically American-born and middle class; and by the post–World War II era, the largely urban church had an increasingly suburban component to it. The Church hierarchy played an important role in this growth, but so, too, did the communities of women religious who provided education, health care, and spiritual and material support. Faithful to the Catholic Church and dedicated to the Institute founded by Catherine McAuley, Sisters of Mercy persisted in staffing parish schools when asked and taught young women in high schools, academies, and at the college level.

This was a period of expansion and growth for the Sisters of Mercy as it was for the American Catholic Church. Hundreds of women entered the Chicago Province each decade between the 1930s and 1950s. The Sisters of Mercy staffed over forty parish schools, with more than thirty in Chicago alone. Sisters taught in over fifty schools, adding nearly half of them in the 1920s. The newly formed Chicago Province owned and administered nine hospitals in three states. They provided safe and affordable housing to young women in five different locations throughout the region. At the same time, religious life became more structured and monastic, and the

Sisters of Mercy operated within a centralized government, which relocated decision-making to provincial and generalate levels. Looking solely at the expanding number of parish schools staffed by the Sisters of Mercy or at the construction of hospital buildings, however, we see only one dimension of the American Catholic Church. While important, a different history comes to the foreground when we look at the people within those institutions. We find instead a complex and dynamic picture of the Chicago Mercys who strove to avoid idleness and were always dignified and self-possessed. The religious reserve stressed in the reminders to avoid "[g]iddiness and levity" belie the true dynamism of the sisters throughout this period, in which they, guided by their vocation, met the challenges of their day.[3]

Unlike the previous era when Mercy life was more decentralized and the formation process diverse, after 1930 and amalgamation, the Chicago Province not only pulled together disparate houses, but also created a new identity. A closer look at the formation process in the mid–twentieth century suggests how this was possible. At the same time, it is important to remember that while the Chicago Province created a new community, it remained faithful to the original spirit of the Institute created by Catherine McAuley.

"This union will mean adjustments"
In his opening address at the first General Chapter of the Sisters of Mercy of the Union in 1929, Archbishop John T. McNicholas told those present that they needed to make adjustments following amalgamation. This was hardly news to the delegates in the audience, nor to those at home in their respective provinces. Faced with the task of truly uniting their sisters, the new provincials, with the generalate's guidance, focused on constructing one identity. For Chicago's provincial council, the railroad helped accomplish this goal. The train, after all, had made discussion and planning for amalgamation possible earlier in the 1920s. Still the quickest mode of transportation in the early 1930s, it had bridged distances between separate motherhouses, from Bethesda to Cincinnati to Milwaukee. It enabled sisters to meet, plan, and forge bonds throughout the country. The railroad would continue to serve in this capacity as the new provincials traveled from one house to the next to meet with all the members of the convents within the new province.[4]

Community correspondence frequently mentions a pass that enabled sisters to travel the Milwaukee Road, the rail line that connected Chicago and Milwaukee, without charge. Mother Sophia Mitchell and other members of the council used it when traveling from one formerly independent motherhouse to the next, becoming acquainted with the women in Iowa, Wisconsin, and Illinois. In 1930, once again, the pass surfaced in a letter from Mother Sophia to Sister Hyacinth English, the local superior of Saint Xavier in Chicago. Mother Sophia directed Sister Hyacinth to give the "'pass' on the Electric road" to Mother Bernardine Clancy, Assistant Mother Provincial and Sister Mercedes Wellehan, Provincial Secretary when the two traveled to Milwaukee in March of that year.[5]

While this correspondence to Sister Hyacinth did not contain the reason for Sisters Bernardine and Mercedes' travel to Milwaukee, their trip coincides with visits to the various former motherhouses. Mother Bernardine Clancy, a prominent figure in the effort for amalgamation, had been the Mother Superior of the Milwaukee community. Sister Mercedes was the Mother Superior of Davenport prior to the merger. They had fought for amalgamation and their presence on the new provincial council was significant. They, along with Mother Sophia and Sisters Augustine Greene (Ottawa), Evangelist Flanagan (Chicago South), Cecilia McGinnity (Janesville), and Margaret Murphy (Chicago West) constituted the first Provincial Council. By drawing members from each area of the Province, they hoped to reinforce the message that they were now one community.

Mother General Carmelita Hartman specifically directed the provincials to "visit the houses of [their] Province as often as possible." The idea behind her directive was to assure sisters that they stood on equal footing with all sisters within the new government system. She advised the provincials:

> See if you can not make the Sisters feel that you love and are interested
> in every member of your Province; that your former community receives
> no more attention or consideration than the communities added to your
> jurisdiction in 1929; that you are familiar with the joys, sorrows, anxieties,
> financial obligations of all your Local Superiors; that you no longer speak
> of the Sisters of your former community as "my Sisters," or "our Sisters."[6]

Visiting the formerly independent houses helped ease the merger and trips like the one Mother Bernardine and Sister Mercedes took started this process. Mother Sophia, as Mother Provincial, made visitations shortly after amalgamation became official. After spending time in Maryland to help harmonize customs of the new Union, she traveled to Iowa to meet with sisters in Davenport and Iowa City. Reporting to Mother Bernardine in 1930 she found that the sisters in Davenport had "splendid spirit" and were "religious first," suggesting that the meeting with these Sisters of Mercy was profitable.[7]

These visits went a long way toward smoothing relations between houses and uniting the province. Yet full unity did not occur overnight. Familiar practices of one motherhouse did not always correspond with those designed by the generalate. The new Chicago Mother Provincial, Sophia Mitchell, attended a series of meetings held in Maryland to work toward a unified religious life in the spring and fall of 1930. For this amalgamation to work, however, provinces throughout the new Union had to conform to one mode of life, no matter how minute the details. For instance, after a daylong discussion of religious dress in March 1930, Mother Sophia wrote Sister Hyacinth that the next day's meetings would center on street cloaks, which "did not stand in favor with all," but would have to "be decided by vote of the Chapter when the discussion . . . ended." Religious dress was just one of many issues that needed attention. During more meetings held in October and November 1930, several days were spent discussing novitiate education and the role of the Mistress of Novices and "sub-mistresses." In the same letter, Mother Sophia remarked that she offered the Mother General Carmelita Hartman the Divine Office the Chicago sisters used. She reported that she heard the Divine Office sung in Maryland and it was "about two tones lower than [the Chicago sisters'] and not uniform pitch at that."[8]

Mother Sophia's letters to her sisters in the Chicago Province reveal not only her sense of humor but, more important, the deep commitment she and others had to make amalgamation work.[9] Her letters continually mentioned long days in meeting and requested prayers to sustain their new Mother General who spent her days in meetings from 8:30 a.m. to after 8:30 p.m. The general council, Mother Sophia feared, had "all aged ten years . . . No one knows the tenth part of what they have to do." Yet, if amalgamation were to work, the different provinces had to adopt a uniform structure of religious life. Dressing in the same habit, saying the same prayers, and observing the same rules were just a handful of ways to encourage a new outlook and identity. These efforts at uniformity were designed to smooth away the differences without destroying the elements of the formerly independent motherhouses that made them unique. The distinct sets of personalities and selfhoods had to blend peacefully into the whole and to come to terms with the merger. Sisters who saw themselves as Iowa City or Milwaukee Mercys had to knit that identity with a new one and develop new loyalties to the Chicago Province. Potential obstacles to unity lay in the demographic dominance the Chicago sisters had. In terms of numbers, they had nearly 70 percent of the population. Compounding this was the location of the provincial house and its new novitiate in Chicago. It was hardly the geographical center of the new province and the sheer number of Chicago sisters had the potential to obscure the identity of those from the rest of Illinois, Wisconsin, and Iowa. Chicago South, however, had contributed to the foundation of all the other communities, and the large city with its college, academy, vast network of parish schools, its hospital, and other resources made it the best choice for the provincial headquarters. Council members who came from Chicago, like Mother Sophia Mitchell, recognized the need to deemphasize their origins in favor of the good of the whole.[10]

Yet, declaring amalgamation did not make it so. As the generalate government worked out how to govern a disparate group of communities across the county, the Chicago Province found its place within the Union. They had to learn how to put no single region over another. While the generalate had to foster an equitable relationship between provinces, at the same time serving the larger needs of the Union, the provincialate had to enforce the same sentiments and government structure at the provincial level. Under the old system, government stopped at the motherhouse of a particular region with the local bishop as the next authority. The mother superior of Janesville or Davenport, for example, had set the horarium for local houses. She gave permission for travel, visiting family, or altering their habits. After amalgamation, sisters in local houses sent their requests to the provincial council for matters related to ministry, convent life, and individual or personal requests. In one instance, Iowa City asked permission to take a loan to build an extension to Mercy Hospital in April 1930. In this case, the council granted permission. Other times, provincials submitted requests to the generalate. At the September 30, 1936, meeting of the provincial council, the members discussed the possibility of a particular sister taking a graduate course in pediatrics at Cook County Hospital. After the council worked out the details of this course of study, including a determination on who would study at the same time and act as companion, they sent the matter to the generalate for permission.[11]

In both these cases, provincials had to make decisions that best served the larger province, not simply one region, ministry, or sister. In the first case, Mercy Hospital, Iowa City needed to expand its facilities to serve its community better. In the second instance, the community required more qualified medical professionals. What was uppermost in the mind of the council was fulfilling its responsibility to the people the sisters served. A month prior to the decision to allow a sister to study at Cook County

Hospital, the council denied the request of another sister. In July 1936, De Paul University asked Sister Mary Therese Flatley to act as coordinator of nursing education and teach a seminar. The council favored granting permission as long as it did not interfere with her duties at Mercy Hospital, Chicago. A month later, however, members of the council reversed their decision primarily because they felt this position would interfere with Sister Therese's teaching at Mercy Hospital. A year later, the council permitted Sister Therese to write a history of Catholic nursing and, in 1938, allowed her to accept a position of chair of an organization affiliated with Catholic Schools of Nursing. In 1939, the council appointed Sister Therese the Director of Nursing Education at Saint Xavier College. All of the requests reflected well on her success as a nursing educator, which ultimately cast a favorable light on the Sisters of Mercy and Catholic nursing in general. The provincials made decisions, however, based upon what served the community's ministries and spirit, not the professional development of one sister.[12]

The Mercys throughout the new Chicago Province needed time to adjust to this new system of centralized government. The professed sisters had to adapt to an increasingly regimented style of religious life. Amalgamation and a new *Rule and Constitutions* (as per the revision of the Code of Canon Law in 1917) were means of eliminating the variations in Mercy life, as discussed in the preceding chapter. In addition, a more monastic style of religious life was forced upon historically active communities like the Mercys, including a more formal rule of enclosure. As discussed in previous chapters, Catherine McAuley had determined that no cloister would hinder the works of her sisters. Since the 1930s, more explicit instructions and regulations of daily life determined how sisters should operate within the bounds of enclosure. Mercy life in the nineteenth century did not have a cloister or enclosure in the traditional sense, but distinctions between laity and religious were maintained. This persisted into the twentieth century as the Sisters of Mercy were not bound by a strict monastic enclosure in the traditional sense (no grate or wall barred their access to the world). The Mercys continued to go out into the world and perform their works of mercy, but they carried with them a spirit of enclosure that "should serve as their grate and their cloister." Within the context of the new restrictions following the revision of Code of Law, Mercys incorporated rules of behavior and restrictions on interactions with lay persons and clergy, even members of their own families.[13]

Sisters of Mercy continued to maintain a barrier between their convent space and the secular world, forbidding the laity from entering their cells (bedrooms), community room, or refectory (dining room), unless "for necessary purposes." The medical needs of an ill sister fell under the category of a "necessary purpose," but the barring of laity from community rooms extended to limiting visitors, whether clergy, lay members of the community, or family from entering sisters' local houses. This included the local parish as well as the hospital convents. Sisters needed the permission of their superiors to receive visitors, and they could only visit with their families (once they were fully professed) about once a month. In the course of their daily ministry lives, sisters interacted with lay men and women, and children. In the same manner they restricted their contact with the laity within their convents, they were required to guard their behavior, keeping the spirit of enclosure with them. This translated into limiting their interactions to their ministerial duties. Sisters working in parish schools did not participate in the activities of the church and those in hospitals did not engage in friendships or relationships outside their duties. Sisters always traveled with a companion, except in extreme cases. If a sister needed to travel alone, the Mother Provincial first secured permission from the Mother General. Once travel by car became more frequent, sisters were not permitted to ride in an automobile alone, even if the driver were a male family member.[14]

While more severe restrictions were placed upon novices and temporary professed sisters, fully professed Mercys also had to guard their access to "seculars," especially with regard to evening activities. Typically, sisters were not permitted to attend events or functions at night, even if they pertained to their ministerial work. For example, parish school teachers could not attend events at the parish for their students. In one instance, a sister requested permission to attend an evening meeting of a nursing organization to discuss the standards of education of student nurses, which directly impacted the Sisters of Mercy's own nursing programs. Sister Therese Flatley of Mercy Hospital, Chicago requested permission to attend, but the Mother Provincial, Genevieve Crane, could not give her approval without first sending the request to the Mother General. In this case, the generalate would not agree to this evening meeting without first winning the approval of Archbishop Samuel Stritch of Chicago. Stritch denied the request stating that he "frankly . . . [did] not like the idea of a Sister attending evening meetings outsider her convent." He went on to remark that "Our Catholics are shocked when they see Sisters outside their convent in the evening at meeting places." The archbishop closed his response to Mother Genevieve with the request that Sister Therese find a way to not attend this meeting, as he was "only trying to protect the best interests of religious life."[15]

The meeting to determine the education standards for nurses had relevance in the professional lives of Sister Therese, future sisters, and lay nurses who attended Mercy nursing programs, and potentially Mercy hospitals. Yet, Sister Therese, the director of Nursing Education at Mercy Hospital, could not attend. She had to find another way to contribute to the meeting, possibly by proxy. Archbishop Stritch's response fit with the thinking behind proper religious comportment and the "necessary" restrictions placed on women religious's movements. Here, Sister Therese was bound by a form of enclosure, but in this sense, without an actual cloister grate. Nonetheless, it set up barriers between religious and lay people. Restricting interaction with the laity and clergy, limiting the use of the radio and later television in convents, and regulating reading material were as good as an actual convent wall or grate. According to the *Customs and Guide*, the intent of these regulations imposed upon women religious was to protect them from the secular world in which they moved. It was "to protect religious institutes and their members from the injury which comes from free communication with seculars," as Archbishop Stritch's response indicates. In this way, the spirit of enclosure, in theory, also helped build up the "interior life" of Sisters of Mercy, keeping distractions and temptations from sisters' daily lives.[16]

Mercys' spiritual life was just as important as their active ministries, with the former inspiring the latter. Yet "reforms" of the early twentieth century re-emphasized the separation between what Angelyn Dries, OSF has called the "inner and outer roles" of religious life, and these reforms imposed a stricter life based on the religious rule. Communities became compartmentalized and were outwardly identified more by their institutional service and less by their founding spirit. Teaching and nursing sisters, like the Mercys, came to be identified solely by a parish school or hospital rather than the deeper prayer life supportive of it. In the end, these changes created an appearance of the inter-changeable sister. The arguably "homogenized" religious life that emerged in the mid–twentieth century put more emphasis on the religious rule of the community and the outward symbols of religious life (the habit), versus the "life experience of prayer and action" typical of the nineteenth century. Furthermore, the "protection" provided by enclosure and the continual need for permissions removed all choice from sisters, which we will see in subsequent chapters was a central element of the reforms of the 1960s and 1970s.[17]

Despite the changes that amalgamation brought to the community, none dismantled the essence, or spirit, of the Sisters of Mercy. Furthermore, this was not a static period of religious life, nor was every sister's experience the same within the congregation. More restrictions were placed upon novices and temporary professed sisters than on the fully professed members of the Mercys. Sisters' lives were also ordered by their ministries. A sister in a parish school had a different experience than a nursing sister as well as a sister who taught at Saint Xavier College. While each decade brought new developments within the Catholic Church and in American life, each generation of sisters, from the individual sister to the leadership of the provincial councils, shifted the landscape of the Chicago Province. The Mercys may have altered their religious life to conform to the demands of the Vatican, but they did so to continue to serve God and each other. By the mid-1960s, the Sisters of Mercy were on the verge of momentous change, and the renewal of religious life of the late 1960s and early 1970s seems radical when examined in isolation. Before we can understand the need for renewal, we must look closer at the preceding decades, particularly the formation process and nature of religious life for professed sisters between 1929 and 1963. This mid-twentieth-century period of Mercy life sheds light on how the dynamic changes of the late sixties and seventies emerged.

"No Sister of Mercy is a finished product until her death"

If one of the goals of amalgamation was to create a uniform identity of the Sisters of Mercy across the new Union, one place to begin was the novitiate. As Mother Sophia discussed in her 1930 letter, the provincials and mistresses of novices meeting in Maryland worked to create one novitiate formation process. For the newly formed Chicago Province, a means of assisting in this process was the creation of one central novitiate. Immediately following amalgamation, novices came to Saint Xavier College when the province agreed to consolidate its novitiate in 1929. Shortly afterward, the location shifted to St. Patrick's Academy in Des Plaines, Illinois. This served as the novitiate until 1956 when it relocated to the new St. Xavier College campus at 103rd Street in Chicago. The novitiate remained here only for a relatively short period. By the end of the 1960s, the novitiate process decentralized and eventually young women lived among professed sisters in an active local house. Up to that point, however, the Chicago Province concentrated its formation efforts in a centralized novitiate.[18]

Women who entered the novitiate right before or right after amalgamation had an advantage over those who had been in the community for

Figure 6. First group of women to enter the Sisters of Mercy after amalgamation: Postulant group 1929. Top (*left to right*): Sisters Josetta Butler, Lucetta Lysaught, Laetare Rooney; Middle (*left to right*): Sisters Noel Grimes, Elaine Ryan, De Rey O'Sullivan; Front (*left to right*): Sisters Bridgetta Hurely and Beata Gibbons.

some time. They did not have to adjust to a new system (see Figure 6). Yet, the new bands[19] of women began their education at the start of a period in Mercy history noted for its heightened structuralized religious life. With one central novitiate, formation could be better regulated and more efficient. For those who supported this idea, their arguments included sharpened training of novices and effective separation of novices from professed sisters to less distraction for the students who could more easily focus on their studies. Another argument touched upon the economical and material benefits to the community. With one location, fewer sisters would operate the novitiate. Under the established system, multiple sisters per province had the duties of training new novices. With a centralized novitiate, only "one or at most two Sisters will suffice as mistresses of novices."[20]

In a letter to Mother Mary Carmelita Hartman, Mother Bernardine Clancy conveyed the essence of the motivation behind amalgamation.

All we want is the opportunity to strengthen our government and train our young religious so that the future members of the order will be religious according to the heart of God, able to cope with the problems facing

them. Surely if the Bishops understand our motives, they will not put an
obstacle in our way.[21]

Mother Bernardine wrote this letter in the midst of the struggle for amalgamation. Despite some opposition from diocesan administrators like
Cardinal Mundelein concerning amalgamation itself, sisters succeeded in
forming the Union, and the Chicago Province proceeded with the plan for
one central novitiate.

The strength of this new facility was its uniformity. If, as Mother Bernardine remarked in her letter, the goal was to train future members of the
community to meet their world with fervor as Religious Sisters of Mercy,
they would have more success if they conveyed one message about daily
religious life and Mercy spirituality. Had they preserved the older system,
then all seven motherhouses (including Aurora after 1937) would have
their own novitiate. Ultimately, this would have run counter to the effort
to foster the new identity as Sisters of Mercy of the Chicago Province.

Almost immediately, sisters felt the change of the central novitiate at
every level. By the spring of 1930, some young women arrived at Saint
Xavier "already clothed" in their religious dress. Mother Sophia expressed
her regret to Sister Hyacinth that they no longer had the ceremony in
which these women received their new clothes. Normally, a woman entered the novitiate in secular dress; only after a formal ceremony did
she put on the religious clothing of a postulant. This development, while
disappointing to the leaders of the new Chicago Province, was only one
by-product of the merger. Among other concerns, Mother Sophia also inquired about the novices who had just arrived and if they fared well at
Saint Xavier. She worried over their homesickness and tears, as well as
sleeping accommodations, indicating the affection she and others felt for
their charges. These new entrants, much more than in years previous, had
left their homes and families and traveled longer distances to the novitiate. They were all young women, possibly leaving home for the first time.
Nearly half of them were under the age of twenty.[22]

While the Union of the Sisters of Mercy worked to normalize their
customs and religious life, the novitiate continued to grow. The Chicago
Province accepted forty-four entrants in 1930. These postulants entered
a community in which the details of formation had not been finalized.
Mistresses of novices, provincials, and generalate continued to work out
the details of the changes. Mother Sophia confessed in a letter to Mother
Bernardine that the Mercys of the Chicago Province "had not done so
badly" when compared to other provinces because they had to make fewer

changes. In April 1930, the provincial leadership continued to discuss the formation process and the revisions to the *Customs and Guide*. Despite this period of change, the Chicago Province continued with its plans to move the novitiate from Saint Xavier College to Des Plaines, Illinois on the northwest suburb of Chicago in the summer of 1930.[23]

A brochure advertising the Chicago Province's novitiate proclaimed, that "no Sister of Mercy [was] a finished product until her death." This meant that sisters continued to grow and learn, even after they left the novitiate and professed their final vows. Their education, however, began at the novitiate. *Mercy* also characterized the profession to religious life as the continuation of God's love for humankind. Issued in 1948, the pamphlet described the Sisters of Mercy as women who "contribut[ed] positively to the society in which [they lived.]" God's love for humanity was acted out through the corporal and spiritual works of mercy. It further stressed the symbolic importance of the Mercys; they represented God's mercy in the world. At the heart of this message was Catherine McAuley. As the foundress, she presented a perfect example of what motivated and inspired Sisters of Mercy from the conception of the religious institute. The desire to do God's will in the world and to help those in need motivated many young women to become Mercy Sisters.[24]

As in the nineteenth century, the Mercys needed women who were dedicated and able to carry out their ministries. A desire to serve God and the poor was a primary qualification but, as in the previous century, women had to be of sound mind and body. While the risk of death due to dangerous ministries declined remarkably in the twentieth century, Sisters of Mercy worked long days, particularly as teachers in classrooms and nurses in hospitals. The Mercys also required applicants have a good reputation, or "be of good character." With the recommendation of clergy and a sense that the individual had a "capacity to learn," women entered the novitiate as postulants for six months and the religious life that lay ahead had to be built from the ground up.

By the 1930s and 1940s, the Catholic Church had grown in strength and size and nearly everywhere parish priests and bishops were eager for new recruits like those who entered the Chicago Mercy novitiate. The demands only increased in the 1950s. The call to religious life that many young Catholic women felt throughout this period came out of a long tradition of honor given to sisters and nuns. Yet, what motivated young women to enter religious life in the face of the ever-expanding array of choices for them in American society between the 1930s and mid-1960s? Throughout this period, Catholic and non-Catholic women had widening

opportunities in education and employment, as well as socially and politi-
cally. They emerged from the 1920s with more equality, including the vote.
Some young women drove cars, and many wore makeup and socialized
in mixed gender groups, attending dances and going to movies. Seemingly, everywhere in 1920s American culture, the young had thrown off
the mores of their parents' generation and embraced modern dress and
sensibilities.[25]

The stock market crash in 1929 shifted the outlooks of Americans. The
1930s in America were fraught with economic depression and dissatisfaction. Following a decade of cultural changes and economic boom, the thirties were years of struggle as unemployment rose, and fortunes, both large
and small, were lost. Unemployment did not affect women as quickly as
it did men, particularly those who worked in offices, but, ultimately, the
widespread economic depression affected both. As many as two million
women were unemployed by 1931 and the number increased by the mid-
1930s. Despite the growing joblessness, many typically "women's jobs"
were protected because clerical work and domestic service were seen as
essential. With jobs scarce and the persistent belief that men were the
chief and sole breadwinners of families, women, especially wives, had difficulties getting employment in certain fields. Not surprising during an
economic crisis such as this, plus the added stress of forced unemployment due to marital status, the marriage rate declined in the 1930s. At the
same time, despite economic disruptions, the numbers of single Catholic
women attending universities and colleges continued to increase. This
trend began in the early part of this century and only steadily climbed. By
the 1940s, the number of Catholic women attending college rose to over
20,000.[26]

While World War II saw a rapid decline in attendance rates in higher
education for Catholic women, the war years brought different and expanding avenues of employment that not only tested their mettle but
provided the opportunity to act heroically for their nation. During World
War II, women's work was needed in munitions factories, military service,
and nursing. If women looked for chances to perform good works while
serving their neighbor and nation, they could find it as seculars and not religious. By the end of the forties and into the emerging post-WWII boom
of the 1950s, modern American life in the suburbs called young Catholic
and non-Catholic women alike as popular culture preached a revival of
domestic bliss. As the twentieth century progressed, marriage, higher education, and a broadening employment field were just some of the choices
women had before them. Upwards of 120,000 Catholic women attended

university by the mid-1960s, and social and political changes reempha-
sized youth culture, particularly stressing a break from traditionalism of a
past generation.[27]

At the same time, Catholic laywomen had more opportunities to find
spiritual enrichment and community support in organizations that did
not include a life-long vowed commitment. While sodalities and parish
organizations had always drawn laywomen to their membership, providing not only spiritual and social purposes, they had also enabled women
to perform acts of charity. In the early 1930s, especially in areas like Chicago and Milwaukee, a new breed of lay activity known as Catholic Action started to emerge, which attracted some lay Catholics. Increasingly,
the message from the Catholic hierarchy was that the laity had distinctive
gifts, which they used in the world. Pope Pius XI in the 1922 encyclical,
Ubi arcano, stressed the importance of the lay apostolate. Lay involvement
in apostolic work and the Church began to expand by the 1930s with the
larger Catholic Action movement, and it became the nucleus for change in
lay participation within the Church. The laity had a sacred ministerial role
and Catholic Action developed in various organizations and movements
like the Catholic Youth Organization, Christian Family Movement, and liturgical reform. While popular in areas like Chicago, which had clergy
that supported these developments, it did not become a larger movement
until the 1950s. Davenport Catholics, particularly those connected with
St. Ambrose University, participated in this movement in the 1950s, and
the Mercys' St. Catherine Residence in Milwaukee engaged in Catholic Action in that city.[28]

With all the cultural, religious, and economic changes impacting their
lives, we may wonder why women chose a religious life and specifically the
Sisters of Mercy. In reality, many women, with all the new opportunities
in front of them, opted for a life-long commitment to a religious congregation. The number of American women entering religious life increased
consistently from the 1930s, reaching over 200,000 by the mid-1960s.
Women who became Mercys participated in this growing trend because
they saw something appealing in this life. With the cornucopia of new opportunities, religious life drew many women who saw no other way to be
a part of the institutional Catholic Church and perform good works. The
Chicago Province saw the number of entrants in 1930 nearly double that
of two years' previous and throughout the decade they received a steady
stream of new applicants, averaging twenty-two a year, and over 200 for
that decade. While there were fluctuations in rates of applications, the
high numbers of applicants continued up until the mid to late 1960s.[29]

For those who entered the Chicago Province, they found something in the Mercy community that attracted them. All had a vocation, or felt a call from God, directing them to this life, but they perceived this call in many personal ways. Some discerned their vocation through their first-hand experience with Mercys, in elementary and secondary schools.[30] Many said that they were impressed with their teachers, particularly at either Mercy High School in Milwaukee or Chicago, or Siena High School and Saint Xavier Academy in Chicago. They also remarked that the Mercys' compassion, charity, sense of hospitality, and joy captivated them. Other sisters entered the community with family members, like blood sisters Elizabeth and Mary Feinberg from Milwaukee in 1918, becoming Sisters Mary Aquin and Mary Philip. This sisterly bond is reminiscent of the nineteenth century example of the McGirr sisters. Biological sisters Lucille and Rose Ellen McKillop also entered together in 1944 becoming Sisters Mary Lucille and Roseline. Still others had aunts who were Mercys, and their desire for religious life in general was fostered by an association with these relatives. Some also came from strong Catholic families and had parents who wished to have a daughter in religious life.[31]

Typical of many aspirants to the Chicago Mercys was Joan Agnes McSloy, who entered Mother of Mercy Novitiate at St. Patrick Academy in Des Plaines on September 8, 1938. She had grown up in Chicago and attended both Catholic grammar and high schools. Her education at Mercy High School in Chicago especially influenced her decision. As a student, she admired the sisters' dedication to their work and religious life and she was attracted to the sisters' spirituality, seeing how their faith and commitment to God led them to care about others. The future Sister Evangeline McSloy, like so many other young women, had come out of a tradition of Catholic education, which proved an important tool in perpetuating Catholicism in the United States.[32]

While not all Mercy aspirants attended Mercy schools, the large majority attended Catholic schools, staffed by women religious. The exposure to religious life and a sound Catholic education had the potential to inspire a vocation, as did family devotions and church participation. The lesson learned from nineteenth-century anti-Catholic sentiments and behavior was that the Church needed an infrastructure of Catholic institutions to prevent the faithful from losing its faith or, even worse, converting to Protestantism. This belief prompted scores of women religious like the Mercys to staff multitude of parish schools, which might in turn produced future aspirants.

The success of these efforts was apparent by the twentieth century. The number of schools grew during the twentieth century. In Chicago, the archdiocese's priests and bishops turned to communities like the Mercys because they were effective and affordable. The minutes of the Chicago Province's meetings are replete with demands for more sisters. How to fill these demands depended squarely upon the availability of sisters, and the provincial council understood that new recruits came remarkably from their high schools. Thus the council directed principals and teachers to look to their students to find and foster vocations. As mentioned, Joan McSloy, the Mercy High School Chicago graduate and future Sister Evangeline, was a product of this effort. Shown the everyday religious life of her teachers, she followed her calling to Mother of Mercy Novitiate in Des Plaines.[33]

The formation process following amalgamation was not fundamentally different prior to 1929. There were some obvious changes, such as the central location and larger band, or class, sizes. More noteworthy was a revised novitiate guide for the entire Union, which shifted some aspects of daily novitiate life. The basic steps essential to becoming a Sister of Mercy, however, had not changed. Aspirants still entered as postulants and remained for six months; following their reception into the novitiate, they began wearing the religious habit with a white veil (see Figure 7). Reception ceremonies occurred in the novitiate's chapel. In the 1950s, the provincial council considered moving reception ceremonies for large bands to a parish church. A public ceremony would not only give more families an opportunity to attend, but they might inspire other young women to follow a vocation. While the council decided in the early 1950s not to relocate these types of ceremonies, within the next decade novices had receptions at places like St. Stephen Church in Des Plaines and Queen of Martyrs Church in Chicago, the neighboring parish to the campus of Saint Xavier College and the new novitiate (see Figure 8).[34]

A continual concern for provincial leaders was whether the young women were sufficiently prepared for religious life. Rarely did a mistress of novices or the provincial council who made final judgment about accepting an entrant question an aspirant's piety. *Mercy*, the booklet advertising the Sisters of Mercy, stated that women did not need to be "notably pious." The purpose of training during the first six months was to "lay the foundation for growth in the spiritual life," and postulants had the time to discover if they wanted to proceed into the novitiate. While they discerned their vocations, the mistress of novices and her assistants assessed the

Figure 7. Postulants and novices: Sisters Patrick Anne (Cathleen) Cahill, wearing a habit of first profession, and Peter Marie (Nancy) Ponzi, wearing a postulant habit. Mother of Mercy Novitiate, Saint Xavier College Campus, 1961.

Figure 8. Queen of Martyrs Reception Ceremony, Band/Class of 1959.

aspirants' character, aptitude, and suitability for the congregation. After another two years of study, novices took temporary vows and exchanged their white veils for a black one. After another three years, sisters took perpetual vows and wore a ring.[35]

The characteristics of a suitable candidate for the Mercy congregation had not changed radically from the nineteenth century. While piety and a desire to serve God were essential elements, they were not the only considerations. The Mercys needed women like the future Sister Evangeline to perform their duties and withstand the difficulties of daily religious life, which also included rich spiritual and communal components. Mercys also considered postulants' background and determined if any impediments barred their admittance. They rejected women if they were not of legitimate birth, or if they were not baptized Catholic and had received certain sacraments. Age was also a consideration. In one instance, the provincial council debated accepting a recent convert of three years as well as a thirty-six-year-old woman. They were both accepted on a trial basis because of their "qualifications for either nursing or teaching."[36]

After an evaluation of aspirants' background, reinforced with positive recommendations from their parish priest or former teachers, the community scrutinized their motivations for entering religious life. The Mercys wanted individuals whose purpose was simply to follow God's desire for them, to glorify God, or to save souls. They did not want women who were motivated by less spiritual reasons. While some women followed a relative into the community, wishing to join the Mercys simply to be with an aunt or friend was not an acceptable reason for seeking religious life. Neither should an aspirant choose the Sisters of Mercy to find economic security or raise one's social status. In reality, people did choose religious life for more "human" reasons. Young women like Sisters Evangeline McSloy may have felt God's call to become Sisters of Mercy, but she and others responded in personal ways, influenced by family, their education, and their immediate experiences with women religious.[37]

Once a postulant moved onto the next level of formation, life continued with study, prayer, and work. The novitiate in Des Plaines and later at 103rd Street in Chicago brought together larger groups of novices who led a structured life. Impressive images are found in the novitiate booklet, *Mercy*, of large groups of postulants and novices working on sewing, in the laundry, praying in chapel, studying, attending classes, and relaxing during a game of croquet, volleyball, or a tennis match (see Figure 9). These images, however staged, indicated to aspirants the full scope of postulants' and novices' lives. Some worked in the laundry or the refectory, while others performed janitorial duties, such as cleaning stairs and mopping floors, and helped take care of elderly sisters in the infirmary. While the Chicago Mercys appear to have found a source of inexpensive labor, manual labor was an essential aspect of the postulants' and novices' formation. Domestic duties, particularly for a community that performed works of mercy, taught obedience and discipline. Their labors also served the common good of the congregation as in the case of Saint Xavier Academy and College's move from the 49th Street and Cottage Grove Avenue location to its new campus at 103rd Street in Chicago. Novices played an essential role packing and then unloading items.[38]

After two years of study as novices, sisters with temporary vows, also known as juniors, entered a period of intensified education and training. The Mistress of Juniors was responsible for monitoring the temporary professed sisters' work and study. The juniors' lives were no less regimented than the postulants, but the purpose was the continued formation of the sisters. Everything, including comportment, letter writing, reading material, and entertainment, was regulated. The Mistress of Juniors, like

Figure 9. Novices and postulants at a picnic at the new Sisters of Mercy Novitiate, Saint Xavier College, at 103rd Street, Chicago, 1956.

the novice mistress, opened all incoming mail and had the authority to withhold any correspondence deemed unwise. Sisters were to read only approved materials outside their work and study. It was also the mistress's duty to be aware of changes, manners, and comportment to ensure that sisters followed the rules of religious modesty. Juniors had weekly lectures based upon the *Constitutions, Customs and Guide,* and other religious writings. The Mistress of Juniors gave these lectures and encouraged sisters to live up to the congregation's expectations. The idea behind this study and lectures was to immerse sisters fully in the Mercys' spiritual foundation, which supported and directed all the works of mercy of the institute. Sisters such as Evangeline McSloy may have been inspired by the hospitality, spirituality, and professionalism of their teachers, but they began to understand how these qualities and characteristics manifested in fully professed Sisters of Mercy.[39]

Religious and spiritual formation was complemented by college courses. Prior to 1955, sisters, however, worked toward college degrees slowly. While juniors took college courses on weekends and during the

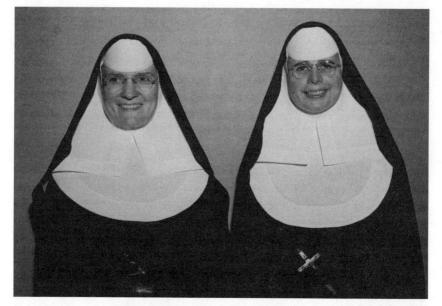

Figure 10. Sisters Evangeline McSloy and Norella Hartnett, Formation Directors, 1954–65.

summers, the province needed them to fill positions in schools, hospitals, and other ministries. In the case of Sister Evangeline McSloy (see Figure 10) who took her temporary vows in March 1941, seven months after her first profession, she began teaching music in a parish school in Chicago. In the midst of this first assignment three years later, she professed her perpetual vows. Sister Evangeline earned credits toward her bachelor of arts in music by taking courses at Saint Xavier College and De Paul University. She completed her degree in 1949. Sister Evangeline's path to full profession and a college degree was typical for most Sisters of Mercy in the 1930s and 1940s. For some, completing their degree took upwards of ten years, as they took one or two courses a semester or in the summer months. Demands of assignments, religious formation, and community life kept both the juniors and fully professed sisters busy.[40]

Despite their full schedules, juniors continued their formation for another three years before professing final or perpetual vows. Concern about sisters' preparation for final profession dot the provincial records. Periodically, sisters had to renew their temporary vows for an additional three to six months or until the Mistress of Novices and the council believed they were ready. In some cases, the postponement occurred to avoid interrupting college course work. This, however, did not allay anxieties that sisters had not prepared fully for final profession. By the early 1950s, concern over spiritual readiness expanded to professional preparation as well. Did completing degrees part-time over the course of five to ten years truly serve the needs of the community? While the continual demands of the clergy for sisters to staff parish schools and the needs of health care pushed provincials to assign juniors prior to completion of degrees, they saw the benefit of more time for study. In March 1952, the provincial council discussed the change in the juniors' course of study. Starting in August, they would spend two years in a house of studies before their first assignment, whether in the classroom or hospital ward. At the May 17 council meeting, Mother Provincial Domitilla Griffin reported that Cardinal Samuel Stritch of the Chicago archdiocese understood the consequences of the creation of the two-year Juniorate House of Studies Program, but hoped that the community would implement this change gradually.[41]

The implications for the parish schools became evident by fall 1952, when the provincial council feared the community would not have the personnel to staff all their schools. The community worked out an arrangement with the Archdiocese whereby parish schools would have a ratio of one lay teacher to every eight sisters, except in the cases of poorer schools. The Sisters of Mercy were not alone in their concern about proper education and formation of their sisters. In an effort to respond to the needs of the Catholic community, particularly in the very public and local setting of the parish school, communities of women religious had stretched their resources to the limit. The compromise with the Archdiocese forced local parish priests to hire lay teachers and pay them higher salaries. Furthermore, standards for teaching certification continued to rise and teachers needed college degrees. Communities of women religious, like the Sisters of Mercy weighed the needs of the laity, the Church hierarchy, and their own sisters and chose to prepare women, not just spiritually, but also professionally for religious life.[42]

The Sisters of Mercy were not alone facing the challenges of fully educating their sisters. A national movement, the Sister Formation Conference, to address these problems arose in the 1950s. An outgrowth the National Catholic Education Association and a 1951 directive from Pope Pius XII that sisters should have complete preparation for their apostolic works, the Sister Formation Conference urged congregations to reexamine and reform religious life. A complete education and more time to prepare spiritually for religious life had long-reaching consequences. Sisters up to this point had a formation and training that stopped well short of equality with that of the clergy. This underscored the gender inequity within the

Catholic Church and sisters across religious congregations by the 1960s outwardly questioned how the larger Church saw them as women and as religious. In the next chapter, I discuss the impact of the Sister Formation Conference and the Chicago Mercys' participation in it.[43]

In the Chicago Province, real change in the training of Mercy sisters began in the 1950s. Those who made their temporary professions by 1952 no longer went straight to their first teaching or nursing assignments. They instead spent two years in the Juniorate House of Studies. From this point, younger sisters took more direct routes to college degrees and professional development. Sisters, who entered in the late 1950s and 1960s, increasingly finished their degrees closer to the date of temporary profession and often before final profession.[44]

Toward the Perfection of Mercy

As stated previously, "no Sister of Mercy [was] a finished product until her death," and her religious formation did not end with profession of final vows. Achieving religious perfection, always the intent of the individual sister, was a life-long process. From the 1930s up to the beginning of the Second Vatican Council, the Chicago Province engaged in its own pursuit of perfection as it knit together the different motherhouses and maintained and expanded its works of mercy. Considering the regional and territorial differences within the Chicago Province, religious life had its own diversity, but the rigid structure appeared to hold everything together. Yet religious life, whether in the formative period of the novitiate or as professed sisters, was far from static.[45]

If cultural stereotypes of women religious of this period are to be believed, then nothing distinguished one community of sisters from another. Those unfamiliar with the nuances of religious life in the mid–twentieth century might see nothing unique about the Sisters of Mercy, their ministries, community life, or spirituality. They were just another cadre of "good sisters." The amalgamation established one province for the different formerly independent motherhouses and the formation process helped forge new identities as Chicago Mercys. From the 1930s through the 1960s, the Mercys consistently maintained the ministries or works of mercy including parish schools, academies, and high schools for girls, a woman's college, residences for young women, and hospitals. Taken as a whole, the consistency of these ministries reveals more than dutiful workers of the Catholic Church. It shows a dedication to the spiritual and material needs of their mid-twentieth American society.[46]

For much of the twentieth century, Sisters of Mercy lived "over the shop" in parish convents, upstairs in high schools and academies, and within the walls of hospitals.[47] Few physical distinctions existed between the sisters' work and their identity, something which they sought to change by the end of the 1960s. Chicago Mercys throughout the mid–twentieth century lived in both small and large convent settings. Those who taught in parish schools sometimes had as few as three or as many as twenty-nine sisters living within local convents, depending on the size of school. More sisters lived at high schools such as St. Patrick's in Des Plaines, or Siena High School on the west side of Chicago. Mercy High School in Chicago had as many as fifty sisters residing in its convent in 1932. The high schools, residences for young women, hospitals, and the provincial house generally had the largest numbers of sisters. Fifty-five sisters lived at Mercy Hospital, Davenport versus the twenty-five who lived at St. Xavier Convent in Ottawa, Illinois.[48]

Regardless of the size of the convents, local houses observed a similar pattern of religious life, depending on the type of ministry of the house. Local convents connected with parish schools followed a different schedule than hospitals. Sisters in parish schools ordered their day with faculty meetings, teaching, the occasional school outing, and the daily preparations for classes. They also had community exercises, such as morning and evening prayers. Local superiors paid attention to the details of the sisters' prayer life, ensuring that they observed community silences, and that prayers were said "devoutly" and "at the same tempo" as the sisters who led them. Sisters within hospital ministries had different schedules and professional roles, but they also conducted their spiritual life in a similar fashion. Within the rhythms of daily life, certain elements were universal, such as religious exercises and daily prayers that united all Sisters of Mercy.[49]

In many ways during this period, convent life continued in the usual structured fashion, with a combination of prayer and work. Days were filled with call bells, permissions granted (or not), and an enforced separation from the laity. Increasingly, outmoded restrictions placed upon sisters' lives, such as whether or not they could drive, visit family, listen to the radio, or talk on the telephone, resulted in dissatisfaction articulated by the early 1960s. Complicating matters was the relationship between church leadership and the average sister. The growing advocacy to fully educate and prepare sisters for their apostolic works was joined by discussions of the role of sisters in modern society. Were they simply interchangeable parts in a Catholic institutional machine? Or did sisters have a deeper purpose to truly imitate Jesus Christ and be with the poor and suffering in new ways? The demands of the laity and clergy for women religious to continue as they always had conflicted with the spiritual needs of the congregation to return to their founding mission as set out by Catherine McAuley.

The Mercys' ministry throughout the 1930s to 1960s provided a vital service to American Catholics, but by the end of this period, the tensions between an increasingly outmoded and highly restrictive religious life born out of the amalgamation and revisions to religious life in the 1910s and 1920s and the desire for a more engaged spiritual and self-directed apostolic life, resulted in pressure from sisters within the province to move in new directions. The seeds of renewal of the 1960s and 1970s were planted in the preceding decades. To understand how and why the struggles for renewal and change occurred, we must consider how the tension between serving the Church and the laity and attending to the needs of sisters within Chicago Province manifested itself between the 1930s and 1960s. The next chapter will examine how the Chicago Mercys attempted to maintain their ministries without sacrificing sisters' spiritual and professional development. The Sister Formation Conference, in particular, played a central role in how the Chicago Mercys negotiated the tug between forming sisters for apostolic work in the spirit of Catherine McAuley and responding to the institutional needs of the Catholic Church in hospitals, schools, and elsewhere in society.

4

Demanding Decades
Mercy Response to the Clergy
and the Laity: 1928–1960s

The Constitutions *require that a number of Sisters sufficient for the works of the Institute obtain diplomas or certificates for teaching and nursing recognized also by the civil authorities (see* Constitutions, *Article 282). The Mother Provincial, with the consent of her Council, provides for the education of the Sisters under her in accordance with the needs of the province. With the consent of her Council, she selects the institutions the Sisters are to attend and designates the field in which each Sister is to work.*[1]

From the late 1920s up to the changes instituted by the Second Vatican Council of the mid-1960s, the Sisters of Mercy of the Chicago Province, like many other communities of women religious in the United States, faced growing demands to staff parochial schools, to expand health care, and to continue to provide for the spiritual and material welfare of American Catholics. At the beginning of this period, the Chicago Mercys began to learn what it meant to be a united province. Amalgamation had created a new name by which Wisconsin, Illinois, and Iowa Mercys identified themselves, but did not change the essence of who they were: Sisters of Mercy. Their novitiate education may have shifted to one location and their government structure centralized, but the spirit that inspired the nineteenth-century communities had not vanished and from 1930s to the mid-1960s, the Chicago Mercys did not stand still. As they conformed to the demands of the Catholic Church to restructure their congregation's government and faced increasing structuralization of their daily life, sisters willingly embraced a religious life that meant obedience to their superiors and to God, as they provided education, health care, and material and spiritual comfort to Catholics and non-Catholics alike.

The women who entered in 1929 (see Figures 6 and 11), just as amalgamation became a reality, joined a community in flux. Without being aware of what had shifted, these early sisters started the journey with the rest of their new sisters that took them from the larger centralized novitiate in Des Plaines, Illinois to their first assignments—chosen as the epigraph to

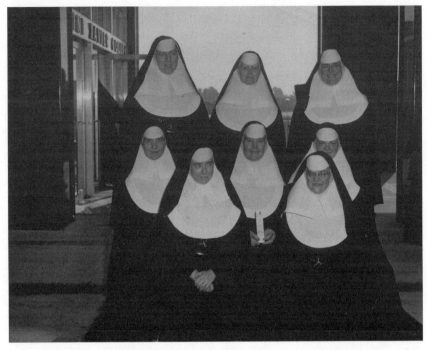

Figure 11. Silver Jubilee 1957, Saint Xavier College. *Top*: Sisters Laetare Rooney, Lucetta Lysaught, and Josetta Butler; *Middle*: Sisters Noel Grimes, Elaine de Rey O'Sullivan; *Front*: Sisters Bridgetta Hurely and Beata Gibbons.

this chapter from the *Customs and Guide* indicates by the provincial superior and her councilors—either in schools or hospitals or possibly in one of the province's homes for women. Throughout the next thirty years, they earned college degrees and in some cases masters and doctorates. They did not necessarily achieve these diplomas in a timely fashion, but often took ten to fifteen years or more, completing courses one or two at a time, on weekends or in the summers. They saw the dawn of the Sister Formation Conference, which stressed the importance of sisters' professional development before assignment in classrooms or on hospital wards. Their community, always attentive to the education of its members, embraced this new movement in the 1950s, and the 1929 band saw newer and younger sisters held back from placements to complete degrees much quicker than themselves. By the end of this period, these sisters observed and joined in the discussion for reform of religious life and many of them lived to see the modification of their community prayers, ministries, and religious government.

So often the perception of religious life in the mid–twentieth century is that of a highly structured and unchanging monolith. In reality, the dynamic changes wrought by Vatican II had percolated for decades before the impact of renewal in the 1960s. Change brewed as parish priests and local bishops placed heavy demands on women religious to provide a cheap labor supply to keep the Catholic infrastructure moving and growing. At the same time, theology of the Mystical Body of Christ and the expanding lay involvement in the Church inspired communities like the Mercys, just as much as the Sister Formation Conference and the push for more and complete education before beginning ministries, to reconsider their role in the Church and in society. Finally, change started with Pope Pius XII's call in the early 1950s for women religious to become more engaged and prepared for their apostolic ministry, echoed in 1962 by Leon Joseph Cardinal Suenens (among others) and his book, *The Nun in World*. Sisters of Mercy and other women religious observers and participants in these and other secular social movements were receptive to the spirit of renewal, which emanated from the Second Vatican Council.[2]

Reexamining this period from the 1930s to Vatican II through the eyes of women religious like the Mercys provides another perspective on the evolving American Catholic Church. The Sisters of Mercys were a part of this institutional Church and were dedicated to supporting and sustaining it. The American church and many of its institutions of the 1930s through early 1960s flourished because of women religious's continued support and proliferation of their traditional ministries, such as health care and education. Parish schools, in particular, needed their presence to maintain the system in that form in the mid–twentieth century. Yet the Sisters of Mercy, while sharing the mission of the institutional Church, were mindful of their charism and their dedication to preserving other ministries, such as homes for young women or a home for unwed mothers and children with developmental disabilities, such as Misericordia in Chicago. The homes, while involving relatively few numbers of sisters, ran counter to an efficient use of personnel in the face of the demands from parish priests and bishops. The Sisters of Mercy, however, understood that these ministries had importance and relevance to the spirit of the Institute and in the context of their age. Navigating the demands of the institutional Church and their own community resulted in a delicate balance between the two during this period. The needs of the community, ultimately, determined the shifts in formation and education that resulted in a modification in attitudes and perspectives about the role that women religious would fill in American society.[3]

"To serve God more faithfully"

In September 1929, Evelyn Grimes entered the Mother of Mercy Novitiate in Des Plaines. Before she was accepted, she had to complete a questionnaire that asked for her personal background, the extent of her education, and whether or not she possessed any impediments that would prevent her from becoming a woman religious. She was also asked to provide her reasons, or "motives," for "leaving the world" and becoming a Sister of Mercy. The future Sister Mary Noel answered that she wanted "[t]o serve God more faithfully." Many applicants articulated similar sentiments. They wished to "save [their] own soul by helping others to save theirs" or "sanctify [themselves] and save souls." The three Rooney sisters, Marguerite, Eileen, and Catherine, who entered the Mercys in 1920, 1927, and 1929, respectively, all believed they could serve God "more perfectly" by becoming religious. While these answers may appear perfunctory, they should not be dismissed primarily because they reflect both what the community wanted in its applicants and what young women sought—a life of service to God.[4]

After the Sisters of Mercy accepted Evelyn Grimes's application, she spent two years at the Des Plaines novitiate before beginning her first teaching assignment at Saint Xavier Academy in Chicago. Sister Mary Noel Grimes spent the next several decades teaching in elementary schools in Chicago, Elgin, Mt. Prospect, Elmhurst, and Seneca, Illinois, with three years in Milwaukee, Wisconsin. Despite her years of teaching (or more likely because of her time in the classroom), Sister Mary Noel did not earn her B.S. in Education until 1954. Beginning her college education in 1933, she completed her degree a handful of classes at a time. In many ways, Sister Mary Noel's story is like numerous other Sisters of Mercy who entered the community during the late 1920s, 1930s, and 1940s. Parish schools expanded as the Catholic population multiplied and moved from traditional urban neighborhoods into the growing suburbs by the 1950s. Demands for sisters to fill slots in parish schools, both old and new, continued to increase and this took precedence over whether or not Mercys had completed their religious formation and their degrees.[5]

Bridget Cecilia Leahy provides another example of a delayed degree, but in health care. Leahy entered the Sisters of Mercy in Aurora, Illinois in 1931, before this group joined the Chicago Province. Born in Ireland, the twenty-one-year-old began her novitiate preparation at Mercyville Convent, working in the Sanitarium performing "domestic duties." By 1934, Sister Mary Andrew Leahy began her nursing education, the same year she received her high school certificate from Visitation High School in

Chicago. From 1937 on, she worked as a nurse, first at St. Joseph–Mercy Hospital in Aurora, then at Mercy Hospital, Marshalltown, Iowa. She was a nurse, then supervisor, at various Mercy-owned hospitals throughout Illinois and Wisconsin the remainder of her career, retiring in 1983. While she achieved her nursing certificate from St. Joseph–Mercy Hospital in 1936 and her state license as a registered nurse from Illinois in 1937, she began a bachelor of science program in nursing education in 1944, earning her BS in 1946. A glance through her records and list of assignments of Sister Mary Andrew reveal that she began her education, like many women religious of this period, "on the job." St. Joseph–Mercy Hospital granted her nursing certificate and she continued to work at this hospital while she earned her RN from the State of Illinois the following year. In contrast to teaching sisters like Sister Mary Noel, Sister Mary Andrew completed her BS degree in two years, using her previous education in nursing school toward her degree. Little time for either woman, however, was available to develop fully their professional talents before beginning their employments.[6]

Sisters Mary Noel and Mary Andrew follow closely the typical trajectory to professional development of Mercys in education and health care and their paths help make clear the challenges faced by many young women as they entered religious life. Granted, most women did not expect a different formation and some sisters have expressed the anticipation or thrill of beginning their apostolic lives quickly. One sister commented that she looked forward to putting on the "black veil" worn by those who worked in classrooms before they officially took temporary vows, the time one traded the novice's white veil for the black one. Yet putting on the religious habit did not guarantee proficiency in the classroom or hospital ward. In one case, Sister Mary Bridgetta Hurley, who entered the Des Plaines novitiate at fifteen, began her first teaching assignment, a first-grade classroom, at the age of eighteen fresh from her temporary profession. Sister Mary Bridgetta's age did not necessarily prevent her from providing a thorough education to her young charges, nor did her superiors within the parish school fail to give her guidance.[7]

These sisters and others desired "to serve God more faithfully" and they wished to do that as Sisters of Mercy. In the mid–twentieth century, how they would serve God was left largely up to their superiors. For the provincial council, this meant assessing the resources within the community, evaluating the abilities and talents of the individual sisters, and matching them with the needs of the Mercy institutions and Catholic Church within the province. And the needs of mid-century Catholics continued to evolve.

Throughout the 1930s and 1940s, the large majority of American Catholics rooted their religious life in their local parishes. Still identified with their immigrant heritage (particularly those closer to the immigration experience), the parish was the center of social and cultural identity, not simply the source of religious obligations and sacramental devotions. That immigrant identity (whether first- or second-generation) started to shift as many assumed a more Americanized outlook, particularly after World War II. This also signaled the beginning of a larger movement away from urban neighborhoods to growing suburban communities. Consequently, while parishes in cities like Milwaukee and Chicago did not close as Catholics moved out to the suburbs, they often changed demographic composition. At the same time, newer parishes developed, adding to the number of sisters required to fill schools and provide religious instruction.

While those who lived in the neighborhoods and parishes served by the Mercys continued to need the same level of assistance, Catholics living in newer and often economically stable suburbs had different, but no less valid needs. Furthermore, much of the laity developed new ways of relating to their communities and their church as Catholics. As Jay Dolan, Robert Orsi, and others have shown, generational distance from the point of immigration and increased American identity coupled with the physical distance from traditional urban neighborhoods diminished the hold and centrality of a national parish with specific ethnic identity in the lives of the laity. The parish was not the sole source of social and religious activity. Still, this did not mean that the laity was any less Catholic or committed to their parish. By the late 1940s and 1950s, the laity embraced alternative avenues for engagement in the form of the growing Catholic Action movement.[8]

Catholic Action developed first in Europe but became a growing American phenomenon by 1930. As a product of the Vatican call to the laity to become more engaged in society in opposition to modernity and growing secularism, from its conception, Catholic Action became an umbrella term under which many social, cultural, and economic concerns fell. Papal encyclicals like Pope Leo XIII's *Rerum Novarum* in 1891, and later *Quadragesimo Anno* issued by Pius XI in 1931, had challenged Catholics to concern themselves with the social order, encouraging the laity, religious, and clergy to work for social and economic justice. Pius X, however, issued *Il Fermo Proposito* in 1905, promoting "Catholic Action" specifically in Italy. *Il Fermo Proposito* also spoke to the entire Catholic Church with the goal "to restore all things in Christ," uniting "all their forces in combating anti-Christian civilization by every just and lawful means." Intended to "restore

Jesus Christ to the family, the school, and society by re-establishing the principle that human authority represents the authority of God," Catholic Action encouraged laywomen and men to attend to the economic and social injustices of their day. By 1930, Catholic Action developed in the United States and included labor unions, interracial justice, and youth organizations among other movements.[9]

Catholic Action was buoyed by the Mystical Body of Christ theology, which began to impact the American Catholic Church by the 1940s. According to this theological interpretation, Jesus Christ is the center of the Catholic Church and each member of the Church is united for the common good of the whole. Individuals furthermore find salvation not simply by escaping the world, but by joining with others to better it. The Church itself is the mystical body of Christ. By this theology, the focus moved away from a strict institutional understanding of its construction toward a more spiritual conception of the Church. Jesus Christ and the celebration of the Mass, consequently, occupied a central position within this view of the Church. The Church as the mystical body of Christ predated this period, but when Pius XII promoted this doctrine with his encyclical *Mystici Corporis* in 1943, the theology fit with a growing trend toward greater lay involvement in the Church and an emphasis on a social spirit. *Mystici Corporis* recognizes that all people, regardless of lay or religious, have talents or gifts, which should be employed to the benefit of the whole body. Pius XII did not advocate ridding the Church of its hierarchy, but he did stress that laywomen and men had an active role to play. In comparison to other regions in the United States, the reforms that grew out of this theology took strong hold in the Midwest, particularly in places like Chicago, Milwaukee, and Davenport, among others. The Mystical Body of Christ stressed the responsibility of Catholics to others in their communities and the larger society and this manifested in increased lay involvement in liturgical reform, the Christian Family Movement, and Catholic Action. This last movement inspired its followers to "observe, judge, and act" in their communities and Catholic Action "cells" developed.[10]

The result of the popularity and dissemination of these ideas affected both lay and religious. While Midwestern cities like Chicago retained elements of a more institutionalized and ethnic Catholicism, the advancement of the twentieth century saw a disruption of traditional settlement patterns. As white ethnic Catholics moved away from their working-class roots locating in the suburbs and middle class status, concerns arose about who they would become and to what extent new materialism and consumerism would alter their Catholic identity. The theology of the Mystical

Body of Christ combated fears over losing their core Catholic values. The various reform movements like Catholic Action, Christian Family Movement, and liturgical reform were the means by which the laity, the clergy, and women religious redefined American Catholicism.[11]

These movements occurred as the larger nation ruminated on poverty and prosperity, the life of the city in the face of increasing suburbanization, and race and the emerging civil rights movement. Catholics did not remain ensconced within their "ethnic ghettos" separate from these questions. By the 1950s, many Catholics, armed with the new sense of communal and social responsibility, joined Catholic Action cells and the Christian Family Movement, seeking to address racial and economic injustices. Catholics of all ages participated in Liturgical Reform to engage fully in the future of their church, while the Young Christian Students (YCS) took hold among Catholic teenagers. Engagement in these various organizations and movements resulted in a more informed and involved laity. Sisters of Mercy, for their part, did not lead lives separate from all these changes. Rather, they were products of the evolving Catholic communities, participated in these changes, and helped usher in these reforms.[12]

Yet theologically, where did women religious fit in the Mystical Body of Christ? They were not yet considered with the laity as they would be after Vatican II, but they were definitely not seen in the same terms as the clergy. Catholic tradition had classified nuns and sisters as something elevated from the everyday life of the laity. Scores of children who filtered through parish schools understood the religious life to be something revered. This reverential status, however, distanced women religious from the laity among whom they worked. Furthermore, the separation between the laity and Mercys was reinforced on the sisters' part as they followed strictly the rule of enclosures, as discussed in Chapter 3. Enclosure had erected a wall (albeit invisible) between sisters and those they served, despite their close proximity in classrooms, homes for women, and hospital wards. The Sisters of Mercy, despite the barriers between them and the laity, were a part of the Church and were aware of the changes growing within it. Sisters throughout the Chicago Province engaged in education, for example, encountered Catholic Action and its accompanying theology of the mystical body of Christ in Summer Schools of Catholic Action in the 1940s and facilitated YCS groups in their schools. Mercys more specifically re-envisioned their religious life by participating in movements like Sister Formation as they addressed their communities' educational and professional needs. Simply because it involves women religious, the 1950s

Sister Formation Conference cannot be seen as something separate from the other developments within the Church like Catholic Action.[13]

The Sisters of Mercy quickly embraced the Sister Formation Conference. The seeds of this new movement to reform the formation of women religious had started to take root in the preceding decade. The Mercys, engaged in organizations like the National Catholic Education Association (NCEA), were present and participated in the Catholic education and hospital professional associations from which conversations emerged about the need to fully prepare sisters for their religious and ministerial life. Mercys from across the Union were present at the pivotal April 1952 national convention of the NCEA where Sister Mary Emil Penet, a Sister of the Immaculate Heart of Mary, gave an inspirational talk, which led to the organization of the Sister Formation Conference. Sister Mary Emil's presentation galvanized her audience (primarily the women religious present in contrast to the clergy amongst their numbers) to unite across congregations to reconstitute their formation process. After remarking on the growing dissatisfaction many women religious felt over their intellectual and spiritual preparation for their apostolic work (or lack thereof), as well as the high demands placed upon them by local bishops and priests, Sister Mary Emil proposed that religious superiors determine when young sisters were ready for ministries, proposing to hold them back for four years, and set a ratio of lay to religious personnel in schools and other institutions. When Sister Mary Emil spoke in April 1952, she spoke to a crowd of educators, but her message and subsequent mission of the Sister Formation Conference had consequences for all sisters, even those intended for medical ministries. The important point of the Sister Mary Emil's talk (and in future conferences and workshops) was that women religious had been barred from the intellectual and spiritual education necessary to act within the larger Catholic Church. The Sister Formation Conference intended to rectify this by elevating the level of education and broadening its content.[14]

Much of the discussion of the necessity of the Sister Formation Conference and the planning that occurred throughout the 1950s was steeped in the same language of Catholic Action and other movements that had engaged the laity. It spoke of women religious as a part of the Church as the Mystical Body of Christ and that, as members, sisters had a right to engage in the world as such. The leaders of the Sister Formation Conference—Sister Mary Emil and Sister Ritamary Bradley, a Humility of Mary sister, among others—promoted a change in curriculum and formation for young sisters. The organization's *Sister Formation Bulletin* enabled them to communicate plans and disperse information to women religious communities throughout the United States and eventually the world. Mercys who had attended meetings like the one in April 1952, including Sister Mary Josetta Butler, who later became a vital liaison to the Sister Formation Conference for her community, continued this conversation at later conferences. In 1956, communities such as the Sisters of Mercy sent representatives to a summer-long conference held at the Sisters of Providence's School of Nursing in Everett, Washington to strategize and share college and novitiate curriculum to develop what was known as the Everett Plan. Following this summer planning session, the Sister Formation Conference sponsored regional conferences to disseminate knowledge and practices in workshop forms.[15]

The Everett summer conference examined all aspects of liberal arts education and brought together experts in each field. The resulting report promoted the idea that sisters, regardless of ministry, needed to have complete educations in all areas, including humanities, social sciences, mathematics, philosophy, and theology. The goal of this education was to provide an "integration of Catholic social thought into the liberal arts and development of a social consciousness and a global awareness along with an effective approach toward effecting structural change in society." As Karen Kennelly, CSJ has asserted, the authors of the report understood this integrated curriculum "as a call to sisters to enlarge their view of the world and to exercise their baptismal call to holiness and leadership as public representatives of the Church." They justified this position or rationale based on the doctrine of the Mystical Body of Christ as articulated by Pius XII in *Mystici Corporis*.[16]

The result of the Everett Report, the ensuing workshops, and circulation of information among different religious communities was a transformation in religious formation. The Sisters of Mercy, for their part, were engaged in this push for education reform and already aware of the need for a change. Four years before the summer conference in Washington State, they had instituted a House of Studies and an extended Juniorate period as of 1952. Those who entered the Sisters of Mercy in this period after the implementation of the Juniorate had a somewhat different educational experience than those who entered a decade previous. The 1952 band began the trend of delayed assignments for an extra two years, and for some within this group, it was both a blessing and a disappointment. After three years in the novitiate, sisters expected to have an assignment. Instead, they had two more years of studies at Saint Xavier College, first at the old location at Cottage Grove and then at the new campus at 103rd Street. This additional education gave sisters more preparation and a chance to finish or come closer to completing their college degrees. By this period, state educational board requirements mandated degrees for certifications and this change enabled sisters who entered in 1952 to complete their degree before the decade ended. On the other hand, for those who eagerly antici- pated their first assignments, this was a frustrating change.[17]

At the same time, those who entered in the mid-1950s had the benefit of more developed theological training. In accordance with the push from the Sister Formation Conference to incorporate theology into the educa- tion of sisters, the Mercys inserted this discipline into the studies of its Ju- niorate and provided opportunities for professed sisters to study theology either at Saint Xavier College by the 1950s or in other Catholic colleges and universities. Those already in ministries prior and through the period of change in the mid-1950s had other opportunities for education develop. While the NCEA conferences provided opportunities for some select sis- ters as early as the 1940s for professional development, similar programs were held at Saint Xavier College throughout the 1950s, which provided opportunities to learn more about Church developments, Mercy spiritual- ity, and Sister Formation for superiors. These continued into the 1960s and incorporated the developing trends stemming from Cardinal Leon Joseph Suenens's *The Nun in the World* (among others) and the Vatican Council. Superiors were not the only ones who benefited from these conferences. Sisters throughout the province traveled to Chicago to Saint Xavier Col- lege for educational conferences. At the Eleventh Educational Conference in November 1957, Gustave A. Weigel, SJ "spoke on the relation between the spiritual and intellectual life. He stated [that the Mercys had an] obliga- tion to develop [their] intellect so that [their] work in the apostolate will be efficient and effectual." This conference at Saint Xavier came three years after the Sister Formation Conference was established in 1954 and spoke to the importance of the total education of the sister for full participation in the world. Cardinal Suenens's 1962 publication continued these ideas by challenging women religious to clarify their apostolic role in society and to participate fully as modern religious, begging the question: How effectual would sisters be without a total education?[18]

Reforms in the educational preparation of young sisters paralleled efforts at Saint Xavier College to broaden and strengthen its curriculum for all its students. Sister Josetta Butler, as Dean of the college, played an instrumental role in these developments. The expansion of college offer- ings to include a theology degree went hand-in-hand with the belief that a Catholic education for women ought to include structured courses in theology. Beginning in the mid-1940s, Saint Xavier College expanded its curriculum to include theology, and the Sisters of Mercy on faculty at the college quickly complained that the studies available to students were not available to sisters. From this point, Saint Xavier College offered summer institutes in theology for women religious. In 1948, a three-year summer course began, which granted certificates in theology to more than 100 women religious from various communities. The purpose of this Theological Institute was "to deepen the understanding of the spiritual life in the individual . . . and to give an adequate background for the teaching of Religion in grammar schools and high schools." By the 1950s, theology was a central part of the college curriculum. Catholic liberal arts education needed to include philosophy and theology, despite concerns among some clergy about lay and religious women acquiring this type of knowledge. The establishment of the Theology Department at Saint Xavier College put the school in position to embrace future theological developments in the ensuing decade, most notably the results of the Second Vatican Council. Sisters of Mercy continued to benefit from these developments as opportunities for spiritual growth occurred at crucial times in the life of the community in the 1960s.[19]

Religious formation of sisters up to this point had not dwelt on theology, but instead focused on the spiritual identity of the community and the practical means of becoming a faithful professed religious. Studying theology, it was feared, might have caused sisters to become "intellectuals" and "overfascinated with the speculative" drawing their attention away from the practical needs of parish schools and other needed ministries. In reality, sisters wanted to keep pace with the laity and their modern times. Many of the sisters discussed at the beginning of this chapter, who entered in 1929 and took decades to achieve their first undergraduate degrees, took advantage of these new opportunities to take courses in theology at Saint Xavier College. Sister Mary Andrew Healey completed twelve credits in theology from 1952 to 1954. Sister Mary Noel Grimes also took classes in theology during these same years. Both sisters' academic records reflect that they earned Theology Certificates in 1960 and 1961 respectively. Sisters Mary Andrew and Mary Noel were not the only Mercys who extended their education beyond the needs or requirements of their professions. A glance through the records of many sisters throughout the 1950s reveals efforts to broaden and amplify the Sisters of Mercy's intellectual and spiritual lives. Significant community-wide reform, however, would not occur

until after the implementation of changes brought on by renewal in subsequent decades. Saint Xavier College, with its curriculum changes and
educational conferences, along with the hospital administrator meetings,
led the community toward the question, which seemingly consumed all of
religious life for sisters in the second half of the twentieth century: Where
did women religious fit within the Catholic Church and in the world?[20]

The provincial council recognized the need for improved education
of its sisters, and throughout this period, the Sisters of Mercy started
to see how it needed to adapt to the changing society. While hospitals,
schools, and homes for women, among other ministries, faced institutional
changes, such as requirements for state certifications and accreditations,
particularly in hospitals and schools, superiors, embracing the agenda of
the Sister Formation Conference, enabled sisters to earn four-year degrees
in necessary programs such as education and hospital administration. Acquiring experience and degrees in these areas enabled the Mercys to continue to maintain a presence in parochial and secondary education and
within their own institutions like many of the Mercy Hospitals throughout the province.

Education and health care dominate the history of the Sisters of Mercy
in the first half of the twentieth century. The largest numbers of sisters
were concentrated in elementary education, followed by health care (including nursing schools), high schools, and Saint Xavier College. Education and health care, however, were just two aspects of the Mercys, and
the community conducted other ministries, despite the fact that fewer
women were assigned to them. The implementation of the Juniorate and
the House of Studies, plus the lessons of the Sister Formation Conference,
inspired the Chicago Mercys to take control over their personnel in ways
that presented staffing problems to diocesan schools. Yet the provincial
council could not let the demands for teachers dictate the placement of
sisters. If external demands were the only factor for the provincial council,
then it would have closed the homes for women and reallocated those staffing these institutions into classrooms and hospital wards. The community,
however, maintained its women's residences, like the Patricia Club on the
west side of Chicago, and the St. Clara Club and St. Catherine's Home in
Milwaukee well into the late twentieth century. These institutions, along
with parish schools, high schools, small and large hospitals, and nursing
schools are reminders that the Mercys understood the purpose of their
community in the same context as Catherine McAuley did in the first half
of the nineteenth century, namely response to need.[21]

Hospitals: "the highest standards of professional excellence"

The care of the sick and Mercy hospitals represented a significant element of the sisters' ministries and identity. Visiting the sick was a founding principle or aspect of the Spirit of the Institute when Catherine McAuley established the Sisters of Mercy in the nineteenth century, and Mercy Hospitals in Illinois, Iowa, and Wisconsin stand as physical reminders of their institutional presence in the different communities. The centrality of this ministry is evident not only in the Mercys' dedication to its institutions, but also in the anecdotal evidence of accounts of visiting the sick in homes. The general council of the Sisters of Mercy of the Union deemed this ministry worthy of documentation and throughout the mid–twentieth century required each house to record the number of visits to the sick in private homes and institutions, as well as the number of visits to prisons.[22]

Catholic health care provided by women religious, furthermore, contributed to the acceptance of the Catholic Church in the United States. Historically, the sister-nurse, whether in the Civil War, the Spanish American War, or Chicago's own cholera epidemics of the nineteenth century, provided moving examples of reasons to rethink popular prejudices of Catholicism among non-Catholics. By the twentieth century, Mercy hospitals in Wisconsin, Iowa, and Illinois represented the community's strength and perseverance. Hospital sisters worked with a more diverse population and did not restrict or bar patients from other faiths, nor did they seek to convert non-Catholics. In contrast, the Catholic parish school and high school were designed to provide education for Catholic children and protect their faith from Protestant encroachments.

Yet hospitals had far fewer sisters engaged in these ministries when compared to the large number of those in education. Chicago's Mercy Hospital had the largest number of sisters assigned to that institution, when compared to the others throughout the province. By 1959, forty-seven sisters worked as nurses, administrators, and other professionals at this South Side hospital. Iowa, however, had a combined sixty-six sisters assigned to its three hospitals in that state compared to the twelve at Mercy Hospital, Janesville in Wisconsin. The Iowa and Wisconsin hospitals, as well as the one in Aurora, Illinois served smaller populations at each institution and faced a different set of problems and changes in comparison to Mercy Hospital, Chicago. In the case of an institution like Mercy Hospital, Marshalltown, the smaller city had fewer resources to support this institution and it closed in 1969 when the Sisters of Mercy could not support and staff it sufficiently. The hospital, furthermore, could not compete with the general hospital in Marshalltown without expanding the facility.[23]

At the beginning of this period, hospital care had become fully modern, and the Sisters of Mercy's nine hospitals embraced the changes of the twentieth century. Increasingly, hospital administration became professionalized and, while the Mercys had superintendents in place by the beginning of this period, a professional and modern hospital administration increasingly required advanced education. By the 1940s, Mercy hospital administrators made connections with other Catholic health care directors and created their own conferences designed to share ideas and methods. Indeed, this and the advances in nursing education promoted professionalization. The provincial council's efforts to send sisters to graduate school to earn degrees in hospital administration enabled the Sisters of Mercy to maintain control of their own institutions, as they endeavored to convey that Mercy hospitals were fully modern health care facilities.

By the 1960s, more sisters like Sister Susan Thomas had received degrees in hospital administration. Thomas received her master's degree from the University of Minnesota in 1966. Sister Susan entered the Sisters of Mercy in 1944 after she had completed her Bachelor of Science in nursing at Saint Xavier College. By 1947, she had taken temporary vows and was assigned to Mercy Hospital, Chicago as a nursing supervisor on a general floor. A year after making her final profession, she began her long career in various Mercy hospitals in Iowa City, Marshalltown, and Janesville as a surgical nurse and supervisor. Once she earned her graduate degree, she held administrative positions at St. Joseph Mercy Hospital in Aurora, and Mercy Hospital, Chicago and Davenport. Valued experiences of sister-nurses on floors, coupled with advanced degrees enabled Mercys to maintain control over the direction of their institutions and not be swayed by external influences either from the hierarchy or male medical professionals. Educational opportunities like those experienced by Sister Susan also opened sisters to prospects beyond Mercy institutions. By the mid-1970s, Sister Susan worked for the Illinois Department of Public Health.[24]

Sister Susan's story reflects the value the Chicago Province placed on education for health care workers. Having thoroughly educated sisters within their own hospitals benefited their health care ministries, and the Mercys could pour their resources back into their institutions, thus preserving them and reinforcing the Mercy identity of these hospitals. Fully prepared and professionally educated sisters like Sister Susan illustrate this point.[25] Returning to the fate of Mercy Hospital, Marshalltown sheds light on a persistent problem faced by the leadership of the Mercys throughout this period. How would the Sisters of Mercy remain faithful to their founding principles, financially support their institutions, and educate their members? Releasing a needed member of a hospital staff, like Sister Susan, to engage in professional development, meant one less sister engaged in this health care ministry. How would the Mercys continue to develop and compete as a network of modern hospitals and to whom would they provide their services? In most of the communities in which the Mercys owned a hospital, non-Catholics equaled or out-numbered Catholics who used their facilities. In places like Marshalltown and Janesville, fewer alternatives for healthcare existed. In a place like Chicago, however, Catholics and non-Catholics alike had more choices when compared to Dekalb or Aurora where the majority of in-patients were non-Catholics. Mercy Hospital, Chicago, in contrast, had significantly fewer non-Catholic patients. As health changed in the twentieth century, Mercys continued to evaluate the health care needs of Catholic and non-Catholic members of their communities and made decisions, as they did in the preceding century, based on how best to serve and where could they do the most good.

This did not mean that practical, difficult questions did not face the community. The history of Mercy Hospital in Chicago illustrates the pressures and challenging questions faced by the community. Mercy Hospital, located on the south side of the city, faced an economically declining neighborhood, which was also increasingly African American. The worsening conditions on the South Side prompted the move of Saint Xavier Academy and College to a further south neighborhood near present-day Evergreen Park at 103rd Street. In this case, the economic and racial conditions of the neighborhood adversely affected the enrollment, as it had with other girls' academies in Chicago. Parents had been unwilling to send their daughters to a school in a troubled neighborhood. The move to the new location also afforded the community the opportunity to expand its novitiate, girls' academy, and college into separate foundations at one location. This move occurred in the mid-1950s, about the same time as the decision not to move Mercy Hospital. This decision to stay, however, came after nearly a decade of discussion and planning to relocate to the north side of the city to Skokie.

By the 1940s, Cardinal Samuel Stritch, as part of his own church-building plans for Catholic Chicago, desired a Catholic health care facility that would include one, centralized location for a hospital and medical school. The Mercys had developed a relationship with Loyola Medical School since 1919 and the construction of a new facility for both hospital and school would solidify this relationship.[26] Mercy Hospital had concerns about its existing neighborhood and its facility needed renovation and modernization. Crime had increased in the neighborhood, including sexual assaults on female employees. As the surrounding South Side neighborhoods changed racially, and white ethnic Catholic residents moved to locations further removed from the center of the city, the Mercys feared that they would lose this patient population now that their commute times from suburban areas increased. Furthermore, the Mercys feared that the growing African American community would not support the hospital. While the clinic attached to Mercy Hospital regularly treated African American patients, the hospital was not integrated until the early 1950s. Still, the large majority of patients treated by Mercy Hospital were white Catholics. Pressure to integrate came from Cardinal Stritch by 1950 and the Catholic Interracial Council in the 1950s. As we will see, community-wide, the Sisters of Mercy confronted the need to integrate their schools at the same time it dealt with racial issues at Mercy Hospital. Community leaders tended to take conservative but forward steps toward racial integration of its schools, hospitals, and its own community. A move north to Skokie would provide the hospital with an opportunity to develop an ideal facility, planning it from the ground up. An association with Loyola, which had changed its name to the Stritch School of Medicine in 1948, would also prove beneficial in that the hospital would have a medical school and more prestige. Could the Sisters of Mercy provide better services in a safer environment?[27]

The benefits of moving seemed to outweigh the reasons for remaining where they were. To add to this, Cardinal Stritch supported this move. Plans developed in 1947 to move Mercy Hospital north. As soon as these plans emerged, problems arose over how this new arrangement would work. A major concern was the relationship with Loyola Medical School. This would still be Mercy Hospital and the sisters did not want to relinquish the administration of it to Loyola, which pushed to control hiring and other aspects of the operation. From the Sisters of Mercy's perspective, Loyola needed only to concern itself with education. Added to this was the difficulty of finding and securing a location in Skokie. While land was more affordable, future neighbors were not happy about a Catholic hospital moving into the area, which meant annexing the property to the city of Chicago. Both wrangling over the price of land and disputes over the annexation and transfer of property to Chicago threw up more barriers to the move. Furthermore, the community faced opposition from some of its medical staff, which felt that the hospital should not abandon an area that desperately needed health care. Surveys of existing staff determined that the hospital would lose all of its established medical professionals if it relocated to Skokie. Plans moved ahead throughout the 1950s, but ultimately, the project collapsed and the hospital announced it would remain were it was in 1959. Despite the problems with staying, the inability to work out an agreement with Loyola, the concerns about losing control of the administration of the hospital, and the pressure to remain outweighed the positives of moving. One further and crucial incentive for staying came from the Chicago city government, which secured surrounding land on the South Side and enabled the hospital to construct a new facility. The promise of urban renewal significantly influenced the decision to stay.[28]

Race circled this entire issue, as it would with questions of staffing parish schools and the location of the college and high schools in Chicago. Race was a delicate issue within the Chicago Mercy community itself as non-white applicants were not accepted at this point and normally directed to other "colored" religious congregations. By the beginning of 1951, the Provincial Council discussed establishing norms "for the acceptance of colored applicants," but at the time, "no definite action [was] taken." Mercy Hospital treated black patients throughout the 1950s, but not in equal number to white patients. Did the proposed move represent another "white flight" from a growing black neighborhood? For those who wished to remain on the South Side, the hospital's inpatient clinic, and other outpatient services fit with what they saw was the original intent of the Sisters of Mercy. The decision to stay resulted in the construction of new hospital that had more beds and better services for the community. This choice ultimately fit with the emerging racial apostolate of the 1960s, where women religious felt called to serve African Americans, regardless of religious denomination.[29]

Schools: "souls . . . precious beyond all calculation"

As with previous periods of Chicago Mercy history, education continued to be one of the fundamental or "characteristic works" of the community. Sisters of Mercy had performed this ministry from the religious institute's beginning in Ireland and according to the *Customs and Guide*, the care and education of children was an integral means of "instructing and saving souls." Changing neighborhoods, urban unrest, poverty, and shifting theology of the mid–twentieth century, however, pushed the Sisters of Mercy to question whether or not they kept faith with Catherine McAuley's founding spirit.[30] In some cases, as in Mercy Hospital, the racial composition pushed the Sisters of Mercy to consider leaving. Ultimately, they did not leave in this instance, just as they did not withdraw in other cases. When the population of Mercy High School Chicago began to transition to include more African American students, the community decided to remain where it was, despite the shift in racial population. Chicago experienced *de facto* segregation for much of its history and the increased movement out of urban centers in the post–World War II era was nothing new. (Chicago was not alone in this experience.) The demographic shift, or white flight, to the new and growing suburbs affected the Sisters of Mercy's education ministry, pushing the congregation again to consider matters of race. The parish schools and the congregation's high schools located in traditionally white Catholic communities shifted as more African American and Hispanic residents moved into these neighborhoods.[31]

Opening its doors to black students was not a universally popular idea from within the Mercys or from laity as well, but the community made the decision to remain where it was and to alter its policies on race. By the mid-1950s, Mercy High School received applications from African American graduates from Catholic elementary schools and observed the Cardinal's wishes for integration of its school. By the early 1960s, Mercy High School maintained a ratio of nine white students to every one black student. As a result of this enrollment, the school began to lose white students and by the mid-1960s, 44 percent of the student population was African American. By this point, the Sisters of Mercy had success with incorporating a limited number of black students into the school, but as the population shifted further, the leadership expressed its concern to the Archdiocese of the consequences to the school. In one letter to the Archdiocesan School Board, Mother Mary Huberta McCarthy wrote:

> We recognize the many problems that the Church, the city, and our schools must face in an attempt to maintain a racial mix of 25.0 per cent negro, which is recognized as a safe factor for preserving an integrated community or enrollment. However, it would seem that this must be our goal; otherwise, for the sake of expediency we are capitulating to segregated neighborhoods, segregated schools, and consequent failure—spiritual, social, and economic.[32]

Mother Huberta expressed concern that Mercy High School would become an African American high school and that the "chances of Mercy remaining an integrated school [were] in serious jeopardy."[33] Despite the changing population, Mercy High School remained open, eventually merging with Loretto Academy, a girls' high school operated by the Sisters of Loretto, in 1972.[34]

Equally important to the Sisters of Mercy mission in the twentieth century were the numerous parish schools they staffed. Elementary education consumed a large majority of Sisters of Mercy personnel resources. The provincial council assigned more sisters to teach in parish schools than any other ministry between the 1930s and 1960s, despite the steady increase in the number of lay teachers throughout this period, particularly in the 1950s. The rise in lay teachers in the 1950s, however, reflects the degree to which the provincial superiors embraced the message of the Sister Formation Conference. The demands placed upon an individual parish school for teachers contributed to the Mercy community's decision to prepare sisters with more education, both secular and spiritual. Within each diocese, the bishop or archbishop had a particular agenda for the parish schools and high schools under its control. The Sisters of Mercy did not own the elementary schools they staffed, as they did in the nineteenth century, and they reached agreements with the diocese and the parish priest. Sisters remained within a particular school as long as both found the relationship and ministry acceptable to each party. When a parish priest needed sisters to staff the school associated with the church, he sent a request to a community. The mother provincial then assessed the community's ability to fulfill that request and responded. The Mercys were more likely than not to respond positively to a priest's request throughout the first half of the twentieth century.

Despite the tendency to respond positively to a request, the provincial superiors did, respectfully, decline invitations to conduct schools. In 1946, the provincial council received a request from Cardinal Samuel Stritch for thirty more sisters to undertake a high school at Holy Angels, a school the community already served at the elementary level. The council resolved to withdraw from Holy Angels because they did not have the resources. Furthermore, Cardinal Stritch wanted one religious community to assume responsibility for the school, because he had dedicated Holy Angels as a "colored" school and a part of the larger ministry to African Americans in Chicago. In September 1945, the school opened its doors to black students for the first time and the Mercys withdrew at the end of May 1946. Leaving Holy Angels, however, freed up more teachers for other schools, including St. James in Chicago.[35]

The placement of sisters in different parish schools throughout the province, again, depended on largely where the council believed personnel could do the most good, especially considering the mounting concern over professional and spiritual formation of sisters by the 1940s and 1950s. As demand continued to increase, the council had to decide how to meet previous agreements to maintain established schools, and to what extent they stayed faithful to the spirit of the Mercy Institute. In the context of parish education in large urban areas like Chicago, was it best to follow the white Catholic population as they settled in developing suburbs? Or should they stay in economically declining parishes whose populations became more racially diverse and less Catholic? The decision was not simply choosing between one or the other, and the Mercys remained in some schools as the neighborhoods shifted away from their traditional white ethnic Catholic population. The shift of sisters from Holy Angels to St. James was not a change away from the black community (see Figure 12). Mercys also remained in West Side neighborhoods as they became racially and ethnically diverse, as in the case of St. Thomas, Resurrection, St. Malachy, Siena High School, St. Finbarr, and Precious Blood. Meanwhile, they also expanded to the newer Chicago suburbs north and west of the city. New parish schools opened in Mount Prospect, Skokie, and Park Ridge, Illinois by the mid-1950s.[36]

To complicate matters further, the Sisters of Mercy had longstanding commitments to schools in Iowa and Wisconsin. In Iowa alone, the Mercys staffed six parish schools, four of which the community had been in since before amalgamation. The sheer number of Chicago-based parish schools might have obscured the needs of more distant locations. The Mercys, however, maintained these schools in Mt. Pleasant, Davenport, Burlington, and West Burlington as long as they had the sisters to staff them because the sisters had a commitment to these parishes that needed their services. The example of these Iowa parishes provides an interesting snapshot at the decision-making process for sustaining this type of mission.

When demand for sister-teachers was greater than available personnel, particularly in the mid- to late 1950s and 1960s, superiors were compelled to disappoint parish priests. Mother Mary Huberta McCarthy, Mother Superior in 1961, wrote the pastor of Holy Family Church in Davenport, Iowa, Monsignor T. V. Lawler, with the news that the community would only assign five sisters for the 1961–62 academic year. According to Mother Huberta, the council faced rapid increase in enrollments and the need to educate sisters for the classroom. As a result of these difficulties, she was "forced to the point of withdrawing complete faculties or of finding some way of apportioning the sisters according to the numbers and needs in the parish. The current situation must be part of God's plan . . ." She hoped that the "clergy, religious, and laity [could] meet the challenge." Monsignor Lawler and his successor Monsignor Barnes apparently met this challenge and hired lay teachers. By the 1962–63 school year, six sisters and five lay

Figure 12. St. James Grade School, Sister Faculty, 1957.

teachers worked in the Holy Family School in Davenport. Apparently, the pastor had dreams of a student population of 1,000 with a ratio of three sisters to one lay teacher.[37]

Mother Huberta's letter to the Monsignor Lawler illustrates the importance of education of sisters to the Sisters of Mercy. The sisters in Davenport, as in Chicago, Milwaukee, Janesville, and other areas, needed to be prepared fully for their ministries. This in part had to do with teaching credentials and state requirements, but the trend toward longer time in the novitiate, the advent of the House of Studies, and the inclusion of more theology furthermore compounded the tensions between satisfying requests for sister-teachers and attending to the needs of young sisters in formation. Ultimately, the changes best served the community.[38]

By the mid–twentieth century, the Sisters of Mercy had taken momentous first strides toward renewal of their religious life. Changes to Saint Xavier College's curriculum (albeit not intended for sisters), conferences for educators and hospital administrators, and the Sister Formation Conference created opportunities for expanded study for women. These first steps were not taken with consciousness of what was to come during and after the Second Vatican Council, but arguably they were just as "radical" as renewal proved to be. While the initial intent of these changes was to educate sisters and increase professionalism to better prepare them for their ministries, they had an unintended consequence; as expressed by one sister, it taught them how to "deal with a world . . . and church that was changing." An education that incorporated both the cultural and theological changes of the mid–twentieth century prepared sisters for the future.[39]

By the early 1960s, administrators and superiors continued to attend conferences, but the subject of these meetings revolved around the issues of the Sister Formation Conference. One August 1963 workshop for superiors and administrators covered basic religious and practical preparation for ministry. It also included sessions given by Reverend George Hagmaier, CSP, Associate Director of the Paulist Institute of Religious Research, such as "Driving Forces of Human Behavior," "Inter-Personal Inter-Action of Community Living," and "Two Basic Approaches to Counseling—an Explanation"[40] At this conference and subsequent ones, local superiors and administrators learned not only how to govern their houses, but how to relate the new theologies and ideas erupting in religious life to the sisters under their authority. With each session or conference, however, these new thoughts altered religious life in the 1960s. For sisters who entered in the early 1960s, the results of Sister Formation had begun to take effect.

Few, if any, of those who entered in 1961 had to wait long to complete their undergraduate degrees before beginning their first assignments. The delay did not factor into the novitiate experience as it had nearly ten years earlier. While in the novitiate, they were exposed to theology in the Juniorate, and they read and studied the theologians who participated in the Second Vatican Council such as Yves Congar and Karl Rahner. A decade of learning had made a difference, and, as the next chapters will show, that education provided the foundation upon which the Mercys of varying generations began to reconstitute their religious life.[41]

Ultimately, the tumultuous events of the 1960s and early 1970s did not begin with the Second Vatican Council and the call to renewal. As with other communities of women religious, the Sisters of Mercy experienced gradual, yet critical, change. This does not diminish the important developments that occurred during and after the Second Vatican Council. The modification of the religious life, changes in community living, withdrawal from traditional institutional ministries, alterations to the habit, and the large number of women who left religious life were revolutionary developments that seemed to come out of nowhere. In reality, they emerged from decades of careful progress from within a structured religious life. Events in the 1970s, an era of tumult, controversy, and heartache, resulted from the changes made in the four previous decades. Progress came with both great rewards and at a great price.

5

"Change Is Blowing Hard"
Renewal of Religious Life in the 1960s and 1970s

Change is blowing hard, and some of us don't know whether to bend—or to lean against . . . You have set us, Lord, in the midst of so much to learn.[1]

In the fall of 1970, the front page of the Chicago Province's newsletter, *Exchange*, contained a copy of the Opening Prayer of Apostolate Day. The prayer asked God for help in accepting the changes in religious life that had developed in the preceding years. It also asked God for inspiration to continue ministries and for each sister to "contribute the best of herself to the well-being of all." It touched upon the concern for each sister's freedom and the right to express herself within the community and the world. The general sense of this Opening Prayer is that change, however difficult, is good. The community, however, needed patience and help from one another, and with God's guidance, each sister would find "a balance of the needs of this group and the needs of the world."[2]

By the time this Opening Prayer had been made, five years had passed since the close of the Second Vatican Council. Those years were dotted with radical events for the community that caused consternation and discord, but the Sisters of Mercy moved tentatively toward change. By 1970, the community had lost more than one hundred sisters and novices and had only professed fifteen women. There had been community surveys and questionnaires, which probed everything from the structure of religious life, to the Chicago Mercys' government, to sisters' habits. Conferences and workshops that promoted new styles of ministry, infused with the teachings of the Vatican Council as well as studies on psychology and group dynamics, abounded for superiors, educators, and hospital personnel. In the wake of the declarations from Vatican II, the Mercys participated in provincial and general chapters, which discussed, debated, and ultimately altered their religious government and life.[3] In the process, younger voices rose to prominence as they pushed and questioned why they and all sisters did not have more choice and freedom. By 1970, the Sisters of Mercy of the Union had formulated a new *Mercy Covenant*, which by 1972 temporarily served as existing *Rule and Constitutions*. Over the next decade and a half, the Union continued to revise and restate its constitution, but all changes stemmed from this period.[4]

The renewal of religious government and life are at the heart of the changes that occurred following Vatican II. By the 1970s, the governmental structure of the Sisters of Mercy had shifted from a strict top-down arrangement where control and authority rested in the hands of a few to a more horizontal and decentralized configuration based upon the principles of subsidiarity whereby the average sister had a closer relationship to and with power.[5] This was not an easy process, and much thought and discussion went into determining what form of government best suited the Chicago Province and the larger Union. The timing of this change places it within the larger political and social upheavals of the 1960s, and many of the sisters who advocated governmental restructuring belonged to the younger generation of members of the community. They had entered in the late 1950s and early 1960s. They had come of age along with their secular "baby boomer" sisters and brothers. The confluence of events, whether popular democratic movements like the student protests, second wave feminism, or the civil rights struggle, along with the renewal of the Catholic Church after Vatican II, implies that the push for governmental change and reform of religious life within the Sisters of Mercy originated from below, from this younger generation of Mercys. A careful consideration of the events and efforts to reform religious life, including governmental structure, suggests something different.[6]

The Sisters of Mercy embraced Vatican II renewal and reaffirmed their commitment to the founding charism given to them by Catherine McAuley. They experimented with new modes of community life and prayer and reimagined their apostolic life to incorporate new ministries. They did all this through a deliberative discussion and cooperation between the existing, traditional religious government and the general population of the community. The times demanded democratic reforms, and change occurred not only from the bottom up, but because the leadership at the top was receptive to a new form of government. The type of government that emerged by the 1980s was radically different from what existed prior to Vatican II. The transition from traditional and highly structured governance to participative decision-making, however, was a prolonged and rocky journey.

"The Goal of *Communion* and *Communication*"

The leading concerns for the Provincial Council in the early 1960s were still to recruit new members and to maintain the ministries of the Sisters of Mercy. All the efforts that went into enhancing the formation process started by the Sister Formation Conference continued into the 1960s, and the Chicago Mercys continued to participate in its programs.[7] Connected to this interest in formation was the growing desire to maintain communication with all the sisters within the province. Up to this point, little communication or interaction between sisters occurred outside their local houses and ministries and often Mercys learned of new developments within the community and the wider Catholic Church from letters read by local superiors or from visitations made by provincial leaders. By 1964, the provincial council recognized the need to deal directly and regularly with each sister and not simply a general circular letter to provide a forum for discussion of the information and developments of the Second Vatican Council and the larger Church. They did this through the publication of a newsletter three times a year during Advent, Easter, and Pentecost. *Agape*, first issued at Advent 1964, responded to the need within the community "for a medium of communication on a province-wide basis in order to allow for a sincere and free exchange of opinions and for the sharing of news and individual accomplishments—in short, the goal of *communion* and *communication*."[8]

Agape also featured the work of the different apostolates of the Sisters of Mercy, dedicating each installment to a specific ministry. The first issue focused on "the work among the poor." The editors planned a feature on health care for the Easter issue and a feature on teaching for Pentecost. *Agape* also published information on jubilarians and deceased sisters. Highlighting individual ministries and updating sisters on the status of the rest of the community stressed the "communion" or the intended unity of the Mercys. Busy lives, a concentrated focus on individual ministries, and distance between local houses might lead to isolation. Changing times and developments within the Church might result in alienation and dissatisfaction. One newsletter did not solve discontent, but *Agape* made an effort to reach out to the individual sister. Sending a copy of the newsletter to each sister, as opposed to one per house, was a part of this effort to provide communication. Its purpose was "to prove to each sister that this magazine [was] hers." This effort spoke to the growing desire that the provincial council recognize the individual person within the greater community.[9]

Agape appeared as the Mercys were in the midst of the debate surrounding renewal. The Sisters of Mercy of the Union convened a general chapter in 1959, five years before this first issue, but few changes resulted from this meeting that significantly altered religious life and government.

While there were modifications to permissions, giving local provincials more authority, and a loosening of regulations around temporal matters such as driving and television, no major developments occurred. The opening of Vatican II, however, pushed the process along. Pope John XXIII had called for the renewal of the Church, and women religious listened and acted. Many sisters, not solely the Sisters of Mercy understood the Vatican Council's call to renewal as a long overdue opportunity to break free of the cloistered restrictions placed upon them since the early twentieth century.[10]

The intent of Vatican II was not simply to loosen restrictions on religious life. Rather Pope John XXIII intended the Council, which lasted from 1963 to 1965, to update the Church based upon the idea that it was "the people of God."[11] More emphasis was placed upon the role of the laity and how the Church could serve and work within the modern world. One aspect of the reforms of Vatican II was the relationship of the governed to those in authority. As much of secular society ruminated on traditional forms of power and government, so did members of the Catholic Church, whether religious or lay. Pope Pius XI's encyclical *Quadragesimo Anno* in 1931 articulated the Catholic Church's support for the dignity of the individual. Pius XI wrote forty years following Leo XIII's *Rerum Novarum*, which concentrated on the condition of labor in the increasingly modern world. Pius XI expanded upon these ideas expressing concern over the preservation of smaller, local communities in the face of concentrated power at higher levels, whether in business or government. Speaking of the principle of subsidiarity, Pius XI defended the rights of individuals to their labors and creativity, but it was equally "a grave evil and disturbance of right order to assign to a greater and higher association what lesser and subordinate associations can do."[12]

Pope John XXIII in *Pacem in Terris* in 1963 and then the subsequent declarations from Vatican II reaffirmed the dignity of the human person. While religious government was just one element of the call to renewal, it factored significantly into how women religious operated. Communities like the Sisters of Mercy had moved tentatively toward this moment in the preceding decade with Sister Formation and they were on the verge of reform of the religious government in the early 1960s. The theology of Vatican II stressed respect for the individual sister and questioned the nature of religious obedience. It asked superiors and everyday sisters to recognize that the Holy Spirit acted "through all the members of the Church, rather than only through those placed in a position of authority."[13] This fits with the idea of subsidiarity and the Mercys came to incorporate it into their discussion and planning for revisions of their Constitutions. It became a part of the process in small ways initially when the leaders merely asked for feedback from the members on religious government and considered the sisters at the local level. Ultimately, the centralized and top-down structure of religious government came into question and many believed that a more decentralized and local form of religious government best suited the needs of the individual sisters within the community.[14]

The reaffirmation of the dignity of the human person did not officially emerge from the Council until December 1965, with *Gaudium et Spes*, and the Vatican had only called for reform of religious government, *Perfectae Caritatis*, in October the same year. When these documents did emerge from the Vatican, they did not offer radical change to religious life. *Perfectae Caritatis*, in particular, did not alter significantly the hierarchal structure of religious government. Yet the new theology that came to dominate Vatican II filtered into presentations not only to the superiors and administrators at workshops and conferences, but also to the novices during the course of their studies. The calling of the Vatican Council was news and the world was focused on the meetings. Sisters, no different than other groups, Catholic and non-Catholic alike, awaited the possibility of reform. In some instances, they engaged in discussions of renewal within their ministries, as in the case of the sisters of St. Alphonsus School in Mt. Pleasant, Iowa. In early January 1964, they encouraged the members of their Young Christian Students (YCS) to read the documents from the Vatican Council and others from the Liturgical Movement. For much of the year, the sisters of this parish reported that they had profitable and rewarding discussions with the YCS group, particularly enjoying hearing other points of view. Furthermore, they were impressed with the level of understanding and engagement of their students.[15]

Mother General Mary Regina Cunningham set in motion the steps toward renewal, however minor, in August 1963. The Union had a general chapter planned for August 1965, and preparations began in 1963. Provincial councils throughout the Union orchestrated studies of government and spiritual life, which resulted in proposals or recommendations for fundamental changes to the Rule. The Chicago leadership met in August 1964 and directed studies on religious government, community life, formation, and the apostolate. By the end of September, the direction of renewal of religious government and community life was still uncertain and the form these would take at the end of the process was unknown. Continued study was in order, and the Chicago provincial council hoped to engage the local superiors and administrators in further discussion in the planned October 1964 Local Superiors workshop. Local superiors from throughout the province came to Chicago for the three-day workshop after which they returned to their houses to share the information and discuss it with their sisters throughout the next four weeks.[16]

Over the course of three days from October 9 through 11, the sisters attended panel sessions on religious government, community life, formation, and the apostolate. Each session had a presentation and time was allotted for discussion based upon prepared questions. The presenters on religious government, for example, asked the attendees to consider everything from what norms they believed needed changing to the nature of religious obedience. The exploration of this latter topic delved into the extent to which obedience "imperil[ed] the human dignity of the religious" and the existence of tensions within community life because of it. The discussion on community life probed related issues to obedience and individual fulfillment in the form of spiritual life, prayer, and how the community environment fostered or hindered commitment to the Mercy life. Throughout the remainder of October and into November, local superiors held similar discussions at their houses. These weekly meetings gave sisters opportunities to provide their views on religious renewal and opened them up to the possibility or hope of change. That sisters who did not serve as local or provincial councilors could offer their opinions was significant and convent chronicles suggest the importance of these meetings to the participants. In the case of the group at Mother McAuley High School in Chicago, for example, sisters remarked in the pages of their convent chronicle that these meetings occurred, but only gave a hint of expectation for positive change on the part of the sisters. The sisters at St. Alphonsus, in Mt. Pleasant, Iowa, on the other hand, passed on that they found them "worthwhile and thought provoking." The sisters of Resurrection convent in Chicago, who had their first meeting October 14, reported more closely the role they were to play in the next chapter. The convent's chronicler reported after the "first in [their] series of discussion on adaptation and renewal," that "[t]he results of these discussions will go to the Provincial House to help in deciding the topics to be discussed at the Provincial and General chapters."[17]

Some sisters "hoped" that the questions they raised would be considered at the general chapter, which began in August 1965. Other sisters, while enjoying their discussions, did not feel they were any closer to "definite solutions." These faint hopes and concerns of progress reflect the distance most sisters had with the process of renewal. Meetings and discussion continued to prepare for the chapter, but sisters in local houses only participated in this removed manner. The real decisions occurred in chapters, which few sisters attended at this point. Ultimately, this separation from decision-making, or lack of participatory government was one of the fundamental problems emerging for the Chicago Sisters of Mercy in the late 1960s.[18]

Meanwhile, the community continued to receive information through *Agape*. Superiors and committee leaders reported their impressions from their workshops in the Easter and Pentecost 1965 issues. In a recurring column entitled, "Currents of Thought," those involved in the preparations for general chapter laid out the pertinent concerns of the community, but often from the perspective of superiors. Readers were reminded that renewal might tear "out all the comfortable security [they found] in conformity to regulations," but they must ask themselves if they were "'religious' more than Christians" and did they "feel a greater guilt in violating silence than in violating charity?" The implication of this question is that by being "good sisters" and observing regulations, they had failed to respond to the needs of their neighbors. The author of this article and that of the next installment focused on "personal responsibility" and the importance of Sisters of Mercy conducting themselves as "mature religious." An essential component to this maturity or personal responsibility was the acknowledgment of the crucial role the superior played in the process of renewal and the growth of the community. As discussed in Chapter 4, provincial superiors had the important responsibility of assigning sisters to positions that best fit their abilities and gifts. They also had to keep in mind the "real goals of the Institute and make sure they [were] being implemented realistically." Individual sisters had a responsibility to understand and keep abreast of the trends of religious life, but they must "subordinate their personal goals to the common goal of the community by living the vows, and they include a high degree of charity and of personal responsibility, in order . . . that they may be free to serve the genuine needs of their day." The pages of *Agape* conveyed the message that renewal would happen, but it would come at a cautious and deliberate pace in order to serve the "common good" of the Sisters of Mercy.[19]

The next installment of *Agape* arrived at Advent 1965 and gave reactions and responses to the first session of the general chapter, which opened in mid-August and lasted until the first week of September. The delegates to this general chapter took a significant step toward renewal when they voted to revise their *Constitutions*. Ultimately, all changes to the *Constitutions* had to be approved by the Vatican, but developments at this and later chapters to this end did much to persuade the larger Union and specifically the Chicago Province that change was on the horizon. Yet the generalate knew the members of the Union needed time to digest the first resolutions on proposed changes to the *Constitutions* and to allow for further discussion and study of issues raised at the beginning of the chapter. They pushed the discussion of the Mercy apostolate to the second session in May 1966. The delegates decided that the group needed more study and long-range planning before making any more changes.[20] The two sessions of the general chapter began the process of renewal of the Mercy government structure and the language of these meetings stressed progress and openness. The Mercys were determined to convey the chapter developments and decisions with the larger membership as they happened.

On first blush, the results do not appear monumental or particularly revolutionary. The delegates' positive votes to modernize the language of the *Constitutions*, to modify the habit, and to give sisters the ability to travel alone if the circumstances required it may seem minor and insignificant. In reality, modification of the habit raised more eyebrows among the laity, and in some cases furrowed the brows of the Catholic Church hierarchy, than other initial changes because those outside the community saw it, while adjustments to permissions and modern language occurred without much notice. Many sisters within the community, however, recorded their pleasure and excitement at the new habit and an overwhelming majority of the Chicago Province voted for a change (see Figures 13 and 14). Yet that did not mean that sisters received their new habit right away. As with most developments or alterations with the Church, these changes filtered down slowly to the Sisters of Mercy. While they knew the shift was coming, sisters had to wait nearly a year before they all had the modified habit. The Mercy High School Milwaukee sisters dutifully informed their students in November 1965, as directed by Mother Provincial. The chronicler of that house noted that "[f]or the most part the students are enthusiastic about it." The chronicles became nearly silent on the subject of the habit as the pages were filled with other events of renewal, lectures, and school business. There is mention of measurements taken in late February and early March. Then in mid-June through August 1, 1966 near daily updates on the status of the changed habit filled the chronicles, including a lengthy description of the formal ceremony blessing them on June 18. Unfortunately, not all sisters received their new religious garb at the same time; some houses had theirs, while others did not. Some within a local convent obtained theirs and others had to wait and watch as sisters fitted their new clothes. The last of the new habits arrived August 1 and the sisters at Milwaukee's Mercy High School finally could wear their new clothes (see Figure 15).[21]

Figure 13. Habit change, 1966: Sister Mary Dominic Merwick (old habit) and Sister Mary Alexis (Ruth) Mutchler (new habit).

Figure 14. Old and new habits worn by sisters in health care ministry, 1966: Sisters Mary Fausta Vorwerk and Mary Eamon O'Malley in Dispensary.

Figure 15. Blessing of the New Habit, Mercy Hospital Chapel, June 1966.

While the excitement expressed by the sisters in Milwaukee is palpable, they were not the only ones to feel this way. Furthermore, this enthusiasm for a change in clothing should not obscure the other developments, both small and big, that when added together had a significant impact on reform of religious life. Companions or partners when traveling, or conducting apostolic work, had been a fact of religious life for over a hundred years. Yet the general chapter made the decision to end this practice. Traveling without a partner was simply more efficient and the decision showed that superiors trusted the members of their community particularly at a time when they asked sisters to consider their "personal responsibility" and act as "mature religious." Modernizing language in the *Constitutions* spoke to the desire to make religious life more relevant to the world.

The first session of the general chapter, begun in 1965, took a first step toward reforming the Sisters of Mercy's government. The delegates voted to limit the terms a sister could serve at the generalate level. The purpose of this decision was to make room for other voices within the community. This vote hardly restructured the religious government nor re-shaped community life. Anyone looking for a revolution and complete participatory government would have been disappointed. The second session, starting in May 1966, pushed government reform a bit farther when the delegates decided temporary professed sisters could have an active voice in provincial chapter delegate elections. This widened the voting base and added a more youthful voice to the government proceedings. In other ways, the general chapter adopted new freedoms for novices and professed sisters. The chapter resolved to give novices more contact with their families as visits became more acceptable. Professed sisters also could revert to their baptismal or family names and novices could keep their original name. These decisions personalized the choice of the individual sister. These measures also relocated some authority or power away from the Mother General and placed it in the hands of either the local provincial or with the individual sister.[22]

Family visits and name selections, along with other developments like relaxed rules on recreation, changes in the Divine Office, and modified habits, began the process toward significant change; they had symbolic meaning and infused in some sisters an excitement for future opportunities. In September 1965, the sisters of the local house at St. Cecilia Convent in Chicago commented upon some of the early changes from the first session of the general chapter. After receiving the information by mail and then at a community meeting at Saint Xavier College, their local house convened to discuss the changes: "Much was discussed in regard to 'recreation'—[travel] 'partners,' [and] 'prayers' etc." While the chronicler gave little detail of the letter and meeting, the excitement about the new freedoms is evident, especially by early October. One member took advantage of relaxed permissions and attended the wedding of the former janitor from St. Matthew Church. Mercys at St. Clotilde in Chicago were also pleased to hear about the developments at the general chapter "concerning Religious Government, Sister Formation, Apostolate, and Religious habit. The Sisters were happy about the decisions made at the Chapter." For many sisters, the anticipation was greater than the actual change. When the same letter from the generalate arrived at the Resurrection Convent on the west side of Chicago, the local superior read it to the community over lunch and finished through dinner. The group was relieved to have received their copy, but had not yet determined the meaning of it for the future.[23]

Communicating to members became an important concern of the provincial council, not only the details of the general chapter, but the general developments within the Chicago Province. Mother Provincial Huberta McCarthy (see Figure 16) continued the practice of writing circular letters to the different houses, keeping the sisters informed of news. In the

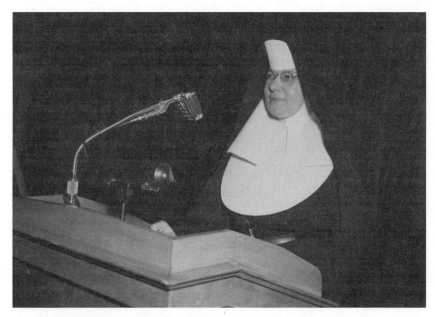

Figure 16. Mother Mary Huberta McCarthy, 1965.

November 24, 1965, circular letter, Mother Huberta announced the formation of a Special Committee "to study the possible structure that will aid in both vertical and horizontal communication within [the Chicago] province and also to explore what means the province might take to be more helpful to the sisters individually and in their work." *Agape* had, in part, started this process. Initially it featured individual ministries, but came to devote more and more pages to a public forum for the community to express itself.[24]

As the implications of renewal filtered to the larger community, the stress on personal fulfillment and "new freedoms" resulted in miscommunication between the leaders and the larger community regarding the nature of the individual autonomy. Mother Huberta's message to the community appearing in the Christmas 1965 issue of *Agape* stressed sacrifice with a guarded tone. She cautiously spoke of the need for individual sacrifice. Of sacrifice, she wrote: "It demands the un-selfing of self, the stripping of our excesses, our pettiness, our rancor, our hostilities, our self-pity, our desire for pleasure, our lust for power, our pride of intellect. Sacrifice connotes holocaust—a holocaust of love for God and for the whole world." Mother Huberta, however, tied individual sacrifice with the process of renewal and self-fulfillment. As sisters developed as individuals, which she referred to as "the process of becoming," they also prayed, worked, and lived within the community. How they developed or what they became as sisters depended upon their relationship with God and how they perceived the world. Mother Huberta closed her remarks with a statement about the need for the community and the individual sister to become their "best selves." She noted that:

> We will become freer to that which God has in mind for us to do. And with true freedom comes genuine renewal. The accidentals of adaptation—horaria, habits, rules, regulations—all fall into place more easily, more securely because they are seen in perspective—a means to the big goal of *becoming* persons, both individually and in community, who love in word and in deed.[25]

Mother Huberta was not against change, nor was she opposed to renewal. Rather, her message struck a delicate balance between tradition and progress.

In another column, "Into One Bread," from the same issue, the editors invited sisters to respond to a question about this "new freedom" and the obligations of the governing and the governed. One respondent commented that with freedom, there had to be restraint. The governed had a responsibility to protect the rights of everyone in the community. With an increased emphasis on individual rights, sisters had to consider the needs of the whole. The author of this piece drew from Edmund Burke to frame this reminder that "[s]ociety cannot exist unless a controlling power upon the will and the appetite is placed somewhere." Nowhere did the pages of the late 1965 publication mention dismantling the existing religious authority.[26]

In contrast to the cautious tone of some of the contributors to *Agape*, the testimony of the sisters within convent chronicles about workshops and in-house discussion suggest that there was excitement and anticipation for renewal. By the end of the second session general chapter in 1966, the renewal process had just begun and much more work and debate was ahead. The workshops and meetings that started the previous fall continued through the winter and, in the spring of 1966, the Easter *Agape* was filled with much more radical ideas about renewal than the preceding issues. The editors, and through them the leaders of the Sisters of Mercy, had created a space or forum for airing opinions and arguing for total renewal, maintenance of tradition, or a combination of the two. Discourse on the emerging "New Breed" of sisters, as one *Agape* contributor called them, who questioned authority and warned against the dangers to religious life of authoritarian methods replaced the quiet, but firm, reminders from Mother Huberta McCarthy of the virtues of authority. In the past, one commentator suggested, sisters had looked to superiors as the ultimate authority; in some cases, they had deified them. The system, which supported and proliferated this conception of authority, led to authoritarianism and bred a lack of trust in the individual sister to make the right choices.[27]

The leaders at the beginning of the process, however, understood that the community and religious life in general needed reform. Change had not happened yet, and norms and the structure of religious life had only begun to shift. Mother Huberta perceived these first efforts as part of the experimental phase and felt compelled to remind the province that any "experimenting with greater freedom" should be accompanied by an examination of the "real purpose of the particular function or activity" in which an individual sister wished to participate. If the new freedoms enabled sisters to attend functions at night or at a location outside the Institute, then "care must be exercised lest the real purpose for granting greater freedom lead to socializing instead of the promotion of a truly apostolic activity." In contrast to Mother Huberta's cautionary language and reminders to maintain religious propriety, the pages of *Agape* were filled with progress and renewal. Some sisters who contributed to the 1966 issues concentrated on the potential for personal fulfillment and freedom, which meant new ministries, new forms of community life, and deeper relationships with all the people of God, regardless of location and time of day.[28]

As the debate in the pages of *Agape* reveals, the community had at least two competing messages as to how to approach renewal. One came directly from religious leadership that gave news of change and the process in which it would slowly unfold. The other also came through the leadership, but indirectly through the community newsletter.[29] *Agape* in 1966 and 1967 continued to provide individual sisters an opportunity to express their views on the results of the 1965 general chapter and the swelling tide of change. While the editors of *Agape* made an effort to publish many different opinions or views of change, the desire for experimentation in religious life and the freedom of expression that led to running debates from one issue to the next, offered a significant message. This debate would lead to a different composition of religious life. By the end of 1966 and the first issues of 1967, a tone of concern rose among the voices that urged caution and issued reminders that all tradition was not bad.

These were not universally "older" sisters, nor were the sisters who advocated change and questioned the place of traditional authority 100 percent among the New Breed, or "younger" sisters recently professed.[30]

Commentary on freedom and the meaning of authority reoccurred in the pages of *Agape* in articles and editorials about ministry and community. Authority and government went to the heart of all other concerns about Vatican II's call for renewal. If the Sisters of Mercy could not figure out how it would order and structure its government, then community life, ministry, and spirituality of the Mercys could not move forward coherently. While some sisters did not question the need for a provincialate or generalate, the other extreme suggested that an authority figure should not exist at all. The debate ranged between the preservation of the existing government structure to the deconstruction of authority by switching to government by consensus. Instead of one authority for a local house, each sister would have a voice in the decision-making process and the manner in which they all lived. Furthermore, each should have responsibility for one aspect of a house's maintenance and operation. The members of that local house would agree upon the decision as to who would perform what duty. When one commentator advocated the discontinuing of a local superior, the next issue contained a response and defense of the preservation of authority:

> There is nothing intrinsically depersonalizing about the exercise of authority, either for the one exercising authority or the one who is working with those in authority. The one in authority, by abusing it, can wreak havoc, not only on the person of his subject, but on his own person as well. But the abuse of authority cannot necessitate the dissolution of the whole concept of authority. Decapitation can get rid of a headache but can hardly be classified as a cure for a headache, any more than the abolition of authority can be classified as a cure for those societies suffering from the headache of authoritarianism.[31]

For this writer, authority was essential to the community's best interests. For her, without some sort of authority governing the whole, an individual sister would not reach her full potential.

As this debate over authority continued in the pages of the community newsletter, some members of the province actively and openly embraced renewal. They wished to have an opportunity to put into practice some of these ideas. This, however, was not yet possible. Real change had come first through experimentation and study (sanctioned by the provincial council and generalate), and then the Sisters of Mercy of the Union had to revise their *Constitutions*. The generalate called another chapter for 1969, which fulfilled the request of the Vatican to address religious government by revising *Constitutions*. By the time of this gathering, however, events had brewed significantly within the Chicago Province and the call for real and practical change had erupted from below.

The faculty at Saint Xavier College, which included Sisters of Mercy and laity, tested the limits of obedience and religious authority. The new theology that inspired and emanated from Vatican II landed squarely at the heart of the Chicago Province's intellectual center with the planning of the John XXIII Symposium at Saint Xavier College in 1966. The symposium, of which Archbishop John Cody did not initially approve, brought leading Vatican II theologians to the campus. College president Sister Olivia Barrett, along with the faculty, planned this conference for March, but Cody's disapproval had the potential for canceling the conference. The dispute over the symposium had become public knowledge when the college faculty issued a press release on February 8 without the approval of the provincial council. Mother Provincial Huberta McCarthy expressed a degree of dissatisfaction with the public handling of the disagreement with the Archbishop by the college. While the Mercys and the Archbishop had settled the matter and had not canceled the symposium, the independent action of the college caused concern and raised issues, which related to the heart of the issue of "new freedom." Upon whose authority had the college acted? The action of the college faculty also raised larger questions about Mercy institutions and how they related "to the canonical structure of the province, the religious institute, and the Church." The faculty asserted its right to academic freedom over the obedience owed to religious government. Ultimately, Mother Huberta learned that the press release was a means of preventing the larger faculty from taking a more drastic and public stance. This very public quarrel was not the last stirring of trouble for provincial leaders. By the next year, all of the Union would know of Saint Xavier College's and the province's "disobedience" when all the sisters in the province received a letter.[32]

The Letter: "These are difficult times for every group in the Church"
On October 14, 1967, the chronicler of St. Gabriel Convent made a notation that "[e]ach Sister in the Community received a letter which caused quite a controversy throughout the Convents."[33] The letter to which she referenced was a short, five-paragraph letter to all the sisters in the Chicago Province. It began:

These are difficult times for every group in the Church and we as Sisters of
Mercy are no exception. For months now many of us have been concerned
about the direction in which we are going. Various groups have been talking from time to time about a concerted plan of action. Recently a group of
us have met and seriously discussed this, and before God we are interested
in doing whatever is best for the community.

Thirteen names signed the epistle, including a member of the Provincial
Advisory Board. The signers were involved in elementary, high school,
and college education as well as hospital ministry. All of the sisters who
put their name to this correspondence, which came to be known as "The
Letter," ultimately wanted the same thing. They stated that "before God
[they were] interested in doing whatever [was] best for the community."
Attached to the letter was a paper, entitled "Some Suggestions for Community Action," which explained their reasons for sending this letter and
made "practical suggestions" as to how to proceed toward real change. The
authors requested that sisters send their reactions to the paper and indicate
whether or not they supported its ideas. The signers directed responses to
the Provincial Advisory Board member within their group.[34] From the perspective of the authors of this letter (and arguably others throughout the
community), the Chicago Sisters of Mercy had reached a point of crisis.
The community had lost a number of sisters and potentially could lose
more. In 1967, the Chicago Province lost thirty-one sisters. The next year,
thirty-two departed, and thirty-eight left in 1969. The rate of departures
decline in 1970, but not by any significant number; twenty-nine left that
year. The number of sisters who left the community dropped to ten in
1972 and held steady around this number until the late 1970s. By the end
of the decade, flow of women in and out of the community stopped. No
one left in 1979, but no one entered either.[35]

According to the Letter, in 1967 the community was in danger of losing sisters "whom [they] regarded as basic to [their] future community."
These valuable persons wanted to stay, but the condition of religious life
was a potential threat to their remaining. The authors of the letter believed
that many who stayed within the Sisters of Mercy felt disenchanted and
discouraged by their current religious life. The existing climate prevented
sisters from understanding why they were a Mercy. The "many *small* restrictions [and] problems" of the community contributed to these feelings
and the growing disconnect. The authors offered "practical suggestions"
as a solution. Of utmost importance was that unfulfilled or discontented
sisters "be encouraged to try to determine explicitly how they can be faith-

October 12, 1967

Dear Sister,

These are difficult times for every group in the Church and we as Sisters of
Mercy are no exception. For months now many of us have been concerned about
the direction in which we are going. Various groups have been talking from
time to time about a concerted plan of action. Recently a group of us have
met and seriously discussed this, and before God we are interested in doing
whatever is best for the community.

The enclosed suggestions for community action express the thought and concern
of the sisters listed below. It seemed important to determine if such
suggestions reflect the thinking and concern of other Sisters of Mercy of
the Chicago Province.

If these suggestions represent the direction of your thinking and you wish
to indicate your interest in bringing about these or similar changes, will
you please sign the statement at the bottom of this letter?

We have asked Sister Mary Sheehan as a member of the Provincial Advisory
Board to present the results of this survey of opinion at the board's next
meeting on October 19. Please return the signed statement to her by
October 18.

Information regarding the response to these suggestions for immediate and
long-term action will be made known to each sister by October 25.

Sincerely in Christ,

S. M. Michaelyn Fleming
S. Virginia Marie Horvath
S. M. Rosalie FitzPatrick
S. M. Jeremy Doyle
S. Margaret M. Madden
S. M. Esther Cronin
S. Marian Michael Chuffo

S. M. Regina Fanning
S. Mary Sheehan
S. Sheila M. Lyne
S. M. Louisa Ruff
S. Marie Raymond Garrity
S. M. Irena Jolie

Return before October 18 to: Sister Mary Sheehan, RSM
                                  Saint Xavier Convent
                                  103rd and Central Park
                                  Chicago, Illinois   60655

The main ideas and concerns expressed in the paper, "Some Suggestions for
Community Action," represent the direction of my thinking and I wish to
indicate my interest in bringing about these or similar changes.

Name _____   Address _____

Figure 17. The Letter, 1967.

ful to their calling." From this perspective the growing crisis of the Mercys
compelled the authors to take action and draw the entire community's attention to the need to act immediately and not through the deliberate and
slow process of another general chapter.[36]

The driving thrust of the Letter was to engage each sister in an exploration of her purpose as a religious and her ministry (see Figure 17). If so many
were unhappy with the current state of the community and its ministries,
then they should evaluate their personal choices for apostolic work. Once
sisters determined how they best could serve, even if it took them outside

Mercy institutions and traditional ministries, then the superiors and community should support that choice. After sisters made a choice in ministry, each person should make the decision as to how and where she should live her religious life. After determining ministry and living, the community would study the results and convey their findings to the various dioceses and institutions. The authors sent the letter in early October, seeking a response before the next Provincial Board meeting on October 19. According to their proposal, by December, the results would be available to the community and the Mercys would make known to local church officials and lay groups with whom they worked how the sisters' change in living and ministry would affect them. If the community followed the proposed plan, small changes could begin as early as the following summer and fall, even if it meant complete withdrawal from schools and other institutions long served by the Mercys. The authors felt confident that the complete realization of this practical solution would take no more than five years.[37]

When the authors wrote the letter, they were aware that their actions were dramatic and expected disapproval from more than their superiors. In an effort to meet objections and criticisms of their proposed plan, they presented possible "difficulties" and their "responses." They suggested that the community and its leadership would have difficulties with everything from how to engage in the process of self-evaluation to the financial feasibility of their program. They, however, went further in listing potential difficulties, which cut to the heart of the traditional Mercy apostolic work in institutions, religious government, and way of life. For example, the possible objections suggested that Church officials and the laity might perceive new apostolic work based on personal choice as irresponsible. The self-evaluation process could result in leaving institutions to which the Mercys had a long-standing commitment. They responded to this point by suggesting that the responsible action would be to commit "the powers [they had] left in a new direction which will be life-giving rather than letting these powers just run out." The other "difficulties and possible responses" spoke to issues of mutual distrust, hurt feelings, and the possibility that they were simply wrong. To each of these objections, the authors reiterated that the desire to serve God, to help their community, and to live an authentic religious life motivated their actions. Furthermore, the possibility that new ministries and community settings might exclude many sisters indicated to the authors that "[i]f many sisters would not be included, then [their] present supposed witness to Christ's love [was] really phony." They hoped that sisters would "trust each other to act in love, or if [they did] not possess this, why not find out and quit pretending?"[38]

The tone in the list of difficulties and responses is filled with a combination of anxiety and anticipation. The authors alternate between blunt proclamations and tactful, diplomatic missives to unite the community around a more aggressive pace toward renewal. Amongst the difficulties listed, one simple statement stands out. The authors suggested turning the very structure of their religious government on its head. They stated that the "generalate [was] only one source of insight in [their] community." This answered any question of why they believed they had the right to develop a program at all. Up to this point, the process of renewal had continued within the accepted government structures. New ideas and attitudes had emerged and dynamic community-wide discussion took place. The Letter, however, was something different. The authors asserted that some, if not a large part, of the authority bestowed upon the offices of the general and provincial councils belonged in the hands of the membership at large.[39]

The Letter had achieved, in part, its intended consequence. Houses took note of the arrival of this unprecedented letter. Along with St. Gabriel's in Chicago, the sisters at Mercy High School in Milwaukee recorded that the letter arrived "without any official letterhead or approbation" and "it created stir and much discussion. It really received reactions!" As the Mercy High School convent chronicle suggests, sisters throughout the province understood that a revision of the *Constitutions* was coming and each local house participated in some way in that process. Each house's discussions had contributed in some way. In the month preceding the infamous Letter's arrival, the Mercy High School community reported that the current Mother Provincial, Paulita Morris, had issued a summary of the community's renewal agenda and its preparation for the upcoming revisions to the *Constitutions* (see Figure 18). Her letter conveyed to the local convents the importance of their discussion to the renewal process for the Mercys. That September, Mercy High School sisters in Milwaukee received a surprise visit from Mother General Regina Cunningham, originally from that city (see Figure 19). During her visit, Mother Regina "spoke freely about latest developments in [the] community, the Church, meetings of the Conferences of Major Superiors in the U.S., adaptation, experimentation, withdrawals, and answered any and all of [the sister's] questions." The sisters in Milwaukee (and in other parts of the province) were quite aware of the developments within the community, the Church, and society around them. The Letter, coming from a group of sisters connected with Saint Xavier College, wanted to move faster.[40]

The Letter was not well received by Mother General Regina Cunningham. Eight days after it was posted, she responded to all the members of

Figure 18. Mother Paulita Morris, 1969.

the Chicago Province, expressing her dismay at the actions of the senders of this correspondence. They had by-passed the usual procedures and authority and went directly to the community with their proposal. Mother Regina made the point that the views expressed by the authors were only a "small minority when compared to the 1062 Sisters listed in the annual statistical report for the Chicago Province." She also reiterated the messages given in the previous communications and in the pages of *Agape* that with the new "freedom [that seemed] to be the word of the moment in the world that it had to exist in conjunction with obedience." The sisters who sent the letter had expressed their religious freedom, but she cautioned that they had acted with impatience.

A singular message that emerges from Mother Regina's letter is prudence. In the midst of all the changes of modern times, the community must not forget that prudence should not be thrown to the wind in [their] efforts to meet the crying needs of the Church, that sometimes an individual must suffer for the common good, that the rights and feelings of others must be considered, that we must keep in touch with reality as it is in our mode of life that patience and humility are still virtues to be cherished. Perhaps one of the most common failings in apostolic and zealous people is their impatience, their intolerance of others who might disagree with them or who might not be equally convinced of the urgency of a problem. This

Figure 19. Mother Regina Cunningham, Mother General, 1954–59.

impatience, this intolerance may point up a problem of selfish ends, of
shortsighted views, or simply a lack of planning.[41]

Amidst words urging the preservation of union and charity, Mother Regina
also characterized the thirteen sisters who attached their names to this Letter as a small percentage of the larger community, imprudent, impatient,
potentially intolerant, and possibly shortsighted. She closed her letter by
referring to the words of their foundress, Catherine McAuley, when she
spoke of the connection between the community's works and the faithful
observation of the rule. Mother McAuley advised her sisters that those
who follow their own desires suffered from "a delusion and artifice of the
enemy, as experience has sufficiently proved."[42]

Considering the strength of this language and the effective use of
Catherine McAuley's words (Mother Regina made a point to mention she
quoted from a copy of text written in their foundress' own hand), one
could assume that would be the end of this matter. The thirteen sisters
and their suggestions for renewal would fade from the Chicago Sisters
of Mercy. This, however, did not happen. A few weeks later in early November, Mother Paulita Morris authored her own letter to the members
of her province to respond to this issue. She did not use the same strong
language employed by the mother general, but she did not praise the actions of the thirteen sisters. She did not reference that they acted outside
the chain of command; she only mentioned the concern, pain, and tension
that the Letter caused. She urged the sisters to come together in prayer
and to trust that a solution to the current crisis would emerge. Remarkably, she announced that the new Renewal Commission created by the
Provincial Council met at the Provincial House to discuss the roughly 200
responses of support to the Letter. The commission and provincial leaders
did not reject the proposed plan, but believed it needed further clarifica-
tion and study. Mother Paulita continued that five of the authors of the
Letter would join four sisters from the Renewal Commission in an effort
to revise the plan and resubmit it for consideration.[43]

Instead of rejecting outright what the authors of the Letter had suggested (and potentially alienating them and their supporters), the Chicago
provincialate worked to incorporate them into the process more fully.
They became a part of the effort to find a solution. The Renewal Commission attached a report to the letter Mother Paulita sent to the sisters.
It clearly stated that the Sisters of Mercy in Chicago were in the midst of
a "critical situation." They acknowledged the desperation of many sisters
and the lack of hope felt by others. The number of young sisters in tem-

porary profession, novices, and postulants had dropped. Many had left in the preceding year and they faced in the future "an alarmingly smaller and older community by August 1968." Ultimately, the Renewal Commission planned to act in the coming year in many of the ways suggested by the authors of the Letter. Despite the conflict and dispute over how quickly the community should act or in what direction (or possibly because of it), provincial leaders made the dissatisfied sisters a part of the preparations for the next general chapter.[44]

"The unique position of being 'first among equals'"

Following the incident with the Letter and the reconstitution of the Renewal Commission in late 1967, the province continued on its path toward this general chapter in June 1969. The Sisters of Mercy of the Union needed to call another general chapter by October of that year because the Vatican required religious communities to revise their constitutions by this date to reflect the directives of the Vatican Council. The Union needed to make those revisions through a special chapter. Once again, provincial chapters had to convene before the general chapter to elect delegates. The Chicago Province (and the others in the Union) prepared proposals for revision to the *Constitutions* and directed further study for the regional governmental assembly at the end of 1968.[45]

In the face of what had occurred within the Chicago Province the preceding year and the desire to rewrite their *Constitutions* to update them for the modern world, committees created by the provincial council pulled together as much information and data to present at the provincial chapter as possible. Along with government, the committees studied Sister Formation, spirituality, the liturgy, and the apostolate of the community. Throughout this period in preparation for the provincial and general chapters, the province undertook self-studies to discern the appropriate form and spirit of religious life for Sisters of Mercy. Any study of this nature had to consider the community's resources, including personnel, and how these fit with the current state of religious life. Along with self-study, the Chicago Province endeavored to operate with more transparency. One means of accomplishing this was to expand the base of participants in the provincial chapter. Another was to maintain a steady flow of communication from Mother Paulita's office to the members of the province. *Agape* had proved helpful following the previous chapter sessions, but it had outlived its purpose; the community needed more than an outlet for discussion. A new and entirely different newsletter replaced *Agape* called *Exchange*. With its first issue in early 1968, *Exchange*'s purpose was to convey to the community the status of proposals for renewal and experimentation. It also provided a consistent and singular outlet of news from the Provincial House and an avenue of communication between the various houses within the province. *Agape* had given the community an opportunity to express ideas at the same time it featured news or ministry developments but it only appeared three times a year. *Exchange*, in contrast, was issued more frequently, nearly every month, and it provided more detailed information about the life of the community. It was less stylized than *Agape*, but what *Exchange* lacked in design, it made up for in content.[46]

By May 1968, the Provincial Council decided that local houses would begin experimenting with forms of participative government and informed the community the next month. How the Mercys envisioned authority took on specific meaning in this process. The Chicago Province had to develop a plan for new government and practical data would help formulate a model. Experimentation revolved around the role of the local superior. The province moved away from a traditional conception of "superior as 'guardian of the rule'" and hoped rather for a local leader who acted as a spiritual guide. The practical, day-to-day responsibilities of traditional superiors distracted them from the more important duty of religious leader. The proposals for experimental government and community living wanted to remove the austere leader from the equation and replace her with a collaborative group who operated with mutual responsibility and respect. Generals and Provincials still existed, but at the local level a coordinator divvied up administrative duties. Experimentation would also give sisters an opportunity to explore important issues about community living. They had a chance to work out community identity, the place of authority, "tensions between personal . . . and community goals," and how all these issues related to the Vatican Council documents.[47]

In practice, superiors would be assigned or elected for a year, regardless of whether they were in the midst of serving longer terms or newly appointed. Within the local houses, the sisters elected the councilors and determined the number and form of councils within their convent. Preparations and elections continued through the summer and each house ideally had its new form of government in place by the fall. The Chicago Sisters of Mercy had moved from discussing the meaning of religious authority to implementing different modes or manifestations of it. This experimentation enabled the community to see if it could effectively conduct meaningful religious life with mutual respect for personal fulfillment at the local level. In essence, the local houses experimented with the principle of subsidiarity spoken of in *Quadragesimo Anno* and developed during the Second Vatican Council.[48]

The results of experimentation in local government became a part of the preparations for the provincial chapter, which began December 30, 1968. While the provincial council had not officially declared an end date to the chapter, they planned for it to close on or near January 6, 1969. The large quantity of information and proposals to consider prolonged the meeting and pushed the sisters to the limit of their stamina. On January 3, the delegates voted to suspend their meetings for two weeks at which time they would resume their deliberations over the course of two weekends. The decision to suspend the proceedings went against the directive from the generalate against adjournments or recesses. Mother Regina meant the chapters to run over consecutive days. No other province had found the need to suspend their proceedings and Mother Regina feared negative reactions from other regions of the Union. After an exchange of letters and telephone calls between Mother Regina and members of the Chicago Provincial Council, the generalate decided that the Chicago chapter was closed and the Chicago Province, thereafter, operated as a "Committee of the Whole." This would prove essential to the course of the revision of the *Constitutions*. The delegates from the Chicago Province needed to continue their deliberations in preparation for the general chapter. Officially concluding the provincial chapter without the chance to complete their tasks would have left them ill-prepared for general chapter.[49]

When it finally met in 1969, the general chapter heard reports and presentations on prayer life, liturgy, spirituality, Mercy charism, ecumenism, formation, religious names, temporalities, the habit, and all manner of apostolic work, but religious government and authority occupied a dominant place in the proceedings. The members of the Government Commission, led by Sister Ignace Garvey of Chicago, stressed the importance of individual freedom and choice, and the need to foster a "person-oriented community," instead of one defined by its "functions" or institutions. Sister Mary Catherine Daly, another Chicago Province member of the commission, drew the important connection between modes of government and the manner of religious lifestyles. The conception of government depended upon the outlook of the community. She stressed that at that moment, the community was divided between those who wished to maintain a traditional view and those who embraced the newer theology of their day. The proposals for governmental reform emphasized models more in keeping with the latter of the two worldviews. Ultimately, the chapter agreed and voted in favor of the newer path when it supported community self-government. Delegates decided that, in terms of local leadership, individual convents would determine for themselves the nature of their community government. They could elect their local coordinator or they could opt for the provincial superior to appoint one.[50]

Sisters of Mercy had expressed dissatisfaction and discontent with religious life of the preceding decades, and the many meetings, forums, self-studies, and provincial and general chapters worked to ameliorate that unhappiness. The decisions of the 1969 chapter, however, would not fix the problem and quell tensions. Yet both the preparations for the chapter and the missives from it stressed mutual respect and cooperation in a common purpose. Just prior to the general chapter, Mother Paulita reminded the sisters of the Chicago Province:

> In response to the Council Documents we accept the principle of collegiality which affirms the interdependence of all those called to build community and the principle of subsidiarity by which each person receives the opportunity to actualize her own potentiality in a given task. These two principles form the foundation of participative government. However, if in our efforts to achieve participative government we fail in love and consideration for our sisters, nothing is accomplished. We—each sister—in true interdependence build community.[51]

This spirit of collegiality and the principle of subsidiarity were fundamental parts of building the new community and the sisters had to transform their thinking on religious government. It was one thing to discuss change, but another to live it. The Religious Government Commission at the 1969 general chapter urged that everyone, regardless of role within the Mercys, "ground themselves in knowledge of religious authority, subsidiarity, shared responsibility, and dialogue." The most meaningful opportunity for change could manifest at the lowest level of government in the shape of the local leader, who was "in the unique position of being 'first among equals.'" Open communication and mutual affection essential to a united community was the responsibility of all members of a house or convent. The local leader, however, would create the opportunity for open dialogue and expression of ideas and feelings. Her greatest role, according to the government commission, however, was "interested listener."

> She should make a genuine, consistent attempt to seek counsel from the group and to have all share in the dialogue. Of course the responsibility

for creating unity does not rest with the leader; all the members including the leader are called to respond to one another in love, in openness, and in cooperation. "The dialogue is not an end in itself; it looks toward decision and directives. In their issuance and acceptance, the Community comes together in a new way." The leader of the local community directs only after true dialogue.[52]

The Sisters of Mercy of the Union emerged from its general chapter in 1969 rededicated to its mission with a new government structure. Another decade of change awaited them, but provinces such as Chicago had to take the necessary steps to sustain themselves in the future. The delegates and observers at the general chapter went back to their provinces to continue experimentation and begin implementing the changes of the assembly. They left with a new *Mercy Covenant,* which would act as an interim *Constitutions* until after the next chapter in 1971. The Chicago Province's plan for a new government structure echoed the model for cooperation and collegiality in Mother Paulita's letter and in the Religious Government Commission report and it conformed with the view of most of the provinces within the Union that the generalate level of government should continue. It should set the directions and goals of the whole community and be the liaison with Rome. At the provincial level, the Chicago community created a new Province Board, which set the goals and agenda specific to the Chicago Province and was "accountable to the province community and to the generalate." The next level of government, the local community, by design, fully enacted collegiality. As per the experimentation, sisters created a mode of government suitable to their house. They set goals for their immediate lives, but also carried out the policies and goals of the province. They were "accountable to the Province Board and to each person within the local community."[53]

The delegates and observers at the general chapter also brought with them new titles or names for leadership. No longer would they use the title "superior" to identify the local or provincial leader. The Mother Provincial from that point forward was known as the Provincial Administrator and Mother General became Superior General. With new names in hand, the Chicago Mercys intended to move forward to implement their plans for a new government. The changes to the religious government made for all of the Union, however, had not received approval from the Sacred Congregation of Religious in Rome and by early 1970, Union and province leaders learned that the office had reservations that their changes did not guarantee a sister in a position of authority. The new structure of government gave an elected body or board the power to make all decisions. The Sacred Congregation for Religious believed an elected body could and should act in a consultative manner, but it could not take the place of a religious superior, meaning only one sister, a mother superior, should have the final authority over community decisions.[54]

The plan for consensus government at the local level did not get approval from the Sacred Congregation of Religious in 1970, and Superior General, Sister Regina, did not appeal this decision. She attempted to continue the dialogue between the Mercys and the Sacred Congregation, but further experimentation was not approved. While frustration rippled through the Union, at the local level, experimentation continued in some form. Houses that had begun experimenting in new ways of governing and relating to one another at the time of the 1969 general chapter, continued even after the Sacred Congregation denied the permission for local government by consensus. Many local houses elected a coordinator and selected or divided duties among a team or "subsidiaries." In smaller settings such as a parish convent like St. Ita in Chicago, the subsidiary team members took charge of housekeeping, cooking, and liturgy and spirituality matters within the local house. In a larger setting like Mercy High School, the coordinator had an administrative team made up of the principal, assistant principal, and two other sisters who took charge of coordinating matters such as students' extracurricular activities.[55]

The changes at the 1969 general chapter were in many respects revolutionary, and the Chicago community needed the ensuing two years to become more comfortable with much of the new structure. The experimentation in local living and participatory government with consensus decision making took time for the sisters to understand and figure out for themselves. With this new method, everyone had a say in the decision, but the process took longer than if one person had authority alone. In the end, with open dialogue, even if it meant conflict and time-consuming debate, the group came to a decision with which most could agree. Despite the extra efforts, many within the community preferred to have a voice, because it (and other responsibilities within the house) enabled the sisters to act and live as mature adults.[56]

This issue of government by consensus did not have a resolution until after the close of the first session of the Eighth General Chapter in July 1971. Following the end of the session, the new Administrator General (formerly Superior General) Concilia Moran and Sisters Doris Gottenmoeller (Cincinnati) and Josetta Butler (Chicago) ventured again to Rome to meet with the Sacred Congregation for Religious to discuss the recent decisions and to open again the debate about government experimentation. As with earlier meetings, the officials objected to the lack of a superior, based on *Perfectae Caritatis* and *Evangelica Testificatio* (Apostolic Exhortation on the Renewal of Religious Life), which emphasized the need for a religious superior. Again, the issue was to whom would the sisters give religious obedience? The Sacred Congregation, seeking to preserve a government structure based upon obedience to a specific and clear authority figure, did not approve of a new form of religious obedience that appeared to leave authority up to the individual sister or the consensus of the group. Despite their continued objections, the Sacred Congregation approved continued experimentation in local government. At the time of this meeting in Rome, the Mercys within their general chapters had discussed what community meant to them and determined for themselves how they constituted religious government. While conversation continued in provinces throughout the Union, the delegates pondered where they as a religious institute wanted to go and whether or not that meant, as historian Mary Regina Werntz, RSM, states "perhaps beyond the limits set by Rome." Fortunately for the Mercys and their evolving conception of religious life, Rome gave room for continued experimentation.[57]

The Sisters of Mercy of the Union continued throughout the 1970s to work through the type of government that best suited their vision of women religious. They started the process of renewal that moved them away from the traditional structured relationships with the Church, one another, and as discussed in the next chapter, the laity. When they embraced renewal, they sought to live a more person-oriented religious life, through their apostolate, their spirituality, and their community life. The Mercys' new religious government enabled them to build their religious life in a manner that made room for personal fulfillment and a mature, cooperative, and collegial community. This, however, did not occur instantaneously. From the chapters in the late 1960s to those in throughout the 1970s, the community worked on the details of the new religious government. The changes of the late 1960s and early 1970s took time to become normal or acceptable to all members of the Chicago Province, like the rest of the regions within the Union. Sisters had to learn how to live peaceably with others; they had to learn a new form of religious life. Conscious of these problems, province administrators sought to make that transition easier by creating offices, such as the Religious Life Council, whose main purpose was to assist in the formation process of the local communities.[58]

Changes in government did not stop with the interim governing document, *Mercy Covenant*, and more work was needed until the Union had an officially approved *Constitutions*. A new *Core Constitutions* did not emerge until the mid-1980s. The renewal process of the 1960s and 1970s, however, had stripped away the elements of religious life that, on the surface, stood between the Sisters of Mercy and a closer relationship with their founding charism. In the years between amalgamation and Vatican II, the Mercys had not abandoned their founding spirit; it was always there, but it was articulated and lived through the structured and monastic religious life. By stripping away of those layers through renewal, as required by the Church and canon law, many sisters found a more intimate relationship with the founding charism originally expressed by Catherine McAuley. The social and political changes erupting in the 1960s intensified this renewal as many sisters embraced feminism, which mingled with their faith in how God had called them to serve. By the early 1970s, the Mercys at every level articulated a renewed dedication to the condition of women in society and especially within the Catholic Church. None of this would have been possible without the revision of their religious government. Their community life, how sisters related to one another, and how they envisioned authority and religious freedom all stemmed from the change in religious government.[59]

When the Mercys amalgamated in 1929, they instituted a generalate government that took decision-making from the local community and gave it to one centralized authority. While this was necessary at the time to conform to Church directives and to preserve their way of life, the renewal that came in the 1960s reversed this process and distributed decision-making among the smaller local communities. This did not do away with the united Mercy community or the Union, nor did it take away the new regional identity of the Chicago Province. The shift returned the Mercys to their original composition designed by Catherine McAuley. When the Sisters of Mercy in Ireland in the 1830s expanded, Mother Catherine did not institute a central motherhouse and government. A new foundation, while connected in spirit and affection with its parent house, stood independent and the local superior governed based upon the circumstances and needs of her house. The new form of government that emerged by the 1970s did not return completely to this model; it could not. Too much had transpired since the nineteenth century and the needs of the sisters were different. The Mercys, by embracing a subsidiarity form of government, had also made room for individual growth and freedom, all the while working to maintain a communal identity. Consequently, the individual sister who needed to live separately or in a small group of two or three sisters apart from a large convent setting could do this with support and blessings of the entire community. It also meant that the individual sister had the freedom to budget her own finances, choose her own clothing, compose her own vows, and have a voice in the direction of the community. To understand fully the consequences or ramifications of revising the Mercys' religious government structure, a closer look must be taken at the community, apostolic, and spiritual life of the Chicago Province of the Sisters of Mercy since the 1960s. In their daily interactions with the laity, the official Church, and each other, the Mercys lived religious renewal.

6

Reinventing Community and Service to the World

[We] bring the word of God or . . . bring and . . . receive God. [I]t's not like we're up here pouring it down. It's mutual . . . we receive as much as we give.[1]

In the summer of 1959, Sister Patricia M. Murphy read an announcement posted on the wall of the sisters' residence at Saint Xavier College for a new mission to Sicuani, Peru. The announcement contained few details about the mission other than the altitude and the purpose of the endeavor: to establish a school and possibly have some sisters work in health care. With a dream from her youth to be a missionary before her, Sister Pat wrote a volunteer letter, ran it across campus to the provincial offices, and slipped it into the mail slot, hoping for the best. The provincial council ultimately selected Sister Pat to join one other sister from the Chicago Province, Sister Mary Johnetta Kaney, and two other Mercys from Baltimore and Omaha, to conduct this South American mission in Peru. Sister Pat left with the three other sisters in January of 1961 full of excitement, but with little preparation for what was ahead of her.

Patricia M. Murphy entered the Sisters of Mercy in 1947 and made her first profession in 1950, taking the name Sister Mary Nivard. (Sister Patricia returned to her baptismal name by the end of the 1960s.) She was soon to take her final vows and was studying at Saint Xavier College to complete her bachelor's degree when she learned about the Peru mission in 1959. The Peru mission was a part of a larger pre–Vatican II mission to evangelize and strengthen the Catholic Church in Latin America. When asked forty-seven years after she left for Sicuani what she expected, Sister Pat reflected that before she left, she did not know the meaning of evangelization or what to expect. She recalled: "Deep down since a little kid [I] felt strongly the call to justice and the poor; everyone had the right to stuff, so I felt these folks were poor, and I was going to see if I could help in any way."[2] Despite rough conditions and uncertain preparation (the sisters had little understanding of Spanish at the beginning of the mission), Sister Pat and the others set about their work, at the same time continuing to keep the Rule of their community. Wearing white church cloaks in the middle of the muddy, rainy season, starching their coifs and guimpes, and attempting to follow the letter of the Rule, however, quickly became anachronistic when faced with the reality of everyday life in Peru. The life of missionaries in Latin America in the 1960s forced questions about the nature of religious life. Everything from the structure of Mercy community life to the habit came under scrutiny. Of deeper significance were the questions that went to the purpose of their religious mission and the relationships and close connections the sisters had with the people they came to "evangelize." Were they to lead or impose upon the Peruvian people a particular religious and cultural standard, or were the sisters to be with them and respond to their needs? The sisters in Peru ultimately had to "create their own way," whether in ministry or community life. While these sisters navigated and negotiated their way through rules and apostolic agendas, the rest of their community back in the Chicago Province asked the same about how they should live, work, and pray.[3]

The experience of Sister Patricia M. Murphy and the other Mercys who participated in the Sicuani mission appears to have been an intensified renewal process. When they first arrived, they and their community had not made concrete changes to their religious life. At the end of the near-decade-long mission in Peru, much had changed. While Sister Pat and others negotiated and experienced change in religious life thousands of miles away from home, their sisters in the Chicago Province, as discussed in the preceding chapter, had their own questions and went through their own renewal process no less significant. The changes wrought by the Sister Formation Conference and Vatican II renewal altered the conception of religious life and ministry. Vatican II stressed the dignity of the person and this idea filtered into all aspects of Mercy life by the end of the 1960s. When the members of the Sisters of Mercy of the Chicago Province considered how they lived, worked, prayed, and related to one another, they pondered the extent to which they recognized this dignity of the person in each other and those they came to serve.

The renewal of religious government underway following the close of the Second Vatican Council inspired experimentation in local living, and ministry rooted in an evolving spirituality. How sister constructed and related to authority affected the very look and location of Mercys' residences, as well as how sisters chose and redefined their ministries. Respect for the individual person was, as we have seen in the preceding chapter, a central element to the reform of religious government and this idea was a central part of the evolving Mercy spirituality of this period. Individual fulfillment as a member of the Chicago Mercys, engagement in one's local house or convent community, and engagement in ministry were elements all tied together, incorporating spirituality. Connected to this was also the ongoing conversation about the meaning and articulation of their vows that the Chicago Mercys (along with other women religious) engaged in throughout this period. While renewal did not change the vows that Sisters of Mercy professed (they still took lifelong vows of poverty, chastity, and obedience), how sisters understood and expressed them did. Religious poverty, chastity, and obedience continued to shape their lives as Mercys, but sisters began to understand them as more than mere negative limitations and boundaries to their lives as women religious.

As with the debate about religious government, *Agape* and, later, *Exchange*, enable the Mercys to begin the conversation of renewal of spirituality (as well as community life and ministry) and the meaning of their vows. The conversation in these publications echoed the debate and discussion going on in the provincial and general chapter meetings to revise their constitutions, as discussed in the preceding chapter. Through the renewal process, the Chicago Mercys offered alternative perspectives on their vows. At the core, poverty, chastity, and obedience had to originate with personal responsibility and individual commitment. In the past, these vows meant for some sisters restrictions, rules, and limitations. In one issue, a sister remarking on the vow of poverty stated that she viewed it as a means of saving or cutting costs. She saw it as "mending and patching," and was tangled up in unrealistic and legalistic rules of religious life. Instead, poverty divided "things of the spirit and things of the world" into "their proper places and the meaningfulness of the spiritual life as the imitation of the living reality of the Person of Christ begins to replace the narrow, confining confusion of a merely material and negative practice of poverty."[4]

The Chicago Mercys' discussion of the vows revolved around personal responsibility and living an authentic life. Acknowledging that poverty, for example, came in many forms, not simply material poverty, sisters needed to engage freely with personal ownership in order to authentically live the vow, not simply acting by the rule for the rule's sake. The vow of obedience could not be authentically lived unless those in power were just and respected the individual person under their authority and sisters turned away from individualism and embraced the community. Celibacy and the vow of chastity, furthermore, had to move away from the negative connotations of abstinence and self-denial. Rather, the vow of chastity provided a gateway toward a more intimate and direct connection to God and the needs of his people.[5]

The Chicago Mercys, while they moved toward a new participative government, experimented with new modes of community life, explored alternative ministries, and contemplated how they as individual women bound their lives to God and to their religious congregation. As we will see, new forms of community and ministry enabled the Mercys to explore these traditional promises, and, by the early 1970s, to understand how they articulated their vows to each other, which respected their uniqueness, but spoke to their commitment to community of women religious.[6] By extension, a new articulation of Mercy charism and the influence of religious, political, and cultural developments redirected changing resources and approaches to apostolates. Many sisters perceived new and different needs and sought a fresh manifestation of their traditional responses as teachers, nurses, administrators, social workers, and religious instructors. Sisters took their talents and decades of experience and applied them as community center directors, pastoral ministers, and psychologists, among other things. Along the way, in the face of declining members due to departures and fewer entrants, they sought a more authentic and meaningful spiritual life by reconceptualizing the formation process and creating new expressions of prayer and liturgy.[7]

The long evolution of the Sisters of Mercy in the Chicago Province (and throughout the United States) did not occur without debate and some discord. As the discussion of renewal of religious government has shown, change did not occur instantaneously nor did each sister move at the same pace. Renewal, for the Sisters of Mercy, meant more than a new form of community government, raising questions about all avenues of their lives. Did changing apostolic works and manner of prayer alter who they were? Did the new forms of community living, especially those that occurred outside traditional convents in apartments and then later in houses purchased by the Chicago Province, represent true religious life? Did maintaining traditional ministries, resident patterns, and prayer indicate a failure on the part of some sisters to change with the times? The Chicago Mercys grappled with these questions at the same time they strove to maintain the essence of the Sisters of Mercy as designed by Catherine McAuley.[8]

"A community of friends is the ideal today, not an assemblage of people"
The year 1967 was difficult for the Chicago Mercys.[9] The "Letter" had caused a stir, and thirty-one sisters left the community that year and the

next year was not any better in terms of retention.[10] Two-thirds of the women who left in 1967 had only been in the community ten years. In 1968, open discord and contention were expressed at community meetings, like the Community Renewal Weekend in January at Saint Xavier College. Mother General Regina Cunningham presided over the weekend-institute, which culminated in a question-and-answer period, where both traditional- and reform-minded sisters expressed their dissatisfaction with the current state of the community. Ultimately, the discord "served to highlight the unrest and divergence of opinion and attitude within the community" and the "weekend had untold consequences." These were heartbreak days for the community and for the many women who chose to leave. The younger sisters felt these departures dearly as they watched their friends leave, but they were not alone in their grief. All members of the community mourned the loss of those who left. What would become of the community and religious life? For those who saw members of their band (women who entered the same year) or sisters from their convents leave, why should they stay? Aware of the unhappiness, particularly among some of the younger sisters who were to be the future of the Chicago Mercys, Mother Paulita Morris and the rest of the council were sympathetic and attempted to respond to the needs of local community life.[11]

The dissatisfaction with the current situation in the late 1960s came from several areas. Sisters who were unhappy with their current living, whether because they resided with forty other women in a convent, or because they lived in a small parish setting, wanted to get away from the rigid and monastic community life that seemed so indicative of their experience. Sisters in larger groups, like those who lived at Mercy High School Chicago, believed that the small group was the start of an answer. Yet most sisters lived in smaller settings and had no experience like those of Mercy High School since their days at the novitiate. More had to happen beyond limiting the number of sisters who lived together. A local convent attached to a parish school could be just as monastic and structured as the larger groups. Some sisters preferred to live with Mercys with whom they did not work. They tired of "living above the store." Sisters in parish and hospital convents could not escape their work; they carried it upstairs or next door to their homes. Living with sisters who performed different ministries might give a respite from their labors and enliven their individual interest in their work. Regardless of how sisters lived, for true experimentation to occur, sisters had to alter their approach to religious life, including implementing the principles of subsidiarity and respect for the individual person so prominent in the theology of the twentieth century.[12]

Sisters who lived through this period of change recall that experimentation seemed everywhere in the late 1960s. Provincials and committee members applied this term to any plan and program designed to alter the structure of religious life, whether as a new type of ministry or an attempt to decentralize government. Initially, however, only a small percentage of the population took radical steps, such as moving out of convents and into apartments or houses. A side effect of sisters' united work and residential life, however, was that they were often unaware of what happened in other locations. Consequently, not all sisters were fully aware of the talk of intentional or small group living. What happened after Vatican II was more complex than appears on first blush. This was not a period of total experimentation or radicalism, nor was it all conservatism. The first efforts were tentative, albeit still dramatic for those involved in them, but they started the Mercys on the road toward new and varied manifestations of community living.[13]

As early as 1966, sisters crafted proposals for experimentation. By 1967, the leadership planned for groups of eight sisters to experiment with government structure, primarily those in parish convents. The leadership gave them few guidelines by which to structure their convent or house government, except that someone had to assume the role of coordinator or superior. The local house voted or determined through discussion their superior and how long she served her term, and then determined what aspects of their daily lives they wanted to change. Slowly, groups of sisters had implemented small changes. The sisters living in the Little Flower convent on Wood Street in Chicago in October 1967 after a discussion of seating arrangements for meals, "decided to permit the Sisters to sit where they choose." Over the next year, sisters living in the Little Flower convent continued to address matters of concern to the entire local house, including whether or not to omit bell-ringing for exercises and how as a group they would divide household duties and chores.[14] While seemingly small issues, group decisions and individual choice about how to conduct their lives were essential. Furthermore, divvying up household chores or setting a rotating schedule instead of having local superiors assign duties had meaning to sisters, especially if one person consistently performed the same unwelcome task, such as sweeping the back stairs of the convent. Respect of the person and fairness were key factors in this process. Many sisters wanted their superiors to treat them like adults, and the traditional structure of religious life had prevented this.[15]

Figuring out the practical day-to-day details of community life within the convent at Little Flower parish is just one example of many and was only one aspect of experimentation. Loosening restrictions on personal finances was another way to give sisters more autonomy. Money and personal responsibility concerned many individual sisters. From the perspective of sisters within local convents, the ability to control one's spending and to have money to make purchases was seen as significant. It meant that the community trusted the individual to manage her own finances. It also meant that sisters did not have to ask permission from a superior for every minor purchase, such as postage stamps. Having control over some money gave sisters the freedom to not only purchase stamps, but mail letters without first submitting correspondence unsealed to superiors for approval and postage.[16]

By spring 1968, selected convents experimented with the budgeting of money. *Exchange* reported in April 1968, that several communities tried out a monthly budget and "convenience money" plans. St. Raymond convent in Mount Prospect, Illinois, for example, experimented with the former. Each sister had $30 a month to spend as she wished on "food (if eating out), clothing, shoes, medicine (other than prescriptions), long distance calls, books, shampoo, and other toilet articles, entertainment, stamp and stationery, [and] personal board while traveling." In October, the sisters at Mercy High School in Milwaukee decided to "to experiment with a small amount of money allotted to each Sister—who wished it—as *Convenience Money*." According to the convent chronicle:

> This gives each person access to $5 or $10 (as she desires) to be used for emergencies, requisitions, travel, etc. When she needs more, she simply turns in the envelope with a general accounting, and gets another $5 or $10. This should make us all now aware of prices, values, and the meaning of our vow of poverty, as well as freeing the Superior from constant requests for small needs.[17]

Exchange reported the results of the survey of the local houses' experimentation and determined that the budgetary plan was far more successful because it was "a realistic plan and that the sisters became budget conscious." Regardless of the financial plan employed, becoming "budget conscious" was an important measure of how sisters lived their vow of poverty.[18]

Tinkering with established houses consisting of sisters in the same ministry was a beginning, but some sisters wanted to take experimentation in new directions. They wanted to establish houses for those of different ministries. Proposals for this type of living existed as early as 1966. The idea was for sisters to live in groups of no more than eight and with those with whom they did not work. Furthermore, the idea advanced the notion that sisters might choose with whom they lived. According to one proposal, "community life gives the truest witness to the love life of the Trinity when the people in the community love and enjoy one another and are actually created by each other."[19] Proposals also took into account locations and finances, and incorporated documents from Vatican II and the existing *Norms* of the community. The authors of another proposal submitted in 1968 wanted to "determine if the identification of the work group with the community group is the only way of living out religious life." While not condemning the traditional model of living with those with whom one worked, they believed it was "not the only workable structure." The authors did not want their proposal to "be a threat to [the Mercys'] way of life of faith and prayer."

> Rather, it is a challenge to this life of faith because it demands a response to a risk, to the future, to the unknown. To give such a response requires as much faith and courage as our present life demands of us, if not more. This response may take the form of actual participation in the experiment or perhaps merely an open attitude toward the experiment. The responses will be different, being determined as they are by the experiences and the particular situation of each sister. All of these responses, however, must and should be based on a deep faith or no true progress will be made.[20]

To make this type of plan work, however, the Mercys needed at least three things. First, the sisters engaged in this type of experimentation needed the permission of the provincials. Without this, they could not proceed. The climate of discord and dissatisfaction, however, made Mother Paulita amenable to these ideas. Second, the plan needed volunteers or a group of like-minded sisters willing to try something new. Of the over 900 sisters in the community by the late 1960s, only 44 put their names on a list of volunteers. The majority of them were elementary school sisters, but hospital, high school, and college sisters and sister-students also volunteered. Last, they needed a place to live. If everyone lived in a ministry-related convent, volunteers had to find a suitable and, more importantly, an available space to conduct their experiment.[21]

Cardinal John Cody compounded the problem of space within the Archdiocese of Chicago. He disapproved of "sisters living in apartments and wanted them to live in 'canonically established houses.'" By 1968, a solution appeared at the same time as Mercys and other religious communities began to withdraw from parish schools. As sisters left a school, they left the convent provided by the parish. Some sisters received permission to form new local communities in these empty buildings. St. Clotilde was one parish where sisters found space to experiment with religious living. In this case, some Mercys still worked within the parish, while others worked at different Mercy schools or other institutions, or they were students.[22]

The sisters who came together at St. Clotilde Convent wanted to implement some of what had been brewing in the community over the preceding few years. The controversial Letter had suggested (among other things) that Mercys chose with whom they lived and two of the sisters who put their names to this correspondence came together at St. Clotilde with four others to experiment for a year. Sister Regine Fanning, one of the signers and a faculty member at Mercy High School Chicago, developed and submitted the proposal, with the intention to "live together in an in-service training program in social spirituality for the purpose of furthering Christian community while engaged in the traditional apostolate of the Sisters of Mercy." Sister Mary Sheehan, the Letter's identified contact person on the Provincial Advisory Board, wanted an opportunity to "follow through on what had been said in 1967," and the location of St. Clotilde made commuting to Loyola University on the north side for her studies convenient. Sisters Mary Alice Pierce, principal at St. Clotilde; Mary Kevin McGrath, teacher at St. Clotilde; Rita O'Sullivan, teacher at Christ the King; and Mary Anne Cranley, religious educator in Confraternity of Christian Doctrine (CCD) rounded out the group.[23]

Other sisters had expressed interest in experimental living, but the location and timing of St. Clotilde only worked for these six. After meeting periodically throughout the summer of 1968 and attending a retreat, the Clotilde group considered the practical and spiritual operation of their new house. This was the essential part of their endeavors (and others who acted in a similar way); they took ownership of every choice and were conscious that they were about to embark upon something new and significant. Working out a house budget and assigning household chores were just as crucial to renewal of religious life as determining the manner in which they prayed and related to one another. Sister Mary Alice filled the position of coordinator (superior), but each member had a role in the maintenance of the house and support of the community. To take this framework one step further, they established "Sister Mary Alice's role of coordinator to be at least that of a contact person for the group with the larger communities with which [they were] affiliated" such as "the Sisters of Mercy, the parish of St. Clotilde, the Archdiocesan Councils, etc." They agreed to monitor this position to understand the extent of Sister Mary Alice's duties.[24]

The manner in which the St. Clotilde group defined Sister Mary Alice's role is significant. As shown in the previous chapter, much discussion around renewal of religious government pushed for the elimination of the local superior. For this local house, the pure participatory democratic model best suited how religious life should evolve. This was truly "revolutionary," particularly considering that when the Mercy Generalate presented plans such as these to the Sacred Congregation for Religious in the early 1970s, the Vatican rejected the lack of a superior. Furthermore, Mother Regina repeatedly reminded sisters through the provincials that experimentation had to have one person in a position of authority. The members of the Clotilde group recognized this and accepted a superior or coordinator, but qualified the position as "at least that of a contact person" with Church authorities.[25]

This structure, while specific to the needs of this group, represented the wishes of many who experimented in an "intentional community." The term itself is noteworthy. These Mercys chose to live together based upon religious and common practical goals (the location was geographically convenient for some). They wanted to share in each other's lives while respecting personal space. Some proposals at this time used the term "family" to describe the manner in which sisters would live together. In many ways, this applies to intentional communities. They created a home in which they shared meals, were aware of each other's lives, celebrated birthdays, and prayed together. At St. Clotilde's and in other small communities, the house became a place to experience new modes of prayer, moving away from the traditional recitation of the Divine Office, or the Little Office of the Blessed Virgin. The sisters at St. Clotilde experimented with Sunday morning meditation and used Leslie Brandt's *Good Lord, Where Are You? Prayers for the Twentieth Century Based on the Psalms*.[26]

While the term "family" may apply because of shared meals, creative prayer services, and birthday celebrations, it is not an accurate description of an intentional community. First, meals, prayers, and celebrations of birthdays and feast days occurred in traditional convents. From the perspective of the sisters who chose the small group, they believed that their free choice to come together in this way, not assigned by a superior and not compelled to order their lives around a horarium, filled a need they had for religious life. This freedom also fit with the breaking down of barriers between themselves as religious and the laity. More important, the intentional community enabled sisters to incorporate their biological families into their religious ones. Many who lived through these experiences, whether in parish convents or apartments, or later in homes purchased by the community, recounted that they had the liberty to invite their relatives for dinner and holiday celebrations, and to create new family traditions in ways that they had previously not been allowed to do.

St. Clotilde was not the only parish convent used for this type of experimentation. Nor were convents the only type of structure in which experiments occurred. The diversity of experience is evident when considering the proposal made by the group planning to live in a part of Mercy Convent in Chicago. From 1968 to 1969, sisters connected to Mother McAuley High School in Chicago established an intentional community in a wing of McAuley Convent called McAuley East. They did not want to live in a large setting, but wanted to experiment within existing facilities and found that they could carve out space in a wing of McAuley Convent to live separately from the rest of the sisters. They, like the sisters at St. Clotilde, wanted to focus on a "person centered rather than work centered" living, despite the close proximity to McAuley High School and other Mercys. While most participants worked at McAuley High, and consequently shared a ministry, they saw themselves as living in a community based upon spirituality rather than ministry.[27]

Ultimately, the spiritual drove experimentation and intentional communities. By 1965 and 1966, discussion of all manner of spirituality became a part of the general chapter proceedings and houses, whether large or small, digested updates from their provincial and generalate leaders. The talk of "new freedoms" crept into discussions of meditations, retreats, and communal prayer. Like other reforms and changes to traditions, once one occurred, more followed as the spirit of renewal inspired sisters to seek new and more personal expressions of their faith.[28]

The changes to the to the praying of the Divine Office, for example, started a discussion of the importance of community prayer. Divine Office consisted of a series of prayers, psalms, and readings led by a cantor and said in common at different points of the day. Sisters had learned that the Office would change in 1964, and in November 1965, local houses received their copies of a new Divine Office in English and Latin. One convent chronicler reported that "Prime has been suppressed, Matins will be said privately, Lauds as morning prayer, one hour of the Little Hours to be said privately, Vespers in the early evening and Compline as night prayers."[29] One change that rippled through convents was that each member of the house took a turn leading the Office, as opposed to one fixed cantor. Yet, this was only one aspect of community prayer and spirituality that started to shift. In a few short years, local houses held discussions about not only how and when they would pray together, but the meaning of communal prayer to each member of a house, apartment, or convent. Sisters who opted for intentional community living also wished to move further away from the rigid schedule of the horarium that had ordered religious life. The horarium set by the provincial and virtually the same for each local house, obligated sisters to recite set prayers at specific times during the day. Traditional daily prayers like the Office had their own means conveying a shared community identity. As experimentation continued at the end of the 1960s and early 1970s, sisters moved away from this type of spirituality and embraced something, which freed them from the constraints of mandatory prayer, as they believed that more authentic spirituality would manifest itself.[30]

Sisters in the Chicago Province conducting experiments in community living found support in the proceedings of the general chapters. The Spirituality and Liturgy Commission of the 1969 general chapter affirmed the ability of the individual sister "to live her religious commitment" and that while daily communal prayer still occupied a central part in their religious lives, it could find expression in unique ways. For example, the sisters at St. Ita convent in Chicago held house meetings in 1970 designed to answer for themselves what community was. A part of that was to allow for a more organic prayer life, exemplified by their practice of putting up a sign to invite members of their local house to pray. The sisters living an intentional community at St. Clotilde convent also included the nature and time of prayer in their house meetings. As with other experimental settings, they valued these times of community prayer, and set a time for prayer that fit the group's schedule. In 1971, they decided to have their year-end retreat at their local house because they preferred quiet prayer.[31]

Changes to traditional communal prayer brought the issue itself into the discussion of renewal of religious life. Prayer life and the Mercys' spirituality were reaffirmed in this process as essential to the congregation's community and apostolic life. Along with new modes of prayer within a local house and opportunities for retreat, sisters were given suggestions for "readings for personal study of prayer" and chances to establish prayer groups outside of their local group, and they developed a House of Prayer. In one case, a summer House of Prayer was established, which brought Mercys together with sisters "of varied background . . . seeking in-depth prayer" for five weeks in the summer.[32]

Those sisters who chose to experiment with religious life were led by the freedom to choose with whom they lived and how they prayed. This

did not mean that these new situations were free of adjustments and difficulties. The June 1969 issue of *Exchange* reported on the process of several
on-going experiments, St. Clotilde among them. The thrust of this update
emphasized the intentionality of the entire process. All believed that the
shared liturgies and prayer life within their "home" made the difference
to their progress. The St. Clotilde group used the term "home" to describe
where they lived. This was not a local house or convent, but their home.
They received support from those who came to the house, such as priests
who said liturgy for them in their living room. They asserted that when
and where they failed stemmed from a lack of honesty among members,
a reticence to communicate, and when "each one of [them] at the times . . .
failed to have responsibility or concern" for their endeavor. At the same
time, "[t]hose who failed to understand the goals [of their experimentation]
and therefore, did not support [them]" also hindered their efforts.[33]

Former parish convents and wings within larger community convents
were not available or desirable to all sisters, especially if their new ministries took them to various locations about the province. It became more
practical to find an alternative in the form of renting an apartment or
house. In other cases, Mercys in parish convents had to find another place
because the pastor or parish congregation wanted the use of the building
for other purposes, including as a meeting space for parish organizations.
In cases like this, sisters who no longer worked in the parish school often
rented the convent space from the parish. Despite the need or desire to
move, relocating to an apartment was a far more radical choice for the
entire community in the late 1960s. Yet as early as 1968, sisters took arguably daring steps to make this happen. In the summer of 1968, Sister Betty
Smith, at that time assigned to McAuley High School, engaged in a chance
conversation with Mother Paulita, expressed to her superior that she did
not believe that "they were meant to live in groups of forty." Mother Paulita, conscious of the unhappiness and discontent among sisters like Sister
Betty, suggested that she "do something about it," effectively giving her
permission to experiment in a new way. For Sister Betty, this planted the
seed to construct yet another new way (and location) in which to create
a community. After forming a group of sisters with similar interests but
different ministries, they determined that they wanted to live in an apartment. After another meeting with Mother Paulita in the spring of 1969,
they found an apartment in Chicago on Honore Street.[34]

The sisters living in the apartment on Honore Street in Chicago were
not the only ones to explore apartment living, and all Mercys who moved
away from a traditional convent, whether a parish, hospital, high school

convent, or some other local house in a Mercy-owned or affiliated institution raised questions about whether or not this was true community living. Asking what could those who lived in apartments possibly want, some Sisters of Mercy questioned the intentions of those who seemed to abandon all that a previous generation had understood. Some wondered, of these new groups in apartments, who was in charge, or who was the superior or coordinator? Or rather *was* there a superior? Were these sisters faithful to their vows of poverty and obedience? What form did their community prayer life take? How could this be community life, when sisters did not live in a Mercy convent? The reality was that over 95 percent of the Mercys still lived in traditional convents in 1970, with apartment living only drawing about 3 percent of the population. From 1970 to the early 1980s, the overall number of sisters living in traditional convents declined steadily, but not by any significant percentage. By 1983, over 70 percent still resided in Church-related or institutional housing, either a Mercy or another religious community's convent, or in a former rectory. Mercys began renting apartments in 1968 and 1969, and by 1970, twenty-nine sisters lived in seven different apartments. This number only increased as the decade advanced.[35]

The first groups of sisters who came together in apartments made decisions about the running of their household and religious government in a similar manner to the St. Clotilde experiment. Like-minded outlooks on renewal of religious life and practicality determined the composition of these apartments. Often, connections made during these early days of experimentation persisted in subsequent housing choices. In 1971, a group of sisters from St. Justin Convent on the south side of Chicago moved together a couple blocks south into a house on Hermitage Avenue. They stayed at this location for two years and then moved four blocks south into a three-bedroom apartment on 80th Street. Six women, two to a bedroom, shared one bathroom in a small apartment, but they did not mind the crowding because they believed they had an opportunity to choose how they wanted to shape their community life. This group consisted of Sisters Sharon Kerrigan, Rita Specht, Jonella Bohmann, Mary Ruth Broz, Emily Kemppi, and Avis Clendenen. Four of the group (Kerrigan, Specht, Bohmann, and Kemppi) taught at Mercy High School Chicago, while Sisters Mary Ruth and Avis were Formation Director and student respectively.

Like the sisters at St. Clotilde, the 80th Street Mercys, while focusing on their ministries, also concentrated on new ways of relating to each other as religious women. They had found life in the larger convents like Mercy High School, and even in the small parish convents, stifling. First in the house at Hermitage, then in their apartment on 80th street, the sisters saw experimentation as "a chance . . . to shape the way [they] wanted to live" whether through creative prayer, or breaking bread together at the Eucharist. They decided together not to say the traditional Divine Office or follow a set horarium, but they made a commitment to have community prayer, albeit in new ways, opting to direct their own prayers. The regular flow of daily ministry life determined schedules, but they made time and held each accountable to be present in their community. The sisters who lived in the 80th Street apartment recalled that Saturdays in the early days of living together became "house days" where sisters performed weekly chores and ran errands for the house. They also had a small-group liturgy in their apartment where their local chaplain presided at the Eucharist, with a shared homily allowing for all members of the community to share their faith. When Mass concluded, the priest stayed for dinner and the sisters described this as their "house night."[36]

Small groups like these suggested that a new and revolutionary Catholic religious life was on the horizon and sisters believed that "the whole Catholic Church was changing overnight" along with them. Women like Avis Clendenen, who entered the community in the midst of these changes, did not have any other conception of religious life. Sister Mary Ruth Broz's role as Avis Clendenen's formation director represented the new direction the community took in educating novices. Newer members to the community went from an orientation program at a local house to a ministry or course of study while living in another small setting. Avis began her orientation at St. Anne's in Chicago, and then went to live at St. Justin and became a part of this group as they moved to Hermitage, then 80th Street. She took classes at Saint Xavier College and participated in community life.[37]

The size and composition of the 80th Street group was somewhat typical of other intentional communities in apartments. By the end of the 1970s and early 1980s, smaller groups of two or three Mercys opted to live together. Throughout this decade, the number of apartments with only two sisters jumped from four to twenty-three by the early 1980s. Sisters opting to live alone or with family doubled from sixteen in 1972 to thirty-two by 1974. By the early 1980s, sixty-three sisters lived alone in apartments. Living in apartments, whether as a group or individually, troubled some within the community and caused province leaders to express concern about the well-being of particularly those on their own. Some judged that a sister's "presence and participation in her local community" was less authentic than the traditional community setting.[38]

Leaders, for their part, worried how sisters would support themselves outside of religious settings. They also wondered if the isolation or separation from the larger community was detrimental to their spiritual life, especially for sisters who lived alone. Requests to live alone began to increase by the early 1970s. While not every sister who wished to live alone met opposition from provincial leaders, they occasionally expressed concern about this choice and wanted sisters to consider alternative options. Provincial leaders concerned about sisters' isolation wanted to establish a schedule of contacts to provide a source of shared community. Furthermore, the Chicago Province continued to lose members. While the number leaving had declined since 1967, sisters still left. Those who participated in experimentation in community living had to justify their choices and prove that they could live as a Sister of Mercy and be a part of the community while residing outside its traditional structures.[39]

One way (and arguably the most effective) was to share the experiences of those in apartments with the larger community. Many informally discussed their new style of community living with other sisters in shared ministries over lunches, or other unplanned encounters of daily life. Another positive means of allaying concerns was to invite the community into their homes. Province officials and individual sisters came to dinner or other celebrations. In the case of St. Clotilde, many who visited the house their first year were sympathetic to their endeavors or were also experimenting in community life. In January 1969, the sisters chronicled that among their guests were six Sisters of Mercy and the 1968–69 Chronicles provide accounts of their effort to share with both the Mercy and parish communities. Open Houses, however, were much more explicit in their intention to allay concerns from within the Mercys. Often a single group held an open house, but in one case, a cluster of houses hosted an afternoon's event. Seven small groups in Oak Park on Chicago's west side held their open houses on the same afternoon in October 1973. *Exchange* published their invitation to the community and included a map and directions for sisters to follow to each home. Those on the home tour could cap their afternoon with coffee cake at four o'clock at Siena Convent and liturgy at five o'clock at Resurrection. Mercys throughout the province welcomed sisters into their new apartments in a similar manner. Two sisters who lived and worked at Mercy High School Milwaukee moved into an apartment in 1973 and held an Open House for sisters in their former residence.[40]

Ultimately, seeing where and how sisters lived helped convince most Mercys of the soundness of experimentation. Sisters who did branch out in the new direction recounted that while others in the community may have questioned their intentions, they always supported them. Those dwelling in apartments and then later in community-owned homes furthermore found that they did not lose the Mercy community as some feared. Most made a point of attending gatherings and the opportunities to reconnect with the larger community became more meaningful.[41]

Community-Owned Houses: "We were renters and owners . . . and livers"

Purchasing houses for the community was a natural progression from renting apartments and living in former parish convents.[42] By moving in this direction, the community further re-conceptualized their place within the Catholic Church and in society. Owning a home, or a series of houses, meant acquiring property and, more important, living among secular people in new ways that challenged stereotypes about women religious and blurred distinctions between sisters and the laity. Observers of sisters and nuns moving into neighborhoods often were surprised by these developments. One sister who experienced these changes reported:

> The one thing . . . about living in a house, you're living in a neighborhood. If you're living in a convent you're really set apart from the people and . . . if we're religious we should not be so set apart from the people we live with or the neighbors. [Sisters were] still isolated [in convents] because you're in a compound of some type and . . . we're over there. Some [lay] people were surprised that the sisters were going out mowing the lawn or watering the flowers or shoveling [snow] and being involved in block parties; that we would socialize.[43]

The Mercys had made many changes to living, governing, and ministry life by the 1970s and being in a neighborhood and living among laypeople was a part of that shift. Community-owned homes and apartment buildings were one more manifestation that change had occurred in religious life. By the mid-1980s, the community owned ten houses with less than fifty sisters living in them. This was still a small percentage of the larger population and each purchase had to receive the approval of the provincial leaders and Housing Committee to determine to what extent it fit within the spirit of the Mercy Institute. Of course, a house made practical and financial sense; it solved a housing concern for sisters in need of place to live. The committee, with the help of building inspectors, determined if the property under consideration was viable and worth the expense. Leadership and committee members also had questions about tax-exempt status, budgeting, and meeting financial obligations with the purchase. They also considered how the larger community would benefit from the transaction and the property's "availability to other sisters of the Province."[44]

Not all properties were approved, as in the case of the purchase of a house on the southwest side of Chicago in early August 1974. Through the course of the month, the provincial leaders evaluated reports on the condition of the property in question, only to determine that because of their reservations, the Chicago Mercys would not obtain the property. Larger concerns arose from this process regarding how the community made its decisions. Specifically, the provincial leaders asked what was "the value to the local community, to other local communities and to the individuals concerned." They felt "that in their review of the request they need[ed] to consider the way in which it effect[ed] Province finance, apostolate, and the affirmation of person over things."[45]

All aspects of the ever-evolving government structure of the 1970s involved itself in these new financial and community endeavors. The provincial administrator acted with other provincial leaders and the various committees and councils pertaining to all aspects of Mercy life to make this decision. Truly, this was more in keeping with a participatory democratic system. Yet it was not nearly effective or efficient enough for the community, and following the 1976 Provincial Chapter, the Housing Committee dissolved, seeing "themselves as an unnecessary intermediary group." The Religious Life Council continued from this point to handle purchases of houses. In an attempt to define how the community would act, it increased the bureaucracy of the process. The provincial government over the next two years redefined its role in housing and acted more as a "clearing-house" for those looking for a place to live. The Provincial Administrative Team (the provincial governing body) provided the information about and funding for the purchases, and facilitated the moves, but individual sisters made decisions as to where they lived and with whom they established local communities.[46]

Unfortunately, the decision to look for a house did not always originate with individual Mercys; sometimes pastors and parishioners motivated sisters to move from their parish convents when the owners wanted to use them for other purposes or sell them. Some turned to house hunting when their apartments were sold (not an unusual happening for any renter). The community purchased a house in 1974 on S. Taylor Street in Oak Park when a group of sisters living in an apartment in that neighborhood needed to find a place because the owner of their building sold it. In this case, the group found their home a block down from another one purchased the year before. Like other small groups, the 1974 Taylor Street group consisted of individuals at work in diverse ministries and from different regions, including one Mercy from the Cincinnati Province.[47]

None of the Sisters of Mercy living at St. Charles Lwanga at 45th Street near the Dan Ryan Expressway worked in the parish. Previous pastors had welcomed the community (who used to teach in the school) to live at the convent paying rent to the parish. In January 1985, a new pastor informed the community that they had to leave by the end of June. He believed that the parish convent should be used by those who worked in the parish and that the "pastor where [they] worked should provide housing for [them]." In contrast to St. Charles Lawanga, other pastors and parishioners alike wanted women religious living in the convents attached to the church, even if they did not work in the school or church. At St. Clotilde, for example, the Mercys had a good relationship with both priest and congregation and they felt a part of the parish. The sisters living at St. Charles Lwanga had invested in the convent and had maintained the building, paid all utilities, and made improvements to the interior. They took care of all the internal improvements, including painting, plastering, carpeting, and creating larger bedrooms from former "cells." They also had a connection to the South Side neighborhoods. Several sisters came from St. James convent (the neighboring church) when that parish sold the convent to raise money for the church in 1981 and continued to work at that school. Others worked at Mercy Hospital, Chicago. Despite their efforts to persuade the pastor to change his mind, they were forced to move and five of them moved into a house purchased by the community on East Avenue in Oak Park.[48]

Similar circumstances motivated Mercys living at the Mary, Seat of Wisdom convent in Park Ridge, Illinois. The community had staffed the school from its conception in 1957, but by the early 1980s, Sisters of Mercy no longer worked in the parish (the last connection ended in 1982). In 1980, the eight who lived in the convent worked in diverse ministries, from pastoral ministry, hospital chaplain, religious education, publishing, office manager, director of residents at Misericordia North, a home for infants and children with developmental disabilities, and elementary education (principal and science teacher in the parish). By September 1982, the number had declined to six and none of the sisters worked at the school. The Mercys paid rent for the use of the convent, but since the late 1970s, had heard "rumbles throughout the parish, at school board meetings, and also at parish council meetings that [the parish] wanted to use the convent" primarily because the Mercys, particularly by 1983, did not work

in the school. Furthermore, parish groups and priests alike failed to recognize that the convent was the Mercys' home. Church clubs used rooms
within the building for meetings with no consideration to the sisters'
needs or schedule, and then expressed surprise when the Mercys wanted
to move.[49]

Sisters' experiences at St. Charles Lwanga and Mary, Seat of Wisdom
underscore the tenuous position all women religious occupied throughout
this period. When sisters, regardless of religious community, moved out
of traditional ministries and dared redefine themselves as religious and
apostolic people, some clergy and laity had a difficult time accepting these
changes. The 1960s and 1970s were tumultuous decades, not just within
the Catholic Church, but all of American society. Where did a community
like the Sisters of Mercy, which had long served an urban and growing suburban, multi-racial population fit and (literally) where should they live?

The Mercys were not the only group to re-envision for themselves a
different role in the Church and America. While the Sister of Mercy's account of neighbors being unaware that women religious mowed lawns is
humorous, it is similar to, although more benign than, the reaction of the
parishioners and priests of Mary, Seat of Wisdom and St. Charles Lwanga.
Some pastors and parishioners accepted the Mercys' presence in their parishes as long as they served a purpose, but they did not necessarily see
them as members of their community. In the case of Mary, Seat of Wisdom, there was a disconnect between parishioners, priest, and sisters as to
why they should leave. The parish needed space and took over the convent
by increments, but they failed to see that sisters gave services to the parish
and were parishioners like the laity. In the case of the St. Charles Lwanga,
the parishioners and priest believed the Mercys simply lived off the parish
in the convent building without ministering to the community because
they were not teaching in the school. This represents a fundamental lack
of respect for women religious as individuals. The Mercys were "pushed"
out as one sister put it and control and ownership of property became an
important aspect of their religious life in order to conduct their ministerial
and communal lives.[50]

By 1973, the Mercys took determined steps toward property ownership, starting in Oak Park with the first of the Taylor Street homes. After
the second Taylor Street home was purchased in 1974, the community
went on to acquire seven more, including a property on Ottawa Street
in Niles for five sisters leaving Mary, Seat of Wisdom in 1983. If sisters
who remained in a traditional convent questioned the commitment of
those living in houses and apartments, the reality was that the Sisters who

Figure 20. Community-owned home, Robert St., Aurora, 1980: Local sisters host get-together of members of their community in their home.

moved out of traditional settings spoke of wanting a more authentic community life. They looked for or constructed a new manner of relating to one another, as Mercys and as women. As sisters "moved out," reasons for coming together to celebrate their shared history as Sisters of Mercy became more important, and with more satisfaction in how one lived her religious life, individuals felt more connected to the larger Chicago Province identity. Community gatherings, such as conferences, Mercy Day, and jubilee celebrations furthermore helped remind members that in the face of change and adaptation, the community still celebrated its past and present (see Figure 20).[51]

The Mercys who moved out of traditional convent-settings spoke of wanting to be treated as mature individuals. Making independent choices about where and how one lived is culturally an "adult" behavior. Moving from renting to home ownership is another step, which historically has reflected stability and permanence, but may run counter to the idea of religious poverty and availability for ministry wherever needed. The Mercys, however, had long owned and often built their high school, academy, and hospital convents, and property ownership was not a new phenomenon for the community. The Chicago Province, however, saw in the changed religious climate the need to have more control, or self-determination, over the manner in which they shaped religious life, and Mercy-owned houses and apartment buildings were a way to accomplish this goal. As time progressed, traditional convents came to serve new purposes, as the Mercys transitioned many of these buildings into assisted living and nursing homes, which enabled the community to protect and respect the individual person as she aged. Those who opted to live in the traditional convents during this period, however, were not divorced from the changes to community life and often "experimented" with and engaged in new modes of relating to one another as sisters, like their sisters who formed intentional communities in rented parish convents, apartments, and community-owned homes. In a similar manner, this respect for the individual sister's choice was reflected in space given to explore and make new ministerial choices throughout the late 1960s and 1970s.[52]

"We are committed to the apostolic mandate"

The September 1970 issue of *Exchange* included a quote from *Mercy Covenant*, the interim *Constitutions* that re-articulated in modernized language the place that Sisters of Mercy had occupied as apostolic beings in the world. It began:

> Both as a community and as individual members we are committed to the apostolic mandate; however, we acknowledge as inherent in any corporate effort the hope that dedicated persons will maximize the possibility of value changes and needed renewal. We recognize the value of extending the apostolate . . . Religious women today are asked to find Christ in society and to hear Him in the needs of His people.[53]

This passage encapsulated both the importance of "individual members" and a "corporate effort" to act in society. While the language fits with the times, the sentiments go right to the heart of the Sisters of Mercy's charism. While they operated from different perspectives and worldviews, Catherine McAuley's nineteenth-century sisters went out into their world to hear the "the needs of [God's] people," just as the Chicago Mercys envisioned doing at the beginning of the 1970s. This issue of *Exchange* went on to report on the various ways the individual members of the Chicago Province acted in the society, from Sister Mary Lou Hogan's volunteer efforts on her brother Mark's campaign for governor of Colorado to Sister Mary Thomasina Kobliska's work as nutritionist and coordinator of the Pinal County, Arizona Nutrition Project Team. Both sisters' efforts, according to this report, emphasized social justice efforts to alleviate poverty, hunger, and illness. Other articles in the same issue featured Mercy Hospital, Chicago's pastoral training program and the hospital's neighborhood outreach program.[54]

The apostolic news presented in this issue of *Exchange* may appear quite different than preceding decades, but in reality, the activities of these sisters fit with the fundamental Mercy spirit. These Mercys went out into the world, maybe not in the same form as their ancestral "Walking Sisters" of Catherine McAuley's age, but guided by those religious principles. The characteristics that make these apostolic endeavors appear new represent important opportunities presented to the members of the community to follow the Mercy spirit where it led them. This is apparent when considering the choices Sister Patricia M. Murphy made after she returned from Peru in 1969 and needed to determine what she wanted to do next. Ten years had passed since she first saw the announcement for a mission in South America hanging in the hallway at Saint Xavier College. When she left, provincials still assigned sisters to their ministry; they still wore the traditional full habit; and Mercys continued to live where they worked. Prior to renewal, personal choice was not in the forefront of superiors' thinking when placing individual sisters in particular spots. Some Mercys described their placements as like being interchangeable parts, going wherever Mother Provincial sent them.[55]

In 1969, Sister Pat and the Chicago Mercys began to have a choice. Still adjusting to her life in the United States, Sister Pat chose to study at Mundelein College on the north side of Chicago. While doing this, she lived in an apartment with three other sisters in Wheeling, Illinois (Sisters JoAnn Persch, Patricia Costello, and Evelyn Derezinski). Although a full-time student, Sister Pat also assisted Sister JoAnn at the religious education center conducted in a nearby parish. Sister Patricia Costello taught biology at an Arlington Heights public school and Sister Evelyn Derezinski taught at a Catholic high school. Here was an intentional community like those formed by sisters at St. Clotilde convent, in the apartment on 80th Street, and in the new community-owned homes.[56]

As with other intentional communities, Sister Pat and her apartment-mates participated in diverse ministries. Many Mercys like this Wheeling group wanted more from their religious lives and sought new ways to follow the call they felt from God. In all four cases, the sisters chose for themselves what form their apostolate would take, and while they did not replicate traditional teaching patterns of previous decades, they were grounded in the Mercy tradition and spirit. For over a hundred years, the Sisters of Mercy of the Chicago Province had dedicated their lives to education, just as teaching was a founding ministry of Catherine McAuley's original community. The parish school or high school, however, had long confined some sisters and prevented them from following the guiding spirit of their foundress as they discerned it. These four sisters perceived a need regardless of Catholic or secular institution and wanted to fill it.[57]

Vatican II renewal and the earlier call for women religious to be "in the world" put many sisters like the Mercys on a new course, as the 1970 *Exchange* illustrates. Investigation and study of Catherine McAuley's founding charism, plus the influence of the religious, cultural, and political events of their age, inspired many to determine how they as individual sisters needed to respond. Sister Patricia M. Murphy and other sisters over the next decades found new ways to become "walking sisters" and followed where they believed God called them, while remaining faithful to their religious congregation. Sister Pat, for her part, was drawn to work that enabled her to work for peace and justice and embodied the corporal and spiritual works of mercy (as many other within the community did). She worked with other Chicago Mercys in community outreach program at Mercy Hospital, Chicago highlighted in the 1970 *Exchange* issue mentioned previously. Sister Pat was not alone in her concern for social justice for the poor, sick, and uneducated of her society and her community supported her actions. Other Mercys took up similar works, but they also followed the Mercy spirit in other directions.[58]

The choices made by Mercys at this time appear highly individualist, with each person following her own path, and from the 1970s onward, Mercy ministries diversified and multiplied. The Mercys, however, strove to support individual growth and fulfillment, even when it might hurt their traditional institutions. The Sisters of Mercy came to articulate about their apostolic lives that:

> The Community is the individual and does not exist separate and independent of the individual. We must develop a mutual respect for the contribution made by all members of our congregation . . . Each person is different and unique; and in order to develop her truest individuality, the Community must be a supportive body. The Community has an obligation to see that the Sisters' basic needs for security, recognition, response, and new experience are being met. This can only be done on a local level, and at times the needs of the institutions might have to be sacrificed.[59]

To satisfy the needs of the individual sisters, the community had to redefine itself, and throughout this period as it re-conceptualized its government and community life, it also had to determine the meaning and identity of the Sisters of Mercy as a group through its apostolic work. The trick was allowing for the realization of the community's needs.

To the outside observer at this time, sisters following a call to a new, and possibly ill-defined, ministry had the potential to threaten the central identity of the Sisters of Mercy. If the Mercys were not in parish schools or working on wards in their own hospitals, what were they to the laity in Illinois, Wisconsin, and Iowa? Some sisters took their talents and employed them in "perhaps less understood apostolates" that articulated anew the meaning of Mercy ministries. They chose to approach ministry in a way that distinguished their apostolate from the institution in which they worked. The individual "must be apostolic" and they were not "persons committed to specific apostolates." Consequently, sisters moved first into areas that grew from more traditional apostolates and then expanded the scope of their ministerial life. They were art teachers, professors of nursing, and dieticians in institutions not only outside their Mercy-owned properties, but also in locations beyond their province and denomination. They did this as individuals and when this shift began, sisters had to justify their work and show they were still connected to the community.[60]

In 1968, however, over 70 percent of the Mercys continued to work in education. The majority worked in Chicago, followed by other parts of Illinois. Wisconsin and Iowa still had a small percentage of sisters in education. Health care drew nearly 25 percent of Mercys, with the largest presence in Chicago. Janesville, Iowa City, and Davenport also maintained their Mercy Hospitals, despite fewer sister-personnel. Long-established ministries such as Saint Catherine Residence for women in Milwaukee and Misericordia in Chicago for children and adults with developmental and physical disabilities also persisted as Mercys continued to respond to needs of their populations as they arose. By the early 1970s, as the manner in which Mercys engaged in traditional ministries started to shift, individuals found new ways to enliven education and health care at the same time they moved into new apostolates like hospital chaplaincy, pastoral ministry, parish religious education, and community activism.[61]

The Chicago Province's Renewal Commission met in the spring of 1968 to "determine a direction for the future of the sisters of Mercy in regard to apostolic works" and to "see if other modes of operation than those currently employed by the community [were] valid." Ultimately, they wanted to understand how they could "most effectively work for the good of the world." The numbers of active sisters, however, had declined due to departures, declining entrants, and age. The Mercys infused with new religious and intellectual sensibilities about the respect for the individual person, no longer compelled its members to fulfill traditional ministries.[62]

What did this mean for the Mercys' long presence in schools, both elementary and high schools? The reality of the decline in active sisters was that they had to make hard choices about retrenchment[63] from parish schools, particularly those located in inner-city neighborhoods. The Chicago Mercys left not only inner city schools, but also suburban parishes at the same time. For inner-city parishes, the decision to leave was difficult, as many of these schools tended to have fewer resources and many feared that if women religious left these Catholic schools, they would close. The Mercys, however, had to consider where and when they as a corporate body would support or continue their presence in a school or other institution. Related to this was the discussion of where individual sisters could be most effective. The answer to this might mean that one sister remained in a parish school, or a group of sisters used their talents as educators to establish a community outreach program like the Austin Career Center on the west side of Chicago that touched a wider population. The Austin Career Center began after the Mercys' Siena High School closed and with the invitation and cooperation of local neighborhood residents.

Finding enough qualified sisters to staff parish schools was a challenge before Vatican II and renewal, and since the advent of Sister Formation, the Chicago Province placed professional development of sisters before satisfying the needs of parish priests. That might mean disappointing pastors who had to either hire more lay teachers to fill positions, or cut programs. Since the late 1960s, the Mercys periodically withdrew a few or all of their sisters from elementary schools. By the end of the decade, the ratios of lay to religious teachers steadily rose and with complete withdrawal of sisters, some schools closed. Parish priest who opted to close their parish schools cited declining enrollment and rising costs. In the case of St. Patrick School in South Chicago, the pastor closed the school for these reasons, plus an "inadequate teaching staff" because of the lack of a sufficient number of Sisters of Mercy to "to adequately conduct classes."[64]

Much study went into leaving or remaining at a particular parish school. To some observers, the Mercys' long association with Irish and other white ethnic parishes linked their decisions to leave some inner city parishes to racism. When the community kept its affiliation with a growing African American or Hispanic parish and left a white school instead, others accused them of being traitors. On the west side of Chicago, for example, the community continued at St. Finnbar, Precious Blood, and St. Catherine of Siena through the 1950s and 1960s, among others, as those schools shifted racially. In 1970, the Mercys announced their withdrawal from ten elementary schools within and without the Chicago Archdiocese by September 1971. Five were suburban Chicago schools and five Chicago city parishes. One of the city schools was St. Thomas Aquinas, a West Side parish. The Mercys began teaching at this school in 1909 and by the late 1960s, it became increasingly African American, reaching 52 percent of the student population in 1968. As a part of the study to determine the community's place in parish schools, the principal completed a questionnaire to determine the effectiveness of the Mercys at the school. The first question asked of the respondent was whether the sisters were successful considering "the cultural background of the pupils in the school." Were the white Sisters of Mercy, despite their decades of work as educators, the right people for this position? For that matter, did they have the right lay teachers, free of prejudice?[65]

The continued presence of the Sisters of Mercy at St. Thomas Aquinas was debatable already in the late 1960s. With difficulties that the community faced in staffing other schools and that the school already had a majority of lay teachers, there was a movement to remove the remaining teachers. From the answers given on the questionnaire, the indication was that the Catholic school offered an alternative to the inadequate public school and the nearest Catholic elementary school was Resurrection (also with a long history of Sisters of Mercy as teachers), which was about four to five blocks from St. Thomas Aquinas. Resurrection was a larger school with better facilities and could accommodate many students from St. Thomas Aquinas if it should close. The respondents, however, reported that a Catholic school filled a need in that neighborhood.[66]

When the Mercys announced in 1970 that they would withdraw from St. Thomas the following year, the associate pastor, Edward McKenna, publicly attacked the community, calling the Mercys racists. McKenna, along with the St. Thomas Home and School Association, used the media to question the withdrawal of the remaining four sisters from the school when another white parish, Little Flower, retained its fifteen sisters. The priest with a small group of parents and children visited this school and another with television cameras in an attempt to compel the Mercys to reconsider their decision. The main argument presented was that if the sisters withdrew, the school would be forced to close because of the substantial cost of hiring lay teachers. Detractors paid little attention to the fact that sisters should be paid the same wages as a lay teacher. For its part, the Mercy leadership attempted to respond to the charge of racism. They

re-asserted that the lack of members to staff schools had forced the community to retrench. They had attempted to make "an equitable withdrawal
from urban, suburban, inner city, and small city schools."[67]

McKenna's accusations of racism came at a time when the Mercy community had taken substantial strides not only to eliminate racist mental-
ity but to actively combat racial injustice in their ministries. The *Mercy
Covenant* includes a resolution to "encourage our own sisters to respond
to the needs of the economically poor, the Black American, and other racial
and cultural minorities and to receive favorably requests from qualified
sisters who wish to serve and to live among those in need." The *Covenant*
urged members to develop a "right social conscience" and to "support and
give leadership to movements which have as their object the eradication
of social and political injustices." A declaration in a constitution did not
necessarily guarantee the eradication of all racist thoughts within the community, nor did it inspire every individual sister to lead a fight against
social and political injustice. The Mercys, however, had taught African
American and Hispanic students in parish schools since the mid-twentieth
century.[68]

Yet the community also had a complicated history in previous decades
with integration of schools and, more significantly, with their own membership. They took tentative steps toward integrating their high schools in
the mid-1950s, but this was not the resounding call to arms voiced in the
1970s *Covenant*. In terms of membership in the Mercys, the Chicago Province in the 1940s and 1950s opted to dissuade or direct African American
candidates to other religious communities consisting of all black sisters.
In a letter to the Mother General, the then Mother Superior, Domitilla Griffin suggested non-white applicants would have a difficult time with white
laity and "older Sisters." The Provincial Council also was against creating
a separate novitiate for "colored subjects" because they "would have little
connection the rest of [the community]." Their position was to deflect the
issue of race.[69]

By the 1960s, the Sisters of Mercy had committed themselves to racial equality. In May 1965, Mother General Regina Cunningham issued a
lengthy document, *The Policies of the Sister of Mercy of the Union on the
Question of Social Equality*, which clarified their position. The document
drew from Catholic theology and social teachings as well as writings of
Martin Luther King, Jr., to shape the Union's policy on interracial relations. Sisters of Mercy would work for racial equality. According to the
policy,

> All action in this sensitive area of race relations must be approached with prudence. But prudence does not mean silence about the moral principles at stake, or a policy of waiting for another generation to right the wrong.[70]

Given the view of the provincials and generalate articulated in the late 1940s and early 1950s and the withdrawal from certain inner-city schools in tenuous positions in the 1970s, one might conclude that, yes, the Mercys were racist, but this conclusion is too simplistic and overlooks the complexity of what motivated the community in the 1970s. Yes, they dealt heavily with white Catholics, but when confronted with dwindling resources, they tried to withdraw somewhat equitably from both black and white parish schools. Along with St. Thomas Aquinas, they also combined or withdrew from largely white parish schools in Streator, Illinois; Davenport, Iowa; and Janesville, Wisconsin among others.[71]

Sisters who continued to work in education, whether in racially diverse areas or not, engaged in more community-wide discussion of how and in what capacity they served with the support of this statement on racial equality. The Mercys had decades of experience and authority as educators, particularly in the Archdiocese of Chicago where most of their schools were located. They reevaluated the best use of their resources, and with individual choice in ministry in mind, they redoubled their efforts in the places and neighborhoods in which they remained.[72]

Concurrent to retrenchment, approaches to teaching, or pedagogical theories, shifted and the Mercys incorporated those developments into their schools. For example, the Student Affairs Committee at Saint James School in Chicago created a school-within-a-school to provide a more concentrated, student-directed learning environment in 1973. The religious education program at the same time incorporated more parental involvement school-wide. The Mercys at Saint James in conjunction with the lay teachers strove to "create the best possible environment for [their] students." They recognized that the classroom was not "the real world." It was "very different from the urban survival hassle of the streets, but [they] also believe[d] that [their] students should cope with the real problems in their world."[73]

The pedagogical developments at St. James School provide only one example of many such advances during the 1970s. This example, however, represented the concerted effort to redefine women religious's presence as educators. They did not want to simply staff schools and await directions. They had been at work in the field and for those interested in pursuing this ministry, they wanted to make sure they had a positive impact. According to Sister Honora McNicholas, "We must stop apologizing for our existence and capitalize on the heritage of value education that we possess." Finding the best use of their resources often meant acting in a supportive role, rather than in control of an entire school. The transition to religious education and CCD centers illustrates this.[74]

Some Mercys felt troubled neighborhoods would be better served from assistance from within, rather than from outsiders like themselves. In cities like Chicago, which had been scenes of racial violence in the late 1960s, little patience existed for white-led efforts for racial justice and women religious active in civil rights understood this. Mercys involved in changing neighborhoods, committed to ensure equal education and opportunities realized they could be present and provide help on the practical level, but they also felt that black and Hispanic teachers and community leaders could have more success. For example, Resurrection School implemented a teacher-training program for African Americans. The existing racial inequality in American society had made earning degrees difficult, and Resurrection hoped its training program would prepare non-degreed black teachers for the classroom and provide the opportunity to earn teaching credentials. The staff of Resurrection believed that black students would benefit from black teachers who had better insights into what they needed in and out of the classroom. This program instituted in 1970 had yielded four successful teachers with the possibility of more by 1972.[75]

Plans like this one at Resurrection typified the direction taken by women religious in the racial apostolate. Mercys laboring in increasingly racially diverse neighborhoods had witnessed the continued poverty of the working class regardless of ethnic origin. They had observed the racial violence throughout the 1960s in their neighborhoods and they offered help to the victims of violence in its aftermath.[76] As the civil rights movement shifted and more militant strains developed offering messages of separatism, sisters' participation in the racial apostolate declined. Many communities of women religious concluded that African Americans should lead efforts to achieve social equality. As Suellen Hoy and Amy L. Koehlinger have argued, sisters and nuns had the competing concern of revision of religious government and self-studies designed to implement the reforms of Vatican II. Community programs to fight racial inequality funded by the Office of Economic Opportunity faced cutbacks during the Nixon administrations. Yet the trajectory of the Sisters of Mercy's activities stemming from the Social Justice Committee suggests that they continued to engage in programs at the local level to combat racism and social inequality.[77]

The Mercys long understood that education provided opportunities and avenues of social and economic advancement. They knew this in the nineteenth century when they provided affordable and free education to Catholic immigrants. They also understood that a community required sound health care. To this end, Mercy Hospital, Chicago had a long-established free clinic, which continued to serve patients in its South Side neighborhood. By the 1970s, the clinic persisted in providing on-going care for those who could not afford regular medical care, thus preserving the institution. Sisters within Mercy Hospital saw a need in addition to the free clinic to take health care from the hospital into neighborhoods with follow-up visits in patients' homes. This community out-reach program (the same one mentioned in the September 1970 *Exchange*) enabled sisters, like June Anselme and Ann Flanagan, to extend the institutional role of Mercy Hospital through its clinic. This out-reach program remade how health care worked and enabled sisters and other lay workers to reach patients as families and individuals and get to know them over time.[78]

Programs like Mercy Hospital, Chicago neighborhood outreach illustrate that health care was required in many forms. While Mercys continued to provide health care in urban settings, both large and small, in Chicago, Aurora, Janesville, Davenport, and Iowa City, others recognized a need in the medically underserved rural areas in Iowa. Two family nurse practitioners, Sisters Annelle Fuczyla and Eleanora Holdgrafer, transferred their skills to small towns and rural communities through clinics in the Des Moines area and nearby Indianola (see Figure 21). They focused on preventative health care in well-elderly clinics, helping those who did not have regular access to medical care. Hospitals and outreach clinics in large urban areas may have served a larger number of people, but "relieving the distress of those in need," in a small rural town in Iowa, was a part of what Mercy meant for some women religious. Those sisters who worked in health care in both Iowa and Chicago understood that fundamentally, there was no difference in their approach to their work. Sisters such as Venarda Lance who served at different times as administrator for both Mercy Hospital, Chicago and Iowa City, saw their work motivated by their faith in God and the life of Catherine McAuley. They saw their religious life as "the union of active (ministry) and contemplative (prayer)" as directed by the Mercy foundress.[79]

These developments in both education and health care in urban and rural areas are not difficult to trace to traditional Mercy apostolates. When the Mercy charism led sisters beyond province institutions to new apostolates, it appeared a natural outgrowth if they went to another religious

Figure 21. Eleanor Holdgrafer, Family Nurse Practitioner, Iowa, 1976–88.

community's school or health care facility, or to one sponsored by their diocese. When sisters continued to work within traditional ministries, but in a non-traditional setting, such as in public schools, this confounded some who believed Mercy institutions should have preference. How did the larger community react to sisters who took positions in wholly new areas? Sister Lois Graver worked for Continental Bank for five years from 1971 to 1976 as a computer programmer. Her work within the Systems Research and Development Division in downtown Chicago determined how "computers [could] reduce repetitive actions and help people at the bank do their jobs better and with less boredom." This did not sound like a traditional or even a new form of the Mercy apostolate. How did computer programming represent the founding charism of Catherine McAuley? Sister Lois's newfound enthusiasm for her work and her commitment to the Mercy community countered any challenge to the purpose of her work "outside the community." She found fulfillment and value in her work, and hoped to "bring back to the community some input on how things [were] done elsewhere." Sister Lois observed in the business world people employed in areas that sisters throughout her community could have easily done. She, furthermore, supported sisters receiving monetary compensation for their work because it showed its worth or value. Accepting a salary or stipend for work ran counter to the decades of experiences Sisters of Mercy (and other women religious) had. The parish priest paid below standard rate. Sisters' vow of poverty, an essential part of their identity, and conditioning to accept a subordinate and silent role in institutional development and ministry (the pastor taking the credit for the school's success), made taking a salary challenging.[80]

Sisters of Mercy who found new life in work outside Catholic institutions brought their Mercy charism with them and viewed their work or employments through the lens of Catherine McAuley's founding spirit. When Sister Tarcissia Moroney became a probation officer for the Juvenile Court in Chicago in 1972, she connected her work with children to that of Catherine McAuley's efforts to care for young women and prevent them living on the streets. Sister Mary Mel O'Dowd also perceived her work outside of the community as bringing the Mercy spirit with her. As a professor of early childhood education at the University of Wisconsin, Milwaukee, when Sister Mary Mel made a connection with her students, she asserted that she was "convinced that Catherine McAuley and her spirit [were] alive and well when [she was] present to them wherever they [were]." Sisters Lois Graver, Tarcissia Moroney, and Mary Mel Dowd were not the first or only sisters to venture into new areas. Initially the women who went into non-traditional work outside the boundaries of Mercy and Catholic circles did so with a degree of community trepidation as to their purpose, much like the first sisters who lived in apartments. Ultimately, they also received the support of their sisters.[81]

While Sisters Lois's, Tarcissia's, and Mary Mel's ministry choices in the 1970s are ground-breaking because they ventured beyond province and Catholic Church based ministries, another group of sisters challenged conceptions of appropriate apostolate for women religious. When presented with the opportunity to explore new ministries and discern where God called them to work in the world, many turned to pastoral ministry in parishes, religious education programs, and hospital pastoral care departments throughout Wisconsin, Iowa, and Illinois in multiple dioceses. In Milwaukee, former Immaculate Conception school teachers, Sisters Mary Monda Elleseg and Mary Virgena Clark, helped coordinate a parish community center, which provided for "religious, social, cultural, and educational needs of the Christian Community on the near south side of Milwaukee." This became a common path for many in education. Sister Mary Loftus made a similar transition from principal of Mary Seat of Wisdom to the administrator of religious education at St. Raymond Church in Mt. Prospect, Illinois in 1972. Working with Sister Jean Shulte, Sister Mary was motivated by a "drive toward the children who needed this kind of service." She had observed as an educator and principal the large number of children unable to find a spot in a Catholic school who still needed Christian formation. Mercys who engaged in this type of pastoral ministry believed that religious education was a better use of their talents than in the traditional classroom.[82]

Increased engagement in parish and community centers led to larger roles at the ministerial level for women religious. They directed prayer groups, ministered to the sick and those who had experienced loss, became Eucharistic ministers, and developed other outreach programs, work typically performed by the male priesthood. Sister Jane Schlosser while director of pastoral ministry and sacraments at St. James Church in Arlington Heights, Illinois, established a "Ministry of Care" program, which trained laity to address the spiritual needs of home-bound women and men in ways formerly expected only with priests. Women religious and lay people were able to move into these positions particularly after they earned degrees in religious education, pastoral ministry, and in the case of health care ministry, a Clinical Pastoral Education (CPE), which gave the similar, if not the same, credentials as male clergy. Further professionalization of their ministry went a long way to advancing the role of women within the Catholic Church.[83]

Sisters within health care perceived the same opportunities to care or minister to patients and their families within institutions. Mercy Hospitals, with the creation of pastoral care departments, more clearly defined the role that women religious and laywomen could play. In Catholic hospitals, chaplains were always priests, but women religious in positions such as nurses, dieticians, administrators, and pharmacists had always had a ministerial presence. Acting in new ways, labeled as "patient visitors" (as opposed to chaplains), as in the case of Mercy Hospital, Iowa City and Davenport, retired Mercys did more than provide company to the sick. Mercy Hospital, Iowa City established its pastoral care department in 1969, and by 1977, it included six Mercys, a priest-chaplain, and a layman. Mercy Davenport created its pastoral care department in September 1971 and Sister Mary Claver Ryan took on the role of Pastoral Associate. Mercys' physical presence within hospitals declined throughout the 1970s but those who assumed pastoral care positions, visiting patients in both Davenport and Iowa City, acted as a counter to the declining number of sisters as floor supervisors.[84]

The "patient visitors" at the Iowa Mercy Hospitals, and elsewhere, earned degrees and received practical training in programs like the one at Mercy Hospital, Chicago or at another hospital, regardless of religious affiliation. By the early 1970s, some sisters who had worked for decades in hospitals as nurses and administrators, considered other ministries partly because they had that option and, in the case of Sister Laurette Betz, it was an opportunity to "spend time with patients, to be with them" in a different way than when she worked as a nurse. Sister Laurette discerned how her ministerial life should evolve beginning in 1974 when she took a year's sabbatical to study theology at Catholic Theological Union. Intending to "update [her] theology," she took classes in Clinical Pastoral Education. Eventually Sister Laurette became certified to work in hospital pastoral ministry and was recognized by the National Association of Catholic Chaplains and the Association of Professional Chaplains. She worked as a chaplain for the Lutheran General Hospital in Park Ridge, Illinois in 1977, later becoming the chaplain for a group of seven parishes at Suburban Medical Center in Hoffman Estates, Illinois in 1979.[85]

As the spiritual representative of Catholic patients in a Lutheran and community hospitals, Sister Laurette was considered the chaplain, using that professional title. This was not possible in Catholic hospitals at this time. Women religious who obtained certificates and degrees to work in hospitals as pastoral ministers received the same education as seminarians and priests and they performed the same work. They could not perform the ritual sacramental duties, such as last rites and absolution of sins, but they could administer the Eucharist and they could listen, console, and provide spiritual guidance. Mercys' education in pastoral ministry enabled them to move into these roles formerly occupied by men, but their titles were Pastor's Assistant or Pastoral Associate, and pastoral minister, assistant chaplain, or patient visitor as in Iowa. Yet their work and education won them the recognition of professional organizations such as the Association of Professional Chaplains (not a Catholic organization). This formalized and institutionalized women's involvement and led to professional and personal growth for sisters engaged in this ministry. Many women in the mid to late 1970s who felt a call to the priesthood believed that the Roman Church would change its position and open holy orders to women. Here were women performing virtually all the duties of the male clergy, but still barred from taking the final steps. Ultimately, female pastoral ministers had to fight for the use of the title, chaplain. Throughout this period, women, however, could not be identified with this title within Catholic institutions and settings.[86]

"The awakened consciousness of women"

Many Sisters of Mercy, such as those engaged in pastoral ministry and those intimately involved in parish communities, wished to expand their role within the Church.[87] With all the ways in which Mercys participated in Church life by the 1970s, the institutional Church continued to bar them and all women from the priesthood. When some Sisters of Mercy expressed a desire for holy orders, the Chicago provincial leaders supported the exploration of this role for women and created a subcommittee co-chaired by Sisters Pat Diver and Teresa Maltby under the Office of Ministry to study women's ordination in 1972.[88]

By the mid-1970s, the leaders of the Sisters of Mercy of the Union made the injustices practiced upon women and the betterment of their human condition a focus of the larger community. The United Nations declared 1975 the International Year of the Woman and Sister Concilia Moran, Administrator General of the Mercys, presented a paper to the National Council of Catholic Bishops Bicentennial Committee identifying the injustices toward women that the Church had not fully sought to redress. Moran stated that "the awakened consciousness of women is here to stay" and "the Church leadership may already [be] four years late in its encouragement and support of this maturation process of half of its members." Concilia Moran had only to point to her own community to illustrate how women religious had evolved and matured since Vatican II renewal. According to Moran:

> I have seen [Mercys] grow from mere observance of the law to responsible creativity with regard to it, from mere membership in the Church to responsibility for it. I have seen more and more move from social integration to social opposition. In other words, I have seen them move from religion to faith. For an increasing number, the choice is no longer between this Church or a better Church, but between no Church or a new Church. For an increasing number, no adaptation, restoration or addition can help any longer. It seems only a total radical upheaval of the existing order, or at least of the existing order as women have experienced it, together with a drastic change of direction can prevent the end of everything.[89]

For some, preventing "the end of everything" meant women's ordination. Within the Chicago Province, a handful of women felt called to prepare for this role or support those who wanted to become priests. In new intentional community groups, as they expressed their faith and spirituality in new ways, going from breaking bread in small-group liturgy with a priest present to without a celebrant, some sisters saw no reason why women should not become priests. In November 1975, eight Chicago Mercys (Sisters Patricia Moran, Teresa Maltby, Evangeline McSloy, Marion Cypser,

Therese Ragen, Avis Clendenen, Mary Ruth Broz, and Judith Hermann) attended the first meeting of the Women's Ordination Conference. This two-day conference in Detroit drew over a thousand (mostly) women and men to discuss the possibility of women's ordination.[90]

The Chicago Mercys, other women religious, and laywomen who attended the conference in Detroit in November went with different agendas and expectations for women and the priesthood. All of the Chicago Mercys in attendance believed that ordination of women should and would happen. Many believed the current male-only-priesthood had its limitations and that the Church failed to touch some people because it excluded women from holy orders. Mercy charism inspired women to respond to the needs of their society, yet the Church prevented them from serving all needs because of their biology or gender. Women by this point, particularly women religious, had stepped into roles performed by the clergy. They acted as pastoral ministers and associate pastors; sisters and nuns had provided comfort to the dying for centuries. In that context, sisters who felt called to the priesthood, or saw others more than fit for that role, had difficulty with the limitations placed upon them by the Church.[91]

The conference in Detroit was a turning point for the Catholic feminist movement and women's ordination. Women in Future Priesthood Now galvanized the women's ordination movement. Hope was in the air, particularly following the steps taken by women in the Episcopal Church. In 1974, two Episcopalian bishops ordained eleven Episcopalian women in Philadelphia. While the Episcopal Church did not recognize these ordinations, it pushed the issue closer to realization in that denomination. The inaugural Women's Ordination Conference in Detroit conference the next year featured feminist theologians Rosemary Radford Ruether, Elizabeth Schüssler Fiorenza, and Sister Margaret Farley, a Sister of Mercy from Detroit. Another Sister of Mercy, Elizabeth Carroll from Pittsburgh, also gave a paper in which she commented on the extent of women's involvement in ministry. Chicago Province's Sisters Terry Maltby and Judy Herrmann did not speak but acted as group facilitators, and Avis Clendenen was a conference task force member. Margaret Farley's paper, while academic, brought the issue of women's ordination to an emotional head. She urged women to listen to the call to the priesthood and to be guided by the Holy Spirit, even though it would be difficult and emotionally draining. She brought much of the audience to tears when she concluded her talk with the primary reason why women should be ordained, "because now ripens the time when they must say to the Church, for all women, words reminiscent of the words of Jesus Christ to his disciples (under the continued query for a revelation of his true reality), 'Have we been so long with you, and you have not known us?'"[92]

After the Chicago Mercys returned from Detroit, they provided their impressions of the gathering. Their tone was cautiously optimistic of the inevitability of women's ordination, but stopped short of the claim that they would all realize this goal in the immediate future. They, however, understood that the Church needed a new conception of the priesthood, where the "horizontal aspects of ministry rather than a hierarchical one, and call for all ministers, both men and women, to evaluate themselves and the character and quality of their ministry."[93]

Of all the sisters who attended the Detroit conference, only Avis Clendenen reported in 1975 to have a call to ordination. She continued to study theology at the Jesuit School of Theology, Chicago and by the early spring of 1977, school officials testified to that she had completed all the necessary requirements for the priesthood. Clendenen did not act alone as a renegade within her community. She had the support of the Province Team and they "agreed to pursue the appropriate channels leading to an appeal to Bishops for her ordination." This was a risky position to take in May 1977, particularly after the Vatican had issued the "Declaration on the Question of the Admission of Women to the Ministerial Priesthood" in October 1976. The Vatican had said that women could not become priests, that it was an office only held by men. Yet the Chicago Provincial Team, Clendenen, and others had not given up hope. They, like other women participating in the national Women's Ordination Conference, believed that the "Declaration" had not yet shut the door on this issue and that continued dialogue or conversation with the hierarchy could further the cause. The Provincial Team, when they voted to support Clendenen, "recognize[d] the risk [they] may be taking and [felt] the process of communication [was] extremely important both intra- and extra-community." The Province Team also understood that many within the American Catholic Church and members of their community did not support women's ordination. They acted in support of women's ordination as the Team, not necessarily as the Province of Chicago.[94]

Throughout the remainder of 1977 and 1978, the movement for women's ordination continued and Clendenen's case in particular evolved. The Provincial Team did not waver in their support of women priests throughout this period, and went so far as to contribute financially to the Women's Ordination Conference in November 1978 in Baltimore at which they would have a display table. They sought continued dialogue with bishops who might prove potential allies or supporters of their cause.

Matters continued to move forward and another member of the community, Sister Mary Ruth Broz, stepped forward wishing to seek ordination following the 1978 conference. In contrast to the Detroit conference, the 1978 convention in Baltimore did not have a unified and universally optimistic tone. The movement had begun to fracture somewhat by this point as segments became more radicalized in their intentions, and contention arose as to how quickly and in what form women would accept ordination. At issue was the nature of the priesthood and many women did not want to become priests without reform of the structure of this office. Despite growing divide, hope still held among the Mercys. The Sisters of Mercy had engaged in study and work throughout this period as to how they ministered and they concluded that women religious had contributed in unique ways as women, ways that were vital to preserve.[95]

The moment for women's ordination stalled after the 1979 visit to the United States by Pope John Paul II. Sister Theresa Kane, Administrator General of the Sisters of Mercy and president of the Leadership Conference for Women Religious (LCWR) took the pope's visit as an opportunity to press the issue of women's ordination. During her formal welcome and greeting, she urged the pope to consider women's ordination. The pope responded with a strong negative response, which reinforced the Vatican's position to bar women from the priesthood. The Church hierarchy told women religious such as Avis Clendenin and Mary Ruth Broz that despite their study, preparation, and spiritual exploration they had incorrectly discerned an authentic call to the priesthood.[96]

Sisters of Mercy (and all women) who wanted ordination had to come to terms with the Vatican's continued declaration against women priests. For some, the Vatican's unyielding stance on women's ordination proved too much and both lay and religious women left the Catholic Church. Women religious who discerned a vocation to the priesthood, like Sister Mary Ruth Broz, had to address the hurt and anger caused by this position because they loved their Church and still felt called to be Sisters of Mercy. With avenues to the priesthood cut off, Sisters Avis and Mary Ruth and others took other paths that enabled them to minister to the spiritual needs of their community and the laity. As hospital chaplains, retreat directors, and pastoral associates, sisters embodied roles once only held by male clergy.

The decades following Vatican II renewal were not easy ones for the Sisters of Mercy. The Chicago Province spent those years reconsidering their religious government, the manner in which sisters related to one another in living and prayer, and new or renewed ministries inspired by the spirit of Catherine McAuley. The Mercys began this period of change determined to undo the rigid structure imposed upon their community at the beginning of the twentieth century. The strict manner in which they lived, governed by religious Rule and *Customs and Guide*, made life unsatisfying and stifling to many. Increased education and a changing religious, political, and cultural society inspired many to question religious authority and seek out new modes of living and working. By the end of this period of upheaval, the sisters who led a rallying cry for change had entered into a new phase of their religious life. Some who signed the famous "Letter" of 1967 assumed positions in leadership, as did those who conceived of new modes of community living and engaged in new and non-traditional ministries. How would those who sought change (and found it) continue the spirit of Catherine McAuley into the late twentieth and early twenty-first centuries? In the 1980s, the Chicago Sisters of Mercy entered into a period of continued contraction of resources and an aging population. The upheaval of the late 1960s and 1970s had passed and calmer waters lay ahead—transitioning to a religious congregation that had developed considerable respect for the individual member's community and apostolic choices.

New Life, New Paths, Same Spirit

Carrying Mercy into the
Twenty-First Century, 1980s–2008

Figure 22. Rally to End Deportation: Institute Chapter 2011, Saint Xavier University Campus.

He can soon bend and change, and form and re-form, any of His creatures to fit them for the purposes He designs. You will, I know be animated and delighted at this opportunity of showing that it is God alone whom you love and serve. And then the promise made to those who follow Christ will be realized—the bitter things will be made sweet, and the sweet bitter, because they [the sweets of this life] are not conformable to our dear mortified Saviour.[1]

Important Dates from the 1980s to 2008

1983: The Sisters of Mercy of the Union's Core Constitution is officially approved by the Vatican.

1983–84: The Heart of Mercy Village, a residential complex for adults with developmental disabilities, is constructed at Misericordia.

1985: McAuley Manor and Convent are built in Aurora on the campus of Mercy Center for Health Care Services, continuing the convent for retired sisters and creating a long-term care facility for Sisters of Mercy, other religious, and lay people.

1985: Sisters of Mercy of the Union votes to replace the Chapter-system of government with the Assembly.

1991: The Chicago Province and the eight other provinces of the Sisters of Mercy of the Union join with sixteen independent Mercy communities to form the Institute of the Religious Sisters of Mercy of the Americas, creating the Sisters of Mercy, Chicago Regional Community.

1992: Saint Xavier College becomes Saint Xavier University.

1992: Fox Knoll opens and the former St. Joseph Mercy Hospital is converted to Mercy Towers and assisted living in Aurora.

1992: The Institute of the Sisters of Mercy of the Americas articulates its Mercy Charism statement.

1996: The Chicago Regional Community becomes one of the sponsoring congregations in the creation of the Provena Health System.

2004: The Chicago Regional Community begins working with the Auburn, Burlingame, Cedar Rapids, Detroit, and Omaha communities to form the West Midwest Community.

2005: Misericordia South closes.

2008: On July 1, the Chicago Regional Community officially joins six other regional communities to become West Midwest Community.

7

"This Far by Faith"
Reimagined Religious Life and the Sisters of Mercy

We carry out our mission of mercy guided by prayerful consideration of the needs of our time, Catherine McAuley's preferential love for the poor and her special concern for women, the pastoral priorities of the universal and local church, and our talents, resources and limitations. We strive to witness to mercy when we reverence integrity of word and deed in our lives. Recognizing our own human weakness, we know that only through God's mercy can we be merciful.[1]

In the Spring/Summer 1983 issue, editors of the Chicago Province news magazine *Dimensions* published a letter from the Chicago Sisters of Mercy to Catherine McAuley. They had not unearthed a previously unseen letter to their foundress. Rather, they published a contemporary letter composed in the spirit and tradition of McAuley's own letter-writing: a means of remaining connected with the recipients of her many epistles. This letter, written 142 years after their foundress died, conveyed their desire to maintain a connection to Catherine McAuley and their need to inform her of how her religious institute had grown. In the spirit of Catherine McAuley's correspondence, this letter also conveyed the news of foundations and described changes since the 1830s and 1840s, while simultaneously connecting the lives of 1980s Chicago Mercys to those of their predecessors and their foundress.[2]

This letter is also significant because the author, Sister Judith Niemet—at that time a member of province leadership and a part-time art therapist—used the dancing imagery that Catherine McAuley employed in an 1840 letter to Sister Mary de Sales White of Bermondsey, England, detailing her visits to Mercy communities in England and Ireland.[3] Niemet wrote under the name "Your Chicago Sisters," describing how some Chicago Province members had moved beyond the Midwest territory to live among other Mercy communities, and how Mercy sisters from other provinces worked and lived among Chicago sisters. Sister Judith informed Mother Catherine that Chicago Mercy Sister Madeleine Perkins now lived and worked in Washington, D.C. as executive secretary to Sister Theresa

Kane, president of the Sisters of Mercy of the Union. Sister Judith also explained that Sister Patricia Sullivan from Windham, New Hampshire, worked in Chicago as assistant dean of graduate nursing and professor of nursing at Saint Xavier College. Sister Judith briefly described Sister Jeremy Buchman of St. Louis, who had headed the Department of Nursing at DePaul University since 1978 and served "on the Boards of St. Xavier College and Mercy Hospital, Chicago";[4] the letter to Mother Catherine continued with other examples of cross-province and cross-congregation exchange.

This letter across the centuries to Catherine McAuley sent the message that much had changed, but the core of the Chicago Province's identity as Mercys had not. In the ensuing decades, the Chicago Mercys faced a changed religious landscape with a revitalized spirituality, which shaped their approach to ministry and to each other. These decades brought new challenges, such as an aging population declining in numbers, which necessitated adaptation and forward thinking to carry the community into the twentieth-first century. Throughout this period, however, they held to and were guided by what they understood to be the Mercy charism. The Sisters of Mercy may have developed new titles for those in leadership, used different names for foundations, dressed differently, and had expanded throughout the world, but the same spirit that inspired their foundress in 1831 lived on among her late-twentieth-century sisters. They were on the move and "dancing into the future." In the preceding months and years, the pages of *Dimensions* had "tripped" back to the past, presenting not only short pieces on Catherine McAuley, but also features on community history, reminding readers that the spirit that brought sisters to the west side of Chicago, to Milwaukee, and to Aurora was shared by all Mercys, and it united them. A clearer understanding of the Chicago Mercys in the closing decades of the twentieth century requires that we look past the realities of an aging and numerically declining population to see a vital and forward-looking population, which had no plans to curtail or cut off their religious life.[5]

The Sisters of Mercy had just emerged from a nearly two-decade journey of renewal. The path had been steep, but not insurmountable. Sister Judith Niemet's letter to the congregation's founder connected the Chicago Mercys to their past; it also, together with many other *Dimensions* articles, pointed them clearly to the future. By the early 1980s, the Chicago Mercys, as part of the Sisters of Mercy of the Union, had a new constitution and a new outlook on community living. The *Core Constitutions*, approved in 1983, fulfilled the charge of the Vatican to revise their religious constitution, but more importantly, it was a product of cooperation and collaboration among themselves and with Mercys across the country.

As religious life in the post–Vatican II, post-renewal era unfolded, the Chicago Mercys adapted. In the 1980s and 1990s, they embraced new forms of ministry and community life, sustained by their spirituality. Personal choice informed post-renewal ministry, community, and prayer life, leading to diversity within the Chicago Mercys. This emerging heterogeneity did not indicate the loss of the essential elements of identity and experience that united them as a community and identified them as Sisters of Mercy. It did, however, require them as a community to understand and accept the diversity of experiences of individual members of the Chicago Mercys. Education and health care, traditional endeavors of the community, remained the primary avenues of ministry, but sisters were also drawn to other, less traditional ministries. Sisters discovered that individual apostolic life did not work against community unity; rather it enlivened it. They came to understand that one did not have to always live in the same place, work in the same ministry, and pray in the same manner to cultivate community.[6]

Sister Lucille McKillop, speaking as Regional Community President, addressed the Chicago Regional Assembly in March 1995 and expressed the community's post–Vatican II, post-renewal climate of mutual understanding and diversity:

> We have moved so far in the past few decades that we now know that we come from different experiences. For each of us, our experience is the truth which we carry in our own persons. We must recognize and respect the truth in the other at the same time that we pursue the COMMON good. Expression of this COMMON good at any moment in time may mean looking for a compromise statement which is acceptable, not because it is perfect, but because it involves thoughtful choice and because it leaves intact, and does not compromise, the real reason we are here . . . We need to learn the story of the journey of the other (whether individual or group apostolate) and where that journey has led them for the time being. So much good is being accomplished! The combined insights, the combined experiences of all who cause the good to happen, the values which impel them, need to be shared with all of us.[7]

Sister Lucille spoke four years after the Chicago Province had become the Chicago Regional Community, joining other Mercy communities from within and without the Union in the Institute of the Sisters of Mercy of the

Americas. She addressed the "assembly" of sisters rather than a gathering of delegates to the provincial chapter and she did that as Regional Community President, as opposed to Mother Provincial.[8] It had been twenty years since Vatican II closed and twelve years since the Vatican had approved the Sisters of Mercy revised constitution. In another decade, the Chicago Regional Community would be planning and transitioning into a larger regional community, West Midwest—a process that was completed in July 2008.

As the preceding chapters have shown, the Chicago Mercys had, in various ways, shared their foundress's "preferential love for the poor and her special concern for women." They had, throughout the nineteenth and twentieth centuries, sought to mitigate and alleviate the injustice of poverty by serving as educators, health care workers, and providers of material and spiritual comfort. Vatican II had modified how the Mercys related to one another and their ministry; it had not altered this central, guiding charism of their community. Faith in this founding spirit had led the community in the past; it guided them through renewal; and in the remaining decades of the twentieth century, it continued to lead them in their ministerial and spiritual lives.

The Chicago Mercys emerged from the renewal period with their gaze on the future. Yet they moved forward with a renewed grasp on their collective history. As they entered the 1980s and this new chapter of their lives, it was unclear what lay ahead. The future was no more clear when Sister Lucille McKillop addressed the Chicago Assembly in 1995. In this post-renewal period, however, the Mercys understood themselves to be fully formed adults within the Catholic Church, capable of making decisions about their spiritual lives and ministering where they believed God called them to respond to needs. Their personal choice required them to engage the world as Sisters of Mercy within the Church.

The Chicago Mercys' post-renewal period was also marked by a new emphasis on justice, reflected in both its traditional and its diversified, non-traditional ministries. This new emphasis manifested in another element unique to post-renewal life: congregational sponsorship of institutions and community corporate response. The sponsorship of institutions was not new to the Mercys, nor was it invented during this period. However, it became one of the more significant developments among religious congregations in the late twentieth century. As communities like the Mercys declined in numbers, both sponsorship and support of public policies and issues that reflected elements of their founding spirit were means of preserving Mercy charism and effecting socially just change.[9]

By the end of the twentieth century, Chicago Mercys understood that they were not growing in numbers, nor were they getting any younger. This understanding was not unique to their community, or to congregations of women or men religious, generally. In 2008, when Chicago Mercys joined other regional Sisters of Mercy communities to form the West Midwest Community, no new candidates had reached full profession since the early 1990s. To provide for their aging members in the future, the Mercy communities consolidated resources and personnel. This was not a quick transition, nor was it a decision made lightly or without contention. Faith in what was Mercy and where they, as women religious, fit into the institutional Church and in the world had led the Chicago Mercys since their arrival in Chicago in 1846. Faith in what was Mercy guided them as both membership and territory expanded. This faith, as preceding chapters have shown, produced neither a uniformity of position nor a unilateral interpretation of how and where the Mercys would serve. Yet faith was the key element that preserved the Chicago Mercys at turning points and during changes. It guided them as they lived out amalgamation, the Sister Formation Conference, and Vatican II renewal. In the closing decades of the twentieth century, the community continued to call upon that faith to carry them into a future with aging members and declining numbers. Chicago Mercys had to determine "with prayerful consideration," how to proceed as individuals and as a community in ministry and in community life.

"We carry out our mission of mercy"

As with preceding eras, how the Chicago Mercys lived their religious life was rooted in their understanding of their charism and guided by their constitutions.[10] The spirit of Catherine McAuley had inspired generations of Sisters of Mercy, and it continued to do so in this new, post–Vatican II era. The renewal process required the Chicago Mercys to closely study their foundress as they explored their community's charism. From the 1980s onward, Catherine McAuley's life, spirituality, and motivations for establishing a religious congregation were not only a source of communal reflection but a serious intellectual pursuit for Mercy scholars across the United States and beyond. The renewed study of McAuley and Mercy history brought to light aspects of their foundress's personality and spirituality that many sisters had not fully understood.[11]

The *Core Constitutions* reflected how the Sisters of Mercy congregations' outlook had changed during the twentieth century, and—more specifically—between the 1950s and 1970s. It stressed that the Mercys "strive to witness to mercy," and asserted that they should be "guided by prayerful consideration of the needs of [their] time," and "Catherine McAuley's preferential love for the poor and her special concern for women." The needs of the Church and their own "talents, resources and limitations" shaped how and in what way the Chicago Mercys strove "to witness to mercy." At the root of this statement of purpose was an understanding of how they as women religious could best serve, with their foundress's spirit guiding their decisions. Respect for the dignity of the human person, strongly emphasized by the Second Vatican Council, was incorporated into their understanding of spirituality and God and articulated in their *Core Constitutions*. While the Chicago Mercys interpreted respect for persons chiefly in terms of their ministry to and concern for the poor, they also understood their own dignity as persons. This new understanding of their own dignity shaped their community relationships and their view of how the larger Church perceived them.[12]

The Vatican II call to all religious to study the founding charism of their religious communities and realign themselves with their founder's original intent was a dominant part of post-renewal Mercy spirituality. Chicago Mercys had turned to Catherine McAuley to connect in a new manner with their foundress's original intent for their religious institute.[13] Sisters of Mercy were not unfamiliar with Mother Catherine; they had read about her life, consulted her *Familiar Instructions*, and studied her *Maxims*. The Vatican's charge to rediscover founding charism, however, inspired sisters to look again at their foundress, through eyes informed by Vatican-II-era theology, as well as the political and cultural ideas of their era.

Sisters in the 1980s and 1990s understood Catherine McAuley's choice to establish a religious congregation through the twentieth-century lenses of feminism and a desire to work for justice in the world. From this late twentieth-century perspective, McAuley had risked much to follow her faith in God and had resolved that nothing should hamper or prevent her sisters' movements in public as they served the needs of the poor, sick, and uneducated of their day. More than a century after Catherine McAuley expressed her intent for her religious congregation, the *Core Constitutions* reiterated her intent in modern language, expressing a strong intent to "respond to the cry of the poor." The Sisters of Mercy, according to this new governing document, sought "Through direct service and through . . . influence . . . to relieve misery and address its causes, and to support all persons who struggle for full dignity." The *Core Constitutions* explained that through their ministries—"education, health care, . . . other ministries that further social, political, economic and spiritual well-being, [and] the special ministry of prayer and patient suffering"—the Sisters of Mercy located themselves squarely in the world, eager to respond to the needs of their time.[14]

The substance of the "Spirit and Mission of the Sisters of Mercy," articulated in the early 1980s, differs little from the "Spirit of the Institute" conveyed in the nineteenth or first half of the twentieth century. The language, however, differs significantly. In the nineteenth century, Catherine McAuley charged her sisters to dedicate themselves "to the service of the poor, sick, and ignorant" and as women religious, they "[became] for life the vowed and consecrated servants, not of the affluent, but of the *'poor, sick and ignorant.'*"[15] Though this nineteenth-century language did not resonate with a late-twentieth century view of the world, Sisters of Mercy espoused the same sentiments and concern for justice in the revised constitutions they published in the early 1980s. By modernizing their language and clearly articulating their purpose, twentieth-century Mercys dismantled any barrier that might stand between the sisters and the world in which they chose to serve. Thus, these revised constitutions fulfilled the intent of Sisters of Mercy from general chapters of the late 1960s and 1970s. The Mercys understood that Catherine McAuley's positive response to the call from God to go out into the world—to put the "walking sisters" on their path in nineteenth century Dublin—continued with them as they strove "to witness to mercy when [they] reverence the dignity of each person, create a spirit of hospitality, and pursue integrity of word and deed in [their] lives."[16]

The emphasis here on dignity, hospitality, and integrity is reflected in the approach to ministry, but it is also present in the fundamental way in which Mercys related to each other in community life and in prayer life. An essential part of Catherine McAuley's charism was the way she wove together spirituality, community, and ministry, without preferring one over the others. At the heart of the charism was mercy. To outside observers, the structural expressions of ministry (i.e. schools and hospitals) had defined the Sisters of Mercy for decades, but as preceding chapters demonstrate, these structures alone did not encompass their identity. They continued to live as women of faith in new and dynamic ways, identifying themselves as Sisters of Mercy. This identity signified that they had a life-long commitment to serve those in need, to follow the example of Jesus Christ, to "profess public vows to live in chastity, poverty, and obedience," and through a shared "faith and mission . . . come to know [themselves] as sisters and to form bonds of union and charity." The renewal process, however, had taught the community that continued conversation about and exploration of the interconnectedness of spirituality, community, and ministry they experienced only enlivened their sense of mercy for the late twentieth century.[17] As Janet K. Ruffing, RSM, Professor Emerita of Spirituality and Spiritual Direction at Fordham University and Sister of Mercy from Burlingame, California, has asserted:

> This path of mercy is one of constant personal and communal transformation because we can only be merciful and do mercy in the measure with which we have experienced ourselves in need of such mercy and received this gift from a compassionate God. The meaning of doing and living mercy changes in every historical period. But it always has to do with an ever deepening capacity to see, feel, act, and respond to misery wherever it appears.[18]

Meditations on Mercy spirituality in the Chicago community's magazine, *Dimensions*, in spiritual reflection during retreats, in everyday community prayer, and at congregation gatherings and celebrations supported this ongoing conversation. In the Spring/Summer 1983 issue of *Dimensions*, Sister Mary Ellen Nolan wrote an article exploring the nature of mercy as described in Pope John Paul II's 1980 encyclical, *Dives in Misericordia (Rich in Mercy)*. According to Sister Mary Ellen Nolan, the encyclical provided "a deepened and enriched understanding of this basic spirit [mercy] of the Sisters of Mercy." Sister Mary Ellen's *Dimensions* article emphasized how the Pope's message of mercy was relevant to the lives of the Chicago Mercys. The New Testament story of the Prodigal Son, in particular, expressed the core spirit of their congregation and the needs of their current age. Using the example of the Prodigal Son, Pope John Paul II detailed the need for those with the gift of mercy to help people in society for whom "poverty, suffering, and illness are often aggravated by a loss of dignity and identity, a loss of the joy of being son or daughter. Mercy restores this joy, repairs and makes whole a person's identity and dignity." Sister Mary Ellen Nolan extended this concept of mercy with which members of her congregation were familiar. The message of *Dives in Misericordia* to be merciful parallels the directive of Catherine McAuley to respond, to be present, and to be one with the poor and suffering.[19]

While *Dimensions* brought discussions or meditations like these to the members of the Chicago Province, sisters developed individual interpretations or understandings of Mercy spirituality or charism. Prior to Vatican II, superiors determined retreat attendance; sisters had no choice about where or when to attend. One new freedom emerging from the post-renewal period was the opportunity to select the location and the style of retreat and to attend individually. This did not end the religious government's practice of providing retreat options or encouraging experiences that furthered a larger community goal. Rather, the province presented listings of retreats throughout the 1970s, which fostered spiritual and community life renewal. In the June 1970 issue of *Exchange*, listings for retreats offered by St. Joseph College in Rensselaer, Indiana, and the Sisters of Notre Dame in DeKalb, Illinois, focused on aspects of renewal emerging from Vatican II, including liturgy, theology, group dynamics, and personal growth in religious life.[20]

Building on the retreat practice that developed in the 1970s, Mercys in the 1980s and 1990s sponsored opportunities for reflection and retreat that focused on themes in the recently published *Core Constitutions*. A two-week retreat, "Experiencing Mercy Program," held at the Mercy-staffed Carmel Prayer Center at Our Lady Mount Carmel Convent in Chicago, had a "social justice emphasis." The goals for this retreat were to "experience Mercy Spirituality, especially in relation to the fourth vow of service." It further engaged the meaning and structure of poverty, particularly as related to women, and related Scripture to social justice. Retreat directors also listed among the retreat goals their intention that participants "share with each other the tradition of Catherine McAuley and Frances Warde."[21]

Not all retreats were as long as this two-week experience at the Carmel Prayer Center, nor did they all center on the theme of Spirituality and the Fourth Vow. A subsequent two-week retreat at the Cabrini Retreat Center in Des Plaines, Illinois focused on "Re-examining the Vows." In this case, Sister Mary Daniel Turner, a Sister of Notre Dame de Namur, directed this retreat, and participants engaged in "the meaning of the vows and the gospel message in the light of contemporary theology and spirituality." In another instance, sisters could attend "Afternoons of Reflection," a series of lectures on a particular theme through the year. Six lectures held from January to November 1988 concentrated on the theme "Poverty in Our Times: Simplicity and Service in Our Lives." The six speakers came from various backgrounds, including women religious from Mercy communities outside the province, from other religious congregations, and a professor from the Institute of Pastoral Studies at Loyola University. The same year, two retreats were offered: "Spirituality of the Beatitudes" in Woodstock, Illinois, and "Women of Mercy—The Power of God in Society," in Milwaukee.[22]

The 1988 lecture series, "Poverty in Our Times," referenced the *Constitutions* and the challenge to Sisters of Mercy to "serve the needy of our time," and "to follow Jesus Christ in his compassion for suffering people." Again, this is a restatement of Catherine McAuley's original intent for her institute. In the 1980s, these lecture series, retreats, and community celebrations, such as jubilees and Mercy Day, reinforced the Sisters of Mercy's identity to those within the community. The September 1985 Mercy Day, for example, included a novena entitled "Women of Mercy, Women of Peace" developed by Sisters Corlita Bonnarens and Jeanette Noonan of the St. Louis Province. The authors drew from *Core Constitutions*, biographies of Catherine McAuley and Frances Warde, and various "contemporary readings on peace." Bonnarens and Noonan designed this novena to resemble other traditional novenas, or nine successive days devoted to prayer to receive special grace. In this case, the prayers for special grace linked their Mercy heritage and traditions to their present age. They sought through prayer to "accept [the] challenge to be women of mercy [and] women of peace." Beginning on September 15 and continuing with prayers until September 23, the novena included reflections on Catherine McAuley or another Sister of Mercy from the long history of the institute, prayers, and selections from the *Constitutions*. The novena merged past with present, celebrating their heritage but conscious of whom they had become.[23]

The conversation about Mercy spirituality and charism, which started in the late 1960s and continued into the 1970s in newsletter articles, retreats, and community celebrations, took on a new tone as the Chicago Mercys and the other provinces of the Union contemplated restructuring into a larger configuration. A shared identity, history, and common spirituality united Sisters of Mercys already; the Union evidenced this. The need and desire to unite all Mercys throughout the United States, which had resulted from the 1929 amalgamation, was revisited in the late 1980s. By the end of the 1980s, the nine Mercy provinces within the Union and the independent Mercy communities began the process of forming an Institute that would unite them in one congregation in the United States. After several years of discussion and preparation, the delegates to the 1988 Union general chapter voted unanimously to form the Mercy Institute. It became official in 1991. At this point, the Chicago Province became the Chicago Regional Community. The development of an official "Statement of Charism" that represented all of the members of the newly formed Sisters of Mercy of the Americas was a part of this transition. The culmination of this study was the 1992 statement of the Mercy charism, which articulated three interconnected points: compassion, hospitality, and respect. This new statement of their charism identified that the "Spirit [of the Institute] is Mercy expressed in compassion for those in need, especially the economically poor, women and children; environments marked by hospitality, compassion, healing, and freedom; [and] a deep respect for the dignity of each individual."[24]

The newly stated Mercy charism echoed the congregation's historic support for the poor, particularly women and children, and folded in the desire to work for justice for all members of their society. Mercys throughout the many provinces, including Chicago, had studied, prayed, and discussed their spirituality. They had reflected on how the legacy of Catherine McAuley and the teachings of Church (for example, documents from Vatican II and Pope John Paul II's 1980 encyclical *Dives in Misericordia*) informed their lives as women religious within the Catholic Church. If the Church advocated the respect and equality of all people, then it had to look to its own proliferation of injustice, specifically in the form of paternalism. The Sisters of Mercy for their part took this message and sought to work through their ministries for the respect and equality within the larger secular society. They also looked to one another in community to foster relationships of mutual respect and support of each other's chosen apostolate.

"Prayerful consideration of the needs of our time"

In the 1984 *Dimensions* article, "Ministry: A Responsible Choice," Sister Lucilla Conway discussed her perception of changes in the community since Vatican II, and reflected on how these changes shaped ministry.[25] Before Vatican II, Sister Lucilla remarked, she was sent where the provincial leaders needed her to go. Since Vatican II, she "no longer [felt] others could decide where [she] could best serve. [She] had to assume responsibility, to decide prayerfully where to be missioned. Freedom of choice brought with it many responsibilities and changes."[26] For her part, Sister Lucilla Conway had prayerfully concluded that, after fourteen years as principal of St. Catherine of Genoa school on Chicago's far South Side, she needed a change. In 1979, she became the director of religious education at St. Kilian Church, also on Chicago's South Side. Upon taking her new position, Conway left a post occupied by Sisters of Mercy for over a century. But she did not abandon the essence of how Sisters of Mercy worked in the world. Echoing the sentiments of the 1983 *Core Constitutions*, she related that she perceived a pastoral need in the local church and found a new place in a parish as an educator, in a new way.[27]

The freedom to choose both ministry and style and size of community residence became central to the Mercys in this post–Vatican II era. Respect for the individual person meant that the sisters had freedom to follow the Mercy spirit where it led them, but this freedom was balanced with the responsibility to make a choice that best fit with their community's identifying charism and the needs of "the universal and local church."[28] Prior to Vatican II, Mercy communities like the Chicago Province had focused primarily on education and health care. While they maintained women's residences and engaged in various social services, teaching and hospital work—at least in terms of numbers—had overshadowed other ministries. Following renewal, apostolates conversation and discernment was dominated by how sisters conducted their ministries and how their charism directed them in potentially new ways.

The Mercys wished to place their charism in the context of the larger world. Chicago Mercys had always been a part of the world—serving since the beginning in classrooms, women's residences, and hospital wards. Yet as they reshaped and redefined how they served, they wished to articulate clearly that, with thoughtful consideration of the spirit of Mercy, they would "bring the mission of the church alive in the world." These sentiments reflected decades of consideration about their place within the Catholic Church and the secular world and a response to the Vatican II call to renew religious life. This reflection, reshaping, and redefinition produced a more engaged attitude, befitting the orientation of the Sisters of Mercy of the late twentieth century.[29]

The Chicago Mercys, as part of the larger Union, engaged in ongoing discussion that, in the late 1980s, moved them toward the Institute of the Sisters of Mercy of the Americas (a new collaboration of Mercy regional communities) and developed the new charism statement of the early 1990s. In the face of the changing demographics of their communities and the needs of their society, how would the Mercys direct their ministries in the future? How would they as a religious congregation determine their priorities and direct their resources and personnel? They met the converging challenges of engaging with society, adjusting to their community's demographic shifts, and directing resources and personnel by reflecting on the historical Mother Catherine. That is, during renewal they rediscovered the significance of Catherine McAuley as a woman and as a religious, and in the late twentieth century they used the historical Mother Catherine[30] to guide their present endeavors. Catherine McAuley had recognized the condition and needs of poor women and children in her early-nineteenth-century context, and she gathered companions to alleviate the consequence of poverty's injustice in Dublin. Chicago Mercys of the late twentieth century followed her example, working with both laywomen and men and representatives of the Church. McAuley was frustrated and stymied by Church hierarchy, but she was also aided by it. Her descendants in her religious congregation shared this experience. McAuley had been led by her faith in God to find a means of ministering to the poor, sick, and uneducated of her day. The Sisters of Mercy who came after benefited from her legacy, the Mercy charism, that guided them in their ministerial lives.[31]

In the late 1980s Mercys in both the Union and the Chicago Province had to answer the fundamental question, "what was God calling [them] to?" As part of the Sisters of Mercy of the Union commission to study and develop ministry stemming from the Twelfth General Chapter of the Union in 1986, the sisters in the Union discussed in small groups the findings of task forces called to evaluate the congregations' historical ministries and the future trends. Through the study of the both historical Catherine McAuley and their traditional role in ministries of education, health care, and social service, the Mercys articulated that they "understood" themselves as "women of the church, working among those who struggle to overcome the limiting realities of poverty, sickness and lack of education." As much as they understood their past, present-day society urged them to respond to the "new and changing context of powerful societal, ecclesial and economic trends" of their day, but within the context of their charism.[32]

By the late 1980s, the Mercys had developed a clearer understanding of themselves as "people of God" and "women of the Church." They found that their shared ministerial experiences as Sisters of Mercy suggested "that we minster to and within the context of church, women, and the poor; that the major thrust in all our ministerial efforts must be toward systemic change; and that the style of our ministry must be genuinely collaborative." Ultimately, these task forces and community studies resulted in the Institute of the Sisters of Mercy of the Americas' "Direction Statement," issued in July 1995. Building on the collaborative efforts across the Institute and informed by the Mercy charism, the Institute declared that, as Sisters of Mercy of the Americas:

> We . . . are impelled to commit our lives and resources to act in solidarity with the economically poor of the world, especially women and children; women seeking fullness of life and equality in church and society; one another as we embrace our multicultural and international reality. This

commitment will impel us to develop and act from a multicultural, international perspective; speak with a corporate voice; work for systemic change; act in harmony and interdependence with all creation; and call ourselves to continual conversion in our lifestyle and ministries.[33]

"We strive to witness to mercy"

As the renewal process ended in the early 1980s, the new structures of and attitudes about ministry did not precipitate a radical shift away from education, health care, and other traditional areas where Chicago Mercys served.[34] Between the end of renewal and creation of the West Midwest community in 2008, Chicago sisters in active ministry continued to cluster in education and health care, and then the newer and growing pastoral ministry. Considering the very public debate and concern that women religious left traditional ministries because of renewal and the upheaval it brought to religious life, it is interesting to note that Sisters of Mercy discerned for themselves where their ministry lay and in some cases, their life-long commitments to education or health care inspired them to persist in these positions, albeit infused with a new attitude toward their positions and a new understanding of their charism. It is helpful, however, to consider how Mercys persisted in traditional ministries; how they articulated for themselves their Mercy charism within their work; and how sisters in active and retired ministries found new, non-traditional, creative ways to follow where they believed God called them.[35]

Although the number of Chicago Mercys declined steadily while the median age of sisters rose, consistently more than half of the population persisted in active ministries throughout the 1990s. Between 1990 and 2000, membership followed this pattern of slow abatement. By the first years of the twenty-first century, numbers dipped below 300 and percentage of sisters in active ministry also fell to a little over 40 percent. This number did not decline significantly to suggest that age presented a barrier to ministry for the Chicago community.

Against the backdrop of this trend in population and active ministry, a consistently higher number of Chicago Mercys engaged in education—whether in higher, secondary, or elementary education—with roughly half of those in active ministry in 1980, but only a little over 20 percent by the early 1990s. While the number of sisters engaged in elementary education declined by the early 1990s, this apostolate topped the list of education ministries. Health care during the same period drew about a third of the population, but this number was lower by the mid-1990s. Pastoral ministry—that is, religious education in parishes, pastoral care in hospitals, and spiritual direction—represented a smaller percentage of the whole, 10 to 15 percent of sisters engaged in active ministry. However, it was a steadily growing area of apostolic work during this period. The remainder of the Mercys engaged in active ministry fell into the "catch-all" category of "diverse" or "other" ministry, or they ministered to the community itself as administrators, leaders, and "community services." Together with the active ministries that the Chicago Mercys reported, they also tracked retired sisters who contributed valuable hours as volunteers in various ministries.[36]

While these numbers encapsulate the ministerial and membership trends of the late twentieth and early twenty-first centuries, they also reflect the ideas and wishes of the community expressed in directives of the Union general chapter in 1986 and the findings of the ministry task forces that stemmed from it. These numbers also illustrate how the Mercy Institute's charism in the early 1990s fit both with its history and resonated with its present ministries. The Sisters of Mercy in Chicago wanted to direct their ministries in a constructive and unified voice. While the diversity of their ministries would not change, they understood that they originated from one single place: the Mercy charism. The new *Core Constitutions* in the early 1980s, into the new Institute of the Sisters of Mercy of the Americas in the early 1990s, helped solidify this idea. A closer look at some of these ministries, however, sheds light on how the Mercys incorporated the changes of renewal and the new "theological reflection . . . of direction in [Mercy] ministry."[37]

"We serve God's People through education"
In the 1980s, Sisters of Mercy worked in all levels of education.[38] As a community they understood, as did their predecessors, the powerful influence a good education had in the lives of children and adults. Most of the Chicago Mercys active in education ministry worked in Catholic elementary or parish schools; the remainder worked either in Mercy-sponsored institutions of higher or in secondary education, specifically Saint Xavier College and Mother McAuley Liberal Arts High School.[39] In contrast to the pre–Vatican II period, Sisters of Mercy educators in the late twentieth century were not appointed to their teaching positions; they applied, interviewed, and competed with other applicants for positions. Furthermore, Mercys were not the only women religious employed by institutions such as Mother McAuley, where Sisters of Mercy worked alongside religious and lay women.[40]

Figure 23. Campion McGuire, Principal, Christ the King School, 1980–93.

Sisters who remained in education after being given the freedom to choose their ministry did so because they wanted to teach (see Figure 23). For some, even after decades of experience in the classroom, teaching continued to be a fulfilling and rewarding vocation and many saw Catholic education as necessary and relevant in the late twentieth and early twenty-first centuries. Sisters like Sister Jeremy Doyle—who taught in small towns in Illinois and Wisconsin for most of her career—connected her teaching to her faith. As Sister Jeremy shared in 1980, she taught "as Jesus did." Sister Jeremy's perspective on teaching as Jesus echoes the views of other sisters, regardless of their ministry, that their lives should be led by Jesus Christ and his example. Sister Jeremy and others looked for the face of Jesus in the poor and were guided by their charism and the Mercys' Constitution. They believed that Catholic education not only gave students religious instruction but also a strong educational foundation that served them all their lives.[41]

Other sisters also shared this view. Sisters Sharon Hamm and Adele Bennett, who were featured along with three other Sisters of Mercy in a 1980 *Dimensions* article, emphasized their reasons for choosing an education ministry. Sisters Sharon and Adele taught in the elementary school attached to Resurrection parish on the west side of Chicago, found their classroom experiences valuable, and held that Catholic education offered an alternative to what secular society offered. Sisters Sharon and Adele, and others like them, cultivated a broad vision for what they hoped to accomplish year after year in their classrooms. They saw themselves as providing children with tools needed to navigate an ever-changing secular world. Their former students, they held, armed with proper discipline and moral foundations, had the potential to positively shape society. Speaking in a 1980 *Dimensions* article about why she taught, Sister Adele remarked that she enjoyed her ministry and believed that it contributed to the betterment of society. She could "help people to learn to think, to make decisions, to love to read, and if [she could] provide some amount of guidance, motivation, and direction, [she was] fulfilling what [she] saw as [her] mission." Sister Adele believed teaching was a means of living the Mercy charism.[42]

While the 1980 *Dimensions* article highlighted only five Sisters of Mercy who continued in education, sisters continued teaching in a number of contexts, among them elementary and secondary schools—parish schools like Resurrection, or Mercy-sponsored high schools like Mother McAuley High School in Chicago.[43] Post-renewal sister teachers differed from their pre-renewal colleagues in the emphasis placed on what Sister Lucilla Conway identified above as "freedom of choice." During the post-renewal period and into the early twenty-first century, Mercy teachers provided quality education and a strong moral and religious foundation, which they believed benefited their students and, by extension, the larger society. They could offer stability and strong formation as young women in an instable world, filled with racism, sexism, and violence. They believed the Catholic education offered by the Mercys at McAuley High School throughout this period (and beyond) helped meet the demands of high school–age students. This also fit with the intentions expressed in the Mercy Institute's "Direction Statement" to "work for systemic change." In the 1990s, Mercys in secondary education expressed concern about the continuation of secondary-education ministry, and hoped to mentor future faculty to continue this work "in a Mercy institution with the declining number of available sisters."

Sisters of Mercy who continued to teach in the later post-renewal period, and who embraced a positive outlook about teaching, were not alone in their desire to effect change in society and impact young people. This is a sentiment shared by many educators, whether religious, lay, or secular. But the Mercys articulated this goal in a way tied to their unique religious identity as Sisters of Mercy.[44]

Teachers at Resurrection and other schools operated in a late-twentieth-century context, but they did so in the spirit of Catherine McAuley and carried on her view of the value of education in the lives of the poor and of young women. Not all students taught by Sisters of Mercy were materially poor, but contemporary sisters did recognize the resemblance their work bore to that of Catherine McAuley and the other founding sisters of their religious congregation. In nineteenth-century Ireland and England, Catholic children and young women needed rudimentary education to secure any measure of a successful future. As previous chapters have indicated, Sisters of Mercy in the United States provided education to a largely immigrant poor population. As the Catholic population matured, was integrated into American society, and became more upwardly mobile, Mercy educators in the 1960s, 70s, and 80s still found places to positively affect the lives of Catholic and non-Catholic children. Indeed, Mercys such as Sisters Adele and Sharon and others continued this ministry by educating new generations of children who were both materially and, as they perceived it, at times spiritually poor.[45]

While some sisters chose an education ministry and entered a classroom, others found new ways to continue in this apostolate—providing the same educational foundation necessary for success in the late-twentieth-century world outside a traditional school setting. Many served in community education centers like the Austin Career Center, established in Chicago in the 1970s. Sister Colette Jolie, who had worked at Siena High School (among other institutions), helped develop this center and direct its efforts through 2008. Others, among them Sister Rosemary Welter, extended their ministerial lives by volunteering in literacy programs such as the Milwaukee Achiever Literacy Services. In 1987, although she already worked as a dietician, Sister Rosemary began volunteering with the Milwaukee Achiever program, tutoring adults in English as a Second Language. As a volunteer, she taught primarily immigrant women, helping them adjust to life in the United States. As a Sister of Mercy, she brought with her to the Milwaukee Achiever program the affiliation and support from her congregation as well.[46]

Sister Rosemary Welter's work, and her support of the Milwaukee Achiever program, illustrates the significant developments among the Sisters of Mercy in the late twentieth and early twenty-first centuries. Sister Rosemary started volunteering when she was in her sixties, continuing to volunteer after she ended her ministry as a dietician. Her trajectory was typical of many retired sisters. New ministries, or second and third careers, emerged after they retired. Religious life offered avenues for engagement in active ministry, whether on a volunteer or part-time basis. Sister Rosemary's involvement in the literacy program not only provided an opportunity for her to continue ministering after retirement, but it also enabled the Mercy community to support a ministry that reflected its charism. Individual sisters—whether semi-retired or retired volunteers like Welter, or Mercys engaged in an active ministry for social justice—acted with the support of their community. In some cases, that support included financial backing, like the funding provided by the community for Milwaukee Achiever. These are just a handful of examples of how the Chicago Mercys' persistence in all aspects of the education apostolate continued through 2008 as a central component of Mercy ministries.

The Mercys' post-renewal focus on working for justice was evident in the manner in which Sisters Sharon, Adele, and Rosemary approached their teaching. As educators—whether in an elementary classroom, a career center, or literacy outreach program—sisters offered their students opportunities to succeed. As a community, Chicago Mercys in the post-renewal period discussed and considered the significance of sisters' involvement in education. Reflecting back the Chicago Mercys' discussions, regional community president, Sister Lucille McKillop remarked in February 1997:

Every problem seems to point again to the need for education if the problem is to be solved. Education to justice is needed among the more affluent who are able to reach into the societal systems to work for systemic change; educations as justice is needed among the less privileged to raise them to the level where they, too, can take their place in society. Education is their key to a non-violent society, not just in the sense of physical violence, but more in the sense of violence to their dignity as persons. It is their key to working for and in a society where every person is respected.[47]

McKillop's message married the Chicago Mercys' traditional educational ministry with the late-twentieth-century emphasis on justice. This focus is also echoed in the community study, "Ministry: Our Story and Our Context." Its authors asserted that "[l]ack of education with corresponding lack of earning power condemns large segments of our society to continuing poverty. Education is recognized today as a powerful tool for effecting systemic change." The Chicago Mercys believed that the Mercy charism positively impacted both new educational ministries such as the volunteer work of Sister Rosemary Welter and that of established institutions. McKillop and Mercys engaged in education ministries understood the need to preserve the Mercy spirit in their educational institutions, even as their actual numbers within the institutions declined.[48]

They turned increasingly to community sponsorship of institutions such as Saint Xavier University or Mother McAuley Liberal Arts High School—institutions they had built, guided, and directed from their nineteenth-century beginnings. By the mid-1970s, *sponsorship* frequently characterized the Chicago Mercys' relationship with institutions that their congregation had formerly owned and solely administered. Sponsorship, for the Sisters of Mercy, meant "the support of, influence on and responsibility for a project, program or institution which furthers the goals of the sponsoring group . . . Sponsorship . . . implies that the sponsoring group is publicly identified with the [entities], and makes certain resources available to them." Sponsorship also enabled religious congregations like the Mercys to concentrate on specific areas of concern such as "projects, programs, and institutions for which the Sisters . . . are corporately responsible."[49]

For the sisters, sponsorship was a means of maintaining a connection—and to a certain extent, influence—over the direction of institutions and ministries once closely identified as Mercy. As the number of sisters within a particular organization decreased, or they ceased to own an organization directly, the Mercys developed a sponsorship relationship in accord with what Sister Concilia Moran, writing as the Mother General of the Sisters of Mercy of the Union, articulated in her 1978 circular letter quoted previously. Ultimately, corporate sponsorship broadened to include a larger network of support for ministries outside of the Sisters of Mercy congregation.

The purpose of sponsorship in the 1970s, 80s, and early 90s, however, was to maintain the community's ideals and spirit in institutions once controlled by the Mercys and in ministries such as education and health care once wholly occupied by the congregation. For example, Mother McAuley High School, despite having its own corporate identity, retained a strong Mercy presence among its administration and faculty throughout the end of the twentieth century. Over time, however, that presence diminished; sponsorship enabled the Chicago Mercys to maintain not only a connection with this educational institution, but it connected the high school with the religious congregation responsible for its founding identity. Saint Xavier University evolved in a similar way. It moved from the college directed by the Sisters of Mercy to the institution separate from the corporate identity of the Chicago Mercys, but tied to the Mercy charism through sponsorship.[50]

Following Vatican II, lay involvement in many religious congregations' ministerial work expanded; that shift made sponsorship a more formal and vital reality. The decline in religious personnel, combined with this increased lay engagement in Church-related ministries, resulted in more cooperation between Mercys and lay workers in education ministry. (This also occurred in health care ministries.) Sponsorship provides a legally binding (in both canon and civil law) relationship among an institution increasingly staffed and led by lay workers; its religious congregation, and the Catholic Church. Sponsorship is one manifestation of this increased cooperation, and it is exemplified in the case of Saint Xavier University. At Saint Xavier, a Sister of Mercy, *appointed* by the Mother Provincial, held the office of the president through 1968, when Marvin G. Osborn, Jr., became the first layperson to occupy this role. Other Sisters of Mercy held this position in subsequent years (as did other laymen and laywomen), but they were not *appointed* officials.[51]

Helen Marie Burns, RSM, writing about sponsorship and its direction, argues that the trend in religious life toward fewer members actively involved in ministry will lead to a greater role for laity in formerly religious-controlled institutions. Even sponsored institutions, she asserts, will no longer have a religious presence on boards or among trustees.[52] Consequently, imparting the importance of Mercy charism became increasingly necessary. In the case of Mother McAuley High School, sisters ensured that the Mercy charism and Catherine McAuley's example were conveyed by commemorating Mercy Day each September; by honoring—with an annual Catherine McAuley Award—individual students, faculty, and staff who emulated McAuley's qualities; and by guaranteeing classroom instruction in the values of Catherine McAuley, the Mercy community, and the Catholic Church (with particular emphasis on the importance of service). Since the 1980s, the percentage of Mercys working in Mother McAuley in some capacity has dropped from more than thirty to just one. Students, however, continued to experience the symbols and the spirit of Mercy through images of foundress Catherine McAuley and Mother Frances Warde, posted copies of the Sisters of Mercy "Direction Statement," and the singing of McAuley's "Suscipe." Saint Xavier University has made similar efforts to maintain a Catholic and Mercy identity. These include pastoral ministry within the Campus Ministry Department and mentoring faculty and staff in the mission of the university. Sister Susan Sanders, RSM, Vice President for University Mission and Heritage, directed the institution's Catholic identity "by drawing even more consciously on the values of the Sisters of Mercy—especially those of compassion, hospitality and service."[53]

With Chicago Mercys' involvement in sponsored ministry came engagement in more collaborative efforts with other Mercy communities across the country, prescribed by the 1980s and 90s thinking on directions for Sisters of Mercy ministries. Although Chicago Mercys had, for decades, belonged to such educational conferences as the National Catholic Education Association, they developed new affiliations "as a means of strengthening [their] impact in ministry." In the early 1980s, for example, the Sisters of Mercy of the Union established a new cooperative network for secondary educators. The Mercy Secondary Education Association (MSEA) was established "to further the Mercy charism in secondary schools" and cultivate a deeper understanding of the purpose of Mercy high school education. The MSEA wished also to expand national conversation and collaboration, advancing a "dialogue among [Mercys] and with others involved in the ministry of secondary education."[54]

"Health care in its many forms"

In a similar way, sponsorship and collaboration across Mercy communities, with other religious congregations, and with laywomen and men was also essential to Mercys' health care ministry.[55] In the 1980s, the number of Mercy sisters serving in health care remained consistent, just behind elementary education, but began to decline by the 1990s. By 1991, thirty-eight sisters in the Chicago community were engaged in health care, nineteen of whom were between the ages of sixty and seventy. This represented only a small percentage of the sisters in active ministries.

By 1990, however, the Chicago community sponsored four hospitals and one long-term nursing care institution, known collectively as the Mercy Chicago Health Care system. Network members included Mercy Hospital and Medical Center, Chicago; Mercy Hospital, Davenport; Mercy Hospital, Iowa City; Mercy Center for Health Care Services and McAuley Manor in Aurora. The 1985 creation of the Mercy health care system enabled the Chicago community to collaborate across the region and consolidate resources; it also ensured that their sponsored health care institutions reflected a Mercy spirit and identity. These were two goals Mercys held across the Union—and later the Institute—toward the end of preserving their ministries for the future.[56]

In the last decades of the twentieth century, the Sisters of Mercy faced constriction of their personnel while they sought to maintain hospitals that, as preceding chapters discussed, spanned the region from Chicago, to Iowa and Wisconsin. The Chicago Mercys, through the voice of the Administrative Team (leaders of the Chicago regional community), issued a "statement of convictions" to all Mercy health care institutions. This statement, developed by the Administrative Team in 1993 as Mercy Center, Aurora and Mercy Hospital, Chicago were "involved in serious considerations regarding future collaboration." In an effort to ensure the preservation of Mercy core values and charism, this statement was distributed to the governing boards of these institutions. At the heart of these convictions was a desire to serve local communities and ensure that the health care was available to the poor. The Administrative Team understood that independent hospitals faced economic pressures that warranted serious consideration of joining resources with other institutions. The statement of convictions, however, asserted that no merger should threaten the moral and ethical position of Mercy hospitals; their "Catholic identity ha[d] been an integral part of [their] tradition. Any decision to change that Catholic identity must be made for compelling reasons."[57] A successful example of consolidation came in 1996, when the Sisters of Mercy combined resources with two other religious congregations, the Franciscan Sisters of the Sacred Heart and the Servants of the Holy Heart of Mary, to form one health system. Mercy Center in Aurora became a part of the larger Provena Health System.

These concerns about Catholic identity and health care also appeared in Iowa in the mid-1990s. Mercy Hospital, Davenport negotiated consolidation with St. Luke's Hospital, an Episcopalian hospital in the same city. Davenport, Iowa, could not support two hospitals. To serve the needs of the local community, the Mercys transferred control, ownership, and Catholic identity of the hospital to Genesis Health. The decision to sell Mercy Hospital, Davenport was difficult and—considering the statement of convictions circulated among Chicago-area hospitals—made with much trepidation. The community administration weighed the needs of the local community against the resources and personnel of the Chicago Mercys. Mercy Hospital was not the only health care facility in Davenport and, in terms of financial and personnel resources, consolidation was the most reasonable course of action for preserving quality health care in the city. While some sisters volunteered to maintain Mercy presence in Davenport, the Chicago community ultimately lacked sufficient personnel to maintain Mercy Davenport. Preservation of health care outweighed the need to immortalize the Mercy presence at the hospital. The new health system in Davenport, Genesis East and West, streamlined services and eliminated duplication. Genesis West, the former Mercy Hospital, preserves such elements of its Mercy heritage as the Sisters of Mercy cemetery adjacent to the hospital buildings, which includes the chapel where Mother Mary Borromeo Johnson, the community foundress, is interred.[58]

Ultimately, consolidation was the best choice for the Chicago Mercys, but Davenport residents mourned the loss of the Mercy hospital in their city; an intangible quality departed when the hospital consolidated with the neighboring Episcopal hospital. The Chicago Mercys, however, continued to sponsor Mercy Hospital, Iowa City. As with other health care facilities, Mercy sponsorship of Iowa City's hospital meant that the Mercy Hospital, Iowa City's board of directors was responsible for the "moral and legal oversight for the business and affairs of Mercy Iowa City and affiliated entities." The board, in this capacity, was required to establish policies "in accord with the teachings of the Catholic Church." The Sisters of Mercy, who acted as "Members-of-the-Corporation," were responsible for assisting the board in maintaining the mission of the hospital and its affiliated services, and for encouraging a Mercy presence among the board and the staff. No change in the hospital's ownership or mission could occur without the consent of the Members-of-the-Corporation. In this way, the board and the Mercys worked in concert to maintain the hospital in the tradition in which it was founded. Mercy Hospital, Iowa City illustrates transference of the Mercy charism to a largely lay population. Mercys maintain a sponsorship relationship at this writing. Although no sisters worked in the hospital in the 2000s, three continue to sit on the Board of Directors.[59]

Consolidation and collaboration with other religious congregations helped the Mercys continue to provide health care for populations they had served for over a century. While the sale of their health care institutions might mean the end of a Mercy identity, it did not mean the end of health care in that community. When a Mercy institution merged with another Catholic community, preservation of Catholic identity was assured. Ultimately, choice in ministry and a declining number of available personnel to serve in their community-owned hospital led the congregation toward this decision to consolidate or sell their institutions. Yet, as health care became more corporate and was dominated by "managed care," Mercys struggled to find the balance between how streamlining services fit with their call to address the decline of affordable services that the poor faced?[60] One answer to this question came through personal or individual ministry choices that some Chicago Mercys—with the support of their religious congregation—made. For example, Sister Ann Flanagan, who entered religious life in 1961, chose nursing over her Spanish major at Saint Xavier College after she observed the care other sister-nurses gave the sick. In the 1980s, after more than a decade of working to gain valuable experience in the general wards and clinics of Mercy Hospital, Chicago, Sister Ann assumed the administration of a community health education program, Mercy Family Center, connected to Mercy Hospital. She sought to bring a Mercy institution and its preventative-care program into the neighborhood surrounding the hospital. In this case, Sister Ann embodied the direction of Mercy ministry in the last decades of the twentieth century. She worked alongside other Mercys, like Sister June Anselme who also worked in the Mercy Family Center and sought to work outside the walls of the hospital, directly with patients and their family and members of the immediate Mercy Hospital neighborhood. Like other Mercys ministering in health care, she wanted to bring the institution into the neighborhood, provide preventive or wellness care, and be with the people in the South Side Chicago neighborhood that surrounded Mercy Hospital (see Figures 24 and 25).[61]

The Chicago Mercys' relationship to health care and health centers continued throughout the late 1990s and early 2000s largely in a sponsorship capacity. However, individual sisters worked in various capacities, serving as administrators, pastoral ministers, and nursing care providers. With this transition to a sponsorship role, the Chicago Mercy community continued to support health care, and they remained primarily concerned about providing health care and wellness services to those who needed it most, particularly as health care corporatized in the 1990s and early 2000s. With

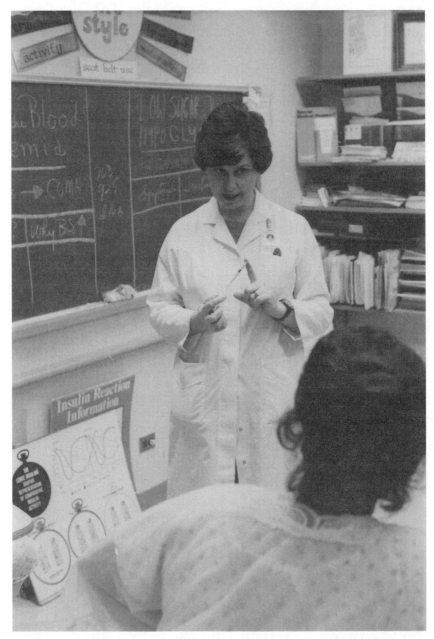

Figure 24. Paulette O'Connell, Nurse Educator, Mercy Hospital Diabetic Education Center, 1986–90.

Figure 25. June Anselme, Mercy Hospital Patient Community Services, 1991.

the increased emphasis on managed health care, concerns arose among many within Mercy health care ministry that the needs of individual patients and their families would be lost amidst potentially impersonal and bureaucratic plans such as an "Integrated Delivery Network" of health services. Furthermore, as Mercy institutions merged or became collaborative

Catholic health care systems, many expressed concerns about the legacy of those changes as they participated in corporate restructuring.[62]

In the wake of these changes, Mercys working in health care ministry wanted their efforts, with the support of the community, to address the decline in access and affordable services within a Catholic context. They wanted to work "with the Church," but also "with churches of all denominations" to "be with the people." They wanted a closer connection with the human aspect of health care and by "listening and engaging" with people, discern what they needed—whether home health care, long-term nursing care, or community wellness programs. The sentiments of those in the health care ministry reflect the extent to which sisters incorporated the Mercy charism and the language of justice in their ministry. They spoke of the Mercy spirit coming first, over whatever institution in which they worked. This did not mean that they saw no use for the institution but they articulated the post-renewal understanding that they were not the hospital or other health care structure.[63]

As fewer Mercys staffed Mercy health care institutions, the community relied on those sisters who were in health care institutions—either as volunteers, nurses, pastoral care ministers, or administrators—to maintain the Mercy and Catholic identity (see Figure 26). In the case of administrators, more than one sister in the post-renewal period began her ministry in nursing care, whether on general ward or as a psychiatric nurse, but by the 1980s had moved into an administrative position in a Mercy-sponsored health care center. By the mid–twentieth century, the professionalization of health care required hospitals that wished to remain successful and competitive engage a more professional administration. Degrees in business management and hospital administration were essential, and community-run hospitals like the Mercy health care system that sought to retain control and direction of their institutions placed members of their congregations in graduate programs.[64]

That Sisters of Mercy occupied administrative positions within their own institutions was not unique to the late twentieth century, nor was it unusual for the preceding 130 years of the Mercy history in the Chicago Province. The presence of Sisters of Mercy in some capacity within their health care institutions helped them to maintain Mercy identity, as did the many sisters who acted as pastoral care ministers or volunteered as patient ambassadors. Sisters who occupied positions within business offices, worked as administrative assistants, and served as administrators also contributed to the maintenance of Mercy identity.[65] Sister Venarda Lance, who worked in hospitals in Chicago, Aurora, Iowa City, and Davenport, for

Figure 26. Rosemary McManus, Pastoral Care Visitor, Mercy Hospital, Iowa City, visits children and their families, 1980.

example, understood her position as emanating from the Mercy charism to serve the needs of the poor. In this case, "[a]n administrator sets the tone of the quality of care which is a ministry to everyone involved in the hospital." Sisters of Mercy who had "set the tone" of their health care institutions for generations, stressed that a Catholic and Mercy identity was imperative, especially as health care changed and their role within this ministry diminished. Women religious had always acted as administrators of their institutions, but what role would Mercys have, and in what way would they continue to influence the Catholic identity of their hospitals, when the institutions passed from their direct control and sister-nurses no longer worked on the floors?[66]

"Catherine McAuley's special concern for women"

The sisters' continued presence as administrators and board members helped maintain the community's ministerial presence in education and health care. However, Mercys also persisted in other types of ministries. They had, for example, a long-established ministry of providing safe and affordable housing since the congregation's early presence in Illinois, Iowa, and Wisconsin. This tradition of keeping Houses of Mercy, started by Catherine McAuley in Dublin, continued in American cities such as

Milwaukee. St. Catherine Residence, in particular, had weathered the twentieth century, emerging as a sponsored institution that provided women with an affordable and safe place to live. For much of its history (and for that of St. Clara's residence prior to its consolidation with St. Catherine), the residence had given young women a beginning to their adult lives.[67] St. Catherine Residence, by the late 1980s and 1990s, offered women more than a safe and affordable place to live. In keeping with the community's post-renewal conception of how and where God led them to serve those in need, the Mercys in Milwaukee offered a home for women "starting over," where they "can reach their full dignity and not be afraid." Consequently, the mission of St. Catherine Residence evolved; it became "a supportive environment for vulnerable women of low-income with diverse needs so that they are able to become more self-reliant and participating members of society." Under the direction of Sister Ruth Mutchler, St. Catherine Residence helped women take the next step to "integrate themselves back into society." Whether single mothers; women who escaped violence; those recovering from addiction or mental illness; or those with limited resources, education, and job skills, St. Catherine offered women an opportunity to move forward.[68]

According to a feature article in the Milwaukee *Catholic Herald*, many of St. Catherine's residents in the mid-1990s were women over twenty-five. "Over 65 percent of the residents work at or below the poverty level," the *Herald* reported. The Mercys' desire to alleviate or mitigate the economic challenges faced by these women who "fall between the cracks" of society stems directly from the Mercys' understanding of where God called them to serve throughout this post-renewal period. Within this woman-centered residential environment, both Mercys and lay staff who collaborated in the mission implemented their new articulation of the spirit of their ministry to women. By addressing the needs of the whole person, St. Catherine Residence provided women with needed educational, financial, spiritual, and emotional support.[69]

"Ministry: Our Story and Our Context," the study conducted in the late 1980s and discussed earlier (which contributed to the 1992 Mercy Institute Charism statement and informed the Direction statement of 1995) identified women as a population of particular interest to the Mercys. This, as preceding chapters have shown, was nothing new to the community. Significantly, however, the language of this Direction statement and subsequent ones focused on the Mercys' intent "to participate in a mutually collaborative way with women, especially poor women, in organizing, consciousness-raising, and learning to use feminist processes." Living and working at St. Catherine Residence enabled them to do just that. Including a learning center in the residence and connecting women with existing social services in Milwaukee, for example, enabled the Mercys "to respond creatively to the needs of women in the areas of job training, adult education, housing, health care and child care." While not always universally successful in their endeavors to help women "start over," the staff of St. Catherine Residence persisted in its mission. Because St. Catherine is a Mercy-sponsored institution, the community maintained its connection with this unique ministry to women, first as staff and later as members of the board of directors.[70]

"All who struggle for full dignity"

Mercys worked in, and the community sponsored, the women's housing ministry in Milwaukee because it was rewarding and because it filled a need for women in Milwaukee. The Chicago Mercys operated Misericordia in Chicago for a similar reason: They were needed. Misericordia, a ministry of the Chicago Archdiocese, began in 1921 as a maternity hospital for married and unwed mothers and a home for children on the south side of Chicago. After the mid-1950s, Misericordia evolved into a home for mentally and physically handicapped children. At first, care was limited to infants and children up to three years old; however, it expanded to create a home for older children in the late 1960s and early 1970s. In 1976, Misericordia expanded, adding a second location on the north side of the city. In 1983, it established multiple residences, such as the Heart of Mercy Village, for adults with mild to profound developmental disabilities.[71]

Misericordia presents an interesting example of Mercys' involvement in a ministry that reflects the community's desire to respect individual dignity; it provides not only a home but also education and job training. The Chicago Mercys do not own Misericordia, nor do they sponsor it in the traditional understanding of sponsorship described earlier. It was not a former Mercy-controlled property or institution that collaborated with laywomen and men to maintain ministry as Mercy populations declined. Rather, it is an ongoing Church ministry administered and staffed by the Sisters of Mercy for over ninety years; it is so identified with the Chicago Mercys that many are unaware it is an Archdiocesan Catholic Charities ministry.

Concern for the human person, regardless of state in life, is present in the community's response at Misericordia and at St. Catherine Residence. It is evident in other housing ministries, including Hesed House and Joseph Corporation (JoCo), two Aurora-based efforts that provide homes for those who need them. Begun in 1985, and initially directed by Sister Rose Marie Lorentzen, BVM, and Sister Catherine Daly, RSM, Hesed House targets marginalized people living in poverty. It is a multi-faith endeavor intended to help people "move beyond the 'band aid' of emergency services and, instead, to provide people with the care, time, and space to hope again and to seek new possibilities for themselves and their families." Similarly, JoCo, a collaborative effort of non-profit and government agencies, builders, and financiers, begun in 1991, made it possible for low- and moderate-income families to purchase a home, either one rehabilitated by JoCo or a home constructed by the organization and its partners.[72]

By the early 1980s, community concerns about providing for senior sisters led the Chicago Mercys to expand their ministry to care for the elderly. Their surveys and studies of sisters' aging, vocation rates into the congregation, housing preferences, and community life needs resulted in a concerted effort to transform existing larger convents into senior housing, assisted living facilities, and nursing care services. By the early 1980s, the Mercys projected, through careful study, that by the first decades of the twenty-first century well over a third of the sisters over the age of sixty-five would require some sort of assistance and would no longer live independently. Comprehensive studies of existing facilities and the projected needs of members resulted in the transformation of existing facilities and later the construction of new buildings to care for senior sisters. In connection with these efforts, the Chicago Mercys also extended their efforts to include men religious and laity.[73]

Mercys planned for the future of their own elderly sisters, and they came to understand the financial, physical, and emotional difficulties involved in senior housing. Chicago Mercys were determined that their nursing care facilities, like Mercy Manor in Aurora, were "safe and adequate to meet [their] own needs" and those involved in planning committees were sensitive to the feelings of their aging members. The needs of this population, for example, complicated earlier efforts to ensure that each sister had a choice in living styles. Sisters having the freedom to live independently or in smaller groups or who resided in one location, such as Milwaukee or Iowa City, might have had apprehensions about moving to an elder care facility in the Chicago area.[74]

In the late 1970s and early 1980s, the community realized the need to expand its community services and to improve the resident care they had. The percentage of the population over sixty increased and the community needed to set aside resources. By 1972, the former St. Joseph Mercy Hospital in Aurora already was the home of retired and infirm sisters, albeit with the new name, Mercy Manor. Mercys also considered cooperating with other religious communities in their areas to provide senior residences to a larger population. The community had places like McAuley Convent, in Aurora, Illinois, but this facility did not provide sufficiently for members needing expanded health care services and the Mercys responded to this need in 1985, constructing at the same time a new eighty-eight bed long-term care facility, named McAuley Manor.[75]

The need for improved elder care for members of the Sisters of Mercy enabled the Chicago community to extend its efforts to include lay seniors as well. Their own experiences with the needs of aging sisters, plus the decades of experience in administering health care facilities, enabled the Chicago Mercys to make this transition to elder care. When the Mercys constructed McAuley Manor, the new facility in Aurora was also opened to lay residents. Aurora, in the vicinity of the medical center, now had a convent, which consisted of assisted living for Sisters of Mercy, and the Manor, which provided full nursing care for both sisters and laymen and women. As discussed, this complex and the services provided by the Chicago Mercys became affiliated with two other religious congregations, the Franciscan Sisters of the Sacred Heart and the Servants of the Holy Heart of Mary, forming Provena Health in 1997. Paralleling the expansion at McAuley Manor was the development of a retirement community for adults over sixty-two. In the space once occupied by the former St. Joseph Hospital, the Mercys renovated what was known as Mercy Tower and constructed Fox Knoll Apartments beginning in 1989. Mercy Tower and the Fox Knoll apartments, also a part of Provena, provided assisted and independent living for seniors. [76]

"Animated by the Gospel and Catherine McAuley"

In addition to sponsorship, more traditional ministries such as education and health care gave the Mercys an institutional platform to express charism in ministerial works, and the connection between long-established ministries and the Mercy spirit is clearly visible.[77] Throughout this period, Mercys also ventured into new territories, alone or with one or two others, engaging in pastoral ministry in a parish, community center, or hospital and communicating to other sisters how they understood their work within the context of the Mercy charism and community.[78]

Open communication to foster a healthier community had been a goal since renewal and articles published in such community newsletters as

Tidings, or such magazines as *Dimensions*, provided context for new ministries such as pastoral services. The series of articles that appeared in *Tidings* in 1995 that reported on various ministries—among them housing, education, and health care—located seemingly newer positions like pastoral associate, chaplain, or director of the feminist spirituality center within the pantheon of late-twentieth-century Mercy ministries. Sharing their ministerial experiences in print enabled Mercys to convey to their community that they were "out there doing the works of Catherine McAuley," in the same spirit as those in more traditional settings. The Chicago Mercys incorporated their foundress's guiding spirit into their ministry and articulated that charism for themselves in new and modern ways. Their faith in God informed their personal choice as teachers, health care professionals, or administrators. Sharing, in writing, their ministerial experiences with others in the community helped to bridge a potential distance between traditional ministries and what the Chicago Mercys identified as "diverse ministries."[79]

For some sisters, transitioning into an alternative or diverse ministry meant beginning a second or third career. The freedom to consider new ministries opened up avenues for sisters to employ their talents in computer science, public policy, as well as pastoral ministry. Still other sisters became psychologists and artists. Others—like Sister Brian Costello, superintendent of Chicago Catholic schools and later administrative assistant to Cardinal Joseph Bernardin—worked in diocesan offices. Sisters who had spent most of their religious lives in classrooms or hospitals, but who believed God was calling them in new directions, found this diversification of ministry a positive change in the lives of Chicago Mercys. Choice, as discussed in previous chapters, re-energized many and inspired others to follow the Mercy spirit into new, and often separate, endeavors.[80]

The sisters' ability to choose, and to discern and follow God's call to serve, was linked fundamentally to how they saw themselves as a religious community—as Sisters of Mercy—and as members of the Catholic Church. This freedom to choose ministry translated to a community-wide acceptance, with mutual respect and trust that sisters could cultivate individual apostolate and remain part of the community. Further, despite constricting Mercy membership, the community did not operate from a point of conservatism. Instead of retreating, sisters sought opportunities to engage in the world. The Chicago Mercys, as a part of the Catholic Church and its mission, chose to live and work where needed, paying particular attention to women and children in poverty, and the transformation of "unjust structures and practices in society, in [their] church, and in [their] sponsored works." The Mercys operated from the perspective that "new modes of relationship marked by mutuality and respect must characterize all [their] ministerial efforts."[81]

Informed by a feminist perspective and by the teachings of the Church, many Sisters of Mercy structured their views on how and where they engaged in apostolic work in order to engage society more fully and to strengthen their dedication to alleviating injustice and poverty. And as sisters traveled their (often individual) paths, their sisters in community accompanied them, albeit in spirit. Often the Chicago Mercys united behind a particular need or cause in prayer, as individual members requested the spiritual assistance of her community for someone she met in her ministry or elsewhere. This cooperative effort in the form of prayer both enabled the Chicago Mercys not in active ministries to engage in apostolic work, and it applied the full weight and power of the congregation to a diverse array of needs.[82]

The Mercys also used their corporate power to tangibly address local and global concerns, and the community recognized that it had the financial power to mitigate the suffering of individuals in need. With established foundations or funds, like the Clark Fund or the Agatha O'Brien Ministry Fund, the Chicago Mercys targeted specific needs. The community created the Clark Fund with a 1981 legacy from former member Theresa Kutschera Clark, and it grew with donations from sisters and laypersons. It was designed to provide economic intervention at the request of a sister when it was most needed, even if the sum of money was minor. (Gifts were normally about $500.) For example, gifts were allocated to individuals who needed assistance paying rent or medical bills—thereby saving them, and by extension their families—from greater economic and personal crisis.[83]

Complementing the personal thrust of the Clark Fund was the Agatha O'Brien Ministry Fund established in 1992 to provide grants to ministries connected to the Sisters of Mercy, Chicago Regional Community. The Chicago Mercys established the Agatha O'Brien Fund with $5 million to support both their ministry projects and projects of non-Mercy organizations. Using the interest from this fund, the community gave both large and small sums to support programs in which Chicago Mercys were directly involved—among them Wellstreams, Center of Feminist Spirituality, and Milwaukee Achiever Program. They also gave to the National Assembly of

Religious Women, Catholic Relief Services, and Call to Action, organizations in which the Mercys had no specific involvement.[84] Financial support was also an active means of asserting the Chicago Mercys' corporate power. Money to pay rent kept some individuals in their homes. In other cases, funding a particular organization furthered its mission.

In addition to financial support, women religious communities like the Mercys have voiced their support for social justice or public policy issues. In doing this, religious congregations of women have declared intentionally that their "name must be known and identified as a group of women committed to address those issues which violate God-given human rights." According to the Leadership Conference for Women Religious, religious congregations should act "based on the social teaching of the Church" and upon the dictates of their charism, taking action by a mandate of their members. The Chicago Mercys have responded to both the Church's social teaching and the dictates of their challenge with corporate sponsorship, financial support, and collective community activism.[85]

Identified as the Sisters of Mercy, Chicago Regional Community, the Chicago Mercys sponsored institutions like Mercy Hospital, Iowa, and used their power to positively affect the availability of health care in the greater Iowa City area. In other areas of the Chicago Regional Community, their financial resources helped sustain housing projects such as the Hesed House. Chicago Mercys also took public stances on issues central to the Church's social teaching and to their charism—among them community-wide letter-writing campaigns and boycotts of companies that, they believed, acted unethically in business and that did not support the human rights of all citizens of the world. Chicago Mercys also joined with the Institute of Sisters of Mercy of the Americas and used their combined strength (both their might as a corporate body and their reputation) to shape society and address needs. In the early 2000s, for example, acting in concert with the Sisters of Mercy of the Americas, the Chicago community took a stand in solidarity with immigrants, and they publicly called for comprehensive immigration reform that respects the dignity of the human person. This type of response to circumstances in the world highlights the societal influence the Chicago Mercys wielded and demonstrates the weight and power their corporate identity had at the end of the twentieth century. Second, it illustrates how the community acknowledged and claimed its agency and place within the Catholic Church and within the larger society. That is, Chicago Mercys perceived that they had a valued opinion and willingly assumed a leadership role in the Church and in the larger society.[86]

"We have struggled together"

A 1986 Provincial Administrative Team Report announced to the members of the Chicago Regional Community:

> We have grown in our respect for the integrity we experience in one another as we have shared stories of our relationship with God, Church, and our relationship with the Sisters of Mercy. We have grown in the realization of the richness of our diversity. We have struggled together, respectfully and painfully, on the conscience choices of our members. We acknowledge differing views among us relative to fidelity to the Church, civil disobedience, political ministry and Our Communal Search for Truth.[87]

That is, the Chicago Province had navigated renewal and had emerged from the period of experimentation accepting of its diversity. They, as a community, acknowledged that they did not all share the same understanding of ministry, political engagement in the world, and what the report described as the "quality of [their] lives together," where they continued "to struggle with [their] complacency, exclusiveness and consumerism." Yet the emphasis on both cooperative, collaborative community efforts and the importance of their faith in the Mercy congregation and God were a message of encouragement from province leaders and a statement of how important the religious community was to the spirit of Mercy. As preceding chapters illustrate, spirituality, ministry, and community life define the Sisters of Mercy. From an outside perspective, ministry and spirituality take a dominant place in the conception of Sisters of Mercy. Yet, as the 1986 provincial report indicates, the bonds of religious community life continued to play an important, sustaining role in Chicago Mercys' lives.[88]

Although community life remained vital to Mercy identity, it had changed during the twentieth century. As preceding chapters demonstrate, freedom to determine how one lived—whether alone, in a small group, in an apartment, a house, or a convent—was the most important alteration to community life. Yet the type of building in which one lived, or with whom, did not determine community life. Neither did participation in such structural elements of community, among them congregational gatherings and celebrations, assemblies and jubilees, alone provide meaning to the word *community*. Ultimately, personal choice and commitment to Sisters of Mercy made community. Sustaining a community of individuals, however, required mutual respect and faith. The 1986 provincial report expressed these sentiments, acknowledging that the Chicago Mercys had "grown in [their] respect for the integrity [they] experience in one another as [they] have shared stories of [their] relationship with God, Church, and [their] relationship with the Sisters of Mercy . . . [had] grown in the realization of the richness of [their] diversity."[89]

In terms of inter-community relationships, these were positive changes for late-twentieth-century Sisters of Mercy.

While Mercys had developed new perspectives on community life, the size of their membership had declined.[90] The Chicago Mercys drew fewer women to their religious community in the late twentieth century, provoking new questions within the community. Was life in a post–Vatican II religious community something Catholic women still wanted? How would community life continue to evolve as members aged and their numbers declined? Religious congregations, in both men's and women's communities, faced declining numbers during the 1980s and 1990s. According to the Center for Applied Research in the Apostolate, the number of women religious nationally totaled slightly more than 115,000 in 1985, down from almost 180,000 in 1965. This 36 percent membership decrease was part of a national downward trend that continued into the first decade of the twenty-first century. The Chicago Mercys' population, however, declined 42 percent over the same period. In 1965, its members numbered slightly more than 900; by 1985, membership had dwindled to 531.[91] Faced with membership attrition and fewer entrants, the Chicago Mercys considered the long-term effects of low interest in their religious institute and explored new ways of presenting religious life as a viable, valued personal choice to modern lay women.

Although sisters did not seek new vocations only with an eye on the future and concern for care of aging members, the lack of new members troubled the Chicago Province. Those who contributed to the discussion of vocations explored various options to attract women to Mercy religious life. Community meetings devoted to discussing vocations and membership raised a myriad of questions and possible solutions. A 1982 meeting resulted in suggestions that ranged from increasing elementary-school awareness to offering tours for prospective members to acquaint them with religious life. Others suggested looking to those who left their community for possible "clues as to what to change" because, as this responder remarked, "we must be lacking something that the younger generation is seeking." In addition to suggesting a more structured formation process and better advertisement, many participants at this meeting inquired whether individual sisters and houses had taken proper initiative, become aware of what they could do to help, and invited women to become a part of the community.[92]

Prior to the 1982 meeting, Chicago Mercys had endeavored to open their community to prospective members, advertising their congregation throughout the twentieth century. In contrast to the photo-heavy *Mercy* pamphlet of the 1950s, which depicted idealized views of novitiate life, 1980s-era mailings stressed the Mercys' heritage and what the organization had become by 1980, and offered a profile of those who might potentially choose religious life. Specifically, the 1980 pamphlet, "Sisters of Mercy: Listen with Us," advertised a "weekend experience" in April 1980, and it informed recipients that the Sisters of Mercy were "persons of faith, women of the Church; sensing a call from Christ, choosing life; growing in celibate love, pursing Gospel values; contemporary, yet valuing tradition; free, for service to others; [and] incomplete, still seeking to be sisters among themselves and with others." After locating the Chicago Province within Mercy history and stressing its members' relevance in their world, the pamphlet explored who should "listen with [them]" through the weekend experience. Chicago Mercys wanted "women beyond high school age, [. . .] drawn to service to share with some RSMs stories of the life choice, questioning, and commitment during an evening and a day in a relaxed and prayerful atmosphere with an opportunity to meet, ask, consider, [and] reflect." The pamphlet's overall tone urged women to recognize that they had choices and freedoms, but that a vowed religious life did not mean an end to independence and choice.[93]

The 1980s ended with no marked increase in candidates, and Chicago Mercys continued to explore how to attract new members to their religious community. "Membership conversations" convened in Chicago, Aurora, and Milwaukee in 1989 debated the viability of the existing efforts and continued to ask if religious life in its current form appealed to laywomen. Did Mercy efforts to advertise succeed? Or had they attempted to employ "business approaches in an area that [dealt] with spiritual values?" One responder stressed that vocation was "a gift from God [and] anything we do is not going to sell it." These questions and conversations directed the Mercys to the question of their relevance to society. Regardless of the diversity of perspectives as to what was wrong, the consensus was that something had to change to draw people to the Sisters of Mercy. As one responder reflected, the "Mercies [they] had in high school didn't run after [candidates], [they] ran after them."[94] Clearly, from the perspective of this responder, the community had failed to properly convey the value of its religious life to laywomen, or it needed to reconsider how individual women embraced Mercy spirituality, community, and ministry life.

If new members did not materialize, what would be the consequence for the Chicago Mercys' future? Other religious congregations facing similar circumstances were also considering this question, often turning to reconfiguration and consolidation with other communities with a shared heritage or similar charism. Among Mercys, the Chicago Province and the larger Union's 1991 decision to restructure its membership into the Institute was part of this larger resource-consolidation movement.[95] Central to the Mercys' reconfiguration and consolidation conversation, however, was an effort to increase membership in the community. To ignore the need for new entrants would mean that they lacked faith in themselves and their future. In a story that Regional Community President, Sister Lucille McKillop, related to the Chicago regional assembly in 1995, Sister Rosalie FitzPatrick cheered the doubting Sister Lucille about the future of vocations to their community. Sister Rosalie remarked, "I don't know what everyone is getting so excited about. We only had four [candidates] in the year that I entered. No one got exited then." Speaking as president, Sister Lucille McKillop continued that she was "put . . . on [a] happier road" when Sister Rosalie FitzPatrick related these vocation "statistics." She, however, entered the community in 1941, when religious vocations were generally high and fluctuations did not provoke nationwide public debate about the decline of vocations. The 1941 membership lull was actually a short-lived downturn flanked by years of robust entrance. (More than 180 candidates entered in the 1940s.) Vocations did not return to 1941 levels until the late 1960s, after which they never returned to pre-1960s highs.[96] Were Sisters Rosalie and Lucille simply blinded by a positive attitude to an obvious pattern of decline? Records of Mercy vocations after 1964 suggest that, more than a temporary downturn, the community had entered a fallow age.

The Chicago Mercys' debate about why and how to attract applicants to the community led it to the conclusion that it needed to adopt a different perspective or approach. The 1991 decision to join the new Institute required members of all Mercy provinces to recommit themselves to each other as a community of women religious and to the larger religious congregation. To belong to the new, recommitted community meant members had a clear articulation of their charism and the "meaning of membership" in the Sisters of Mercy. The Chicago Mercys suggested that if they offered "an apostolic image closely attuned to the changing needs of the Church and society," new members would come to the community. In a sense, if they operated from a position of strength and confidence in each other and their ministry, they would offer an attractive alternative for Catholic women and expand their membership.[97]

The reality, however, was that applicants did not dramatically increase; only five women entered the Chicago regional community in the 1980s and no one entered and reached first profession in the 1990s. Although they made little headway in garnering new vocations, the Mercys did not cease to encourage interest in religious life, nor did they return to the pre–Vatican II structure of religious life. They moved forward, stressing quality of vocation rather than quantity of applications. Arguing that authentic religious life had more importance than impressive numbers, they refrained from admitting women incompatible with religious life.[98]

The Mercys had renewed and modernized their religious life to fit with a late twentieth century understanding of women and their place in the Catholic Church and the larger society. The Mercys expected candidates to embrace this new religious life. Consequently, women in formation read revised or updated Mercy history, informed by a more contemporary understanding of women's history, feminism, and an intense dedication to social justice. The Mercys wanted women to become members who understood McAuley's original intent for her sisters in 1831 within that historical context. They also wanted candidates and future sisters with more maturity, or life experiences. They wanted individuals who "understood the importance of career choices and life options, [who believed] that such choices and options [were] best examined with others and in a prayerful context, [who strove] to live Christianity in a valid, contemporary style, [and grow] as person[s], as wom[e]n, as Christian[s]."[99]

In the post–Vatican II era, those seeking a spiritual relationship or form of religious association with the Sisters of Mercy could enter the community as a candidate or could affiliate with the community as a Mercy Associate. The community continued, of course, to encourage women to formally profess religious vows and make a life-long commitment to "the service of the Church in the community of the Sisters of Mercy."[100] For candidates, neither elements of the formation process nor steps toward final vows had altered significantly since Vatican II. Women still completed stages, or levels, of commitment—candidacy, novitiate, temporary vows, and final vows. The content of the process, however, had changed in the later twentieth century; rather than requiring the candidate to conform, it was shaped to the individual candidate. This orientation toward the individual in formation was both an effort to respect the person and a byproduct of the low numbers of entrants. (Fewer than ten women entered in the 1970s and only five women who commenced formation in the 1980s made their first profession.) With fewer women in formation each year, candidates and novices spent their years before professing their vows in singular endeavors. In Chicago, religious congregations like the Sisters of Mercy had so few young candidates and novices that they organized an intercommunity novitiate training so that women in formation could meet weekly to enhance their education and connect with others of a similar age group.[101] Furthermore, while the Sisters of Mercy did want women to seek them out, the renewal process had led them to understand ministry, spirituality, and community life differently, and they did not want anyone pursuing a false or outdated understanding of religious life.

Traditionally, religious congregations, particularly those with large teaching ministries, inspired their female students to consider a vocation for the religious life. Daily engagement with sisters in classrooms and parishes, combined with the efforts of sister teachers to "foster" vocations wherever they might see them, inspired young women to consider entering a religious congregation. Because there were far fewer Mercys in classrooms in the late twentieth century, the community developed innovative ways to introduce young women to religious life. For example, women who felt religious life might be a choice for them spent several years exploring their vocation. Women did not formally become candidates (formerly called postulants) until after a period of exploration that could last up to four years. With each new level of commitment to the formation experience, women took on more of religious life, including living in a local community house, extensive theological study, and full-time ministry. The process was designed to develop in the candidates a full understanding of "the vows, Mercy history, and spirituality." Furthermore, women spent longer time in formation with the entire process stretching over a decade, as opposed to the roughly six years prior to Vatican II.[102]

Formation, as the Chicago Mercys directed it, belonged in the context of community life. They could not "develop and sustain its new members apart from the real challenges, strengths, and difficulties of [their] life together as a community of believers." Aspiring Sisters of Mercy had to experience or live the spirit of Mercy. Sisters, for their part, were responsible to assist in this formation process. As with every generation, formation was also the time for future sisters to learn about the spirit and history of the Sisters of Mercy. Like nineteenth- and early-twentieth-century novices, late-twentieth-century candidates studied the spirit of the Institute and underwent spiritual preparation.

While the focus on the spirit of the Institute, or charism, in formation had not changed, the way that the Mercys expressed that spirit had. As discussed, the Mercys had re-articulated their founding spirit, and they included that new language in the education of their candidates and novices.

These new members were women rooted in their contemporary, modern age, and they intended to meet the world on its current terms, facing the challenges of "a time of social crisis," which needed "a commitment to continual heightening of . . . social awareness."[103]

Those not called to, or not fitted for, a life-long commitment as a professed Sister of Mercy, could affiliate with the community as Mercy Associates. In contrast to professed sisters, Mercy Associates did not join the congregation. Mercy Association, open to women and men, indicated an informal relationship based upon support of the Mercy mission. Associates, while supporting the Mercy mission, are not bound in the same way as sisters to the religious life. They can marry if they choose, and many Associates have. The 1981 draft of the *Core Constitutions* created the role of Mercy Associate, which enabled men and women who were "committed to another state of life to share with [the Mercys] in various aspects of Mercy life and ministry." As an associate, an individual shared a spiritual connection with Mercys and entered into a "formal agreement with a living group, ministerial community, and/or personal RSM friends." Individuals twenty years of age or older could become associates, if they had a connection or friendship with members of the Sisters of Mercy. Through this connection, a sister could recommend a man or woman to the associates. Once they entered into an agreement, associates participated in gatherings and celebrations and received communications from the Sisters of Mercy. While sharing in Mercy spirituality, ministries, and some aspects of community life, associates were not members of the Sister of Mercy.[104]

Many women and men who became associates were educated in parish schools staffed by Sisters of Mercy, attended a Mercy high school, or graduated from Saint Xavier College (Saint Xavier University after 1992). Others connected with Sisters of Mercy professionally, as did one male associate who served on the board of a Mercy hospital in Indiana, or one woman who studied nursing at Mercy Hospital, Iowa City's nursing program and, over the decades, developed close relationships with sisters there. Many were married, had children, and led a life separate from the Sisters of Mercy, but they shared in the "spirit, values, and life of the Mercy community."

Initially, the Chicago Mercy Associates accounted for only a small percentage of associates nationally. By the early 1990s, Chicago membership hovered around 20, whereas the St. Louis Associates numbered 101, and Erie Associates 256. By the early 2000s, however, Chicago membership increased; at the creation of West Midwest in 2008, Chicago Mercy Associates numbered 71.[105]

The newsletter *Associates* commenced publication in 1987. Its first issues introduced associates, sharing their personal histories and connections with the Sisters of Mercy, as well as insight into how these individuals perceived their connection to the community and its spirituality. By the newsletter's third issue, articles shifted in tone, describing in greater detail the nature of associates' ministry and spirituality. This third issue concentrated on associates living in Aurora, Illinois; *Associates* described their affiliation with the Sisters of Mercy, their involvement in their parishes, and how Sisters of Mercy inspired their engagement in ministry. Mercy Associates observed individual sisters who shaped the lives of lay people. One associate commented that the Sisters of Mercy got "things started, [enabled] others to take leadership and then [moved] on to another call. Letting go," she continued, "is an essential element of this approach to ministry, but is not always easy to do." This woman was inspired by the legacy of sisters' compassion and ministerial lives to become an associate.[106]

In the early 1990s, associates brought new a component to the Mercys, but they did not necessarily represent a younger force of women and men ready to take the reins of Mercy ministries. In 1992, most associates within the Institute were between forty and seventy and came from the same cultural and generational background as the sisters. Neither was assuming control over and extending Mercy ministries and institutions their intended purpose; associates were not the community's auxiliary organization. Indeed, of those surveyed in 1992, the elements of the Sisters of Mercy most important to associates were Mercy charism and communal and personal prayer. Participation in Mercy ministries, while meaningful to associates, was a secondary concern.[107]

According to the 1996 Mercy Association Handbook, associates desire a formal connection with the Sisters of Mercy. Inspired by God's mercy, "they wish to cultivate a deeper Mercy spirituality in their daily lives." They are women or men who have been quickened by Sisters of Mercy and their ministry, and "they want to have a special connection with a group that will enable them to grow in prayer, Mercy community, and service." Associates annually renew their commitment to the Mercys and share their faith, talents, and time with the community. Responsibilities listed in the Handbook for both sisters and associates requires both parties to collaborate in relationship. The Mercys welcome associates into ministries and community celebration, as well as spiritual support. The associates commit themselves to "sharing faith, prayer, and talents," and time as they develop and sustain relationships with sisters and volunteer their service.[108]

Mercy associates represent an important element of the continuing spirit of the Sisters of Mercy. In one regard, they are the ongoing legacy of the community; Sisters of Mercy have been invested in associates' progress and development from their inception in 1981. Yet they cannot replace the Sisters of Mercy. As they have grown and developed as a group, they have articulated a unique identity distinct from the Sisters of Mercy.[109]

"We are Sisters of Mercy"

According to a faith statement drafted at the turn of the twenty-first century, the Sisters of Mercy of the Chicago Regional Community "dedicate themselves to God by the traditional vows of poverty, chastity, and obedience and by a fourth vow of service." They "are women of the 21st century who hearken to a sense of a call and who want to make God's enduring mercy visible in [the] world." For the Chicago Sisters of Mercy, their lives begin with faith in God and what God calls them to do. From this faith, they are inspired in their ministry and form their community (see Figure 27).[110]

What motivated women to join the Sisters of Mercy in the twentieth century was no different from what brought them in previous generations: They shared faith in God and the desire to be a part of something larger, part of a community of religious women. This motivation manifested differently in the nineteenth and early twentieth centuries than it did in the later twentieth century. Unlike their nineteenth-century counterparts, women did not enter or choose to remain as Sisters of Mercy because they sought a life different than that prescribed for a wife or mother. Rather, they chose life with the Sisters of Mercy because they believed they had a calling to be a religious. The women who make up the Chicago Sisters of Mercy at the end of the twentieth century understand themselves as women of faith; through their faith, they engage in works of mercy. Their spiritual life informs their ministerial life, which in turn, feeds their spiritual and community life. What will inspire and inform the Mercys as the twenty-first century unfolds? Some indication emerges from broader post–Vatican II trends.

Following Vatican II renewal, American women religious found new satisfaction in religious life by restructuring it away from an institutional model and by dedicating themselves and their corporate communities to both new and long-established ministries. "New forms of simple living, community life, ministry, and prayer" emerged, and sisters determined for themselves how they wanted to be "present to life as they find it," though this contradicted the more institutional and structured understanding of being "in but not of" the world.[111]

Figure 27. Jubilee, 2012, Sixty-Year Celebrants.

The hard work of renewal in the preceding decades had yielded more than a restructured religious life. The Sisters of Mercy had emerged from renewal confident in their identity as valuable members of the Catholic Church in the world, not simply as servants or handmaids of the Church. Prior to Vatican II, the Mercys couched their strength and confidence in their purpose as a religious community in more traditional language. Their struggles to strip away the rigid structures of religious life had resulted in a clearer articulation of their identity. This new clarity was evident in the revised constitutions, updated charism, and the direction statement that informed and directed their religious lives. Mercys applied this new perspective to their ministries, reassessing such traditional apostolates as health care and education and embracing new, diverse ministries informed by efforts for justice and systemic change.

Regarding the "common good" of her community, Sister Lucille McKillop, president of the Chicago Mercys, observed in 1995 that, "at any moment in time [it] may mean looking for a compromise statement which is acceptable, not because it is perfect, but because it involves thoughtful choice and because it leaves intact, and does not compromise, the real reason we are here."[112]

As the twentieth century drew to a close, the Chicago Regional Community drew on its faith in God and each other to discern the common good for all that Sister Lucille had described. By the mid-1990s, faced with declining numbers and an aging population, the Chicago Regional Community began to discuss merging with other Mercy regional communities to combine and centralize resources. It began the deliberate process of reconfiguring its regional territory into a new, larger region: West Midwest. The 1991 formation of the Institute had, in some respects, modeled the restructuring and resource-merging process. In the midst of this consolidation, many wondered, what was the future of Mercy?

The question was not a new one. The process that resulted in the 1991 formation of the Institute had required numerous meetings, assemblies, and group reflections on the meaning the Sisters of Mercy and what further centralization would mean. When the Chicago Regional Community began the meeting and reflecting process, this time for the creation of larger regional community, the Chicago Mercys "prayerfully consider[ed]" their needs and how they should respond. Ultimately, the community understood, a larger regional configuration offered more benefits than drawbacks for Chicago Mercys. Yet many wondered what this change—which required the end of the Chicago Regional Community and its government—would mean for their identity as women religious and as Sisters of Mercy. Coming together with other regional communities, however, was not an end to the Chicago Mercys, but a new beginning. As affiliations shifted and the center of government relocated to Omaha, the Chicago Mercys maintained the essence of their identity as women religious.

Epilogue
West Midwest and the Legacy of the Sisters of Mercy Chicago Regional Community

How rapidly the days, weeks, and months are passing. Another month ended, that seemed but a few days begun. If we have not forfeited the friendship of Almighty God, but have been trying to love Him more and more, and to serve Him faithfully, they were blessed days for us. Oh let us endeavor to make these days such as we should wish the past to have been . . . The simplest and most practical lesson I know . . . is to resolve to be good today—but better tomorrow. Let us take one day only in hands—at a time, merely making a resolve for tomorrow. Thus we may hope to get on—taking short careful steps, not great strides.[1]

Catherine McAuley wrote the preceding passage in a letter to Sister Mary de Sales White in Bermondsey in February 1841, a few months after her previous correspondence in which she ruminated on the impermanence of individual Sisters of Mercy. In that earlier letter, McAuley's "little tripping about" placed emphasis on the centrality of God in her community's religious life. She echoes these sentiments in her February letter, which she wrote within the season of Lent. While the most of the letter deals with Catherine McAuley's suggestions for a practical approach to Lenten fasting and other sacrifices while conducting ministry, we can take her words and apply them within the context of endings and new beginnings. In the months leading up to the formation of the new West Midwest Community, Catherine McAuley's words adorned the pages of the community newsletter, *Tidings*. As the publication prepared the Chicago Mercys for the upcoming merger, the quote stood as a reminder to readers of the passing of time, and the importance of loving God and serving "Him faithfully."[2]

In preparation for the Sisters of Mercy Chicago Regional Community coming together with other regional communities into the new West Midwest Community, sisters reflected upon the changes to come in the months ahead. In one sense, they had been preparing for this new affiliation of Mercy communities for over a decade. Since the creation of the Institute of the Sisters of Mercys of the Americas in the early 1990s, sisters had engaged in dialogue about the meaning and structure of the Sisters of Mercy. The Institute meant the dissolution of the Union in order to become a part of a new configuration of communities making up the Sisters of Mercy of the Americas. With this transition, the regional identity of the Chicago community founded in the 1930s remained relatively unchanged since its formation in the 1930s. In the years following the creation of the Institute, Mercys across the country contemplated the meaning of their religious congregation in its new form, and looked for ways in which they could collaborate in their efforts in ministry, spirituality, and community. The Mercy educational associations and the movement toward a combined novitiate education discussed in the previous chapter are just two examples of this process. By the end of the 1990s, the Institute moved its individual regional communities toward reconfiguring its twenty-five regions into new and fewer associations in an effort to create more efficient and streamlined structures.[3]

In the first years of the twenty-first century, Mercys from the Auburn, Burlingame, Cedar Rapids, Detroit, Omaha, and Chicago regional communities contemplated if and how reconfiguration would occur and shape them into a new West Midwest identity. They participated in gatherings and engaged in inter-regional conversations in an effort to build relationships across the expanse of territory that divided them. Each regional community had its own history and identity, and many wondered if merging had the potential consequence of diluting each region's distinction. While some Chicago sisters did not see the need to change their existing structure, others worried that the Institute leadership was imposing reconfiguration on them, effectively removing the decision-making from the local level. Despite disagreement with the reconfiguration process, most Mercys accepted that some change had to occur to preserve and carry their religious congregation into the future, not in passive retreat, but as a viable and life-giving force. While many individual sisters voiced concerns about a merger of the six regional communities into one, they formally agreed in 2004 to work in concert to become West Midwest. One question remained: How would a new and considerably larger geographical territory draw everyone into one West Midwest community?[4]

In many ways, the Institute reconfiguration of regional communities was reminiscent of the amalgamation that occurred nearly eighty years earlier. In 1929, Mercys had united their identity with sisters from different locations and perspectives. They ceased to be Milwaukee, Davenport, or Chicago Westside Sisters of Mercy, and while still retaining their local orientation, they merged their hearts with sisters across a new province. This close affiliation did not happen immediately and it took years to reconceptualize themselves as more than the Milwaukee, Iowa, or Chicago sisters. In a similar fashion, the Chicago Mercys of the late twentieth and early twenty-first centuries began the process of uniting separate identities. The meetings and discussions prior to the 2004 decision continued in the ensuing years up to the official 2008 merger. Sisters gathered in small groups known as Sacred Circles and larger committees to prayerfully contemplate and dialogue about the meaning of reconfiguration and how these changes affected "their understanding of identity and what it means to be apostolic women religious in the 21st century." As the discussions and relationship-building continued, one question emerged: if the Chicago Regional Community ceased to exist, did that alter or diminish the identities of the Chicago Mercys who constituted the community?[5]

The Sacred Circles' dialogues and other gatherings between 2004 and 2008, helped the Chicago Mercys (along with the other Mercy communities with whom they were joining) move toward unification that laid the foundation for a new period of the Sisters of Mercy of the Americas generally and the Chicago Mercys specifically. The goal of the new, larger regional community was to "consolidate their funds and resources" to respond more efficiently and effectively and "so they can better care for their aging members and free up more sisters from leadership roles . . . for ministry." In the process, duplicated resources merged into a single office or team, and government centralized and relocated in Omaha, Nebraska. Sisters in the configuration had a community contact person at the local level within the larger West Midwest structure. Prior to the creation of West Midwest, each regional community had its own justice, ministry, and finance office, among others. To avoid duplication, one team for each department was created to coordinate efforts throughout the new territory.[6]

Without a local leadership team in Chicago, the central office of the Sisters of Mercy Chicago Regional Community changed its name from Chicago Regional Center to the Mercy Meeting Place on July 1, 2008. This was hardly the first time this building had a name change. At one time, it was the Provincial House, where the Provincial Council resided. Constructed in the mid-1900s after the college and girls academy moved south from 49th and Cottage Grove to 103rd and Central Park in Chicago, the building was the governmental center of the Chicago Mercys. Initially intended to be the office and convent of the Provincial Council, in subsequent years, other sisters have lived there and served as the central meeting place for various organizations sponsored by the Chicago Regional Community. After 2008, with the new name Mercy Meeting Place, this former governmental center became a center of hospitality for members of West Midwest visiting Chicago. It will continue to provide meeting space for different

Mercy-related organizations, committees, and ministries and serves as an identifiable center for the Sisters of Mercy living in the former regional community.

The evolution of this building is reminiscent of the growth and continuance of the Chicago Sisters of Mercy. While the Mercys are not their buildings, structures like this one have meaning both to the Chicago Mercys and to the larger society in which they live and serve. The legacy of the Chicago Mercys is larger than one building or even one ministry. When the first five Mercys arrived in Chicago, they established schools, but they did not limit themselves to education. They also expanded to new areas beyond Chicago—western Illinois, Iowa, and Wisconsin—and responded to the needs there. Quickly they added hospitals, care of orphans, and Houses of Mercy to their growing number of parishes and academies. Like the structure that was the Chicago Regional Center, the sisters did not stand still, unmoving or unchanging. They adapted and altered buildings, institutions, and themselves over the course of their 162-year history. They took whatever resources they had at a particular time, and worked with them to the best of their abilities. They created hospitals out of derelict hotels and apartment buildings, as in the case of Chicago's first Mercy Hospital and Aurora's first St. Joseph's Mercy Hospital. When faced with certain end to one of their ministries, they found alternatives to persevere, as in the case of St. Catherine and St. Clara Residences for women in Milwaukee. In this case, urban renewal in the mid-1960s meant the destruction of their building, and the Mercys found a workable solution by moving to another location and combining resources.

The Mercys also understood that leaving a place or ministry, while painful, was often the only solution, as in the short-lived foundation at Galena, Illinois in the late 1850s and the withdrawal from selected parish schools in the second half of the twentieth century. In Galena, sisters were isolated in the western part of the state and the community was overextended. The same thinking applied when superiors withdrew sisters from parish schools; to conserve resources, retrenchment was needed. When religious life changed with Vatican II, both individual sisters and the larger community made thoughtful and prayerful choices about how best to serve God and work in the world. Since the 1980s, as the size of the community has shrunk and sisters have aged, few sisters live outside of the Chicago area. Less than a dozen still lived in Milwaukee and only one remained in Davenport as of 2008. Regardless of period and circumstances, the Mercys adapted and responded. In a similar spirit, the building that is Mercy Meeting Place will continue to occupy an important role for the Chicago Mercys, despite the relocation of the seat of government to Omaha (or perhaps because of these changes). While it will provide a place for meetings, space for the administration of local support services for sisters, and home for some archival records, Mercy Meeting Place will continue as the center of communication and the heart of the Mercy community. The Mercys' buildings and institutions matter, but the spirit that fills the people who work in them has a deeper significance.

In many ways, the history of the Mercys is not that different from other religious communities throughout the United States. In the nineteenth century, women religious provided much of the basic educational, health care, and social welfare services needed by American and immigrant Catholics. For the church hierarchy, these often-free services were the foundation upon which the American Catholic community flourished. For much of this early period of American Catholic history, women had a handful of respected choices: marriage and motherhood; the single life and care of parents, unmarried brothers, and other aging relatives; or entrance into a religious community and they could look to religious life as a viable option and a revered calling. For those who had a religious vocation, this path led to education, life-long employment, the shared experience of community living, and spiritual fulfillment. It also might mean adventure or danger, or both.

Many women who chose a life within the Sisters of Mercy in the nineteenth century acquired an education and engaged in ministries until their deaths (some earlier than others). They traveled to faraway places, originating in Ireland and journeying to Pennsylvania, Illinois, Iowa, and Wisconsin. Sometimes, they worked independently of male authority, other times in partnership with it, and at times in direct conflict with it. While some laywomen became pioneers and lived autonomous lives, more often the demands of marriage and family constricted laywomen's movements and choices. Filial bonds, present for women religious, did not prevent them from leaving them behind to follow God. In some cases, family connections encouraged young women to follow aunts, cousins, and sisters into the same community.

With over a hundred years between nineteenth-century women religious such as Mothers Agatha O'Brien, Mary Borromeo Johnson, and Mary Evangelist Holcomb (foundresses of Chicago South, Davenport, and Milwaukee respectively) and their early twenty-first century counterparts, it appears easier to understand (or presume to know) why women opted for religious life. The outsider might believe that these women did not want marriage and family or to remain the servants of their brothers and fathers. Potentially, religious life offered sisters freedom from these domestic entanglements and a chance for economic and social improvement. While a higher status and deference came with a religious vocation, it would be shortsighted to conclude that these things alone attracted women. The reality, as we have seen, is that women chose the Sisters of Mercy because they believed God called them to this life, and they wanted something more than what was presented to them as wives and mothers.

Clearly, women who became Sisters of Mercy in this early period found "something more" and spiritual fulfillment within religious life as is evidenced by the large number of women who entered the community throughout the nineteenth and early twentieth centuries. The Chicago Mercys grew to over 1,000 members by the mid–twentieth century. It is equally clear to the outsider as to why the Sisters of Mercy responded to the needs of their co-religionists during this same period. The mission-ary church that was the American Catholic Church of the 1800s and early 1900s needed women religious. Immigrant Catholics faced nativist attacks, poverty, and exclusion from the tools of advancement such as sound edu-cation, adequate health care, and employment opportunities. The mission was clear; the laity needed sisters. Sisters of Mercy, along with other apos-tolic communities, understood their godly mission to build the Church and sustain children, women, and men. For Catherine McAuley's daughters in America, educating immigrant Irish children in Chicago parish schools, caring for the mentally ill in Davenport, and providing safe and affordable housing for young single women in Milwaukee fit with their founding charism and the purpose of their Institute.

A closer look at the nineteenth and early twentieth century Sisters of Mercy has revealed a more complex picture. Yes, religious life offered ma-terial advantages and connection to a larger purpose. The negative impact upon health and safety was a consequence many willingly risked as in the case of Mother Agatha O'Brien and three other Sisters of Mercy's death from cholera in 1854. The missing and challenging element to consider and document is faith. The historian observing from a distance the words and deeds of women religious often struggles to uncover evidence of per-sonal choice and spiritual devotion to God. While theological and spiritual writings may exist for some, little remains from the nineteenth and early twentieth century that explains the motivations of women like the Sisters of Mercy. We must look instead at the tangible works performed by Sisters of Mercy to attempt to "quantify" their faith in and commitment to God and to Catherine McAuley's vision of religious life. It is also the element that continually reappears in subsequent generations of sisters.

As the American Church matured, and along with it the Sisters of Mercy, religious life became more structured and rigid. The revisions to the Code of Canon Law in 1917 and the move toward more centralized government and control of women (and men) religious in the first decades of the twentieth century created more uniformity and pushed for greater anonymity among sisters. At the same time, women religious continued to assume an otherworldly and revered status. Perceived as the "good sisters," many believed these women were not like regular Catholics in the pews. They may have once been simply biological sisters and daughters, but by donning the habit and professing their vows, they took on another, separate identity. The rules and norms of the highly structured religious life reinforced those perceived barriers. Again, a closer examination of how Mercys lived their religion, whether as educators, health care workers, administrators, or as providers of shelter, material aid, spiritual direction, and pastoral care, illustrates that all women religious were not alike, nor were Mercys of this period lacking in diversity. Amidst the strong leaders such as Mothers Bernardine Clancy, Mercedes Wellehan, and Huberta Mc-Carthy, there were dedicated professionals and religious. Both the known leaders and unknown Sisters of Mercy had ordinary flaws and faults as well as talents and gifts.[7]

The triumphant Catholicism expressed by the American Church of the mid–twentieth century required much of women religious like the Sisters of Mercy. In the case of the Chicago Province, the need was more often than not for teachers to fill slots in the ever-expanding parish school system. Mercys continued to provide health care and other material and spiritual support, but parish priests demanded a larger number of sisters to fill classrooms than hospital wards. Mercys once again responded, but they also discerned a need among themselves to educate and to prepare young sisters for their religious and professional lives. Superiors had balanced the needs of their sisters with that of the laity prior to this period, but the tug from the institutional Church was strong. Negotiating the demands of cardinals, bishops, and parish priests presented challenges to various leaders of the Chicago Province.

Religious life continued to draw young women in high numbers throughout the twentieth century to the 1960s. The economic and educational needs of American Catholic women could still be met by religious life as they were in the previous century, but by the mid–twentieth century, they could also be met as laywomen. As we have seen, the emergence of a Catholic middle class competed with religious communities for laywomen's attention, but it was not until the cultural and theological upheavals of the 1960s and 1970s that the number of entrants declined significantly. By the mid–twentieth century, American Catholic women had many more options than in the nineteenth century, including more educational opportunities (often provided by colleges and universities owned and operated by congregations like the Sisters of Mercy) and a wider range of employments. Women, however, continued to become Sisters of Mercys throughout the twentieth century because other women religious inspired them; they wanted a life dedicated to service of others; and they believed that God had called them to this life.

With Vatican II, Sisters of Mercy tore down the perceived barriers that separated them from other Catholics, the world, and each other. Religious life in the mid-1960s and 1970s was tumultuous and not for the faint of heart. Renewal shook up life, and to outsiders and insiders alike, how a woman could or should serve God and live a spiritual and communal life appeared in flux. Women continued to enter religious life, albeit in fewer numbers as young women of faith found they were able to serve God and others as either single or married persons. From this period of renewal, however, emerged a new way of life radically different than the preceding sixty to seventy years. Mercys and other communities altered the appearance of some familiar elements, such as habits and traditional ministries, but they did not cast away the fundamental characteristics of the Sisters of Mercy. They infused the Mercy charism into new forms of decentralized and participatory government, diverse ministerial lives, and dynamic community life in new settings, such as apartments, community-owned houses, and other manifestations of intentional group living.

Chicago Mercys moved forward in the last decades of the twentieth century, committed to a religious life inspired by the spirit of Catherine McAuley and placing justice for the poor and oppressed and women's equality in the Church and world at the forefront of their apostolic lives. Vowed religious life, however, does not resonate with as many Catholic women in the same way that it once did, and the number of candidates for entrance into communities like the Sisters of Mercy has declined to only a handful nationwide. The Chicago Mercys, since the formation of the Institute, has not professed any new members. More women (and men) seek to become a part of Mercy life as associates. They are connected to and inspired by the Mercy charism, but they are also free to marry if they wish (among other distinctions). Associates numbered twenty-one in 1991 and rose to seventy-six by the West Midwest merger in 2008. At the time of the new configuration, the larger West Midwest community had nearly 900 sisters and over 500 associates. In comparison, in 1965 the American Catholic Church had nearly 180,000 women religious and the Chicago community had a little over 900 members.[8] The decline in membership is not specific to the Chicago or West Midwest Mercys. According to the Center for Applied Research in the Apostolate (CARA), roughly 15 percent of American Catholic women have considered entering religious life in 2003 and that percentage declined further by 2008. A little over 59,000 women are nuns and sisters as of 2009 and CARA reports that the median age of sisters and nuns is seventy-five.[9]

The Chicago Mercys, as a part of West Midwest and in concert with the Sisters of Mercy of the Americas, did not give up on the goal of increasing their membership or their belief in the appeal that their religious life could have to Catholic women. In collaboration with West Midwest regional communities, the Chicago Mercys asked themselves how they could increase members and in what ways they could connect with laywomen. They understood that the traditional population of young women from "blue collar two-parent working-class" families had declined and most twenty-five to fifty-year-old Catholics came "from the most affluent Christian group" in the United States. Religious life, consequently, needs to offer something different than it has traditionally done for generations. The Mercys have developed programs where they reach out to high school, college-age, and young professional women. They have "Come-and-See" weekends, offer retreats, and hopefully attract women with whom they have forged relations in ministerial work. In one program, vocation ministers within each area of West Midwest invite women who have expressed an interest in Mercy life to come and spend the day with the community. This "Nun Run" created by California-based Sister Bernadette Hart has spread to Chicago and through presentations to high school students at Mother McAuley High School. They have actively embraced the Internet, including providing informational videos on the Sisters of Mercy of the Americas website, and they have established a Facebook page; the West Midwest community has its own blog. The message of vocation ministers is to connect with women to show their relevance in the twenty-first century, stressing that they are forward-thinking professional women who want to help women, children, and the impoverished, and who are buoyed and sustained by their spiritual life and their relationships in community with other Sisters of Mercy.[10]

While the Mercys move into the twenty-first century, the reality of religious life continues to be that fewer numbers and an aging population continue to be a topic of debate within the institutional Church, religious communities, and frequently in news media. Social commentators ask: What will become of the nuns and their ministries and institutions? If women religious are no longer able to act as leaders or models of Gospel ministry, to whom will the Church turn to carry on their charism of service? Pages of newspapers and magazines such as *America* and *The National Catholic Reporter* debate the answer to that question at the same time the Vatican launched an investigation into religious life.[11] Popular news magazines report that young women of the Pope John Paul II generation in growing numbers have entered religious communities and opted to wear a religious habit. Communities with a focus on prayer and contemplation also show a relative increase in vocation. Neither conservative nor liberal religious communities, however, are receiving record numbers, as in the peak of the mid–twentieth century.[12]

It is unclear where religious life is going in the early twenty-first century and if it will persist in its current form. Chicago Sisters of Mercy, deeply invested in their future, are also mindful of their history and are concerned with present societal needs and what they leave to subsequent generations of Catholics. While they wish to preserve and safeguard their history, they recognize that, as one sister put it when asked her perception of her community's future: "Mercy is important, but the People of God served well is more important than Mercy."[13] The Chicago Mercys continue as Catherine McAuley intended—with their lives "centered in God—for whom alone [they] go forward—or stay back."[14]

Appendixes

A Parish Grade Schools, Academies, High Schools, Universities, and Alternative Schools

Parish Grade Schools in Illinois

School	Location	Years
St. Mary Free School for Girls	Chicago	1846–1849
St. Joseph Free School for Boys	Chicago	1846–1858
St. Mary Free School for Girls	Galena	1848–1857
St. Joseph Free School for Boys	Galena	1848–1857
Holy Name School[1]	Chicago	1850–1856
St. James Free School[2]	Chicago	1852–1858
St. Joseph School	Chicago (North Side)	1852–1858
St. John School for Girls[3]	Chicago	1863–1893
St. James School[4]	Chicago	1866–2003
St. Louis School[5]	Chicago	1870–1871
St. Mary Free School[6]	Chicago	1874–1880
All Saints School[7]	Chicago	1875–1949
St. Gabriel School	Chicago	1881–1990
St. Patrick School	South Chicago	1883–1967
St. Agnes School	Brighton Park, Chicago	1883–1967
St. Malachy School	Chicago	1883–1976
St. Elizabeth School	Chicago	1885–1925
St. Rose of Lima School	Chicago	1885–1971
Holy Angels School	Chicago	1887–1948
Our Lady of Mount Carmel Academy	Belmont, Chicago	1888–1904
St. Sylvester School	Chicago	1889–1907
St. Anne School[8]	Chicago	1893–1969
St. Mary Academy	Libertyville	1897–1907
St. Finbarr School	Chicago	1900–1969
Corpus Christi School	Chicago	1901–1928
St. Cecilia School[9]	Chicago	1901–1971
St. Joseph School	Libertyville	1902–1986
Our Lady of Mount Carmel School	Belmont, Chicago	1903–1986
St. Ita School	Chicago	1904–1993
Precious Blood School	Chicago	1908–1979
St. Thomas Aquinas School	Chicago	1910–1971
Resurrection School	Chicago	1911–1981
St. Lucy School[10]	Chicago	1912–1971

St. Patrick School	Seneca	1915–1967
St. Joachim School	Chicago	1916–1978
St. Mary of the Lake School	Chicago	1916–1977
Holy Rosary School	Chicago	1917–1970
St. Justin Martyr School	Chicago	1917–1977
St. Mary School	Lake Forest	1917–1977
St. Catherine of Siena–St. Lucy School[11]	Chicago	1917–
St. Catherine of Genoa School	Chicago	1924–1977
St. Mary School	Sycamore	1925–1958
St. Paul of the Cross	Park Ridge	1925–1970
St. Ann School	Barrington	1926–1933
Little Flower School	Chicago	1926–1975
St. James School	Arlington Heights	1927–1934
Holy Family School	North Chicago	1927–1971
St. Ethelreda School	Chicago	1927–1979
St. Catherine School	Dundee	1929–1977
St. Clotilde School	Chicago	1929–1978
St. Lawrence School	Elgin	1929–1986
Christ the King School	Chicago	1937–1992
St. Raymond School	Mount Prospect	1949–1970
St. Monica School	Chicago	1950–1978
St. Irenaeus School	Park Forest	1952–1972
St. Joan of Arc School	Skokie	1953–1971
Queen of Martyrs School	Chicago	1953–1993
St. Stephen School	Des Plaines	1953–1993
St. Patrick School	McHenry	1956–1978
Mary, Seat of Wisdom School	Park Ridge	1957–1975
Mary Queen of Heaven School	Elmhurst	1957–1985
St. Joseph the Worker School	Wheeling	1959–1971
St. Matthew School	Glendale	1960–1966
St. Emeric School	Country Club Hills	1960–1995
St. Charles Lwanga School	Chicago	1971–1984
St. Angela School[12]	Chicago	1983–
Frances Warde School[13]	Chicago	1989–2002

Parish Grade Schools in Iowa

School	Location	Years
St. John School	Independence	1869–1881
St. Mary School[14]	Davenport	1869–1902
Holy Family School	Davenport	1898–1975
St. Francis School	Keokuk	1900–1903
St. Patrick School	Burlington	1902–1970
St. Alphonsus School	Mount Pleasant	1914–1968
St. Mary School	West Burlington	1916–1970
Sacred Heart School	Manilla	1930–1932

Parish Grade Schools in Wisconsin

School	Location	Years
St. Patrick School[15]	Janesville	1870–1971
St. Patrick School	Milwaukee	1885–1975
Immaculate Conception School	Milwaukee	1886–1987
St. Matthew School	Shullsburg	1918–1968
St. William School	Janesville	1953–1983
Our Lady of Assumption School	Beloit	1955–1975
St. Eugene School	Fox Point	1959–1981

Academies, High Schools, Alternative Schools, and Universities

School	Location	Years
St. Francis Xavier Academy[16]	Chicago	1847–1956
St. Agatha Academy	Chicago	1854–1912
St. Angela Academy	Chicago	1857–1863
Notre Dame Seminary	Independence, Iowa	1869–1881
St. Xavier Academy	Ottawa	1874–1949
St. Joseph Academy	DeWitt, IA	1875–1881
St. Joseph Academy	Cedar Rapids, Iowa	1875–1881
St. Catherine Academy[17]	Chicago	1883–1895
St. Patrick Academy[18]	Chicago	1884–1928
Academy of Our Lady of Mercy	Milwaukee	1894–1925
St. Catherine High School[19]	Chicago	1895–1925
St. Cecelia Academy	Burlington, Iowa	1902–1920
St. Xavier College[20]	Chicago	1912–1992
Mercy High School	Chicago	1925–1977
Siena High School	Chicago	1925–1977
St. Patrick Academy	Des Plaines, Illinois	1928–1969
Mother McAuley Liberal Arts High School	Chicago	1956–
Austin Career Center	Chicago	1977–c2008
Saint Xavier University	Chicago	1992–

B

Hospitals, Facilities, and Residences Owned and/or Sponsored by the Sisters of Mercy, Chicago Regional Community

Hospitals in Illinois, Iowa, and Wisconsin

Hospitals	Location	Years
Mercy Hospital, Chicago	Illinois	1852–
Mercy Hospital, Davenport	Iowa	1869–1993
St. Elizabeth Hospital for the Mentally Ill, Women[1]	Davenport, Iowa	1872–1950
St. John Hospital for the Mentally Ill, Men[2]	Davenport, Iowa	1872–1950
Mercy Hospital, Iowa City	Iowa	1883–
St. Thomas Mercy Hospital	Marshalltown, Iowa	1903–1969
Mercy Hospital, Janesville	Wisconsin	1906–1975
St. Joseph Mercy Hospital	Aurora, Illinois	1911–1971
Mercyville Sanitarium	Aurora, Illinois	1912–1971
St. Mary's Hospital	De Kalb, Illinois	1922–1965
Mercy Center[3]	Aurora, Illinois	1971–

Women's Residences in Illinois, Iowa, and Wisconsin

Residence	Location	Years
House of Mercy	Chicago	1873–1948
St. Catherine Residence	Milwaukee	1894–
St. Clara Club	Milwaukee	1926–1968
Patricia Club	Chicago	1930–1969
McAuley Residence	De Kalb, Illinois	1965–1975

Senior Housing, Residences, and Other Facilities in Illinois and Iowa

Facility/Residence	Location	Years
McAuley Hall	Davenport	1902–1943
Mercy Home	Ohio, Illinois	1904–1957
Misericordia South	Chicago	1921–2005
Misericordia North	Chicago	1921–
Mercy Infirmary	Chicago	1940–1971
Mercy Hall	Chicago	1968–
Mercy Manor	Aurora	1971–1985
Mercy Center Tolentine	Olympia Fields, Illinois	1984–2004
Mercy Rehabilitation Center	Homewood, Illinois	1985–2001
McAuley Manor[4]	Aurora	1985–
Fox Knoll[5]	Aurora	1992–

Notes

Introduction: "One Solid Comfort"

1. M. C. McAuley to Sister M. de Sales White, Bermondsey, December 20, 1840, in *The Correspondence of Catherine McAuley, 1818–1841*, ed. Mary C. Sullivan (Washington: The Catholic University of America Press, 2004), 332.

2. Ibid.

3. This study uses the terms "sister" and "women religious" to identify members of the Sisters of Mercy and active communities like it. The more common term "nun" refers to women who profess solemn vows, live more contemplative lives, and are bound by rules of enclosure (which prohibit movement and interactions with the laity) or cloister (the area of a convent that is reserved for members of the community). These rules signify the limits or barriers between the religious and the laity, and most women religious prior to McAuley's period were bound by these rules. The lack of enclosure was a fundamental element of the Sisters of Mercy's culture.

4. Religious congregations' constitutions must also be approved by the Vatican. At various times in the Chicago Mercys' history (as well as other communities), the congregation had to revise or update their governing documents to adapt to the dictates of the institutional Church. This happened in the early 1920s and then again following the changes of Vatican II in the mid-1960s.

5. McAuley's prayers and letters appear in books, in pamphlets, and on websites devoted to Mercy spirituality and ministry. For example, a simple Internet search for the first sentence of the quotation that opens this introduction results in nearly 300 websites that use it in some way. Most are websites owned and controlled by the Sisters of Mercy. For example, the West Midwest Community, of which the Sisters of Mercy Chicago Regional Community is a part, includes this quotation on its page for the lay volunteer organization Mercy Volunteer Corps. Mercy High School in Burlingame, California includes these words (and others) on its pages devoted to Campus Ministry. The Mercy International Association, an affiliation of leaders of Mercy communities throughout the world, includes it with other quotes from McAuley on the association's website.

6. At the same time that this new middle class emerged, a large number of Irish tied to traditional culture and language died or immigrated during the potato famine, which began in 1845 and continued through 1855. Some scholars

have argued that, as a result of the famine, possibly 1 million people died and about 1.8 million left Ireland. Wealthier Catholics, consequently, had a larger impact on Irish culture than the peasant class, who either died or left Ireland.

7. "Lady Bountiful" refers to the nineteenth century wealthy woman volunteer whose philanthropic endeavors have been characterized as trivial and inconsequential. See Kathleen D. McCarthy, ed., *Lady Bountiful Revisited: Women, Philanthropy, and Power* (Newark: Rutgers University Press, 1990); and Lori D. Ginzberg, *Women and the Work of Benevolence: Morality, Politics, and Class in the Nineteenth Century United States* (New Haven: Yale University Press, 1992).

8. This view of the role of women religious in the Irish Devotional Revolution challenges the understanding of Emmet Larkin and other scholars who suggest that the rise of Irish communities of sisters and nuns came about because of the modernization of Ireland through the middle class and the urging of Catholic Church leadership. Mary Peckham Magray argues that women religious communities existed before the eighteenth century and grew at the same time. They also aided the growth of this new modern Irish Catholic culture. See Mary Peckham Magray, *The Transforming Power of the Nuns: Women, Religion, and Cultural Change in Ireland, 1750–1900* (New York: Oxford University Press, 1998), 5–6, 11, and 16–20 passim; Kerby A. Miller, *Emigrants and Exiles: Ireland and the Irish Exodus to North America* (New York: Oxford University Press, 1985), 280; Mary Sullivan, RSM, "Catherine McAuley in the Nineteenth and Twenty-First Centuries," in Elizabeth Davis et al., "'Fire Cast on the Earth-Kindling': Being Mercy in the Twenty-First Century" (International Mercy Research Conference, November 9–12, 2007), 90 and 91–92. Sullivan states that this "voluntary poverty" is reflected in the Rule, chapter 3, "Of the Visitation of the Sick," section 1. "Mercy, the principal path pointed out by Jesus Christ to those who are desirous of following Him, has in all ages of the church excited the faithful in a particular manner to instruct and comfort the sick and dying poor, as in them they regarded the person of our Divine Master, who has said, 'Amen, I say to you, as long as you did it to one of these my least brethren, you did it to Me.'" "Rule and Constitutions of the Religious Sisters of Mercy," in Mary C. Sullivan, *Catherine McAuley and the Tradition of Mercy* (Notre Dame, Ind.: University of Notre Dame Press, 1995), 297.

9. The history of the Chicago Regional Community is long and involves various manifestations of and names for the individual communities that came to form the Chicago Regional Community. This book uses "foundation" and "community" to identify the individual motherhouses, or central convent that governed other local houses or convents, within their territories in the nineteenth and early twentieth centuries before the amalgamation and the creation of the Sisters of Mercy of the Union. When discussing the community after amalgamation, I use "Chicago Province." Once the Union becomes the Institute in 1991, I use "Chicago Regional Community." I also use the term "Chicago Mercys" to signify the larger Chicago Regional Community's long history in the various

periods. Additionally, while Chicago is the lead name in this title, it represents the diverse area encompassing northern Illinois, Iowa, and Wisconsin. The following chapters describe this history in more detail.

10. Suellen Hoy uses the phrase "journey out" to describe the immigration of Irish women in the nineteenth century to the United States in her chapter of the same title. Hoy sheds light on the pattern of female immigration from Ireland to America, and shows that many of the single women who journeyed to the United States did so to join religious communities in that country. See Suellen Hoy, "Journey Out: From Ireland to America," in *Good Hearts: Catholic Sisters in Chicago's Past* (Urbana: University of Illinois Press, 2006), 11–34.

11. The Chicago Regional Community consisted of foundations that originated from the first Chicago South Side community such as Ottawa, Illinois in 1859, and Davenport, Iowa in 1867. Sisters from Davenport expanded to Janesville, Wisconsin in 1870 and Iowa City in 1873. Sisters of Mercy from Davenport went first to Sterling, Illinois, then on to Janesville. Six years later, Janesville sisters established a motherhouse in Fond du Lac and later in Milwaukee in 1885. Sisters of Mercy from Nashville, Tennessee sent five sisters to the west side of Chicago in 1883 to establish a new community there, which worked independently of the South Side Mercys until the late 1920s. Sisters of Mercy from Council Bluffs, Iowa, another independent motherhouse, sent a small group of sisters to Aurora, Illinois in 1911.

12. See Deborah Gray White, *Ar'n't I a Woman?: Female Slaves in the Plantation South*, revised edition (New York: Norton, 1999).

13. Some of the first and most groundbreaking women's histories have drawn connections between women's agency and participation in the women's rights movement and church membership. See Mary P. Ryan, *Cradle of the Middle Class: The Family in Oneida County, New York, 1790–1865* (New York: Cambridge University Press, 1981); Carroll Smith-Rosenberg, "Beauty, Beast, and the Militant Woman: A Case Study in Sex Roles and Social Stress in Jacksonian America," *American Quarterly* 23, no. 4 (October 1971): 562–84; and Kathryn Kish Sklar, *Florence Kelley and the Nation's Work* (New Haven: Yale University Press, 1995).

14. Carol Coburn and Martha J. Smith, *Spirited Lives: How Nuns Shaped Catholic Culture and American Life, 1836–1920* (Chapel Hill: University of North Carolina Press, 1999); Amy L. Koehlinger, *The New Nuns: Racial Justice and Religious Reform in the 1960s* (Cambridge: Harvard University Press, 2007); Mary J. Henold, *Catholic and Feminist: The Surprising History of the American Catholic Feminist Movement* (Chapel Hill: University of North Carolina Press, 2008); and Kathleen Sprows Cummings, *New Women of the Old Faith: Gender and American Catholicism in the Progressive Era* (Chapel Hill: University of North Carolina Press, 2009). Scholars of women religious history in Britain and Ireland are also contributing much to the narrative. In particular, see Carmen Mangion, *Contested Identities: Catholic Women Religious in Nineteenth-Century England and Wales* (Manchester, UK: Manchester University Press, 2008).

Part I. "Charity Embraces Those Who Abound": The Spirit of Mercy Comes to America, 1846–1929

1. Italics in text. "The Spirit of the Institute," *A Guide for the Religious Called Sisters of Mercy. Amplified by Quotations, Instructions, Etc.* (London: Robson and Son, 1886), 1.

1. "The spirit of our Institute is mercy, as its name denotes": The Nature of Mercy in Nineteenth-Century America

1. Directory for Novices, Spirit of the Institute, n.d., 2, Archives of the Sisters of Mercy Chicago (hereafter ASMC).

2. A novice is a woman in a period of probationary membership in a religious congregation. Sisters of Mercy became novices after a six-month period as a postulant. They remained novices until the first or temporary profession after a year.

3. Lived religion refers to a sociological and cultural anthropological conception that examines the everyday religious practices of groups of people. Fundamental to this approach, and how I use it here, is that an individual's faith directs everyday actions. The faith of women religious is apparent, arguably, because they wore habits, but often overlooked in women's history (and the wider field) is that religious belief informed the actions and sentiments of believers in tangible and often intangible ways. For further discussion of lived religion, see David D. Hall, ed., *Lived Religion in America: Toward a History of Practice* (Princeton, N.J.: Princeton University Press, 1997); and Robert A. Orsi, "Is the Study of Lived Religion Irrelevant to the World We Live In? Special Presidential Plenary Address, Society for the Scientific Study of Religion, Salt Lake City, November 2, 2002," *Journal for the Scientific Study of Religion* 42, no. 2 (June 2003): 169–74.

4. A branch house was a secondary convent that answered to the motherhouse (or parent house) from which it originated. When a mission developed to the point of self-sufficiency, particularly if it fell within a different diocese, a branch house became an independent motherhouse. In the nineteenth century, the Sisters of Mercy did not have a central motherhouse. Joy Clough, RSM, "Yesterday's City: Chicago's Sisters of Mercy," *Chicago History* 32, no. 1 (Summer 2003): 42, 45; and Mary Martina Schmomas, RSM, "History of St. Xavier Academy Written for Provincialate Archives," (March 14, 1951): 1, ASMC.

5. Maria Monk, *The Awful Disclosures of Maria Monk, or, The Hidden Secrets of Nun's Life in a Convent Exposed* (Manchester: Milner, 1936); Rebecca Reed, *Six Months in a Convent* (Boston: Russell, Odiorne, & Metcalf, 1835); and Nancy Lusignan Shultz, *Fired & Roses: The Burning of the Charlestown Convent, 1834* (New York: The Free Press, 2000).

6. The first congregations of women religious to arrive in the Americas were Ursulines and Poor Clares in 1639 and 1793. The Sisters of St. Joseph of Carondelet arrived from France in 1836. Elizabeth Ann Seton established the first

American community, the Sisters of Charity at Emmitsburg, Maryland in 1808. The Sisters of Loretto at the Foot of the Cross began in Kentucky in 1812.

7. George C. Stewart, Jr., *Marvels of Charity: History of American Sisters and Nuns* (Huntington, Ind.: Our Sunday Visitor Inc., 1994), 87.

8. Stewart, 87; and Registry Database of Sisters of Mercy Chicago Regional Community (hereafter Registry Database), ASMC.

9. Evangelical Protestantism emerged in the eighteenth century in America and focused on the personal piety, complete reliance upon Scriptural authority, and included a conversion experience. Evangelicalism emerged in America with the First Great Awakening in the eighteenth century and then the Second Great Awakening in the first decades of the nineteenth century. See George M. Marsden, *Fundamentalism and American Culture, New Edition* (New York: Oxford University Press, 2006), 3; Suellen Hoy, *Good Hearts: Catholic Sisters in Chicago's Past* (Urbana: University of Illinois Press, 2006), 17; Jay P. Dolan, *Catholic Revivalism: The American Experience 1830–1900* (Notre Dame, Ind.: University of Notre Dame Press, 1978), 24; and Colleen McDannell, *The Christian Home in Victorian America, 1840–1900* (Bloomington: Indiana University Press, 1986), 13–14.

10. Mainstream antebellum American society accepted Protestant women who strove to save souls through prayer and church organizations. This was an acceptable use of their time. When they aggressively challenged female prostitution, laying the blame more on men than the "fallen" or "erring women," they traversed into uneasy public territory. When some argued that women needed the vote to make reform stick, both women and men believed that they had tainted their cause by involving themselves in the corrupt world of politics. Carroll Smith Rosenberg, "Beauty, the Beast, and the Militant Woman," 564–65; Lori D. Ginzberg, "'Moral Suasion Is Moral Balderdash': Women, Politics, and Social Activism in the 1850s," *The Journal of American History* 73, no. 3 (December 1986): 608; and Hoy, "Walking Nuns," *Good Hearts*, 43.

11. Hoy, 43; and Joseph Mannard, "Converts in Convents: Protestant Women and the Social Appeal of Catholic Religious Life in Antebellum America," *Records of the American Catholic Historical Society of Philadelphia* 104, no. 1 (1993): 80.

12. During this period, what was considered American Catholicism was really Irish American Catholicism. See Dolores Liptak's discussion in *European Immigrants and the Catholic Church in Connecticut, 1870–1920* (New York: Center for Migration Studies, 1987) and *Immigrants and Their Church* (New York: Macmillan, 1989) of the idea that Irish American domination of the hierarchy in the nineteenth century affected the tone and shape of American Catholicism, but it was just as "ethnic" or immigrant as any other group.

13. Colleen McDannell's *The Christian Home in Victorian America, 1840–1900* makes this point.

14. McDannell; and Hoy, 43.

15. McDannell, 52–55 passim; and Kathleen Sprows Cummings, "Chiefly among Women: The Old Faith, the New Woman, and the Creation of a Usable Past," *New Women of the Old Faith*, 17–58 passim.

16. George Deshon, CSP, *Guide for Catholic Young Women, Especially for Those Who Earn Their Own Living*, Fourteenth Edition (New York: The Catholic Publication Society, 1871), 9–19 passim, and 20 (quote).

17. The prescriptive literature directed toward women that came to dominate Catholic presses lauded the long-suffering wife and mother who sacrificed her life (or nearly) to save her husband or son from various evils, such as alcoholism. McDannell, 74. Often articles offered famous female martyrs as exemplars for married women, such as St. Cecelia who maintained her virginity while converting her husband, or St. Agnes of Rome who welcomed death rather than marry. Normally, their sacrifice converted others. See "A Woman's Influence: Leo XII in Reply to a Deputation of Ladies," *Donohoe's Magazine* 1, no. 3 (March 1879): 224. Irish and Irish American women religious felt a closer connection to the conditions of this population because they often came from similar backgrounds. Maureen Fitzgerald asserts in her book *Habits of Compassion: Irish Catholic Nuns and the Origins of New York's Welfare System, 1830–1920* (Urbana: University of Chicago Press, 2006) that in the struggle between Protestant benevolent volunteers and Catholic women religious in nineteenth-century New York City for the souls of the largely Catholic and immigrant poor, class and ethnicity played just as important a role as religion. Women religious shared similar origins to those they sought to help.

18. A Customs and Guide was a handbook that elaborated on the constitution of a religious congregation, providing explanations of rules, regulations, and customs, and in this case it was specific to each foundation of Sisters of Mercy. For example, *The Customs and Minor Regulations of the Sisters of Mercy in the Parent House, Baggot Street*, Dublin: J. M. O'Toole & Son, 1869), *Customs & Regulations, Sisters of Mercy, Grand Rapids*, 1890.

19. "Lectures" as it is used here means an address or reflection given by the retreat director, a priest, or the mother superior. Deshon, 41.

20. McDannell, 85–6. George Deshon was not the only Catholic priest to write advice guides for young women in the nineteenth century. Bernard O'Reilly, SJ, wrote *The Mirror of True Womanhood: A Book of Instruction for Women in the World* (New York: Collier, 1878). Laywomen added types of manuals with stories and other guides. Mary Ann Sadlier published texts such as *The Young Ladies Reader* (1882) and *Bessy Conway, The Irish Girl in America* (1861).

21. Isidore O'Connor, RSM, *The Life of Mary Monholland, One of the Pioneer Sisters of the Order of Mercy in the West, by a Member of the Order* (Chicago: J. S. Hyland & Company, 1894), 19–20.

22. According to her official biographer, by this point, Monholland had rejected several marriage proposals because of her vocation to religious life. By this

account, her father was a relatively successful grocer in New York City and her suitors wished to marry the woman and the grocery. (O'Connor, 16)

23. Hasia Diner, *Erin's Daughters, Annual Announcement of Rush Medical College of Chicago, Illinois, Session of 1849–50* (Chicago, 1849), 14; Joy Clough, RSM, *In Service to Chicago: The History of Mercy Hospital* (Chicago: Mercy Hospital and Medical Center, 1979), 17 and 19; and Marie Pillion, RSM, "Remembering 120 Years of Cooperation, Sisters of Mercy 1831–1981: The Ottawa Story," *Dimensions* (Summer 1980).

24. O'Connor, RSM, 19, 22.

25. A postulant is a candidate for admission to a religious congregation. Postulancy, or the period of candidacy, usually lasted about six months.

26. Carol Coburn and Martha Smith, *Spirited Lives: How Nuns Shaped Catholic Culture and American Life, 1836–1920* (Chapel Hill: University of North Carolina Press, 1999), 38–39.

27. Single Irish women, especially after the Potato Famine, became increasingly mobile throughout the nineteenth and twentieth centuries primarily because they had fewer choices for marriage and an increasing need for wages. Many found they had better prospects leaving home either for urban centers in Ireland or abroad and they struck out on their own. *Record of Subjects Admitted to the Convent of Mercy Novitiate from 1868 to 1929*, DeWitt and Davenport, Iowa, 1, 8, ASMC.

28. Female religious communities in both Ireland and the United States continued the practice of dowries throughout the nineteenth century. Dowries, however small, contributed to the upkeep of the community. In some cases, religious communities operated academy schools to help fund their charitable endeavors. We will see that the Sisters of Mercy did this in Chicago with Saint Xavier Academy. Rev. H. Hohn, *"Vocations": Conditions of Admission, Etc. into the Convents, Congregations, Societies, Religious Institutes, Etc., According to Authentical Information and the Latest Regulations* (Cincinnati: Benziger Bros., 1912), 326; Hoy, 16, 161 n28; Coburn and Smith, 71; and Timothy J. Meagher, "Sweet Good Mothers and Young Women Out in the World: The Roles of Irish American Women in Late Nineteenth and Early Twentieth Century Worcester, Massachusetts," *US Catholic Historian* 5, no. 3/4 (Summer–Fall 1986): 326; and Hoy, 28–29.

29. Hoy, 14, 12; Brigid Condon, RSM, *From Obscurity to Distinction: The Story of Mercy Hospital, Iowa City, 1873–1993* (Iowa City: Mercy Hospital, Iowa City, 1991–1993), 35–6; and Registry of Entrants, Iowa City, ASMC.

30. Registry Database; Brigid Condon, RSM, *From Obscurity to Distinction: The Story of Mercy Hospital, Iowa City, 1873–1993* (Iowa City: Mercy Hospital, Iowa City, 1991–93), 35–6; and List or Manifest of Alien Passengers for the United States, SS Albania, from Queenstown, Ireland, October 16, 1921, National Archives, Washington, Ancestry.com; New York, Passenger Lists, 1820–1957 [database on-line], Provo, Utah: Ancestry.com Operations, Inc., 2010.

31. Registry Database.

32. Condon, 23.

33. Catherine McAuley, RSM, "The Spirit of the Institute," in Mary C. Sullivan, RSM, *The Correspondence of Catherine McAuley, 1818–1841*, 458–59.

34. "Office" refers to the Divine Office, or Liturgy of Hours, a set of daily prayers, readings, and psalms recited at specific times of the day. See Fernand, Cabrol, "Divine Office," *The Catholic Encyclopedia* 11 (New York: Robert Appleton Company, 1911), http://www.newadvent.org/cathen/11219a.htm; and "Office," Dictionary.com. Dictionary.com Unabridged. Random House, Inc. http://dictionary.reference.com/browse/office; and Agatha O'Brien, RSM, to Elizabeth Strange, RSM, June 28, 1851, ASMC.

35. *Book of Customs for the Sisters of Our Lady of Mercy*, transcribed by Agatha O'Brien, RSM, 1852, ASMC. It is unknown what volume or edition of the *Customs and Guide* Mother Agatha O'Brien transcribed. Compared with other published *Customs and Guide*, O'Brien's text does not follow the same order of items, such as *The Customs and Minor Regulations of the Religious Called Sisters of Mercy in the Parent House, Baggot Street and Its Branch Houses* (Dublin: J. M. O'Toole and Son, 1869). The opening paragraph of O'Brien's handwritten volume notes that their foundress, Catherine McAuley, had died and without her, the various houses had to depend upon a book of customs.

36. "Object of the Institute," *Rule and Constitutions of the Religious Called the Sisters of Mercy* (Pittsburgh: J. Porter, 1852), transcribed copy found in Janesville. This passage is the same in the 1890 edition published by H. L. Kilner & Co., Publishers, 1890 in Philadelphia, and only slightly different in the 1913 edition published by Browne & Nolan, Ltd., in Dublin, Ireland.

37. McAuley, "The Spirit of the Institute," in Sullivan, *The Correspondence of Catherine McAuley, 1818–1841*, 458–59. These words of Catherine McAuley come from a letter believed to be addressed to the Bermondsey Community in England in 1841.

38. Mary and Martha reference the Biblical account of these biological sisters who were disciples of Jesus. Mary sat and listened to Jesus, while Martha did domestic chores. *Customs and Regulations of the Sisters of Mercy, in the Dioceses of Providence, RI* (Providence, R.I.: J. A. & R. A. Reid, Printers, 1886), 10.

39. A more detailed discussion of lack of religious enclosure for the Sisters of Mercy and its implications is the subject of the next chapter. Mary C. Sullivan, RSM, *Catherine McAuley and the Tradition of Mercy* (Notre Dame: University of Notre Dame Press, 1995), 258, 260; and Arthur Vermeersch, "Cloister," in *The Catholic Encyclopedia* (New York: Robert Appleton Company, 1908), from New Advent, http://www.newadvent.org/cathen/04060a.htm.

40. Mary C. Sullivan, RSM, argues that Catherine McAuley's adaptations of the Presentation Sisters' rule indicate that she had a greater respect for sisters and trusted them to comport themselves as proper religious women. Consequently, she refrained from including extensive regulations or laws to manage their lives.

McAuley did not want religious regulations to prevent sisters from spending their time better in service of God. Sullivan, 289. See also Chapter 17, "Of Union and Charity," *Rule and Constitutions of the Religious Sisters of Mercy* (Dublin: Browne & Nolan, Ltd., 1913). Other editions of the *Rule and Constitutions* also contain this chapter.

41. Registry Database; Gabriel O'Brien, RSM, *Reminiscences of Seventy Years (1846–1916) Sisters of Mercy, Saint Xavier's, Chicago* (Chicago: F. J. Ringley, 1916), 298; and O'Connor, *Life of Mary Monholland*, 95.

42. Quotation comes from the section "Lectures for Solemn Retreat," in *Novice Guide*, Convent of Our Lady of Mercy, Saint Francis Xavier's, Chicago, September 1, 1849, ASMC. Handwritten lectures believed written/transcribed by Mother Agatha O'Brien.

43. Ibid.

44. Statistics based upon database of the Registry Database of Sisters of Mercy of the Chicago Regional Community, ASMC.

45. *Rule and Constitutions* (1913), 22; *Book of Customs for the Sisters of Our Lady of Mercy*, transcribed by Agatha O'Brien, 1852; and *Novice Guide* (Chicago: St. Xavier, 1949), transcribed by Agatha O'Brien, RSM, 82, ASMC.

46. Editions of the *Rule and Constitutions* varied somewhat in terms of length of time in temporary profession. The volumes published prior to 1900 examined for this study assign two years for temporary profession, or the length of time the "Young Professed . . . remain[ed] under the direction of the Mistress of Novices." The 1913 edition published in Dublin allowed for three years, and renewal of temporary vows for another three years, or however long it took for the young woman to reach the age of maturity, twenty-one. In this later volume, this period of temporary profession, however, could not be renewed again. Sisters of Mercy, Rule and Constitutions of the Religious Called the Sisters of Mercy (1852), n.p.; Sisters of Mercy, *Rule and Constitutions of the Religious Sisters of Mercy* (1890), 19–22; and Sisters of Mercy, *The Rule and Constitutions of the Religious, Called Sisters of Mercy* (1913), 20, 25–26, and 31–33.

47. Mary Monholland's birth year is recorded in community records as 1811, making her thirty-five when she entered. According to her biography, she was born in 1816. Monholland was not the only thirty-five-year-old to enter in the 1840s. Sister Mary Monica Maher entered at that age in 1849 at Galena, Ill. See O'Connor, *Life of Mary Monholland*, 10.

48. In the nineteenth century and into the early twentieth century, class distinctions continued in religious congregations, which were reminiscent of enclosed and cloistered nuns, namely with choir and lay sisters. A choir sister entered a religious congregation with a dowry, was normally better educated, and once professed was a full voting member of the community. She also recited the Divine Office in Latin and performed the ministries of the congregation, such as teaching and nursing. Lay sisters, on the other hand, came to a community without a dowry and with little formal education. They performed the domestic

chores or duties of the community and did not engage in the congregation's ministries. There was a definite internal class distinction between choir and lay sisters, as lay sisters did not have a vote and could not hold office in the community. These distinctions were unpopular in the United States, as they were seen as undemocratic, and most religious congregations did away with them by the end of the twentieth century. The Sisters of Mercy, who rarely admitted anyone with these distinctions, officially did away with them by 1930. Margaret Susan Thompson, "Sisterhood and Power: Class, Culture, and Ethnicity in the American Convent," *Colby Quarterly* 25, no. 4 (September 1989): 151–52.

49. Sister Gertrude McGuire died of tuberculosis in Galena in 1848. Registry Database; Sisters of Mercy, *Rule and Constitutions of the Religious Called the Sisters of Mercy* (1852); Sisters of Mercy, *Rule and Constitutions of the Religious Sisters of Mercy* (1890), 19–22; and Sisters of Mercy, *The Rule and Constitutions of the Religious, Called Sisters of Mercy* (1913), 20, 25–26, and 31–33.

50. Mary Kennedy, who became Sister Mary Ignatius, was born in County Tipperary, Ireland, March 4, 1850. She entered the Convent of Our Lady of Mercy, Janesville on July 9, 1872, and was received January 13, 1871. She made her final profession in Fond du Lac on August 17, 1876. She died in 1901. "History of St. Joseph Convent, Janesville, Wisconsin, 1870–1951," St. Patrick Convent and School, Janesville, Wisconsin, n.d., ASMC; Patricia Illing, RSM, *History of the Sisters of Mercy: Regional Community of Chicago* (Chicago: Sisters of Mercy of the Americas Regional Community of Chicago, 1994), n.p.; and Register of Receptions and Professions in Saint Joseph's Convent of the Religious called Sisters of Mercy, Janesville, Rock County Wisconsin, 27, ASMC.

51. Directory for Novices, Spirit of the Institute, n.d., 37–38, ASMC. For a larger discussion of the purpose of the formation process in the nineteenth century, see Carmen M. Mangion, "Laying 'Good Strong Foundations': The Power of the Symbolic in the Formation of a Religious Sister," *Women's History Review* 16, no. 3 (September 2007): 403–15.

52. The horarium listed by time the daily activities. It was determined by the Superior of the community. In the case of the Sisters of Mercy, local superiors needed the approval of the Mother Superior of the foundation to make any changes to the horarium. It included a detailed list of the times the community rose, prayed, ate, performed their duties, recreated, and retired for the evening. The novices who remained separate from the rest of the community had a different schedule than professed sisters. "Horarium," Oxford English Dictionary Online, http://www.oed.com/.

53. *Directory for Novices, Spirit of the Institute*, n.d., 4–5, 610, 13; ASMC; and Sisters of Mercy, *Customs and Minor Regulations of the Religious Called Sisters of Mercy in the Parent House, Baggot-Street, and Its Branch Houses* (Dublin: J. M. O'Toole and Son, 1869), 118–19.

54. The *Directory* also listed the number and type of items each sister could possess. This included six tunics, six stockings for summer and winter, eight

pocket handkerchiefs, two pairs of Stays, five towels, one bathing, three flannel vests, three summer vests, three night coifs, two black veils, two white dominos, six coifs and guimpes, one visitation cloak, one bonnet, one church cloak, four winter drawers, four summer drawers, one visitation boots, one visitation veil, two pairs of gloves, one stuff petticoat, two flannel petticoats, one black apron, two dusters, two pairs of shoes, one check apron, one or two black shawls, one cincture, and two habits. *Directory for Novices, Spirit of the Institute,* 18–19.

55. St. Joseph's Novitiate (Chicago, St. Xavier Academy, July 20, 1889), 5, 75, and 77, ASMC; and Catherine McAuley, *Familiar Instructions of Rev. Mother McAuley* (St. Louis, Mo.: Vincentian Press, 1927), 32–34, 99, 101, and 112–13.

56. "Self Will and Obedience," St. Joseph's Novitiate, 78 and 85–7.

57. Postulants read selections from the Spiritual Retreat Book, such as "The end of a vocation to the religious life," "the Mystery of the Incarnation," and "the crucifixion of our Lord," as well as studied the Rule and the purpose of the Institute of the Sisters of Mercy. *Novice Guide,* 85–89 passim.

58. Personal Retreat Notes of Sister Mary Isidore O'Connor, RSM, August 1857, Mercy Hospital, Iowa City, ASMC. This document is found among the Mercy Hospital, Iowa City records. O'Connor carried her retreat notes to DeWitt, and remained with the Iowa City community. It is reasonable to suggest that these notes may have been used in the same manner as Mother Agatha's transcribed Customs book and other documents in lieu of other spiritual readings.

59. Josephine Donnellan, RSM, "Early Times to 1925: Chronicle of the Mercy Convent, Milwaukee, Wisconsin," ASMC.

60. According to Sister Mary Francis de Sales Monholland's biographer, two Sisters of Mercy visited a Chicago prison and inadvertently were locked in for the night with the female prisoners. They spent the evening counseling inmates and praying the rosary. O'Connor, 61–62.

61. Mary Brigid O'Connor, RSM, *From Obscurity to Distinction: The Story of Mercy Hospital, Iowa City, 1873–1993* (Iowa City: Mercy Hospital, Iowa City, 1993), 63.

62. Pope Leo XIII issued Conditae a Christo in 1900, which made communities with simple vows seek papal approval, and Normae in 1901 responded and clarified Conditae pushing apostolic communities to "conform their constitutions and customs to minute and rigidly-codified criteria before Rome would grant its approbation." The 1918 Code of Canon Law applied to men religious as well as women religious. See Margaret Susan Thompson, "The Validation of Sisterhood: Canonical Status and Liberation, in the History of American Nuns," in Margot H. King, ed., *A Leaf from the Great Tree of God: Essays in Honour of Ritamary Bradley, SFCC* (Toronto: Peregrina Publishing Co., 1994), 45–46; and Mary Ewens, OP, "Removing the Veil: The Liberated American Nun," in Rosemary Ruether and Eleanor McLaughlin, eds., *Women of Spirit: Female Leadership in the Jewish and Christian Traditions* (New York: Simon and Schuster, 1979), 273.

63. Justine Sabourin, RSM, *The Amalgamation: A History of the Union of the Religious Sisters of Mercy of the United States of America* (Saint Meinrad, Ind.: Abbey Press, 1976), 35.

64. In the years leading up to amalgamation in 1929, Davenport and Iowa City completed a merger of its own, forming one community, with the Davenport motherhouse becoming the parent house of Iowa City in 1928. The merger occurred as part of the larger push toward amalgamation. The bishop of Davenport, Henry P. Rohlman supported the efforts of the Sisters of Mercy throughout the United States as well as within the Diocese of Davenport to unite in a general government. Mother Mercedes Wellehan, the Mother Superior of the Davenport community, was an early advocate of amalgamation. Both houses, Davenport and Iowa City, had to agree on the merger and they took a vote, which favored uniting both foundations. The unification of the two foundations under the government of the Davenport motherhouse officially took place in January 1929, but Bishop Rohlman sent word of the Vatican approval in August 1928. See Henry P. Rohlman, Bishop of Davenport, to Sisters [of Davenport and Iowa City motherhouses] March 14, 1928; and Henry P. Rohlman, Bishop of Davenport to Mother Mercedes Wellehan [Mother Superior of Davenport] August 15, 1928, ASMC.

65. *Directory for Novices, Spirit of the Institute*, 2, ASMC; and *Book of Customs for the Sisters of Our Lady of Mercy*, transcribed by Mother Agatha O'Brien (Chicago: Convent of Mercy, February 13, 1852), 70–71, ASMC.

2. "Not Bound by Enclosure." The Sisters of Mercy Respond: 1846–1929

1. "Book of Customs for the Sisters of Our Lady of Mercy," 70–71, ASMC.

2. Wolfgang Schivelbusch, *Railway Journey: The Industrialization of Time and Space in the 19th Century* (Berkeley: The University of California Press, 1986), 38, 40–41; and William Conon, *Nature's Metropolis: Chicago and the Great West* (New York: Norton, 1991), 76. Ironically, Pope Gregory XVI condemned trains in 1832 as an evil of modernization calling them *chemins d'enfer* (ways of hell), which was a play on the French term for railroad, *chemin de fer* (iron road) and prevented the development of rail lines in the Papal States. James M. O'Toole, *The Faithful: A History of Catholics in America* (Cambridge, Mass.: Belknap Press, 2008), 89.

3. For a larger discussion of the Penal Laws and their aftermath in Ireland, see Mary Peckham Magray, *Transforming Power of Nuns: Women, Religion, and Cultural Change in Ireland, 1750–1900* (New York: Oxford University Press, 1998); Emmet Larkin, *The Pastoral Role of the Roman Catholic Church in Pre-Famine Ireland, 1750–1850* (Washington: The Catholic University of America Press, 2006); and *The Historical Dimensions of Irish Catholicism* (New York: Arno Press, 1984).

4. The state of the Catholic Church in Ireland needed religious personnel who could help educate its membership. Catherine McAuley was one of many who desired something different and she and the Sisters of Mercy, despite struggles

with Catholic Church authorities who often wanted nuns and sisters to confine or limit their activities to life within a cloister, or enclosure, responded to what they believed was the authentic authority in their lives: God.

5. "Book of Customs for the Sisters of Our Lady of Mercy," 2.

6. "Book of Customs for the Sisters of Our Lady of Mercy," 71.

7. While communities of men religious and priests combated these "difficulties," women religious staffed more schools, hospitals, and orphanages and conducted more social service works than brothers and clergy. Catholic male leadership contributed differently to combating nativism and educating generations of American Catholics. See Coburn and Smith, *Spirited Lives.*

8. Suellen Hoy argues that Chicago's Progressive era reformers like Jane Addams are given credit for creating the first institutions to address the needs of the poor. Catholic women religious in Chicago and elsewhere have been overlooked in this history. See Hoy, *Good Hearts*, 3, 45.

9. Maureen Fitzgerald argues rightly that class, ethnic identity, and religious affiliation united sisters in nineteenth-century New York City with the Catholic immigrant poor, women religious being in positions of authority, like Protestant benevolent reformers. See Fitzgerald, *Habits of Compassion*, 4–6.

10. Agatha O'Brien, RSM, to Charles O'Brien, September 4, 1851; and Agatha O'Brien, RSM, to Elizabeth Strange, RSM, June 28, 1851, ASMC. The "Saint" in Saint Xavier Academy and Saint Xavier College (the future Saint Xavier University) often is spelled out, as opposed to the St. Xavier Academies in different cities, particularly in the twentieth century. For purposes of continuity, when discussing Saint Xavier Academy, College, and University in Chicago, I use Saint.

11. See David J. O'Brien, *Public Catholicism* (Maryknoll, N.Y.: Orbis Books, 1996); Steven Avella, *This Confident Church: Catholic Leadership and Life in Chicago, 1940–1965* (Notre Dame, Ind.: University of Notre Dame Press, 1993); and Jay P. Dolan, *The American Catholic Experience: A History from Colonial Times to the Present* (Notre Dame, Ind.: University of Notre Dame Press, 1992) for a discussion of institution building and Catholic infrastructure to combat anti-Catholicism and threats that Catholic immigrants in particular would lose their faith in an American Protestant society.

12. "Chapter II: Of the Schools," *The Rule and Constitutions of the Religious Sisters of Mercy* (1890), 4–5.

13. See Appendix A for a list of schools staffed and owned by the Sisters of Mercy. Patricia, Illing, RSM. *History of the Sisters of Mercy: Regional Community of Chicago* (Chicago: Sisters of Mercy of the Americas Regional Community of Chicago, 1994); 1870 Federal Census, Fond du Lac, Wisconsin; and 1910 Federal Census, Milwaukee, Wisconsin; and Registry Database.

14. In 1884, along with mandating the creation of parish schools within two years, the Third Plenary Council, held in Baltimore, also produced a uniform catechism, known as the Baltimore Catechism, used in Catholic schools and Sunday Schools until the 1960s. *The Rule and Constitutions of the Religious Sisters*

of Mercy, 5–6; Jay P. Dolan, *The Immigrant Church: New York's Irish and German Catholics, 1815–1865* (Notre Dame, Ind.: University of Notre Dame Press, 1975), 113–14; O'Brien, *Public Catholicism*, 49; and Janet Nolan, *Servants of the Poor: Teachers and Mobility in Ireland and Irish America* (Notre Dame, Ind.: University of Notre Dame Press, 2004), 91–92.

15. Reprinted chapter, "The Few and the Many: The Diocese of Chicago, 1844–1870," from Roger J. Coughlin and Cathryn A. Riplinger, *The Story of Charitable Care in the Archdiocese of Chicago, 1844–1959* (Chicago: Catholic Charities of Chicago, 1981), 10; and Joy Clough, RSM, "Yesterday's City: Chicago's Sisters of Mercy," *Chicago History* 32, no. 1 (Summer 2003), 44.

16. The first St. James Church was at 26th and Prairie in St. Agatha Academy, established by the Sisters of Mercy in 1854. St. James built another, albeit temporary, structure in 1858 at 27th and Prairie. Eventually, the parish constructed its current building in 1884 at 29th and Wabash Ave. "The History of the Sisters of Mercy Encompasses the History of St. James," n.d., St. James Convent, ASMC.

17. Sophia Granger was born in Bernice, Canada, and spoke both French and English. Her family migrated to Illinois, settling in Bourbonnais, and she entered the Mercy community in Chicago in 1849 at the age of seventeen. While the Bourbonnais mission was short-lived, Sister Genevieve Granger remained in the community, and quickly moved into an influential role within the community, beginning with her appointment as Mistress of Novices in 1853. She later became Superior in 1873, a position she held until 1904. Sister Mary Fidelis Convey, RSM, "Mother Agatha O'Brien and the Pioneers" (Master's Thesis, Loyola University, Chicago, 1929), 198, 199, 201, 203; and O'Brien, 87.

18. Gertrude McGuire entered the Pittsburgh Sisters of Mercy in 1845 at the age of nineteen. She was only twenty-two when she died in 1848. She, like Mary Francis de Sales Monholland, RSM, rose quickly through the ranks of the sisters to leadership because of skill and necessity. Mother Agatha O'Brien, only four years older than Sister Gertrude, was not yet a fully professed sister when McGuire entered. The affection with which Mother Agatha wrote about her departed sister in religion in her 1850 letter to another Sister Gertrude of the same Galena community was real. The religious language of the nineteenth century can distract the "modern" reader as to its true meaning. Sister Veronica (Eva) Schmidt entered the Mercys in Pittsburgh and was also one of the first group of five sisters to go to Chicago. She had not made her final profession when she went to Galena. See Agatha O'Brien, RSM, to Gertrude Gibbons, RSM, November 12, 1850, ASMC. Convey, 199.

19. The Chicago Mercys were only thirteen years old at this point and their numbers, while increasing, were not great. Roughly, sixty-five sisters were in the community at this time. Chicago, by this time, had Mercy Hospital, Saint Xavier Academy, Saint Agatha Academy, and numerous parish schools to run, not to mention its other Works of Mercy to conduct.

20. "Act of Chapter of Discreets," August 18, 1859, Chapter Book, St. Xavier Academy, 1855–1929, ASMC; Marie Pillion, RSM, "Remembering 120 Years of Cooperation," *Dimensions* (Summer, 1980). Ottawa was reachable in 1859 by train, whereas Galena was not until 1854.

21. Pillion.

22. M. Jane Coogan, "The Redoubtable John Hennessy, First Archbishop of Dubuque," *Mid-America* 1, no. 1 (1980): 23; Aquinas Healey, RSM, "Mercy Hospital Davenport, Iowa: Briefly Reviewed 1869–1959," n.d., ASMC; Mary Josephine Donnellan, RSM, "Chronicle of Mercy Convent, Milwaukee, Wisconsin: Early Times to 1925," typed transcript, 7, ASMC; and Mary Brigid Condon, RSM, *From Simplicity to Elegance: The Story of Mercy Hospital, Davenport 1869–1994* (Davenport: Genesis Health System, 1997), 6.

23. Charles Blanchard, "Religion in Iowa—the Catholics," *Annals of Iowa* (Des Moines: Iowa State Historical Department, 1962), 389–90; and Stephen J. Shaw, "The Cities and the Plains, A Home for God's People: A History of the Catholic Parish in the Midwest," in Jay P. Dolan, ed., *The American Catholic Parish, A History from 1850 to the Present, Volume II, The Pacific, Intermountain West and Midwest States* (New York: Paulist Press, 1987), 289. Bishop Hennessy, despite his conflicts with the Sisters of Charity of the Blessed Virgin Mary, or perhaps because of them, continued to seek out communities of women religious with whom he was familiar. In 1871, he brought the Sisters of the Visitation from St. Louis, the same city in which he attended seminary. He also sought out Irish communities, returning to Ireland to recruit Sisters of the Presentation from Waterford in 1874. He brought Mercys from Mercy Hospital, Davenport to establish a hospital in Dubuque in 1873. Coogan, 23–24.

24. Donnellan, 8–9. Conflicting accounts exist regarding Father Doyle's connection with the Sisters of Mercy. Josephine Donnellan reports that he was Mother Borromeo Johnson's spiritual director when he was the assistant at Saint John's Cathedral in Milwaukee. He directed the then Elizabeth Johnson to the Chicago Mercy community. Brigid Condon, RSM, however, states that Johnson remained in Ireland up to her entrance in the Chicago community. She had a vocation and when she heard of the Chicago community in 1854, she went directly to that convent. Condon, *From Simplicity to Elegance*, 14.

25. *Rule and Constitutions of the Religious Sisters of Mercy*, 6; and Sullivan, *Catherine McAuley and the Tradition of Mercy*, 297n8.

26. Sullivan, 5–6. Pension school is the nineteenth century term for schools that charged a fee for attendance, and were often convent schools or academies such as Saint Xavier Academy. The Sisters of St. Joseph of Carondelet in St. Louis is a particularly excellent example of this, as are the many convent schools established by the Ursuline Sisters. For a larger discussion of Catholic female academies, see Carol Coburn and Martha Smith, *Spirited Lives*; and Tracy Schier and Cynthia Russett, eds., *Catholic Women's Colleges in America* (Baltimore: The

Johns Hopkins University Press, 2002). For the specific discussion of Ursuline and Sisters of St. Joseph of Carondelet, see Nancy Lusignan Schultz, *Fire and Roses: The BUring of the Charlestown Convent, 1834* (Boston: Northeastern University Press, 2000), 12–13; and Coburn and Smith, 50–52, 160–63.

27. Illing; and Alfred Theodore Andreas, *History of Chicago from the Earliest Period to the Present Time, Volume 3* (Chicago: A. T. Andreas Company Publishers, 1886), 774.

28. Agatha O'Brien, RSM, to Elizabeth Strange, RSM, June 28, 1851; and Hoy, 39.

29. Graduation programs from Saint Xavier Academy in the nineteenth century provide summaries of the type of courses or subjects studied by students. The prizes and awards bestowed upon graduates also indicate the attributes and accomplishments valued by the school. Furthermore, these types of documents and alumnae roles indicate the careers or future paths of graduates, whether as married or single professional women, or as members of the Sisters of Mercy. Schools such as Saint Xavier and other Catholic high schools proved to be gateways to the religious life, which was one of the desired outcomes of Catholic education. See Cummings, *New Women of the Old Faith*. "Catalogue of Pupils of Saint Xavier's Academy, Chicago, for the Academic Year, 1878–9," ASMC.

30. Mercy High School Chicago, "Dedication of the Mercy High School, November Sixth, 1924, Souvenir Book," in "Events: Dedication Book, 1924," ASMC; Mercy High School Academic Program, n.d., Mercy High School, Chicago, Ill., ASMC; Edward R. Kantowicz, "Cardinal Mundelein of Chicago and the Shaping of Twentieth-Century American Catholicism," in *Catholicism, Chicago Style*, ed. Ellen Skerrett, Edward R. Kantowicz, and Steven M. Avella (Chicago: Loyola University Press, 1993), 75; and Harry C. Koenig, "Mercy High School, Chicago," *A History of the Offices, Agencies, and Institutions of the Archdiocese of Chicago* (Chicago: Archdiocese of Chicago, 1981), 613.

31. Sullivan, 5–6, 10.

32. *Rule and Constitutions*, 13. Later Constitutions and particularly the 1957 *Customs and Guide* does not use the term "distressed" and focuses on the creation of Homes for Women as places for young girls and women, albeit of "good character." Sisters of Mercy, *Customs and Guide of the Institute of the Religious Sisters of Mercy of the Union in the United States of America* (Bethesda/Washington: Sisters of Mercy General House, 1957), 49.

33. Janet A. Nolan in *Ourselves Alone* asserts that between 1880s and 1925, single women traveling alone dominated the numbers of immigrants from Ireland. Janet A. Nolan, *Ourselves Alone: Women's Emigration from Ireland, 1885–1920* (Lexington, Ky.: University of Kentucky Press, 1989), 1–3.

34. Nineteenth-century female benevolent reformers commented on the sexual double-standard facing prostitutes. Society condemned women's behavior, but excused or ignored men's actions. These reformers (often Protestant middle class women) sought to hold men accountable for their sins, but they did not believe

that women escaping prostitution could be completely rehabilitated in society. This was also an attitude shared by Sisters of the Good Shepherd. Women who came to their houses of refuge found sanctuary, but their rehabilitation was to reputable domestic service or life within religious community, like the Magdalen Sisters. See Fitzgerald, *Habits of Compassion*, 73–76. For a Chicago example of the Good Shepherd Sisters, see Suellen Hoy, "Caring for Abandoned Women and Girls: The Sisters of the Good Shepherd, 1859–1911," *Good Hearts*, 47–70.

35. The rate of women working in offices rose from 4.5 percent in 1870 to 40 percent in 1880. 10,000 women worked as sales clerks in 1870 and by 1890, 100,000 women were salesgirls in shops. Nancy F. Cott, *No Small Courage: A History of Women in the United States* (New York: Oxford University Press, 2000), 317–18 and 320–21. "Departure to Chicago," Copy of original in the Sisters of Mercy Nashville archives; Joanne Meyerowitz, *Women Adrift: Independent Wage Earners in Chicago, 1880–1930* (Chicago: University of Chicago Press, 1988), xvii; Rosenberg, "Beauty, Beast, and the Militant Woman," 562–584; and Ginzberg, *Women and the Work of Benevolence*.

36. For a larger discussion of the New Woman and Catholic women, see Cummings, *New Women of the Old Faith*, specifically, 17–58.

37. "Helping Milwaukee Working Girls," *Milwaukee Free Press*, June 11, 1916.

38. For a complete list of women's residences, see Appendix B: "Hospitals, Facilities, and Residences Owned and/or Sponsored by the Sisters of Mercy, Chicago Regional Community." Donnellan, 91, ASMC; and Report of the St. Catherine's Council, Milwaukee, Wisconsin, 1919, ASMC.

39. The respect of non-Catholics' faith did not prevent women religious and Catholic priests who worked in hospitals from encouraging anyone interested in the Catholic faith in the same way as sister-teachers did not discourage Protestant students' curiosity in the Catholic Church. Hoy, "Walking Nuns: Chicago's Irish Sisters of Mercy," *Good Hearts*, 36–40. See Mary Denis Maher, *To Bind Up the Wounds: Catholic Sister Nurses in the U.S. Civil War* (New Orleans: Louisiana State University Press, 1999).

40. *Rule and Constitution*, 6–12.

41. Clough, *In Service to Chicago*, 17–19.

42. Coogan, 22–3. DeWitt and Davenport at this time were a part of the Dubuque diocese. The Diocese of Davenport was established in 1881. Early histories of Davenport Mercy Hospital describe Bishop Hennessy's reaction to the request to take over hospital care in Davenport as supportive. Mother Borromeo Johnson joined Mary Francis Monholland during the Civil War and led the group of nurses in Missouri. Given the chance to conduct hospital work may have influenced Johnson to forego a select school for girls. The need for health care was greater than a girls' academy. This ran counter to Bishop Hennessy's plans and the larger movement to provide Catholic schools within the diocese.

43. In 1915, the Sisters of Mercy in Aurora, Illinois also established a mental hospital called Mercyville Sanitarium. The Aurora Mercys originally came

from Council Bluffs, Iowa, a separate foundation from the Davenport and Iowa City communities. They arrived in the Rockford Diocese in Illinois in 1908. Illing; Lynne M. Getz, "A Strong Man of Large Human Sympathy": Dr. Patrick L. Murphy and the Challenges of Nineteenth-Century Asylum Psychiatry in North Carolina," *North Carolina Historical Review* 86, no. 1 (January 2009): 34–35; Juliann Sivulka, "From Domestic to Municipal Housekeeper: The Influence of the Sanitary Reform Movement on the Changing Women's Roles in America, 1860–1920," *Journal of American Culture* 22, no. 4 (December 1999): 1–7; and Frank B. Norbury, "Dorothea Dix and the Founding of Illinois' First Mental Hospital," *Journal of the Illinois State Historical Society* 92, no. 1 (March 1999): 13–29.

44. Schools of nursing developed throughout the late nineteenth century and they normally required two to three years of training before completion. As nursing and its educational process became more professionalized, the trend moved away from two- or three-year certifications toward four-year bachelor of science degrees. Consequently, the school of nursing housed at Mercy Hospital, Davenport transferred to a local four-year institution, St. Ambrose College, in 1951. For a larger discussion on the history of nursing in the United States, see Barbara Melosh, *The Physician's Hand: Work Culture and Conflict in American Nursing* (Philadelphia: Temple University Press, 1982). Gayle M. Voelcker, "A Recording of Nursing's Past: A History of the Mercy School of Nursing, Davenport, Iowa, 1895–1931," 7, ASMC; Condon, 24–25, and 27; *The Catholic Church in the United States of America, Undertaken to Celebrate the Golden Jubilee of His Holiness, Pope Pius X, Volume II: The Religious Communities of Women* (New York: The Catholic Editing Company, 1914), 388–89; Condon, 34; "Pride in Our Past: Faith in Our Future: 1869–1994" (Davenport, Iowa: Mercy Hospital, Davenport, 1994); and Illing.

45. Illing.

46. Diomede Falconi, Cardinal Prefect, February 13, 1905, quoted in Sabourin, *The Amalgamation*, 21.

47. Sabourin, 24.

48. Sabourin, 35.

49. Ultimately, Aurora voted not to join the Union in 1929. It entered the Sisters of Mercy of the Union in 1937 as a part of the Chicago Province.

50. The revisions to the code of Canon Law in 1917 and the subsequent directive from the Vatican in 1918 to religious communities to revise their rules and constitutions resulted, for many women religious, in a more structured and uniform life. The discussion of amalgamation came out of this directive as Mercys wishing to be obedient to the Holy See requested the help of other Mercys.

51. The changes brought by amalgamation and the revision of the rule and constitutions did alter, to some extent, the initial intentions of Catherine McAuley when she established the Sisters of Mercy. The decision in the 1920s to amalgamate can be viewed as an effort to play an active role in those changes

by the Mercys. This issue will be discussed further in a larger discussion of the amalgamation in Chapter 3.

52. Sabourin, 116; and Evangeline McSloy, RSM, Telephone Interview with Author, April 23, 2009.

53. Mother Sophia Mitchell to Mother Carmelita Hartman, December 1927, in Sabourin, 73–74.

54. There were 9,308 Sisters of Mercy spread over sixty independent communities in the United States. Mary Regina Werntz, RSM, *Our Beloved Union: A History of the Sisters of Mercy of the Union* (Westminster, Md.: Christian Classics, Inc, 1989), 1.

55. Mother Sophia Mitchell to Mother Carmelita Hartman, June 6, 1928, in Sabourin, 126. Cardinal Mundelein was not the only ecclesiastical opposed to amalgamation. Pittsburgh's Archbishop Hugh C. Boyle also opposed the merger. Sabourin, 42.

56. Sabourin, 173; and Illing.

Part II. "This Mutual Love and Union": From Amalgamation to a Post-Vatican II World, 1929–1980s

1. *Constitutions*, Article a160, quoted in *Customs and Guide of the Institute of the Religious Sisters of Mercy of the Union in the United States of America* (Bethesda/Washington: Sisters of Mercy General Motherhouse, 1957), 215.

3. New Community, Same Spirit

1. Article 156, *Constitutions of the Institute of the Religious Sisters of Mercy of the Union in the United States of America* (Bethesda/Washington: Sisters of Mercy General Motherhouse, 1941).

2. Another stereotype of women religious is the stern nun who ruled her classroom with fear. Both of these images remain locked in our collective memories, particularly among those who attended parish schools in the mid–twentieth century. These images of women religious have found a renewed presence in American popular culture with the omnipresent calendars of "Nuns Having Fun." Earlier images came from movies like *The Bells of St. Mary's* (1945), *The Nun's Story* (1959), and *The Sound of Music* (1965). The persistent stereotypes of women religious in habits is the subject of a recent documentary. See Bren Ortega Murphy, dir., *A Question of Habit*, January 2011.

3. Sisters of Mercy of the Union, *Customs and Guide*, 192.

4. The quote that begins this section is from John T. McNicholas, "Address, First General Chapter of the Sisters of Mercy in the United States," August 28, 1929, ASMC.

5. Sophia Mitchell, RSM, to Hyacinth English, RSM, March 15, 1930, ASMC. "Pass" appears in quotations in the letter.

6. Carmelita Hartman, RSM, to the Mother Provincials, September 25, 1933, quoted in Mary Regina Werntz, 17.

7. Sophia Mitchell, RSM, to Bernardine Clancy, RSM [1930], ASMC.

8. Sophia Mitchell, RSM, to Hyacinth English, RSM, March 20, 1930; Mitchell to Clancy, RSM [1930]; and Mitchell to Clancy, November 10, 1930, ASMC.

9. In the same letter that she commented on the singing of the Maryland Mercys, she also hoped that the host community would "not be so Puritanic in these parts as to hold this [the meetings] over Sunday." Sophia Mitchell, RSM, to Bernardine Clancy, RSM, [1930], ASMC.

10. *Registry Database*; and Werntz, 10.

11. Werntz, 10; and *Book of Minutes Provincial Council*, Chicago, Sisters of Mercy of the Union in the United States of America (1929–39), 5 and 57, ASMC.

12. Werntz, 54–55; Minutes of the Provincial Council of the Chicago Province (1939–51), 6, ASMC; and Provincial Council Minutes, 1, ASMC. Sister Therese (Katherine) Flatley went on to become the Superintendent of Mercy Hospital, Chicago in 1946 and a coordinator of nursing education for the state of Illinois in 1952.

13. *Customs and Guide*, 73–74. Nineteenth-century editions of the *Customs and Guide* and the *Rule and Constitutions* prior to amalgamation did not have a separate subheading for enclosure and cloister. They did refer to regulations of religious life, including a separate space for sisters within the convent that laypeople could not enter. Conversely, the Union's *Customs and Guide* had a separate chapter on "The Enclosure."

14. *Customs and Guide*, 83.

15. Mother Provincial Genevieve Crane, RSM, to Archbishop Samuel Stritch, October 31, 1942; and Archbishop Samuel Stritch to Mother Genevieve Crane, RSM, November 2, 1942, ASMC.

16. Samuel Stritch was at this time Archbishop of Chicago. He became Cardinal in 1946. The then Archbishop Stritch's response was not unusual for a bishop at this time and his answer apparently pleased Mother Genevieve Crane who felt the same way about Sister Therese Flatley's attendance at the meeting. Mother Genevieve Crane to Archbishop Samuel Stritch, November 4, 1942; and *Customs and Guide*, 73–74, 76–77, and 82–83.

17. Angelyn Dries, OSF, "The Americanization of Religious Life: Women Religious, 1872–1922," *U.S. Catholic Historian* 10, no. 1 and 2 (1989): 20–21; Stewart, Marvels of Charity, 377; and Margaret Susan Thompson, "To Serve the People of God: Nineteenth-Century Sisters and the Creation of an American Religious Life," *Working Paper Series, Cushwa Center* 18, no. 2 (Spring 1987): 40. Both Thompson and Stewart use the term "homogenized" to characterize the period following the revision of the Code of Canon Law in 1917 to the Second Vatican Council in the mid-1960s.

18. Saint Xavier Academy also moved to the new property at 103rd Street and changed its name to Mother McAuley Liberal Arts High School. See Appendix A.

19. Band was the name given to a class or group of novices per year.

20. D. Falconio Arch. Of Largissa, Apostolic Delegate to Rt. Rev., February 24, 1905, ASMC.

21. Bernardine Clancy, RSM, to Carmelita Hartman, October 20, 1927, found in Sabourin, RSM, 53–54.

22. Mitchell to English, March 20, 1930, ASMC.

23. Sophia Mitchell, RSM, to Bernardine Clancy, RSM, n.d. c1930; and *Book of Minutes Provincial Council* (1929–39), 5, ASMC.

24. Sisters of Mercy, Chicago Regional Community, "Mercy" brochure (Des Plaines, Ill.: Mother of Mercy Novitiate, 1948), ASMC.

25. Kathy Peiss, *Hope in a Jar: The Making of America's Beauty Culture* (New York: Henry Holt, 1998), 119, 188.

26. Most notable were the school systems that would not hire married women or that fired those who got married. Similar hiring and firing practices occurred in the insurance and banking industries as well. The federal government reinforced this attitude with the 1932 National Economy Act, which contained a prohibition on more than one family member employed in the civil service. Women, often paid less than their husbands or other male relatives, lost their jobs. Susan Ware, *Holding Their Own: American Women in the 1930s* (Boston: Twayne Publishers, 1982), 28; and Thomas M. Landy, "The Colleges in Context," in *Catholic Women's Colleges in America*, ed. Tracy Schier and Cynthia Russett (Baltimore: The Johns Hopkins University Press, 2002), 69.

27. Ware, 16, 28, and 36–37; and Landy, 69.

28. I return to Catholic Action in the next chapter and its impact on the Mercys' own path to renewal. Debra Campbell, "The Heyday of Catholic Action and the Lay Apostolate," in *Transforming Parish Ministry: The Changing Roles of Catholic Clergy, Laity, and Women Religious*, ed. Jay P. Dolan, R. Scott Appleby, Patricia Byrne, and Debra Campbell (New York: Crossroad Publishing Company, 1990), 224; George William McDaniel, "Catholic Action in Davenport: St. Ambrose College and the League for Social Justice," *Annals of Iowa* 55, no. 3 (Summer 1996): 239–72; and "Catholic Action Program Chosen, Mar. 10, 11, 12 Dates Picked for Convention," *The Sketch* 1, no. 3 (February 1950): 1.

29. George C. Stewart Jr. generated these statistics based upon his survey of the *Official Catholic Directory*. He, however, asserts that the numbers of 1960 and 1965 are inaccurate and he provides close estimates of the real numbers. Stewart, 565. For the Sisters of Mercy, the 1930s were a high point for entrants during this period. The 1940s saw roughly 13percent fewer aspirants than the preceding decade. While the number rose in the 1950s, it declined by roughly 50 percent by the 1960s. See the Registry Database.

30. Numerous Sisters of Mercy were interviewed during the writing of this book or participated in group discussions relating to their reasons for joining the Sisters of Mercy, views on community life over time, and Mercy spirituality. These focus groups and individual interviews consisted of Sisters who entered

the community throughout all decades of the twentieth century after amalgamation, from the 1930s through the 1970s. All sisters stated that they had a call to the religious life as the primary or fundamental reason for becoming a Sister of Mercy. The secondary reasons for entering the Mercys consisted of family association, exposure to Mercys in school, and general admiration for this particular community over others of their acquaintances.

31. Elizabeth and Mary Feinberg were Jewish immigrants from Russia, who converted to Catholicism and then entered the Sisters of Mercy. Their conversions occurred independently of one another, each hiding her religious transformations from her family. They both entered in Milwaukee prior to the amalgamation in 1929. The McKillop sisters were born in Chicago and, entering after amalgamation, completed their formation at the novitiate in Des Plaines, Illinois. A consistent statement of the sisters who participated in these focus groups was that they found the Mercys to be hospitable and knew how to enjoy life, which suggests that an element of "giddiness" surfaced despite warnings against it in the *Customs and Guide*. See Registry Database and Sisters of Mercy, Focus Groups with author, Mercy Convent, Chicago, Ill., October 13, 2006, and Provena McAuley Manor, Aurora, Ill., April 10, 2007.

32. Evangeline McSloy, RSM, interview with author, June 7, 2007.

33. In one instance, the then Assistant Provincial Bernardine Clancy wrote to Sister Mary Dominica Mullin at Mercy High School Milwaukee, directing her to "look to our high schools." Clancy, formerly of Milwaukee High School, was well aware that it had been "fruitful in vocations in the past" and she and others needed it to "continue to bear fruit in abundance." Bernardine Clancy, RSM, to Dominica Mullin, RSM, October 3, 1932, ASMC; and Cummings, 112–13, 115–16.

34. The initial discussion to move the reception ceremonies to a parish occurred at the November 23, 1952, meeting of the Provincial Council. *Book of Minutes Provincial Council*, Chicago, Sisters of Mercy of the Union in the United States of America (1929–39), 121, ASMC. Joy Clough, RSM, informed me in March 2010 that her reception ceremony in 1962 occurred at Queen of Martyrs and was "broadly attended." Joy Clough, RSM, conversation with author, March 13, 2011.

35. Mercy brochure.

36. Along with Catholic baptism, candidates also had received their first Confession, Holy Communion, and Confirmation. Minutes of the Provincial Council of the Chicago Province (1939–51), 127–28, ASMC; and *Customs and Guide*, 61–62.

37. As mentioned previously, family was a strong motivation for joining a religious community. While some followed aunts or cousins into a congregation, whether the Chicago Province or elsewhere, initially choosing the Sisters of Mercy because of their example, in most cases, family connections were coupled with a desire to serve God. Family might also inspire a daughter to enter

religious life because of the status a vocation brought. This was not simply social status, but the larger Catholic culture understood religious life as something special, and young Catholic women chose a better path becoming sisters or nuns. Some Sisters of Mercy interviewed explained that they had selected the Mercys because a parent had specifically praised these sisters over others or expressed a wish they discern a vocation. Carol Coburn and Martha Smith discuss these motivations and conceptions of religious life in their study of the Sisters of St. Joseph of Carondelet. See *Spirited Lives*, 68–71. McSloy, interview; Focus Group, Mercy Convent Chicago; and Mercy brochure.

38. Mercy brochure. Many of the sisters interviewed who were in the novitiate during this period spoke of their role in Saint Xavier's move to 103rd Street. A consistent memory is the assembly line, which passed furniture and other items on and off moving vehicles. Once established in the new location, novices continued to participate in the upkeep of the new college and high school.

39. *Customs and Guide*, 314 and 316.

40. Depending on the type of degree pursued or the staffing demands placed upon the congregation, some sisters interviewed for this study, such as Madeleva Deegan and Laurette Betz, took eight to ten years to complete their degrees whether in education or nursing. *Book of Minutes Provincial Council* (1939–51), 38, ASMC; McSloy, interview; Membership File, Sister Mary Evangeline Mc-Sloy, ASMC; Madeleva Deegan, RSM, interview with author, Mercy Convent, Chicago, Ill., January 9, 2007; Membership File, Sister Mary Madeleva Deegan, ASMC; Laurette Betz, RSM, Mary Ruth Broz, RSM, Cathleen Cahill, RSM, and Jane Schlosser, RSM, Pastoral Care Ministry Focus Group, audio recording, Mercy Meeting Place, Chicago, Ill., July 29, 2008; and Membership File, Mary Laurette Betz, ASMC. McSloy and Deegan's educational development and work as temporary professed follow the traditional path for teachers. Betz's experience is similar, even though her education and work lay in nursing and hospitals.

41. *Book of Minutes Provincial Council* (1951–54), 81 and 218.

42. Ibid., 114.

43. Stewart, 444–45; and Koehlinger, 30–31.

44. See Membership Files and assignments for this period, ASMC.

45. Mercy brochure.

46. The Mercys' health care facilities included general care as well as hospitals for the mentally ill, totaling eight institutions spread across three states. In terms of number of ministries, education far surpassed that of health care and residences. In Illinois alone, the Mercys staffed forty-eight parish schools. In addition, there were two parish high schools and six academies and high schools for girls. Outside of Illinois, the community taught in one high school for girls in Milwaukee, eleven parish grammar schools in Wisconsin and Iowa, and one high school in Iowa. The community owned and staffed three residences for young single women, two of which were in Milwaukee, the third in Chicago.

47. The term "over the shop" was used by several Sisters of Mercy who participated in focus groups and interviews when discussing experimentation in small
group living at the end of the 1960s and 1970s.

48. *Book of Minutes Provincial Council* (1929–39), 20–21, ASMC.

49. The uniformity of prayer life was one element of debate during the Renewal process. Sister Mary Leo Clark, RSM, Report to Mother Provincial, n.d.
[c. 1940–45], Holy Angels Convent, Chicago, Ill.; and St. Lucy Convent Local
Council Meetings, 1961–68, Chicago, Ill., ASMC.

4. Demanding Decades. Mercy Response to the Clergy and the Laity: 1928–1960s

1. Sisters of Mercy of the Union, *Customs and Guide*, 5.

2. Pope Pius XII and Cardinal Suenens were not the only sources of motivation for women religious to become more engaged in the world. Suenens's book,
published in 1963, had a popular following and is often pointed to as the book
that inspired action among many women religious. Pope Pius XII's authority as
the head of the Church is also important to consider. Leon Joseph Suenens, *The
Nun in the World*, trans. Geoffrey Stevens (Westminster, Md.: The Newman Press,
1963); "June 10, 1952," and "March 15, 1953," Minutes of the Provincial Council Meetings (1951–54), 88 and 157, ASMC; Regina Siegfried, ASC, "Religious
Formation Conference: 'Educating for Deepening Relationships: Theological/
Communal/Societal/ Cultural/Ecological,'" *American Catholic Studies* 120, no. 1
(2009): 55; and Koehlinger, *The New Nuns*, 8–9.

3. If placement of sisters and efficient use of personnel were of the highest
concern of the community, then making time for individual works of mercy,
such as visiting the sick in private homes and visiting inmates in prisons, would
have been anomalies as opposed to a constant presence of the annual statistics
reported to the Mother General. In reality, Mercys, whether in parish schools or
hospitals, were required to record these types of numbers on their fact sheets
submitted to the Mother Provincial. Some sisters had more opportunities to
visit in homes than others, but this does not diminish the importance to the
larger community. See fact sheets for Annual Reports to the Mother General,
1930s–60s.

4. Impediments listed on the form were "marriage, illegitimate birth, epilepsy,
tuberculosis, or any contagious malady, defamation by judicial sentence, a notable natural deformity, a bad reputation or insanity in the family." Furthermore,
"no one who has left another community, whether Novice or Professed, [could]
be admitted." Evelyn Grimes (Sister Mary Noel), Personal Statement/application
to Postulancy, 1929, Personal File Deceased Sisters; and Application forms of
Marguerite, Eileen, and Catherine Rooney, ASMC. The Rooney sisters came from
Washington, Indiana and all worked as teachers within various elementary and
high schools throughout the province, but mainly Chicago and Milwaukee.

5. Sister Mary Noel Grimes, Membership File, ASMC.

6. Sister Mary Andrew Leahy, Membership File, ASMC. Sister Mary Andrew changed her name to Sister Brideen Marie in January 1967.

7. Sisters who worked in hospitals wore a white habit. Sister Imelda Byron remarked that when she was a novice, she spent half a day at St. Paul of the Cross School in Park Ridge, Ill. and found it "thrilling to wear a black veil for the first time, and have the kids address [her] as 'Sister.'" Mary Imelda Byron, Survey, March 20, 1979, and Membership File, ASMC; and Mary Bridgetta Hurley, Membership File, ASMC.

8. Dolan, *The American Catholic Experience*; and Robert Orsi, *Madonna of the 115th Street: Faith and Community in Italian Harlem* (New Haven: Yale University Press, 1988).

9. *Rerum Novarum* condemned socialism, but supported the rights of labor to organize in unions and the individual right to private property. Leo XIII stressed the importance of a cooperative (and mutually beneficial) relationship between workers, capital, and the state. Pius XI's *Quadragesimo Anno* was issued on the anniversary of *Rerum Novarum* and continued Leo XII's message on the condition of labor, but also discussed the principle of subsidiarity. Leo XIII, *Rerum Novarum* (*On Capital and Labor*) May 15, 1891, http://www.vatican.va/holy_father/leo_xiii/encyclicals/documents/hf_l-xiii_enc_15051891_rerum-novarum_en.html, August 23, 2011; Pius X, *Il Fermo Proposito* (*On Catholic Action in Italy to the Bishops of Italy*), June 11, 1905, http://www.vatican.va/holy_father/pius_x/encyclicals/documents/hf_p-x_enc_11061905_il-fermo-proposito_en.html, August 23, 2011; Pius XI, *Quadragesimo Anno* (*On the Reconstruction of the Social Order*), May 15, 1931, http://www.vatican.va/holy_father/pius_xi/encyclicals/documents/hf_p-xi_enc_19310515_quadragesimo-anno_en.html, August 23, 2011; and see Burton Confrey, *Catholic Action: A Textbook for Colleges and Study Clubs* (New York: Benziger Brothers, 1935) for a practical guide to Catholic Action.

10. R. P. Chenu, OP, "Catholic Action and the Mystical Body," in *Restoring All Things: A Guide to Catholic Action*, ed. John Fitzsimons and Paul McGuire (New York: Sheed & Ward, 1938), 8–9; Dolan, 395–96; 408–9; James T. Fisher, *The Catholic Counterculture in America, 1933–1962* (Chapel Hill: University of North Carolina Press, 1989), 51–52; and Colleen McDannell, *The Spirit of Vatican II: A History of Catholic Reform in America* (New York: Basic Books, 2011) 88.

11. Andrew Greeley, *The Church and the Suburbs*, Revised Edition (New York: Paulist Press, 1963), 57–59. Chapter 5 will deal with how women religious implemented religious renewal following the Second Vatican Council.

12. Dolan, *The American Catholic Experience*, 389, 395, and 407.

13. This divide between sisters and the laity was something that women religious sought to bridge by the end of the 1960s. Council Meetings, Mercy High School Convent, Milwaukee, Wis. (1938–46), ASMC. For a larger discussion on the Sister Formation Conference, see Karen Kennelly, CSJ, *Religious Formation*

Conference 1954–2004 (Silver Spring, Md.: Religious Formation Conference, 2009).

14. Kennelly, 14–16.

15. Nine Mercys from the Chicago Province representing elementary to college-level teachers attended a November 1952 NCEA meeting in Atlantic City, including Sister Josetta Butler. Minutes of the Provincial Council Meetings (1951–54), 112, ASMC; and Kennelly, 30.

16. Kennelly, 29–30.

17. Telephone Interview with a Sister of Mercy, February 23, 2010. This sister was a part of the first band to be held back for extra studies before first assignments. She received her Bachelor of Arts in 1959 from Saint Xavier College. By 1955, the 1952 band expected profession in March, but their ceremony was pushed to August and only one ceremony would occur per year as opposed to the years previous with two (March and August). For the sisters in this band, the disappointment came from not seeing family and a lack of explanation as to why such a change occurred. Some were eager to start their ministerial work and the extra years of education without a clear explanation was off-putting.

18. For a discussion of conferences for superiors, see "Opening of the Workshop notes," Conferences & Workshops, 1957–76, ASMC. Sisters from various regions within the province attended educational conferences. Convent chronicles record both small group attendance, as in the case of groups from Iowa, and arrangement of larger trips, as in the case of Mercy High School Milwaukee. For example, see Council Meetings, Mercy High School Convent, Milwaukee, Wis., 1953–56. The quotation comes from the St. Gabriel convent chronicle in Chicago. Chronicles of St. Gabriel Convent, October 1955 to September 1960, 82, ASMC. See Suenens.

19. "Annual Brochures for the Theological Institute at SXC," 1948, quoted in Joy Clough, RSM, *First in Chicago: A History of Saint Xavier University* (Chicago: Saint Xavier University, 1997), 208. Clough shows that opponents of the study of theology for both lay and religious women were concerned that this type of knowledge was beyond women. For a larger discussion of the creation of the Theology Department at Saint Xavier College, see Clough, 207–11.

20. Mary Andrew Healey and Mary Noel Grimes, Educational Record and Membership File, Mary Andrew Healey, and Mary Noel Grimes, ASMC; Sister Ritamary Bradley, ed., *Spiritual and Intellectual Elements in the Formation of Sisters*, quoted in Angelyn Dries, "Living in Ambiguity: A Paradigm Shift Experienced by the Sister Formation Movement," *Catholic Historical Review* 79, no. 3 (July 1993): 478.

21. St. Clara's Club in Milwaukee by the 1960s experienced this downturn and ultimately lost its home to eminent domain and Marquette University's urban renewal plans for their neighborhood. St. Catherine's Home still exists at the time of this writing.

22. Quotation, *Customs and Guide*, 32. Sisters of Mercy have reported that observing the hospitality and kindness of sisters of their youth, particularly visit-

ing sick family members or members of their neighborhood, influenced their decision to enter the community. See focus groups, Mercy Convent and McAuley Manor.

23. It is interesting to note that the Sisters of Mercy discussed closing this hospital in the years leading up to 1969. As late as September 1968, the Archbishop of Dubuque, James Byrnes, would not hear of closing Mercy Hospital, Marshalltown unless the community could not staff it properly. Minutes of Provincial Council Meetings, Province of Chicago, 1965–67, Volume II, Issue I (January 1, 1968–December 31, 1969): 262–63.

24. Susan Thomas, RSM, interview with author, April 26, 2007, Chicago, Ill.; and Sister Mary Susan Thomas, Membership File, ASMC.

25. While Mercy hospitals in Aurora and Davenport benefited from Thomas's education, her path in the late 1960s and 1970s, when she worked for the State of Illinois, points to the direction sisters' education and response to need took Mercys in the post renewal period, which is the subject of Chapter 6.

26. According to a history prepared by the community for Cardinal Albert Meyer in 1958, Mercy Hospital began its affiliation with Loyola School of Medicine in 1919, but severed it in 1935. Joy Clough, RSM, in her history of Mercy Hospital, states that this relationship did not end at this time and continued up through the plans to establish a new health care facility and medical school in the late 1940s and 1950s. Mother Regina Cunningham, RSM, "A Brief History of Mercy Hospital," February 1959, ASMC; and Joy Clough, RSM, *In Service to Chicago: The History of Mercy Hospital* (Chicago: Mercy Hospital and Medical Center, 1979), 66.

27. Mercy Hospital was also not the only health care facility in the area; Michael Reese Hospital, established in the late nineteenth century, was only a few blocks south. According to the 1952 Annual Report, Mercy Hospital admitted 400 African Americans, 191 Jews, 2,373 Protestants, and 7,457 Catholics. Barbara Mann Wall suggests that Mercy administration of its Chicago hospital feared the loss of doctors if the hospital fully integrated its services. Barbara Mann Wall, *American Catholic Hospitals: A Century of Changing Markets and Missions* (New Brunswick, N.J.: Rutgers University Press, 2011), 76–75; and Clough, 73–75.

28. Steven Avella argues that Cardinal Stritch ultimately did not want the Sisters of Mercy to move and was instrumental in keeping the hospital on the Southside. Avella suggests that the Mercys pushed for the move to Skokie, but that due to the Cardinal's influence and other city government political maneuvering, Mercy Hospital remained where it was. See Steven Avella, *This Confident Church: Catholic Leadership and the Life in Chicago, 1940–1965* (Notre Dame: University of Notre Dame Press, 1992), 198–200. Avella, however, concentrates on the issue of urban renewal and Mercy Hospital in the late 1940s prior to the real debate and effort in the 1950s. The minutes of the Provincial Council meetings of the 1950s show that the Sisters of Mercy did desire to move to Skokie and that the racial and economic composition of the surrounding area played a

part in this decision. The minutes also indicate that the plans to move had begun with Cardinal Stritch and they had his support. While council meeting minutes are sanitized to include only the most pertinent issues with sparse documentation of meetings, they do show that the Provincial Council had reservations about this project. They were cautious of Loyola Medical School's potential interference and ultimately the medical staff of Mercy Hospital did not want to move. Only sixteen of ninety-three hospital staff surveyed in 1954 wished to move to Skokie. The Provincial Council minutes state that the younger, less established physicians would move to Skokie and the senior medical staff did not wish to move because they were established on the south side, with relationships with local industry. They also feared Loyola's interference in the hospital administration. See Minutes of the Provincial Council of the Chicago Province (1939–51) and (1951–54) and Minutes of the Provincial Council of the Chicago Province, October 7, 1954 to April 29, 1958, October 1947 through December 1962, ASMC. The October 14, 1954, Provincial Council meeting, in particular, mentioned that about 90 percent of the doctors would not move. See Minutes of the Provincial Council of the Chicago Province, Volume III, 284, ASMC. See also Clough, *In Service to Chicago*, 76.

29. Barbara Mann Wall suggests that poor relations existed between the Cook County Physicians Association for black doctors and Catholic hospitals in general. The organization's president argued that Catholic hospitals did not support a national health program because it would require desegregation of their facilities. Wall does not specifically indicate that only Mercy Hospital, Chicago segregated patients by race, but all Catholic hospitals. Barbara Mann Wall, "Catholic Nursing Sisters and Brothers and Racial Justice in Mid-20th Century America," *ANS Advances in Nursing Science*. 32, no. 2 (2009): 7. For a discussion of the racial apostolate, see Amy Koehlinger, *The New Nuns*. Quotations from Minutes of the Provincial Council of the Chicago Province, Volume II, 1939–51, 265. See Chapter 6 for more discussion of the Sisters of Mercy's policies on integrating the congregation.

30. *Customs and Guide*, 8.

31. John F. McDonald, *Urban America: Growth, Crisis, and Rebirth* (New York: M. E. Sharpe, 2007), 13–14; Lilia Fernandez, *Brown in the Windy City: Mexican and Puerto Ricans in Postwar Chicago* (Chicago: University of Chicago Press, 2010), 131–70 passim; Dionne Denis, "Chicago School Desegregation and the Role of the State of Illinois, 1971–1979," *American Educational History Journal* 37, no. 1 and 2 (2010): 55–73.

32. Transcribed copy of letter. Huberta McCarthy, RSM, to Rt. Rev. Msgr. William E. McManus, January 5, 1965, Mercy High School, ASMC.

33. Ibid.

34. For more history of Loretto Academy, see Suellen Hoy, "No Color Line at Loretto Academy," *Good Hearts*. Mercy High School Chicago was only one of several high schools owned and operated by the Sisters of Mercy at this time.

As previously discussed, the west side of Chicago had Siena High School. Saint Xavier Academy, after its move to 103rd in the mid-1950s, became Mother Mc-Auley High School. There was also Mercy High Milwaukee. For a complete list of secondary schools see Appendix A.

35. Mother Provincial Chicago to Mother General, Bethesda/Washington, May 6, 1946, Holy Angels Academy, ES1–1; and May 13, 1946, Minutes of the Provincial Council of the Chicago Province (1939–51), 107–8, ASMC.

36. The Sisters of Mercy ultimately left St. Finbarr parish school in 1968. Sisters who worked here and at Precious Blood dealt with the changing west side racial composition of both African American and Hispanic residents. By the 1950s, Precious Blood served a Puerto Rican and Mexican community. See St. Finbarr's Chronicle, March 1956–June 1957; St. Finbarr's Chronicle, June 1957–January 1960; and "Most Precious Blood Parish Marks Golden Anniversary," *The New World*, November 29, 1957, 3. Sisters of Mercy began their tenure at St. Raymond School in Mt. Prospect in 1949, St. Joan of Arc School in Skokie in 1953, and Mary, Seat of Wisdom School in Park Ridge in 1957.

37. Mother Mary Huberta McCarthy, RSM, to the Rt. Rev. Msgr. T. V. Lawler, Holy Family Rectory, April 1, 1961; and Sister Mary Owen, RSM, to Mother Huberta McCarthy, RSM, September 13, 1962, ASMC. According to Sister Mary Owen's letter, the pastor paid the sisters $100 a month salary, $10 more than the Diocese of Davenport required of pastors.

38. Agreement between Holy Angels Parish Chicago and Superior of the Sisters of Mercy, Chicago, Ill., September 7, 1920, ASMC.

39. Interview with Evangeline McSloy, RSM, October 15, 2006.

40. "Workshop for Superiors and Administrators," August 3–8, 1963, Conferences & Workshops, 1957–76, ASMC.

41. Superiors and administrators read these same theologians at the "Institute on the Theology of Religious Life," held at the Mother Mercy Novitiate, Province of Chicago, on February 19–21, 1965. The readings suggested to the attendees included Congar's *Power and Poverty in the Church*, Thomas Merton's *Life and Holiness*, Pope Paul VI's *Ecclesiasm Suam*, and Albert Plé's *Communal Life*. The 1961 band of novices were also given freedom to implement this new theology in spiritual life within the novitiate, which informed this younger generation of sisters' entrée into religious life as a professed sister. Telephone interview with Ann Flanagan, RSM, February 25, 2010; and "Institute on the Theology of Religious Life," February 19–21, 1965, Conferences & Workshops, 1957–76, ASMC.

5. "Change Is Blowing Hard": Renewal of Religious Life in the 1960s and 1970s

1. "Opening Prayer on Apostolate Day," *Exchange* 25 (October 23, 1970), 1, ASMC.

2. Ibid.

3. Chapters are assemblies where religious meet to make decisions or vote on issues pertaining to the congregation. Prior to renewal of religious government, sisters at the local level within the Chicago Province voted for delegates to a provincial chapter, who in turn selected delegates to the general chapter. All sisters, including temporary professed sisters, had a vote, but only sisters who had taken perpetual vows could be elected. General chapters decided on issues for all of the Sisters of Mercy of the Union. Mother Generals issued in the form of a letter to the provinces a notification of the date of the general chapter and instructed houses to begin the process of electing delegates three months prior to the event. It was this type of government that was the subject of government reform during renewal. *Customs and Guide*, 268 and 272.

4. Registry Database; Sisters of Mercy of the Union, *Mercy Covenant, Special General Chapter Proceedings* (Washington: Sisters of Mercy Generalate, 1969); and Sisters of Mercy of the Union, *Mercy Covenant* (Bethesda, Md.: Sisters of Mercy of the Union/Sisters of Mercy Generalate, 1972).

5. Subsidiarity is "a principle of social doctrine that all social bodies exist for the sake of the individual so that what individuals are able to do, society should not take over, and what small societies can do, larger societies should not take over." In the Roman Catholic tradition, it is attributed to Pope Pius XI in *Quadragesimo Anno*. Vatican II built upon Pius XI's writings, highlighting and condensing this principle in the documents emanating from the council. "Subsidiarity," Dictionary.com. *Collins English Dictionary—Complete & Unabridged 10th Edition*, HarperCollins Publishers. http://dictionary.reference.com/browse/subsidiarity.

6. "Baby boomer" refers to the generation born in the United States from 1945 to 1964. Those who participated as young adults and college students in the protests and demonstrations of the 1960s are often associated with this generation. George Brown Tindall and David E. Shi, *America: A Narrative History, Brief Sixth Edition* (New York: Norton, 2004), 1048.

7. Mother General Mary Regina Cunningham was elected the National Chair of the Sister Formation Conference in 1961. By 1967, Sister Evangeline McSloy became the Executive Secretary of the organization and worked in Washington, D.C. Minutes of the Provincial Council of the Chicago Province, May 1, 1958 to December 18, 1964, 186–87; and Minutes of Provincial Council Meetings, Province of Chicago, 1965–67, Volume I, Issue II (October 18, 1965–December 26, 1967), 114–15, ASMC.

8. Underline in text. *Agape* 1, no. 1 (Advent 1964): 2, ASMC.

9. *Agape* 1, no. 1 (Advent 1964): 2, ASMC.

10. Werntz, 237–38; and Michael Novak, "The New Nuns," *The Saturday Evening Post* (July 30, 1966): 22.

11. "People of God" refers to the understanding of the Catholic Church as constituted by its members articulated during the Second Vatican Council. While the term was employed prior to Vatican II, the council document, *Lumen Gentium*,

describes the Church as the "new People of God," breaking down an extreme "juridical, institutional image of the church," building upon the theology of the Mystical Body of Christ. Jay Dolan, *American Catholic Experience*, 425; Mark S. Massa, SJ, *The American Catholic Revolution: How the 60s Changed the Church Forever* (New York: Oxford University Press, 2010), 8–9; and Pope Paul VI, *Lumen Gentium* (Dogmatic Constitution of the Church) (November 21, 1964), http://www.vatican.va/archive/hist_councils/ii_vatican_council/documents/vat-ii_const_19641121_lumen-gentium_en.html.

12. Pius XI, *Quadragesimo Anno*, no. 79, in *The Church and the Reconstruction of the Modern World*, ed. Terence P. McLaughlin (Garden City, N.Y.: Doubleday, 1957), 246–47, quoted in Christopher Wolfe, "Subsidiarity: The 'Other' Ground of Limited Government," in *Catholicism, Liberalism, and Communitarianism: the Catholic Intellectual Tradition and the Moral Foundation of Democracy*, ed. Kenneth L. Grasso, Gerard V. Bradley, and Robert P. Hunt (London: Rowan and Littlefield Publishers, Inc., 1995), 87; and Thomas C. Kohler, "In Praise of Little Platoons, Quadragesimo Anno (1931)," in *Building the Free Society: Democracy, Capitalism, and Catholic Social Teaching*, ed. George Weigel and Robert Royal (Grand Rapids, Mich.: William B. Eerdman Publishing Co., 1993), 35.

13. Mary Charles Borromeo Muckenhirn, CSC, ed., *The Changing Sister* (Notre Dame, Ind.: Fides Publisher, Inc. 1965), 7.

14. Pope John XXIII quotes *Quadragesimo Anno* in his 1963 document. See *Pacem in Terris*, 47, http://www.vatican.va/holy_father/john_xxiii/encyclicals/documents/hf_j-xxiii_enc_11041963_pacem_en.html (March 29, 2010). In one instance, the superiors and administrators discussed the manner in which the horarium was set. Superiors were "encouraged" to call upon the sisters in their local houses for suggestions. Sisters, too, were to be reminded that they had a duty to participate in this process as well for the "common good, and the goals of the Institute, in general, and of the particular institution." See "Practical Implementation of General Chapter Decisions," October 9, 1965, Superiors and Administrators Chapter Preparation Workshops, 1963–65, Religious Government, ASMC. Also see Muckenhirn, 7.

15. Amy L. Koehlinger, *The New Nuns*, 45–47; Mary Olga McKenna, "Paradigm Shift in a Women's Religious Institute: The Sisters of Charity, Halifax, 1950–1979," *Historical Studies* 61 (1995): 142–43; Ann Flanagan, RSM, telephone interview with author, February 25, 2010; and January 19 and 30, 1964, March 7, 1964, Chronicles of St. Alphonsus Convent, Mt. Pleasant, Iowa, 1959–65, ASMC.

16. The Provincial Council instructed the local superiors to discuss a single issue a week, for the next four weeks. August 18, 1964, Minutes of the Provincial Council of the Chicago Province, May 1, 1958 to December 18, 1964, 289–90, ASMC.

17. Discussion Questions: Religious Government, Community Life, from Workshop for the Local Superiors, Mistresses of Formation, Provincial Advisory Board, October 9–11, 1964; McAuley High School Convent Chronicles, Chicago,

Ill., 1963–69, 32; October 16 and October 29, 1964, Chronicles of St. Alphonsus, 1959–65; and October 14, 1964, Resurrection Convent Chronicles, Chicago, Ill., 1963–68, 17–18, AMSC.

18. McAuley High School and Resurrection in Chicago and St. Alphonsus in Iowa were not the only local convents gathering for discussions. Conferences held monthly had been going on in the years prior to these meetings in preparation for the general chapter in 1965. While often these conferences were conducted solely for the local house, in other cases, groups from more than one convent came together to share information and for socializing as in the case of Chicago suburban parishes like St. Raymond in Mount Prospect and St. Joseph the Worker in Wheeling, Illinois. Sisters from various local convents also came together for conferences at Saint Xavier College. McAuley High School Convent Chronicles, 1963–69, 32; and October 16 and October 29, 1964 Chronicles of St. Alphonsus, 1959–65, ASMC.

19. "Currents of Thought," *Agape* 1, no. 2 (Easter 1965); and Mary Ignace Garvey, RSM, "Currents of Thought," *Agape* 1, no. 3 (Pentecost 1965), ASMC.

20. By studying the nature of their apostolate, the Mercys considered how they would serve the Church and the world. The time between the first and second sessions gave the leadership a chance to digest the new declarations from Vatican II. At the second session in May 1966, the delegates and leadership had their individual provincials' studies and reports on which to base their decisions, but they considered all these in the context of Vatican II document, *Lumen Gentium*. See Chapter 6 for a larger discussion of renewal and ministry. Werntz, 246–47.

21. The negative reaction to the change tended to come from adult laity and clergy. The students at Mercy High School in Milwaukee, however, reacted positively to the news as mentioned. Sisters at various stages of their religious life, both young and old, appreciated the change in habit, often surprising the younger generation of sisters by their eager embrace of this modification. The Mercys conducted extensive study into the new design of the modified habit. Images of the new habit appeared in print prior to the official change, which caused consternation among some Churchmen and laity. November 11, 1965, and June–August, 1966, *Chronicle of the Sisters of Mercy*, Mercy High School, Milwaukee, Wis., 93, 103–8 passim, ASMC; Mother Mary Paulita Morris to Myron D. Weigle, Assistant City Editor, *Chicago American*, March 2, 1967, ASMC; and Clough, conversation.

22. Werntz, 244–48 passim.

23. Chronicles, St. Cecilia Convent, Chicago, Ill., August 1964–September 1968, 28; *Chronicle*, St. Clotilde Convent, Chicago, Ill., 1960–89, 100; and *Resurrection Convent Chronicle*, 1963–68, 34, ASMC. While constitutional changes awaited approval from Rome, changes to norms, customs, and permissions did go forward. Mother Provincial Huberta McCarthy officially informed the community that Rome had accepted the habit modification in November 1965. The same month

she warned sisters "[u]ntil further notice, please do not purchase pumps to be worn with the new habit." Burlingame, Cedar Rapids, Albany, Auburn, Newfoundland, and Hartford Sisters of Mercy adopted the same style proposed by the Union along with the Chicago Province in June 1966. Sisters did not begin to wear the modified habit until after local bishops saw it and priests knew of the shift. See Huberta McCarthy, RSM, Circular Letters to Chicago Province of the Sisters of Mercy, Ferial Day, November 5, 1965, Feast of St. John of the Cross [December 14], November 24, 1965, and June 15, 1966, ASMC.

24. Huberta McCarthy, RSM, Circular Letter to Chicago Province of the Sisters of Mercy, Feast of St. John of the Cross.

25. Huberta McCarthy, RSM, "Currents of Thought," *Agape* 2, no. 1 (Christmas 1965), ASMC.

26. Edmund Burke, "A Letter to a Member of the National Assembly 1791," quoted in "Into One Bread," *Agape* 2, no. 1 (Christmas 1965): 18, ASMC.

27. Sister Miriam Therese Callahan, RSM, "That 'New Breed' in Community," *Agape* 2, no. 2 (Easter 1966); and Sister Paul Marie [family name unknown], "Christian Authority: The Law of Liberty," *Agape* 2, no. 3 (Pentecost 1966), ASMC. The term "new breed" was not specific to this article. Andrew M. Greeley labeled a minority group of Catholics in their twenties in the mid-1960s who challenged authority and who demanded and expected change within the Catholic Church. According to Greeley, the new breed wanted "a Church that is relevant to its own needs and the needs it sees in the world, and it want[ed] it now, not next week." The new breed was not simply the laity; it was also in seminaries and convents. See Andrew M. Greeley, "The New Breed," *America* (May 23, 1994), http://www.americamagazine.org/content/article.cfm?article_id=11803, March 15, 2011. Miriam Rooney, OP also references this concept in her December 1964 article in *Cross & Crown*. See Miriam Rooeny, OP, "The New Breed Enters the Convent," *Cross & Crown* 16 (December 1964): 396–405. Joseph P. Chinnichi, OFM, "The Catholic Community at Prayer, 1926–1976," in James M. O'Toole, *Habits of Devotion: Catholic Religious Practice in Twentieth-Century America* (Ithaca: Cornell University Press, 2004), 75.

28. Circular Letter, Mother Mary Huberta McCarthy, RSM, Ash Wednesday, February 23, 1966, ASMC.

29. The editorial board of *Agape* included some provincial leaders, like Sister Ignace Garvey.

30. *Agape* editors advertised that they could only publish a few editorials, but that they selected those that represented larger groups of opinions of those they had received.

31. In this way, *Agape* truly became a forum for discussion across the community. Instead of debating issues within one house or one ministry, the periodical allowed views to be aired from various places within the province. Mary Mateo Fearon, RSM, from "Dialogue on Community," *Agape* 3, no. 2 (Pentecost 1967), ASMC.

32. Minutes of Provincial Council Meetings, Province of Chicago, 1965–67, Volume I, Issue II (October 18, 1965–December 26, 1967): 15–16, ASMC; Joy Clough, RSM, *First in Chicago: A History of Saint Xavier University*, 74, 86, and 145–47. At the time of the symposium, the provincial council still appointed the president of Saint Xavier College. The province's disobedience and the Union's awareness of it refer to Mary Regina Werntz, RSM's history of the Union. See Werntz, 250.

33. Michaelyn Fleming, RSM, et al to Sisters of Mercy of the Chicago Province, October 12, 1967, hereafter "The Letter," Religious Government, ASMC. When speaking about this correspondence, current Sisters of Mercy, who were members in 1967, refer to it as "The Letter." Chronicles of St. Gabriel Convent, Chicago, Ill., September 1960 to June 1968, ASMC.

34. Mary Sheehan, RSM, was that provincial advisory board member.

35. Quotations from the Letter. The numbers of departures are drawn from the community registry.

36. The Letter; and "Some Suggestions for Community Action," 1. The accompanying paper refers to Sister Michael Marie O'Brien, RSM, "Adapting to the Needs of the Contemporary Problem," in *Looking Forward to the New Constitutions: A Comprehensive Analysis of a Spirituality of Mercy* (Sisters of Mercy, 1967).

37. "Some Suggestions for Community Action," 1–2.

38. Ibid.

39. Ibid.

40. Chronicles of the Sisters of Mercy, Mercy High School, Milwaukee, Wis., 1967–73, 2, 10–11, 13, ASMC.

41. Mother General Regina Cunningham, RSM, to the Community of Sisters of Mercy of the Province of Chicago, October 20, 1967, ASMC.

42. Catherine McAuley quoted in Mother Regina Cunningham, RSM, to the Community of Sisters of Mercy of the Province of Chicago, October 20, 1967. Some of the local communities commented on the letter from the Mother General. They acknowledged the intent of her correspondence was to calm fears and anxieties that may have arisen due to the Letter. Others, while noting Mother Regina's purpose for writing the letter, also expressed sympathy for the thirteen sisters who had acted with the best intentions. Chronicles of the Sisters of Mercy, Mercy High School Convent, Milwaukee, Wis., 1967–73, 13; and Mary Seat of Wisdom Convent Chronicles, Park Ridge, Ill., 1961–70, 108–9, ASMC.

43. Mother Provincial Paulita Morris, RSM, to Sisters of Mercy, November 7, 1967, ASMC.

44. Renewal Commission, Supplement to Some Suggestions for Community Action, found in Mother Provincial Paulita Morris to Sisters of Mercy, November 7, 1967, ASMC.

45. John Courtney Murray, "Freedom, Authority, Community," *America* 115 (December 3, 1966): 740 quoted in "Religious Government Commission: Local

Leader," Special General Chapter Proceedings 1969. See also "Revision of the Constitution," (Bethesda: Sisters of Mercy Generalate, 1967), ASMC.

46. Sisters of Mercy Chicago, Minutes of Provincial Council Meetings, Province of Chicago, 1965–67, Volume I, Issue II (October 18, 1965–December 26, 1967), 149–50; Mother Provincial Paulita Morris, Circular Letter, c. February 1967 [n.d.]; Werntz, 257; and *Exchange* 1 (1968): 1, ASMC.

47. Government Committee, "Special Insert: Local Government Experiment," Sisters of Mercy, Province of Chicago, July 1968, Religious Government, ASMC.

48. Sisters of Mercy Chicago, Minutes of Provincial Council Meetings, Province of Chicago, 1965–67, Volume I, Issue II (October 18, 1965–December 26, 1967): 215–16; and Paulita Morris, RSM, Circular Letter, August 14, 1968, 3, ASMC.

49. Mother Mary Regina Cunningham to Mother Provincial and Councilors, January 8, 1969; and Mother Paulita Morris, "Opening Speech," January 18, 1969, ASMC.

50. Quotation attributed to Sister Andrea Harvey (New York). Running Minutes of the General Chapter found in Werntz, 266 and 269–70.

51. Mother Paulita Morris, RSM, Circular Letter, Trinity Sunday [June 1], 1969, ASMC.

52. Murray, "Freedom, Authority, Community," 740.

53. "Structural Design for government Plan," September 14, 1969, ASMC.

54. Werntz, 269, 277; Sisters of Mercy, Chicago, Minutes of Provincial Council Meetings, Province of Chicago, 1965–67, Volume III, Issue I (January 1, 1970–December 31, 1970): 388–89, ASMC; and Edward Heston, CSC, Secretary Sacred Congregation for Religious, to Reverend Mother, February 26, 1970, ASMC.

55. September 22, 1968, Chronicle of St. Ita Convent, Chicago, Ill., 1959–76, 185; May 29, 1970 and June 2, 1970, Chronicles of the Sisters of Mercy, Mercy High School Convent, Milwaukee, Wis., 1967–73, 85, ASMC; and Margaret (Peg) Barrett, RSM, Madeleva Deegan, RSM, and Kathleen McClelland, RSM, Changes in Community Living and Purchase of Community-Owned Property Focus Group with author, audio recording, Mercy Meeting Place, Chicago, Ill., July 3, 2008. Most sisters interviewed for this study who experimented in community living established their small group of four to six people in 1968 or 1969 and maintained that core group through 1973. In the 1970s, for those who made changes, most often it had to do with a change in their ministry. Their ministry may have taken them to another location and a switch to another house or apartment became necessary. A more in-depth discussion of community experimentation appears in Chapter 6.

56. Focus Group with Deegan et al, Changes in Community Living and Purchase of Community-Owned Property.

57. George C. Stewart Jr. describes the collection of conciliar and post-conciliar documents intended for women religious between 1965 to 1978 including *Evangelica Testificatio* as causing "considerable confusion." See Stewart, 455–56;

Werntz, 303 and 310; Elizabeth M. Cotter, *The General Chapter in a Religious Institute: With Particular Reference to IBVM Loreto Branch* (Bern: Peter Lang Ltd., 2008), 88; and Kenneth Briggs, *Double Crossed: Uncovering the Catholic Church's Betrayal of American Nuns* (New York: Doubleday, 2006), 195–96.

58. The Religious Life Council was created in 1974. Werntz, 295–96.

59. Werntz, 349–51.

6. Reinventing Community and Service to the World

1. Patricia M. Murphy, RSM, interview by author, Mercy Meeting Place, Chicago, Ill., December 4, 2008.

2. Sister Patricia M. Murphy is referred to as Sister Pat. Murphy, interview.

3. Sister Patricia quoted Sister Serena Gallagher, Mistress of Novices from 1928 to 1957, "Keep the Rule, Sister, and the Rule will keep you." Ibid.

4. Other sisters stressed that keeping the vow of poverty required a mature individual woman religious, making decisions about what is necessary. Others saw that religious poverty was not kept in the community because of how the congregation and Church provides for sisters, especially with the little personal "luxuries" such as hobbies, television programs, and books. Others believed living in an "affluent society of mid-twentieth century America," with all their food, clothing, and board provided. "Into One Bread: Is the Practice of Poverty a Vital and Meaningful Part of Your Daily Living?" *Agape* (Easter 1965), ASMC.

5. "Currents of Thought," *Agape* (Easter 1965), ASMC; Mattias Neuman, OSB, "Religious Vows as a Pilgrim Stewardship," *Sisters Today* 45, no. 3 (November 1973): 124–25, 127, and 132; Rev. Robert Morneau, "'Aboutness': Religious Life Once-Removed," *Sisters Today* 45, no. 3 (November 1973): 136–39 passim, quotations, 138–39; and Patricia Wittberg, SC, *The Rise and Decline of Catholic Religious Orders: A Social Movement Perspective* (Albany: State University of New York Press, 1994), 243–44, and 246.

6. By the early 1970s, sisters scripted their own vow statements, professing promises that reflected their individual experience, but underscored their commitment to the Sisters of Mercy. A 1972 issue of *Exchange* published excerpts from the vows professed at four Chicago Mercys' "permanent commitments," or final professions. These statements were individual and personal expressions of the four women's vows. "Four Sisters Express their Permanent Commitment," *Exchange* 41 (September 1972), ASMC.

7. Their expression of Mercy spirituality and meaning of religious life was in flux, not fully "renewed" until a more formal statement of the congregation's charism in the 1990s. The "new" statement of Mercy charism was not issued until 1992, after the dissolution of the Sisters of Mercy of the Union, of which the Chicago Province was a part, and the formation of the Institute of the Sisters of Mercy of the Americas in 1991. Chapter 7 addresses this change and the formation of the Mercy Charism statement.

8. The discussion in the early 1960s that filled the pages of the community newsletter, *Agape*, faded once implementation of experimentation occurred. *Exchange*, which replaced *Agape*, had a different purpose; initially, it was not a forum for discussion, but rather a source of news. It began to incorporate sisters' comments as it evolved. "Greatest Weakness in Formation Program," *Exchange* 44 (December 1972), ASMC.

9. The quotation in the heading that begins this section is from "Background," Sister Formation Issue, *Exchange* 6, Special Issue (June 1968), ASMC.

10. The number of sisters who left is based upon those who had made it to first profession, and does not include the numbers who left before temporary vows.

11. At this January 1968 renewal weekend, a group from Father Adrian Van Kaam, CSSp, Ph.D.'s Graduate Institute of Formative Spirituality at Duquesne University in Pittsburgh presented a discussion on a new form of religious life. Sisters of Mercy from Chicago (and other religious communities) attended this Institute at Duquesne. Van Kaam's work pertains to the psychology of religion, and in the 1960s, how that pertained to Catholicism. See the Epiphany Association, http://www.epiphanyassociation.org/default.asp (November 19, 2007). Some of the younger sisters expressed frustration with the panel presentations, including the flight attendants present to instruct sisters on how to get in and out of cars while wearing shorter skirts. The Mercys switched to the modified habit about this time. June Anselme, RSM, Mary Ann Bergfeld, RSM, Lois Graver, RSM, and Mary Elizabeth "Betty" Smith, RSM (hereafter Betty Smith, RSM), 7800 Honore Street Focus Group with author, audio recording, Regional Community Center, Chicago, June 30, 2008; quotes: Chronicles of the Sisters of Mercy, Mercy High School Convent, Milwaukee, 1967–73, 18–19; and Resurrection Convent Chronicles, 1963–68, 57, ASMC. In terms of departed or dispensed sisters, by the late 1960s, women who departed the community did not simply vanish from convents, never to be spoken of again, as in previous decades. Provincial communications and newsletters published these departures and asked sisters to pray for them. Furthermore, contact with those who left was not forbidden.

12. Rita Specht, RSM, 80th and Wood Street Focus Group with author, audio recording, Regional Community Center, Chicago, June 23, 2008; and Betty Smith, RSM, 7800 Honore Street Focus Group. The Focus Groups, which drew together sisters who lived in apartments on Honore Street and at 80th and Wood, reflected on the intentionality of their prayer life, ministry, and leisure time, including birthdays and guests for dinner. The Honore Street Focus Group consisted of Sisters Betty Smith, Lois Graver, Mary Ann Bergfeld, and June Anselme. The 80th and Wood Street focus group consisted of Sisters Rita Specht, Sharon Kerrigan, Mary Ruth Broz, Emily Kemppi, and Avis Clendenen.

13. Mary Ann Bergfeld, RSM, 7800 Honore Street Focus Group; and Regine Fanning, RSM, Cora Finnane, RSM, Evangeline McSloy, RSM, and Mary Shee-

han, RSM, St. Clotilde Convent Focus Group with author, audio recording, Mercy Meeting Place, Chicago, July 2, 2008.

14. Prior to this period, bells were rung to call sisters at various points in their day, based on the set horarium. A sister in each convent was assigned to ring the bell in a different manner for each exercise. For example, the bell-ringer tolled the bells twenty times for Mass, twelve for Office, and three for night prayers. Lecture, private spiritual reading, recreation, and meals, as well as rising, all were preceded by a "tinkle without interval." Call bells, or a series of tolls of the bells for individual sisters, were employed in some convents or local houses and each sister had "a duty . . . to answer her bell promptly." Sisters of Mercy of the Union, *Customs and Guide*, 194–95.

15. Sisters always had chores in a local house, but they were assigned duties and often with little variation. Feelings of resentment might have developed if an individual sister were always given the same regrettable chore. Minutes of Provincial Council Meetings, Province of Chicago, 1965–67, Volume I, Issue II (October 18, 1965 to December 26, 1967), 116; and Local Council Meetings, 1961–69, Little Flower Convent Chronicles, Chicago, 97, ASMC.

16. Smith, 7800 Honore Street Focus Group. Sister Betty Smith was one of six sisters, who moved into an apartment near the Little Flower Convent on Honore Street in Chicago in 1969. These sisters were not the first nor the only ones to live in apartments at this time.

17. "Temporalities Commission," *Exchange* 3 (April 29, 1968), ASMC. By the April 1968 issue of *Exchange*, St. James, Immaculate Conception, St. Ann, and Holy Rosary in Chicago; St. Joseph, Libertyville; and Christ the King and St. Patrick, in Milwaukee experimented with a monthly budget. Our Lady of Mt. Carmel, St. Catherine of Genoa, Resurrection, Siena High School, Little Flower, Mother McAuley High School, and Mercy High School in Chicago, and St. Patrick Academy in Des Plaines experimented with a sum of money for convenience. Quotes from October 1968, St. Raymond Convent Chronicle, 167; and Chronicles of Mercy High School Milwaukee, 1967–73, 42, ASMC.

18. "Temporalities Commission."

19. Rose Marian Trahey, RSM, "Proposal," December 28, 1966, Proposals for Experimentation and Related Materials, Local Living, ASMC.

20. "Diverse Work Groups Living Together," n.d. Proposals for Experimentation and Related Materials, Local Living, ASMC.

21. "Sisters Volunteering for Diverse Work Groups Living Together," n.d. Local Living, ASMC; and "A Communication from Sister Virginia Marie Horvath," *Exchange* 1 (1968), ASMC.

22. Cardinal John Cody expressed his "misgivings about experimental living in a June 23, 1969 letter to Mother Paulita. He was "not at all convinced of its value." John Cardinal Cody to Mary Paulita Morris, RSM, June 23, 1969, ASMC; and *Exchange* 1 (1968), ASMC.

23. Mary Anne Cranely and Rita O'Sullivan both left the community by June 1969. Mary Alice Pierce left the Sisters of Mercy for the Poor Clare Sisters in 1978. "The Letter," October 12, 1967; St. Clotilde Convent Chronicles, 1968–69, ASMC; and Mary Sheehan, RSM, St. Clotilde Convent Focus Group. This focus group consisted of five sisters who discussed experimentation in community living. Four of the five lived at St. Clotilde: Sisters Mary Sheehan (1968–69), Regine Fanning (1968–74), Marie Shefchik (1968–89), and Evangeline McSloy (1971–72). The fifth participant, Sister Cora Finnane lived in the convent until this experimentation/program began in 1968, when she was assigned to Christ the King convent, but continued to work in St. Clotilde's school.

24. Several participants in the focus groups conducted for this study commented on their impressions of experimenting in small group living. Most recounted that they felt deeply the significance and newness of what they were doing. 80th and Wood Apartment Focus Group; 7800 Honore Street Apartment Focus Group; and St. Clotilde Focus Group. For the division of chores and daily life of the St. Clotilde experiment, see St. Clotilde Convent Chronicles, 1968–69, ASMC.

25. Regina Cunningham, RSM, to Mother Provincial and Sisters, August 14, 1968; and Paulita Morris, RSM, to Sisters, August 14, 1968, ASMC.

26. The point of shared meals was doubly significant because sisters prepared the food themselves. Prior to this, many local houses employed a cook. October 6, 1968, St. Clotilde Convent Chronicles, 1968–69, ASMC.

27. Initially, the group hoped to have women religious from other communities. *Exchange* 7 (July 15, 1968); and Sister Mary Joyce, "Proposed McAuley East Experiment," *Exchange* 16 (June 2, 1969), ASMC.

28. Werntz, 246.

29. Ibid., 109. The Divine Office includes the recitation of certain prayers throughout the day at specific times. Prayers come from the Breviary, or prayer book. Divine Office is also called the Breviary and Canonical Hours. The parts of the Divine Office are Lauds (Prayer at dawn), Prime (early morning prayer), Terce (mid-morning prayer), Sext (midday prayer), None (mid-afternoon prayer), Vespers (evening prayer), Compline (night prayer), and Matins (prayer during the night, also known as Vigils or Nocturns). Ferdinand Cabrol, "Divine Office," *The Catholic Encyclopedia* (New York: Robert Appleton Company, 1911), from *New Advent*, http://www.newadvent.org/cathen/11219a.htm (accessed on November 23, 2012).

30. McAuley High School Convent Chronicles, 1963–69, 75–76, ASMC; and Sisters of Mercy of the Union, *Mercy Covenant*, W-4.

31. St. Ita Convent Chronicle, 1959–1976, October 21, 1970, 215; and St. Clotilde Convent Chronicle, 1960–89, 138–39, ASMC.

32. Some of the suggested readings for the Mercys were an 1961 reprinting of the 1911 edition of Evelyn Underhill, *Mysticism: A Study in the Nature and*

Development of Man's Spiritual Consciousness, Hall Bridges, *American Mysticism*, 1970, the 1971 reprinting of 1941 edition of Alan Watts, *Behold the Spirit: A Study in the Necessity of Mystical Religion*, and Louis Dupres, *The Other Dimension: A Search for the Meaning of Religion*, 1972. The House of Prayer appealed to others in Chicago, with Sisters of the Blessed Virgin Mary, Sisters of Providence, Sisters of St. Joseph, Franciscans, Holy Spirit Missionaries, Adrian Dominicans, and the Adorers of the Precious Blood also participating in this movement. Sister Mary Laureen Kenny, "Summer House of Prayer '72," *Exchange* 39 (April 1972); Sister Sharon Burns, Generalate Prayer Committee, "Suggested Readings for Personal Study of Prayer," *Exchange* 41 (September 1982), ASMC; and *Mercy Covenant*, W-5.

33. "Evaluation of Community Living Experience at St. Clotilde, 1968–69," *Exchange* 16 (June 2, 1969), ASMC.

34. Often the need to move from a parish convent came from pastors and parishioners who wanted to use the buildings or sell them. Mary Catherine McDonagh, RSM, Changes in Community Living Focus Group, Regional Community Center, Chicago, June 23, 2008. This focus group consisted of Mary Catherine McDonagh, RSM, Ann Sullivan, RSM, and Helen Weinfurter, RSM. Joella Cunnane, RSM, Community-Owned Homes Focus Group with author, audio recording, Mercy Meeting Place, Chicago, July 23, 2008. This focus group consisted of Dorothy Burns, RSM, Joella Cunnane, RSM, Conleth, Foley, RSM, Margaret Lyons, RSM, and Judith Niemet, RSM. The conversation between Mother Mary Paulita Morris and Sister Betty Smith occurred when the Provincials were staying at McAuley for the upcoming Provincial Chapter. Sister Betty was serving a meal in the dining room and Mother Paulita casually inquired after the young sister's health. Sister Betty's reply was daring because she spoke in a pointed manner about her discontent. The details of the conversations used here come from Sister Betty's recounting of the events forty years after the meeting took place. She also recalled feeling trepidation upon approaching Mother Paulita a second time with her proposal for apartment living. Smith, 7800 Honore Street Focus Group.

35. 7800 Honore Street and 80th and Wood Street Focus Groups; and "Sisters of Mercy Province of Chicago Residency Data, 1970–1983," Local Living, ASMC.

36. A homily is a sermon and given traditionally during the Mass by the celebrant (priest) following the Liturgy of the Word (first and second readings, and Gospel). A concelebrating priest or deacon may give the homily. It is normally an exposition on the readings during the liturgy. For the late 1960s, it was unusual for women religious to give the homily. For a description of the parts of the Mass, see "The Structure and Meaning of the Mass," United States Conference of Catholic Bishops, 2011, http://www.usccb.org/prayer-and-worship/sacraments/eucharist/structure-and-meaning-of-the-mass-backgrounder.cfm. 80th and Wood Street Focus Group; and "Our Newest Members," *Exchange* 17 (October 30, 1969), ASMC.

37. Avis Clendenen commented that at the time, she did not understand fully the changes that occurred when she was first going through formation. She was not aware that how unique it was that she had an individualized formation experience or that she could select her own retreat, for example, because she entered as these changes evolved. Clendenen made her first profession in 1973 and departed ten years later in 1983. 80th and Wood Street Focus Group, "Our Newest Members." See October 6, 1968, Minutes of Provincial Council Meetings, Province of Chicago, 1965–67, Volume II, Issue I (January 1, 1968 to December 31, 1969): 264; and February 13, 1970, Minutes of Provincial Council Meetings, Province of Chicago, 1965–67, Volume III, Issue I (January 1, 1970 to December 31, 1970): 391–92, ASMC.

38. "Sisters of Mercy Province of Chicago Residency Data 1970–1983"; Inviolata (Catherine) Gallagher, RSM, "Concerns from the Viewpoint of Provincial Administration," *Exchange* 48 (April 1973), ASMC; and 7800 Honore Street Focus Group.

39. For numbers of departures, see the Registry Database. One sister who caused the provincial leaders concern about living alone was Sister Patricia M. Murphy, who had returned from Peru a few years earlier. In this case, provincial leaders were concerned that Sister Patricia would feel isolated particularly as she adjusted to life in the United States after Peru. Religious Life Council, Minutes of Provincial Council Meetings, Province of Chicago, 1972–1973, Vol. I (January 1, 1972 to December 31, 1972), 46, ASMC.

40. Inviolata (Catherine) Gallagher, RSM, "Concerns from the Viewpoint of Provincial Administration," *Exchange* 48 (April 1973), ASMC; 80th and Wood Street Focus Group; "Open House October 27th at All West Side Houses," *Exchange* 50 (October 1973), ASMC; and 7800 Honore Street Focus Group. The two sisters from Mercy High School Milwaukee who moved into an apartment in 1973 were Sisters Mary Barbara Cantorer and Mary Hanseder. Both sisters attended Mercy High School and later taught there in the two years prior to moving into their apartment in 1973. See December 18, 1973, Chronicles of the Sisters of Mercy of Our Lady of Mercy Convent, Milwaukee, Wis., 1973–83, 4, ASMC.

41. Sisters participating in focus groups presented to the author both a sense that these were challenging times in terms of interpersonal relationships, but also that they came out on the other side of this period a stronger community. The effort to protect community ties continued throughout the remainder of this period. 7800 Honore Street Focus Group.

42. Margaret Lyons, RSM, and Dorothy Burns, RSM, Community-Owned Homes Focus Group.

43. Joella Cunnane, RSM, Community-Owned Homes Focus Group. Sister Jonella Bohmann reported that while there were always people who commented that those who lived in apartments were not acting as real sisters, she found that most perceived "nothing negative" in what they did; they were "just people."

Jonella Bohmann, telephone interview with author, June 26, 2008. Sister Jonella lived with the group at 80th Street in Chicago, but at the time of this interview, resided in Milwaukee, Wis.

44. Province of Chicago Administration Minutes, Resource/Service Council (June 22, 1973 to June 4, 1976), 28.

45. Sisters of Mercy, Chicago, Executive Department Minutes, 1973–76 (July 6, 1973 to June 8, 1976), 83; and Sisters of Mercy, Chicago, Province of Chicago Administration Minutes, Resource/Service Council (June 22, 1973 to June 4, 1976), 28, ASMC.

46. As local groups determined with whom they would live, friction could arise if all could not agree or if a house did not have room for a sister. Executive Department Minutes, 1973–76, 86; Province of Chicago Administration Minutes, Resource/Service Council, 30; and "Residency Policies and Committees," Sisters of Mercy Chicago Province, December 2, 1982, ASMC.

47. Margaret "Peg" Barrett, RSM, Changes in Community Living and Purchase of Community-Owned Property Focus Group with author, audio recording, Mercy Meeting Place, Chicago, July 3, 2008. This focus group consisted of Peg Barrett, RSM, Madeleva Deegan, RSM, and Kathleen McClelland, RSM.

48. The pastor of St. Charles Lwanga sent a certified letter and gave the sisters until June 31, 1985 to leave, which caused a degree of mirth among the sisters due to the nonexistence of this date. The parish located at Garfield and Wentworth on the south side of Chicago was created when St. Anne and St. Cecelia merged in 1971 and served African American Catholics. St. Anne's had been a predominantly black parish since the 1940s. There were nine women religious living at St. Charles Lwanga by 1985: Sisters Mary Ellen Nolan, RSM, who worked at Mercy Hospital; Peg Barrett, who worked in the parish and in the Catholic School Board for the Archdiocese; Marion "Dolly" Cypser, RSM, who worked at St. Catherine of Siena in Oak Park as principal; Mary Catherine McDonagh, RSM, who taught eighth grade, was a youth minister, and assistant principal at St. James; Margaret "Marge" Lynes, who was the principal at St. James; Dorothy Burns, who was the vice president of Mercy Hospital; a Sister of Notre Dame de Namur, and two others. Barrett, Community-Owned Homes Focus Group.

49. Nadine Hargadon, RSM, "Many Ministries; One Convent," *Dimensions* 2, no. 1 (Winter 1980): 13, ASMC; Sarah Coyle, "Progressive Nuns: Sisters of Mercy Break Free of Tradition to Be CPA's, Chaplains in Business World," *Park Ridge Herald*, December 17, 1981, 17; July 14, 1983, Mary Seat of Wisdom Chronicles, 1961–70, 139, ASMC; and Deegan, Community-Owned Homes Focus Group.

50. Cunnane; and Barrett.

51. June 15, 1973, Minutes of Provincial Council Meetings, Province of Chicago, 1972–73, Vol. II, 51–52, ASMC. These properties include four on the south side of Chicago, one other in Aurora, and an apartment building in Oak Lawn;

"Recall, Respond, Reach Out: Present, Future Depend on Past," *Exchange* 58 (February 1975), ASMC; and 80th Street Focus Group.

52. In subsequent decades, places like Mercy Convent in Chicago, offered more options for elderly sisters who required some nursing assistance, but did not need full-time care. The province also developed a similar assisted living residence in Aurora, Illinois, which they opened to the lay and other religious as well. Aurora became the site of the province's full-time nursing care facility, McAuley Manor. See Chapter 7 for a discussion of this transition.

53. *Mercy Covenant*, n.p., quoted in *Exchange* 24 (September 15, 1970), 1, ASMC.

54. *Exchange* 24 (September 15, 1970), ASMC.

55. Smith, Honore Street Focus Group.

56. Catherine Maura Holan, RSM, "Activities at the Wheeling Apartment," *Exchange* 18 (December 16, 1969), ASMC.

57. Ibid.; and Murphy, interview.

58. Other sisters who worked at Mercy Hospital's community outreach program were Sisters June Anselme and Ann Flanagan. Sister Pat went on to work with the Little Brothers—Friends of the Elderly, at Su Casa Catholic Worker with refugees from Latin America, taught at the Austin Career Center on the west side of Chicago, and worked at Casa Notre Dame for homeless women. Murphy, interview.

59. The Sisters of Mercy were not the only ones taking new steps in ministry at this time. The reference to "in the world" comes from Cardinal Leon Joseph Suenens, *The Nun in the World* (1962), which inspired many communities of women religious to re-conceptualize their ministry. This quote comes from a subcommittee of the Hospital Apostolate Commission in 1968. This is one of many subcommittees and commissions developed in this period that were short-lived or were remade into a different part of the evolving reformed government of the post renewal period. Hospital Apostolate Commission, *Exchange* 8 (September 8, 1968), ASMC.

60. *Exchange* 30 (March 1971) featured examples of new apostolates. Quotations come from "Sister Audrey Stech, Clinical Care Coordinator, Psychiatric Nursing at West Side VA Hospital," *Exchange* 30 (March 1971), ASMC.

61. *Exchange*, Issue 8 (September 8, 1968), ASMC.

62. *Exchange*, Issue 2 (April 8, 1968), ASMC.

63. Retrenchment was the term given to the process of withdrawing of sisters from parish schools.

64. July 16, 1958, Resurrection Convent Chronicle, 1956–58, ASMC; and Karen Hansen, "End of the Line for 8 Catholic Schools," *Chicago Daily News*, June 28, 1968.

65. St. Thomas Aquinas Survey, n.d, ASMC.

66. Ibid.

67. John Linstead, "Teacher Shortage: Nuns to Leave 10 Schools," Chicago Daily News, July 14, 1970; "The Facts on the Sisters of Mercy Pull-Out," December 17, 1970; and Sister M. Honora, "Letters to the Editor: Mercy Sisters Deny Charles of Racism," December 30, 1970.

68. *Mercy Covenant*, 95–97.

69. Mother Provincial Domitilla Griffin received a request by a Chinese woman for admittance, but with the approval of Mother General Bernardine Clancy, she directed the young woman to a community of Chinese women. See Domitilla Griffin, RSM, to Reverend John S. Quinn, December 8, 1950. In January, Mother General Bernardine Clancy addressed the question of admitting African American women into their novitiate and asserted that they should not speak directly to this issue, or deny a candidate based upon race, but instead deflect the application based upon individual merits and ability to fit into the community. In the early 1950s, due to the inequity between whites and blacks in the United States, the presumption was that "the question of the background of a colored applicant would, no doubt, require closer scrutiny than that of our usual applicants." Mother General Bernardine suggested in 1951 that if African American women were to be admitted, the community would accept her as a domestic servant. See Domitilla Griffin, RSM, to Bernardine Clancy, RSM, November 27, 1949; and Bernardine Clancy, RSM, to Domitilla Griffin, RSM, January 17, 1951, ASMC.

70. Sisters of Mercy of the Union, *The Policies of the Sisters of Mercy of the Union on the Question of Social Equality*" (Bethesda, Md.: Sisters of Mercy Generalate, 1965), 5, quoted in Werntz, 202.

71. By 1980, the Sisters of Mercy continued to work in fifteen parish schools, and by 1990, that number declined even further. For a full list of parish schools and dates the Sisters of Mercy withdrew from them, see Appendix A.

72. One or two sisters remained at Mary Queen of Heaven in Chicago and Immaculate Conception in Milwaukee into the 1980s. Mercys remained at the Immaculate Conception convent long after they no longer taught at the school in the 1980s.

73. From the description of the "mini" school, the plan appeared to take on many of the characteristics of the Montessori method. Margaret Lyons, RSM, "Saint James School!" *Exchange* 48 (April 1973), ASMC. The Mercys at St. James had been dealing with "real problems" for a couple of decades. In the 1950s, the faculty of Saint James School worked to address the needs of their students while they dealt with a shifting neighborhood population. By 1950, St. James was part of the larger Archdiocesan mission to African Americans. The 1950s language emanating from the parish focused on the "instruction and care of large Negro Population" and the successful baptism of this "neglected race" who the Sisters of Mercy served. Throughout the 1950s, the sisters faced declining enrollments and increasing petty crimes and vandalism. In one case in May 1957, the convent discovered their lawn mower, two typewriters, a phonograph, and four suitcases missing and "[t]wo sisters, a bell and a bat [kept] vigil" that night. Reports of

shootings and other violence in the neighborhood filtered into the chronicles by the end of the decade. In the 1960s, the sisters at St. James attended lectures and meetings regarding inner-city schools and new programs to help children. They went to a Catholic Inter-Racial Meetings and heard Martin Luther King speak, attended Urban Apostolate meetings, prayed for civil rights workers in Alabama in 1965, and set up a HeadStart program. "Saint James Catholic School," October 1950; St. James Chronicles, 1954–57, 192; August 3 and 6, 1958, St. James Chronicles, 1957–59; St. James Chronicles, 1959–64, 175, 179; and St. James Chronicles, 1964–71, 13, 35, 42, and 44, ASMC.

74. Mary Honora McNicholas, RSM, "Education as Ministry," *Exchange* 47 (March 1973), ASMC. CCD stands for Confraternity of Christian Doctrine, an association within the Catholic Church established to provide religious education programs for children. Religious education classes for children commonly were referred to as CCD.

75. Mary Sullivan, RSM, "Social Justice Activities: Resurrection," *Exchange* 38 (March 1972), ASMC; and Hoy, 150–52.

76. Many of the sisters serving Chicago parish schools in the 1960s experienced racial rioting in the 1960s, particularly after the assassination of Martin Luther King, Jr. in 1968. Sisters at schools on the west side of Chicago, in particular, had rioting in their neighborhood. Sisters at St. Patrick Academy were relocated because of potential fire. Other sisters in convents like St. Malachy School on Washington Boulevard faced similar dangers. In the midst of the rioting, sisters from St. Clotilde on the south side brought food and blankets to St. Catherine of Siena parish for victims of the riots. Sisters also dealt with growing gang violence among their students. In one instance, sisters at Precious Blood School navigated growing tensions between their students and those at the neighboring William H. Public School in 1962. Chronicle of St. Ita Convent, 1959–76, 152; Joella Cunnane, RSM, "Partners in Service, 1883 to the Present," *Dimensions* 4, no. 3 (Spring/Summer 1983), 4; Chronicles, St. Clotilde Convent, 1960–89, 128; and Chronicles, Precious Blood School, 1958–63, 122, ASMC.

77. Koehlinger, 227.

78. *Exchange* 24 (September 15, 1970), ASMC; and "Focus: Mercy Hospital Clinic: Who Says Service Is Impossible within Our Institutions?" *Exchange* 54 (March 1974), ASMC; and Ann Flanagan, RSM, telephone interview with author, February 25, 2010.

79. Laurus Gannon, RSM, Eleanora Holdgrafer, RSM, and Vernarda Lance, RSM, Iowa Focus Group with author. Chicago Regional Community Center, Chicago, June 4, 2007; and "Iowa Paper Features RSM Family Nurse Practitioners," *Exchange* 8, no. 4 (April 1977), ASMC. In 1988, Sister Brigid Condon continued the legacy of Catherine McAuley when she created the House of Mercy in Des Moines for pregnant women.

80. Joy Clough, RSM, "Focus: Sister Lois: Extending the Apostolate," *Exchange* 52 (December 1973), ASMC.

81. "The Whole Idea: To Keep Kids from Getting a Number," *Exchange* 60 (May 1975); and "Focus: Mary Mel O'Dowd," *Exchange* VIII, no. 3 (February 1977), ASMC.

82. *Exchange* 25 (October 23, 1970), 6, ASMC; and Mary Loftus, RSM, interview with author, October 28, 2008, Mercy Meeting Place, Chicago.

83. Julie Neal, RSM, "Pastor—It's a Verb, Not a Noun," *Dimensions* 1, no. 3 (Summer 1979): 3, ASMC; and Jane Schlosser, RSM, Pastoral Care Ministry Focus Group with author, audio recording, Mercy Meeting Place, Chicago, July 29, 2008. This focus group consisted of Laurette Betz, RSM, Mary Ruth Broz, RSM, Cathleen Cahill, RSM, and Jane Schlosser, RSM.

84. "Mercy Hospital, Davenport," *Exchange* 46 (February 1973), ASMC.

85. Laurette Betz, RSM, Pastoral Care Ministry Focus Group.

86. At the time of this publication, the Catholic Church continued to define chaplain as solely a male clerical role. Women also cannot act as chaplains in Veterans Administration hospitals, despite the Denver court ruling that barring women from these positions is illegal. According to the VA, chaplain applicants must receive approval from their particular church authorities. See "Catholic Women Chaplains: Yes and No," *Christian Century* (May 19–26, 1993), 547.

87. The quotation in the heading that begins this section is from Concilia Moran, RSM, "Women in World and Church," *Exchange* 59 (March 1975), ASMC.

88. For the sub-committee to study women's ordination, see November 12, 1972, Minutes of Provincial Council Meetings, Province of Chicago, 1972–73, Vol. I, 91, ASMC.

89. Concilia Moran, RSM, "Women in World and Church," *Exchange* 59 (March 1975), ASMC.

90. Mary J. Henold, Catholic and Feminist: The Surprising History of the American Catholic Feminist Movement (Chapel Hill: University of North Carolina Press, 2008); 80th and Wood Street Focus Group; and "RSM's Discuss Women's Ordination," *Exchange* 62 (December 1975), ASMC.

91. "RSMs Discuss Women's Ordination."

92. "RSMs Discuss Women's Ordination"; Jason S. Lantzer, "Hoosier Episcopalians, the Coming of Women's Ordination and the 1979 Book of Common Prayer," *Anglican & Episcopal History* 72, no. 2 (2003): 234; and Margaret Farley, RSM, "Moral Imperatives for the Ordination of Women," quoted in Henold, *Catholic and Feminist*, 125–26.

93. Executive Department Minutes, 1973–1976, 176; and "RSMs Discuss Women's Ordination."

94. They had done this in March 1977 when they contributed funds to support a Quixote Center study, "Will the People Ever Be Ready," whose purpose was to ascertain the readiness of Catholics for women priests. Sisters of Mercy, Chicago, Province Team Minutes (June 1976 to June 1979), 90–92, 106–8, and 118; and Henold, 167–69.

95. Province Team Minutes, 157–58, 180, 185–86, 198, 249, and 254, ASMC.

96. Henold, 230–31; Heidi Schlumpf, "Call Waiting: The Stories of Five Women Who Want to Be Priests," *US Catholic* (February 2001), 17; and Mary Ruth Broz, RSM, Pastoral Care Ministry Focus Group.

Part III. New Life, New Paths, Same Spirit: Carrying Mercy into the Twenty-First Century, 1980s–2008

1. This is an excerpt from a letter from Catherine McAuley to a sister at Kingstown, Ireland paraphrased by Mother Austin Carroll in the first of four volumes, *Leaves of the Annals of the Sisters of Mercy*. The original letter is believed lost. The passage is used and further paraphrased by numerous communities of Sisters of Mercy, including the Chicago Mercys on their newsletters in the months leading up to the West Midwest reconfiguration. I wish to give a special thank you to Mary Sullivan, RSM, for finding the source of this passage. Mary Teresa Austin Carroll, *Leaves from the Annals of the Sisters of Mercy, in Four Volumes, Volume I: Ireland* (New York: The Catholic Publication Society, 1881), 73.

7. "This Far by Faith": Reimagined Religious Life and the Sisters of Mercy

1. Sisters of Mercy of the Union, *Core Constitutions* (1986), 7–8, ASMC.
2. Judith Niemet, RSM, "Dancing into the Future," *Dimensions* 4, no. 3 (Spring/Summer 1983): 7–11, ASMC.
3. This same letter is used to open the Introduction of this book.
4. Niemet, 8–9.
5. *Dimensions* debuted in the late 1970s and many of the volumes of the first years of publication did contain features on the community's history. The Mercys celebrated the 150th anniversary of the founding of their congregation in Ireland in 1981 and many of the articles touched on that legacy. See Joy Clough, RSM, "Mercy: The Unifying Spirit," *Dimensions* 3, no. 3 (Summer 1981): 6–10, ASMC.
6. Lucille McKillop, RSM, "Address to RSM Assembly," March 4, 1995, ASMC.
7. McKillop, 2.
8. As part of the revision of their government, Mercys convened assemblies to review and discuss issues upon which the community decided. In the past, local houses voted to name delegates to the provincial chapter where one of the main and at times only duties of the delegates was to elect delegates to the general chapter. As discussed in Chapter 5, this system of government gave way to the more participatory style of democratic government in the post-renewal period.
9. Sister of Mercy, telephone interview with author, June 8, 2011.
10. The quotation in the heading that begins this section is from Sisters of Mercy of the Union, *Core Constitutions* (1983), 2, ASMC.
11. In focus groups and interviews, Chicago Mercys discussed that they had access to Catherine McAuley's *Maxims* and *Familiar Instructions*, as well as bio-

graphical writings while in formation, but that increased in the post–Vatican II period, with new scholarship, including studies conducted by Sisters of Mercy themselves. For examples of Sisters of Mercy scholarship on their foundress, see Janet Ruffing and Theresa Moser, "An Option for Women?" *The Way* (Summer 1992): 89–100; and *Catherine McAuley: Timeless Legacy, The MAST Journal, The Journal of the Mercy Association in Scripture and Theology* 6, no. 2 (Spring 1992). This volume of *The MAST* was dedicated to the manner in which Catherine McAuley's construction of a religious institute and her spirituality in the nineteenth century resonated in the late twentieth century in the various manifestations of Mercy ministries, community, and prayer life and includes contributions from Angela Bolster, RSM; Helen Marie Burns, RSM; Mary Celeste Rouleau, RSM; Julia Upton, RSM; Grace Leggio Agate, RSM; Megan Brown, RSM; Ann Marie Caron, RSM; Marilyn Sunderman, RSM; and Mary Rose Bumpus, RSM.

12. Ruffington and Moser, 93, 95–96; and Angela Bolster, RSM, "Catherine McAuley: From the Edges of History to the Center of Meaning," *The MAST Journal* 6, no. 2 (Spring 1992): 1–2.

13. This re-examination of Catherine McAuley's founding charism was not unique to Chicago and all Mercys throughout the United States and internationally engaged in this type of study.

14. Dolores Liptak, RSM, "A US Sister of Mercy Dialogues with Tradition," 1; "Spirit and Mission," *Core Constitutions*, Sisters of Mercy, 1983, 1; and Margaret Susan Thompson, "Charism or Deep Story? Toward a Clearer Understanding of the Growth of Women's Religious History in Nineteenth Century America," *Review for Religious* (May/June 1999).

15. Italics in original. "The Spirit of the Institute," *A Guide for the Religious Called Sisters of Mercy. Amplified by Quotations, Instructions, Etc.* (London: Robson and Son, 1886), 1; and Liptak, 2.

16. Sisters of Mercy of the Union, *Constitutions* (Silver Spring, Md.: Sisters of Mercy of the Union, 1986), 4. Regina Werntz, RSM, discusses the "reflection on the Mercy charism" in the early 1970s in her work, *Our Beloved Union*. Werntz argues that in the general chapters, discussion of the charism revolved around Catherine McAuley's original intent and how that historically fit with their ministerial life. See Werntz, 316–17.

17. *Constitutions*. See Sullivan and M. Michael Lappetito, RSM, "Our Life Together in Mercy: Toward an Apostolic Spirituality" (Federation of the Sisters of Mercy of the Americas, 1980), 4–5, and 9–10. See also David D. Hall, ed., *Lived Religion in America: Toward a History of Practice* (Princeton: Princeton University Press, 1997).

18. Janet K. Ruffing, RSM, "The Burning of the Heart on Account of Creation," *The MAST Journal* 5, no. 2 (Spring 1995): 23. Ruffing's essay is a revised version of the 1994 Mercy Day (September 24) address given at Hartford, Connecticut.

19. Mary Ellen Nolan, RSM, "'Rich in Mercy': A Shared Meditation," *Dimensions* 4, no. 3 (Spring/Summer 1983): 24–25, quote 24; Mercy Health Conference

Task Force, *"Dives in Misericordia (Rich in Mercy)*: A Guide to the Encyclical," (Farmington Hills, Mich.: Mercy Health Conference, 1983), 1; Carol Estelle Wheeler, RSM, "Catherine: A Reflection on Values from the Mercy Tradition" (Baltimore: Mercy High School, 1991), 4–5; and Mary C. Sullivan, RSM, "Catherine McAuley in the Nineteenth and Twenty-First Centuries," ed. Elizabeth Davis et al., *"Fire Cast on the Earth-Kindling": Being Mercy in the Twenty-first Century, International Mercy Research Conference 9–12 November 2007* (Mercy International Association, 2009), 90.

20. *Exchange* 21 (June 1970), 3–4, ASMC.

21. Kathy Thornton, RSM, "Presentation to Mercy Continuing Formation: Goals for Experiencing Mercy 1986," October 1985, ASMC.

22. "Re-examining the Vows: A Call to Conversation," and "Poverty in Our Times: Simplicity and Service in Our Lives, 1988 Program," ASMC.

23. "Poverty in Our Times"; and Corlita Bonnarens, RSM, and Jeanette Noonan, RSM, "Women of Mercy, Women of Peace: Novena for Mercy Day, September 1985," ASMC. Joseph Hilgers, "Novena," *The Catholic Encyclopedia*, Vol. 11 (New York: Robert Appleton Company, 1911), http://www.newadvent.org/cathen/11141b.htm, June 20, 2011.

24. Statement of Mercy Charism, April 11, 1992.

25. The quotation in the heading that begins this section is from *Core Constitutions* (1986), 7–8.

26. Sister Mary Fearon, RSM, "Ministry: A Responsible Choice," *Dimensions* 5, no. 3 (Summer 1984): 22.

27. Ibid., 22–24.

28. Core Constitutions, 1986, 7–8.

29. Gilmary Bauer, RSM; M. Irenaeus Chekouras, RSM; Karen Donahue, RSM; Agnes Mansour; Margaret S. Thompson; and Linda Werthman, RSM, "An Examination of the Context of Ministry," Task Force on Our Context, Sisters of Mercy of the Union, September 1988, 19, ASMC.

30. By historical Catherine McAuley, I mean the study of who Catherine McAuley was within the context of her time, culture, and society as opposed to the timeless nature of who she is as the spiritual founder of the Sisters of Mercy.

31. Sisters of Mercy of the Union, "Ministry: Our Story and Our Context," December 1988, 1–2, ASMC.

32. "Ministry: Our Story and Our Context," 3.

33. Institute of the Sisters of Mercy of the Americas, "Direction Statement," July 1995, ASMC.

34. The quotation in the heading that begins this section is from *Core Constitutions*, 1983, 2. Active renewal of the Mercys' religious life "ends" with the approval of the new Core Constitutions in the early 1980s. The growth and development of the Mercys religious life, however, does not end; rather, it continues to evolve throughout the end of the twentieth century.

35. "Ministry: Our Story and Our Context," 5.

36. Membership numbers and percentages in ministry are drawn from the Registry database and provincial and regional community reports to the Union and Institute governance, and reports to the Chicago members. There are discrepancies in reporting the number of members by year, due to the time of year a report was submitted. For example, the 1980 report submitted at the beginning of the year reports that there were 603 sisters in the Chicago Province, but a later report that same year gives 593 as the membership number. The number in active ministry for both reports is 393. Often sisters who were fully retired and not drawing a wage or salary volunteered. The various reports to leadership and the community did not consistently break down the retired sisters into retired volunteers and retired non-volunteers. By comparison, the Chicago community's ministry statistics are slightly higher for active ministry than those for the entire Sisters of Mercy of the Union and its membership is one of the larger communities for the Union and its successor, the Institute in the 1990s. The population remained one of the larger ones as it came together with the other communities of West Midwest in 2008.

37. "Ministry: Our Story and Our Context."

38. The quotation in the heading that begins this section is from *Core Constitutions*, 1983, 2.

39. Saint Xavier College became Saint Xavier University in 1992.

40. Lourdes Sheehan, RSM, Mary Bender, and Stephen O'Brien, *A Study of Opinions and Attitudes of the Sisters of Mercy, Members of Mercy High Education Colloquium, Mercy Secondary Education Association, and Mercy Elementary Education Network* (Silver Spring, Md.: Sisters of Mercy of the Union, 1986), 48–50; Annual Statistical Report: Ministry, 1985–89; Chicago Annual Statistical Report: Ministry, Sisters of Mercy of the Union, July 1, 1989 to June 30, 1990, ASMC; and Sister of Mercy, telephone Interview with author, June 8, 2011. At the time of the writing of this book, only one Sister of Mercy currently teaches at Mother McAuley Liberal Arts High School.

41. Colette Jolie, RSM, "Unsung Heroines of the Classroom," *Dimensions* 2, no. 1 (Winter 1980): 3, ASMC. Janet Ruffing, RSM, "Enkindling the Embers: The Challenge of Current Research on Religious Life," *The MAST Journal* 4, no. 2 (Spring 1994): 8; and Sheila Carney, RSM, "The Constitutions: Our Corporate and Corporeal World," *The MAST Journal* 14, no. 1 (2004), 4–5.

42. Jolie, 3.

43. By the 1980s, many former high schools owned and staffed by the Sisters of Mercy had closed. St. Xavier Academy in Ottawa had become Marquette High School in the 1950s, a co-educational diocesan school, and Mercys continued to work here up to 1980. St. Catherine of Siena, or Siena High School in Chicago closed in 1977. Mercy High School in Chicago had merged with Loretto Academy in 1972 to become Unity High School. In 1980 Unity became a part of the VAUT Catholic school system, which consisted of Aquinas, St. Thomas Apostle, Visita-

tion, and Unity. Unity ultimately closed in 1988. Mercy High School Milwaukee closed in 1973.

44. Jolie, 4–5; Joy Clough, RSM, "25—and Quite Alive!" *Dimensions* 3, no. 1 (Winter 1981): 2–7; "Direction Statement"; "Notes from Ministry Meetings with RSMs Working in Secondary Education," November 3, 1994; "Ministry Meetings: Secondary Education, March 14, 1996," *Tidings* April 1996, ASMC; and Sister of Mercy, telephone interview with author, June 8, 2011.

45. Marilyn Sunderman, RSM, "Dream Shaping/Dream Sharing: The Educational Vision of Catherine McAuley," *The MAST Journal* 6, no. 2 (Spring 1996): 54–56.

46. Mary Catherine Daly, RSM, "Moving Along—Together," *Dimensions* 2, no. 3 (Summer 1980): 3, ASMC; Mark Zambrano, "School a Beacon of Hope in Austin," *Chicago Tribune*, May 27, 1985; "Thank You for Your Service," *Catholic New World* July 17, 2011; "Around and About," *Tidings* 44, issue 4 (July 2007): 4, ASMC; and Rosemary Welter, *Milwaukee Sentinel*, May 4, 2009, http://milwaukeeachiever.org/blog/2009/05/11/sister-rosemary-welter-rsm/.

47. In Sister Lucille's address, she touches upon the on-going community discussions about the centrality of working for systemic change within the community before articulating this importance of education as a means of working for mercy and justice for all members of society. Emphasis in text. Lucille McKillop, RSM, "Assembly," February 8, 1997, ASMC.

48. McKillop, "Assembly"; and "Ministry: Our Story and Our Context," 8.

49. Circular Letter, Concilia Moran, RSM, to the Sisters of Mercy of the Union, quoted in Helen Marie Burns, RSM, "Reflections on Sponsorship: One Congregation's Perspective," in *Sponsorship in the US Context: Theory and Praxis*, ed. Rosemary Smith, SC, Warren Brown, OMI, and Nancy Reynolds, SP (Alexandria, Va.: Cannon Law Society of America, 2006), 9.

50. Burns, 9; and Helen Amos, RSM, "A Moral Quandary for Sponsors: Like the Family and the State, Sponsorship Is an Institution," *Health Progress* (January–February 1996), 22.

51. The last sister appointed to the position of president was Sister M. Olivia Barrett, RSM (1963 to 1968). Sister Irenaues Chekouras, RSM, was the next Sister of Mercy to assume the role in 1972 to 1982. A Sister of the Sacred Heart of Mary, Sister Colette Mahoney, RSHM acted as interim president in 1994. Since this hiring, laymen and laywomen have been the university's president. For a list of past presidents, see: http://www.sxu.edu/Administrative/President/past_presidents.asp. Presentation Annual Meeting, Mother McAuley High School, November 18, 2002; Presentation McAuley Board Retreat, August 14, 2004; Presentation McAuley Sponsorship Consultation, September 21, 2004; and Presentation: The Journey Continues: Mother McAuley Annual Meeting, September 19, 2005, ASMC.

52. Helen Burns, RSM, is a Sister of Mercy from the Detroit Regional Community, and she wrote on sponsorship in general, speaking to a larger audience

beyond the Mercys, using examples from the Sisters of Mercy's history. A close sponsorship relationship with laywomen and laymen proved necessary for the Chicago Mercys. Since 1999, they engaged in cultivating lay and religious persons who support and understand the Mercy charism and seek to act in a sponsorship role within institutions. This type of discussion dovetailed with the plans to reconfigure the regional community and to merge territory as in the case of West Midwest. Burns, 6–7; Terry Maltby, RSM, "Sponsorship: A Matter of Heart, A Matter of Law," 2001, ASMC; Regional Leadership Team (Joy Clough, RSM, Ann Flanagan, RSM, Carlotta Oberzut, RSM, and Terry Maltby, RSM) to Sisters and Associates, November 2005, ASMC; and "Sponsorship Pilot," n.d., ASMC.

53. See the 2004 press release of her appointment to this office, http://www.sxu.edu/Administrative/Media_Relations/Press_Releases/press_release_05262004.asp. Clough, "25—and Quite Alive!" 5–7; and Sister of Mercy, interview with author, June 8, 2011.

54. A parallel affiliation and collaboration occurs at Saint Xavier University, which belongs to the Conference for Mercy Higher Education, an affiliation of over a dozen colleges and universities sponsored by the Sisters of Mercy. See the Conference for Mercy Higher Education, http://www.mercyhighered.org/index.html. "Ministry: Our Story and Our Context," 7–8; and Sister Judith Heberle, RSM, "Mercy Secondary Education Association History Through 2010," Network for Mercy Education: MSEA—Historical Documents, http://www.netmercyed.org/MSEA.html, July 9, 2011.

55. The quotation in the heading that begins this section is from *Core Constitutions* (1982), 2.

56. In 1991, 435 sisters were in the Chicago community, and of that number 268 actively engaged in ministry. Annual Statistical Report: Ministry, Chicago, Sisters of Mercy of the Union, July 1, 1989 to June 30, 1990; "Number of Sisters Serving in Each Apostolate, Age Distribution in Each Apostolate, Sisters of Mercy, Province of Chicago as of January 3, 1991"; Report Chicago Sisters of Mercy of the Americas, August 1993, ASMC; Bryan T. Froehle and Dominic J. Perri, "Cara Report, Sisters of Mercy of the Americas Regional Community of Chicago: Pathways Toward the Future" (Washington: Center for Applied Research in the Apostolate, Georgetown University, March 1998), 28; and "Ministry: Our Story and Our Context," 8.

57. Administrative Team, "Statement of Convictions: Health Care," Sisters of Mercy of the Americas, Regional Community of Chicago, December 1993, ASMC.

58. Ludmilla Benda, RSM, Al Hathaway, Peg Hathaway, Ed Schloemer, and Helen Wunderam, Mercy Hospital Davenport Focus Group with author, Genesis West Health Center, Davenport, Iowa, June 13, 2007; Elizabeth Smith, RSM, interview with author, Regional Community Center, Chicago, Ill., June 19, 2007; and for Mercy Iowa City's current status, see *Mercy Iowa City*, http://www.mercyic.org/?id=1&sid=1.

59. Laymen and women who participated in this focus group remarked that since the Sisters of Mercy had left the hospital, they missed the presence of the sisters in the hospital. Having lived and worked within the Mercy Hospital, Davenport community, laymen and women shared their dismay at the change in the hospital's identity. By the time of the transfer of the hospital to Genesis, very few sisters remained in Davenport. At the time of this conversation with the author, only one sister, formerly a hospital administrator, lived in Iowa and she conducted an outreach ministry to the homeless. This same group also regretted the lack of sisters in the classrooms and remarked that their children did not have the same discipline from their education. Mercy Hospital Davenport Focus Group.

    Similar transitions in ownership occurred in Janesville, Wisconsin, as the community transferred Mercy Hospital, Janesville to the municipality. Mercy and Catholic images adorn Mercy Hospital, Iowa City to signify that this hospital still has a connection to its past, and its mission (printed on various public relations documents and annual reports) identifies itself as Catholic in the Mercy tradition. According to its mission statement: "Mercy Iowa City heals and comforts the sick and works to improve the health of the community in the spirit of Jesus Christ and the Catholic tradition of the Sisters of Mercy." Annual Meeting, Mercy Hospital, Iowa City, October 26, 2004; Sponsorship Agreement, Mercy Hospital, Iowa City, Iowa, October 26, 1999, ASMC; and Ronald R. Reed, interview with author, Mercy Hospital, Iowa City, Iowa, June 14, 2007.

60. Managed care refers to "collective decision making in health care" where health insurance companies and health care facilities worked in concert to "manage" the care of those sick in a more efficient and arguably more cost-effective manner. Manage care developed by the 1990s. See James C. Robinson and Paul B. Ginsburg, "Consumer-Driven Health Care: Promise and Performance," *Health Affairs* 28, no. 2 (January 27, 2009): w272.

61. Ann Flanagan, RSM, telephone interview with author, February 25, 2010; and Stephanie Szuda, "Ottawa Native Honored for Dedication to the Sick, Elderly, and Poor," *The Times*, April 19, 2010, http://www.mywebtimes.com/archives/ottawa/display.php?id=402260.

62. Integrated Delivery Networks refers to a network of health care facilities and providers that is designed to work collaboratively to give a continuum of care, with an effective use of resources. Often health care institutions work in conjunction with health insurance companies to manage care efficiently. In 1994, thirty Sisters of Mercy from the Chicago community participated in a discussion of their involvement in health care ministry, what they perceived the problems were, and what they hoped would occur in the future. Several participants expressed concern about losing sight of patients and their families in "direct service" systems. Others mentioned that health care was the Mercys' responsibility, "not just someone else's responsibility," that Mercy health care should include

"wellness versus sickness," and that the "future of health care won't be in with in-
stitutions." Comments were listed anonymously. "Health Care Ministry Meeting,"
Mercy Hospital and Medical Center, Chicago, Illinois, December 8, 1994, ASMC;
M. Cathleen Kaveny and James F. Keenan, SJ, "Ethical Issues in Health-Care
Restructuring," *Theological Studies*, 56 (1995): 139–40; and Clarke E. Cochran,
"Sacramental and Solidarity: Catholic Social Thought and Health Care Reform
Policy," *Journal of Church and State* 41, no. 3 (1999): 476–77.

63. Prior to Vatican II and renewal, Sisters of Mercy did not necessarily construct their identity as the institution, but most outsiders to the Mercy community and other women religious congregations did not distinguish sisters from
their institutions. Mercys after Vatican II and renewal consistently verbalized
their identity as women religious separate from the institutions in which they
performed their ministry. "Health Care Ministry Meeting," December 8, 1994;
and "Health Care Ministry Meeting," *Tidings*, June 1996, ASMC.

64. Melosh, *"The Physician's Hand,"* 163–64; and Christopher Kauffman,
"Catholic Health Care in the United States: American Pluralism and Religious
Meanings," *Christian Bioethics* 5, no. 1 (1999): 56–57.

65. There are a number of examples of Sisters of Mercy whose service was
essential, but not necessarily on the front lines of ministry as administrators.
Their efforts, however, are as valuable as those who are more known. Margaret
Mary Hinz, RSM, worked in payroll at Mercy Hospital, Davenport, was Director
of Finance at Mercy Health Care and Rehabilitation in Chicago, was the Director
of Finance at Oak Park Hospital, Marian Joy Rehab, and Misericordia South in
Chicago, and was the Assistant Administrator of Provena Villa Franciscan in Jo-
liet. She became the Associate Director of Graduate Programs, Graham School of
Management, Saint Xavier University in 2003. See Membership File, ASMC, and
McDonagh, RSM, 4. Others join Sister Margaret Mary Hinz with their contributions, including, Sister Mary Columba Finnegan, RSM, who was an administrator
at Mercy Manor for much of the 1980s. See Membership File.

66. Sisters continued to act as directors of their health care facilities throughout this period, including Sister Dorothy Burns, who earned degrees in business
and hospital administration in the 1950s and 1960s and worked in Aurora.
Sister Sheila Lyne occupied administrative positions at Mercy Hospital, Chicago
throughout the 1970s through 2008, with a temporary interruption when she
worked for over a decade as head of the Chicago Public Health Office in the
1990s. Dorothy Burns, RSM, telephone interview with author, February 22, 2010;
Mary Catherine McDonagh, RSM, "'Behind-the-Scenes' in the World of Hospi-
tals," *Dimensions* 2, no. 4 (Autumn 1980): 2–6; Virgena Clark, RSM, "Today's
RSM, 'Mutual Support and a Strong Sense of Belonging,'" *Dimensions* 3, no. 4
(December/January 1981–82): 5–6; Linda Muston, "She Would Have Many Job
Offers," *Dimensions* 6, no. 1 (Fall/Winter 1984): 5–7; Sisters Sheila Marie Lyne,
RSM, Membership File, ASMC; Jean Latz Griffin, "Nun Picked as City Health
Chief," *Chicago Tribune*, February 8, 1991; Deborah Rissing, "A Healing Minis-

try after 10 Years of Crusading for Public Health, Sister Sheila Lyne Returns to Running a Hospital, the Job She Believes she was Called to Do," *Chicago Tribune*, Jan 3, 2001; and for a consideration of the role of congregational sponsorship, see Helen Marie Burns, RSM, "Reflections on Sponsorship: One Congregation's Perspective," in *Sponsorship in the US Context: Theory and Praxis*, ed. Rosemary Smith, SC, Warren Brown, OMI, and Nancy Reynolds, SP (Alexandria, Va.: Cannon Law Society of America, 2006), 4.

67. St. Catherine Residence survived Milwaukee's urban renewal plans, but to do so, it had to merge with the Mercys' other home for women, St. Clara Residence, and relocate to a new site in the city.

68. Maryangela Layman-Roman, "St. Catherine Residence for Women: 'Home' and 'Family' to Thousands for 100 Years," *Catholic Herald*, January 12, 1995; and Annual Meeting, St. Catherine Residence, November 20, 2002, ASMC.

69. "Ministry: Our Story and Our Context," 6; and Layman-Roman.

70. St. Catherine Residence Board of Directors has in the past had four to five Sisters of Mercy serving on it. See St. Catherine Residence, "Development Office Report, 1990," and St. Catherine Residence, "Annual Report 2009–2010," for a list of members of the Board of Directors. The Statement of Mercy Charism, April 11, 1992, also echoes the 1980s Ministry handout, as does the 1995 Direction Statement.

71. Under the direction of Sister Rosemary Connelly for over forty years, Misericordia offers "a lifetime home" to over 600 residents. Since 2005, all of Misericordia's services have been transferred to the north side location, when the original South Side institution was sold. "A Brief History of Misericordia Homes," n.d., ASMC; "Who We Are, Why We Are, What We Hope to Become," n.d. ASMC; "Sisters in Charge," *Chicago Tribune*, February 1920; "Misericordia Reconversion, Begin Care, Tests for Retarded Tots," *Brighton Park/McKinley Park Life*, January 20, 1955; Jeff Truesdell and Sandra Sobieraj Westfall, "A Nun's Haven for the Disabled," *People* 73, no. 7 (February 22, 2010): 117.

72. "Hesed House's Ideal, Goals, and Objectives," September 1987, ASMC. Christopher Julka, "Top Need: Affordable Housing," *Beacon-News*, August 9, 1989; Tom Parisi, "Old Well House Foundation of Hope, City Trades Class, JoCo Join to Build a Home," *Beacon-News*, March 25, 1993; Hal Dardick, "A Home of Their Own: Joseph Corp. Gives People a Hand Up, Not a Handout," *Chicago Tribune*, July 17, 1994 and Joseph Corporation of Illinois, Inc., Business Plan, January 1–December 31, 1996, 1, ASMC.

73. Susan M. Sanders, RSM, "Planning for the Housing Health Care Needs of Senior Sisters of Mercy, Province of Chicago: A Progress Report," June 1983, ASMC; Jay Copp, "Residence Planned for Retired Religious," and Jay Copp, "Housing Needed," *New World*, March 13, 1992.

74. Brigid Condon, RSM, paraphrased and adapted an anonymous poem, "What Do You See," about aging and invisibility to convey the feelings of some elderly Sisters of Mercy for the Advisory Retirement Planning Committee in

May 1982. The poem urged the observer to see past the failing and possibly "crabby old nun," to remember the individual and all her devotion to the community and the Church.

75. Marcian Deisenroth, RSM, "The Fox Knoll Story, Tenth Anniversary," September 15, 2002, ASMC.

76. The Mercys' association with Mercy Health Care and Rehabilitation Center was short-lived. For a larger discussion of this institution, see Benedicta McCorry, RSM, "Does Sponsorship Make a Difference?" *Dimensions* 4, no. 1 (Spring 1982): 2–6, ASMC. Not everyone could afford or sustain this quality of care and the Chicago Mercys proposed "enlarging [their] focus to housing for all of the elderly will allow [them] to address a significant need in society while providing alternative living and ministry options for Mercys." In conjunction with these actions, the Mercys expanded ministries to care for senior adults, which also fit with their own community's needs. "Proceedings: 15th Provincial Chapter, Session I," February 13, 1982; Administrative Report to Members (Institute of the Sisters of Mercy Chicago Regional Community, 1994), 15; Gary Hoppenworth, "A Study of Mercy Manor Residents and How They Relate to the Population of the Province," c. 1980; Advisory Retirement Planning Committee, "Housing Patterns," November 7, 1980; and Intercommunity Retirement Project for Women Religious, October 22, 1987, ASMC.

77. The quotation in the heading that begins this section is from Sisters of Mercy of the Americas, "Direction Statement," 1995. The full line is "Animated by the Gospel and Catherine McAuley's passion for the poor."

78. Prior to renewal, sisters in various ministries, consumed with their daily activities, did not know what others were doing on a regular basis. Yet, traditional ministries like education and health care afforded more familiarity across the community. It is not surprising that a sense of unfamiliarity with individual ministries persisted after renewal, particularly in newer "diverse" apostolates outside Mercy institutions. Community publications such as *Tidings* attempted bridge distances between sisters by publishing the results of ministry meetings of different groups, such as education, health care, and pastoral services workers. See "Report of Pastoral Services Ministry Meetings," *Tidings* 18, no. 5 (March 1995): 1–2, ASMC.

79. Twenty sisters participated in discussion of the pastoral services ministry on February 9, 1995 at Mercy Hospital, Chicago. The results of this meeting were published in the March 1995 *Tidings*. The majority of those gathered were engaged in parish ministry as pastoral associates, members of the pastoral team, directors of religious education, and pastoral musicians. Others worked in hospice and as chaplains in a hospital. The remaining group of sisters were drawn from more diverse ministry such as Youth Office of the Chicago Juvenile Court, "Ministry of Presence with Victims of Torture" at Su Casa, a home for refugees from Central America, and Wellstreams, a Feminist Spirituality Center in Chicago. One sister, as the Director of Religious Education at St. Luke Parish in

Milwaukee, expressed her wish to let her sisters know she was doing the work of Catherine McAuley. "Report of Pastoral Services Ministry Meetings," 1–2.

80. Sister Madeleva Deegan, for example, taught in elementary schools nearly two decades before becoming a principal. She remained in education as a school administrator for another twenty-six years, before taking a sabbatical in 1988. The following year she began an eleven-year career as a pastoral associate. She retired in 2001, but remained an active member of the community as a volunteer. Sister Madeleva volunteered in her community's archives up until she died in 2010. Membership File, ASMC. Administrative Report to the Members (Institute of the Sisters of Mercy of the Americas Regional Community of Chicago, 1994), 11; Bryan T. Froehle, and Dominic J. Perri, "Sisters of Mercy of the Americas Chicago Regional Community, Pathways toward the Future," (Washington: Center for Applied Research in the Apostolate, Georgetown University, March 1998), 28; "The Sisters of Mercy—Contemporary Profiles," *The Defender— West, Chicago Defender*, Sunday March 21, 1981, 13; Marj Holbrook, "'Ordinary People' Called by God," *The Beacon-News*, December 13, 1981; "The Mercy Action Cunningham Award," *Mercy Action Annual Report*, 1971–96, *Silver Jubilee*; Focus Groups: Provena McAuley Manor, April 10, 2007; and Regional Center, Chicago, April 17, April 24, 2007; Non-Traditional Ministry, Mercy Meeting Place, July 28, 2008; Pastoral Ministry, July 29, 2008; and Interview with Dorothy Burns, RSM, February 22, 2010; Sister Survey Worksheet, 1981, 2, 4, 6, 10, 17, and 18; and Sisters of Mercy Province of Chicago, "Into the 21st Century: Planning Document," February 20, 1990, 11, 13, ASMC.

81. This attitude or outlook of the Chicago Mercys was expressed by sisters who participated in the various focus groups for this study. Retired sisters reflecting upon their history and the future of their community, while concerned that their legacy was preserved, focused more on how they currently might contribute or were connected to the Mercy charism. Many sisters who participated in focus groups who were of retirement age were engaged in some form of ministry, whether in full or partial employment, or as a volunteer. Mercy Convent Focus Group, Chicago, October 13, 2006, and Milwaukee Focus Group, St. Catherine Residence, Milwaukee, May 16, 2007. See also, Susan Perschbacher Melia, "Continuity in the Lives of Elder Catholic Women Religious," *The International Journal of Aging and Human Development* 48, no. 3 (April 1999): 175–89 for a discussion of perspectives of aging women religious. "Into the 21st Century: Planning Document," 5.

82. Bauer et al., 3–4; and "Ministry: Our Story and Our Context," 5.

83. For examples of Clark Memorial Fund, see "Say," February, 1983, ASMC. See "Clark Fund Requests," *Tidings* 43, no. 8 (December 2006): 3 and 9, ASMC.

84. Agatha O'Brien Ministry Fund, General Ledger, 1993–2008, ASMC.

85. Rita Hofbauer, GNSH, ed., *The Corporate Response: Why and How* (Silver Spring, Md.: Leadership Conference of Women Religious of the USA, 1988), 1, 3–4.

86. Administrative Report, 1986–1990, Sisters of Mercy Province of Chicago, Mercy 1990, ASMC; and "Sisters of Mercy Oppose Arizona Immigration Law," May 5, 2010, http://www.sistersofmercy.org/index.php?option=com_content&task=view&id=2664&Itemid=180.

87. "We Have Come This Far by Faith: Sisters of Mercy, Province of Chicago Administrative Team Report: 1982–1986," April 1986, ASMC.

88. Ibid.

89. Ibid.

90. The significant modifications and upheaval in religious life, compounded with societal change, constricted the numbers within the province by the early 1980s. Between 1966 and 1980, 130 sisters chose to leave the Sisters of Mercy in the Chicago Province. They cited various reasons for leaving, most often stating they had found another manner of life to serve God. After 1980, the exodus subsided and only a handful of women departed the community. (Fifteen sisters left between1980 and 1989.) However, total membership declined significantly as sisters died. The community lost over 340 members between 1960 and 1980; by 1990, Chicago Mercys numbered a little over 450 sisters. Registry Database.

91. "Frequent Requested Statistics," *Center for Applied Research in the Apostolate*, http://cara.georgetown.edu/CARAServices/requestedchurchstats.html, June 21, 2011. The number of Chicago Mercys from 1965 is drawn from a circular letter from Mother Provincial Huberta McCarthy at the time of the elections for delegates to the Provincial Chapter held in the local houses on May 3, 1965. Statistics for 1985 come from the Sisters of Mercy Province of Chicago Administrative Report, 1986–1990, March 1990. Both numbers are supported by the Registry Database.

92. One responder wished the Chicago Mercys "would advertise as the [other congregations] do," but thought the sisters doing publicity at the time were doing "a splendid job." In this case, she referenced a "block" they had in the new Archbishop's photo issue, finding this type of advertisement "superb!" Responses like this one were somewhat contradictory. Sisters hoped for more entrants to the community and believed more should be done to attract women, but their responses were a mixture of support of current efforts and reticence to become too aggressive in recruiting. "Responses from September 25th Presentation (Community Meeting)," September 1982, ASMC.

93. "Sisters of Mercy: Listen with Us," 1980, ASMC.

94. The "membership conversations" were part of the province-wide preparation for the provincial assembly convened in 1990. Responses ranged from the need for a clearer articulation of their spiritual values, definition of community life, and the need for more structured formation to stressing the importance of apostolic works, the need to update or modernize their language, and whether or not the Mercys' moment had passed. This last point resonated with some sisters who felt they were a dying community. Planning Committee Members (Sister Peg Barett, Donna Hayes, Sister Carol Mucha, Sister Judy Niemet, and Sister Jane

Schlosser), "Conversations on New Membership and Personnel Needs," January, 1989; and Membership Conversations, East. Ave., January 5, 1989, Milwaukee, January 19, 1989, Laurel Drive, Aurora, January 19, 1989, and Province Center, January 26, 1989, ASMC.

95. The Institute meant the dissolution of the Union, not merely the addition of Mercy provinces that had not amalgamated in 1929. On the eve of this new amalgamation in 1991, Mercys faced with all religious congregations in the United States a potential period of crisis, but the out-going president and vice-president of the Union, Helen Amos, RSM, and Helen Marie Burns, RSM, described the ensuing nineties "as an opportunity for transformation and new life." Helen Amos, RSM, and Helen Marie Burns, RSM, "Restructuring the Sisters of Mercy," *Human Development* 12, no. 2 (Summer 1991): 16. The Leadership Conference of Women Religious (LCWR), with National Association for Treasurers of Religious Institutes (NATRI), and the National Religious Retirement Office (NRRO) studied reconfiguration of religious institutes and their viability in the late 1980s and early 1990s. They concluded that while early efforts to merge communities had had some problems, this was the direction of the future. Margaret Cafferty, PVBM, "The Think Tank on the Viability of Religious Institutes," in LCWR, NATRI, and NRRO, A Critical Juncture: Assessing the Viability of Religious Institutes (Silver Spring, Md.: LCWR, NATRI and NRRO, 1996), ii–iv.

96. According to the community registry, seven entered religious life in 1941. In February 1941, three women had entered the community. Sister Rosalie entered in September 1941 with three other postulants, as they were known then. At that time, there were two general entrance periods, late winter and early fall. (See Registry Database.) The decline in vocations was discussed in national newspapers and magazines, such as the *LA Times* November 1986 article, "Shortage of Priests, Nuns, US Bishops Report on Decline in Religious Vocations," by Russell Chandler reprinted in various papers throughout the country, such as the *Gainesville Sun.*

97. Sister Survey Worksheet, 1981, 18; and "Planning Document / Into the 21st Century: Proposed Task Forces from Implementation," ASMC.

98. The numbers of vocations are based upon those who entered and remained. After joining the Institute, the Chicago Mercys and other religions communities continued to have the responsibility to direct formation. It was not until 2001 that the Institute established a central novitiate in Laredo, Texas. Sister Survey Worksheet, 1981, 18; "Planning Document / Into the 21st Century."

99. While the transition to the Institute in the early 1990s changed some of the language of the formation process (the use of regional community and institute), it did not alter the philosophy or purpose of formation. It also did not change the location of formation, which was directed at the local regional level. When women professed their vows as Sisters of Mercy, they entered the Sisters of Mercy of the Institute, but whether they made it that far was determined by local

regional formation directors and presidents. "Sisters of Mercy: Listen with Us, Weekend Experience, April 11–12, 1980," ASMC.

100. "Come and See: Membership in the Sisters of Mercy," October 1979, ASMC.

101. The Chicago Mercys also participated in a collaborative novitiate with other Mercys throughout the country. Developed in the early 1980s, the Mercy Collaborative Novitiate started in 1985 with three novices in Cincinnati, Ohio. Eventually, the Institute relocated their novitiate to Laredo, Texas in the early 2000s. "History of the Mercy Collaborative Novitiate," n.d., ASMC. Sister of Mercy, telephone interview with author, 8 June 2011.

102. "History of the Mercy Collaborative Novitiate."

103. Sisters of Mercy, "Chicago Province Formation Program," 1983 Revision, ASMC.

104. Sisters of Mercy, Province of Chicago, "Mercy Association," 1988, ASMC.

105. For examples, see *Associates: Sisters of Mercy Province Chicago*, No. 1 (June 1987), No. 2 (February 1988), and No. 3 (November 1988), ASMC.

106. *Associates* No. 3 (November 1988).

107. Mercy Associate—Sister Conversation, Worksheet I, December 17, 1993; and Rosemary Jeffries, RSM, "Report on the Associate Survey for the Institute of the Sisters of Mercy of the Americas" (June 15, 1993), 12, ASMC.

108. Sisters of Mercy of the Americas, Regional Community of Chicago, "Mercy Association Handbook," 1996, ASMC.

109. Committee Concerning Membership, Meeting Minutes, April 10, 1997, ASMC.

110. Joy Clough, RSM, "Draft of Faith," n.d., c.1998–2002 ASMC.

111. USIG, "Summary of the Questionnaire Responses—USA," Fall 1982, 1.

112. McKillop, 2.

Epilogue: West Midwest and the Legacy of the Sisters of Mercy Chicago Regional Community

1. M. C. McAuley to Sister M. de Sales White, Bermondsey, February 28, 1841, in Mary C. Sullivan, ed., *The Correspondence of Catherine McAuley, 1818–1841*, (Washington: The Catholic University of America Press, 2004), 365.

2. Ibid.

3. Lisa Schulte, "Six Regional Mercy Communities to Merge," *National Catholic Reporter*, February 23, 2007; and Sisters of Mercy of the Americas West Midwest, "A New Mercy Moment," 2008, ASMC.

4. While the West Midwest Mercys contemplated merger, other Mercy regions did the same. Northeast became the first to merge in 2006 combining the Albany, New York; Connecticut; Portland, Maine; New Hampshire; Providence, Rhode Island; and Vermont communities in 2006. Mid-Atlantic followed in 2007, merging Dallas and Merion, Pennsylvania; Watchung, New Jersey; and Hartsdale and Brooklyn, New York. In January 2008, New York, Pennsylvania, Pacific West

was created from Buffalo and Rochester, New York; Erie and Pittsburgh, Pennsylvania; and the Philippines. In September of the same year, Baltimore, Maryland; Cincinnati, Ohio/Jamaica; St. Louis, Missouri; and North Carolina/Guam were reconfigured into South Central. Katherine Doyle, RSM, "West/Midwest Region Imagines New Life in Mercy," *Tidings* 22, no. 17 (August 2001): 6; and David Ramey, "Sisters of Mercy of the Americas: Institute Membership Survey Report," (Dayton, Ohio: Strategic Leadership Associates, Inc., October 14, 2003), ASMC.

5. The merger process, much like the creation of the Institute, required the Sisters of Mercy to consider their future as women religious. This manifested in each period of change in collaborative discussions, like the Sacred Circles. "Assembly Outcomes: April 24, 2004," *Tidings* 41, no. 4 (May 2004): 1, 4; "West Midwest Area Updates," *Tidings* 42, no. 2 (March/April 2005): 4–5; and "Vowed Members Invited to Contemplate Identity in *Sacred Circles*," *Vita* 15, no. 7 (July 2006): 12, ASMC.

6. Schulte, 17a.

7. Mothers Bernardine Clancy and Mercedes Wellehan from Milwaukee and Davenport were superiors at the time of the amalgamation in 1929. Mother Paulita Morris played an important role in the renewal process as Mother Provincial from 1966 to 1970.

8. Associates were not instituted until over a decade later.

9. Registry Database; "Ordination and Vocations," *Center for Applied Research in the Apostolate*, 2008, http://cara.georgetown.edu/ordvocation.pdf, July 18, 2011; Ilia Delio, "Confessions of a Modern Nun: Reflection on a Religious Divide," *America* (October 12, 2009): 11.

10. Sisters of Mercy Regional Community of Chicago, "Into the 21st Century: Planning Document," November 27, 1995, ASMC; Institute of the Sisters of Mercy of the Americas, "Vocation Program in the United States," July 1, 2007, ASMC, 5; Sisters of Mercy of the Americas, "Think Mercy," Become a Sister of Mercy, http://www.sistersofmercy.org/index.php?option=com_content&task=blog category&id=59&Itemid=101; and Sisters of Mercy West Midwest Community, http://sistersofmercywestmidwest.wordpress.com/.

11. In December 2008, the Vatican's Congregation for Institutes of Consecrated Life and Societies of Apostolic Life began a Visitation of apostolic institutes of women religious in the United States. According to the Vatican, this process was initiated to "look into the welfare of a particular aspect of the Church." "About Us," *Apostolic Visitation of Institutes of Women Religious in the United States*, http://www.apostolicvisitation.org/en/about/index.html, accessed April 14, 2011.

12. Most women seeking a vowed religious life, however, come to this commitment with more experience and more education than in previous decades. What is known is that women who have made a commitment to religious life in the 2000s are more likely to have completed an undergraduate degree, if not graduate degree, and have had some work experience, many within a ministry setting. "State of the Sisters," *America* 204, no. 4 (February 14, 2011): 8; Lisa

Takeuchi Cullen and Tracy Schmidt, "Today's Nun Has a Veil—And a Blog," *Time Magazine*, November 13, 2006, http://www.time.com/time/magazine/article/0,9171,1558292-4,00.html, July 15, 2011; and "You've Come a Long Way, Sister: The Editors Interview Sister Doris Gottemoeller, RSM," *U.S. Catholic* 65, no. 5 (May 2000): 18.

13. Betty Smith, interview with author, June 19, 2007.

14. M. C. McAuley to Sister M. de Sales White, Bermondsey, December 20, 1840, in *The Correspondence of Catherine McAuley, 1818–1841*, 332.

Appendix A: Parish Grade Schools, Academies, High Schools, Universities, and Alternative Schools

1. Behind the Cathedral
2. Madison and Clark Street
3. 18th and Clark Street
4. 28th and Wabash
5. Destroyed by fire
6. Wabash and Eldridge
7. 25th and Wallace
8. Merged with St. Cecilia and became St. Charles Lwanga
9. Merged with St. Anne and became St. Charles Lwanga
10. Merged with St. Catherine of Siena
11. Merged with St. Lucy
12. Massasoit Avenue
13. Formerly Old St. Patrick on Des Plaines Avenue and Holy Name Cathedral
14. Formerly Clay Street School
15. Originally St. Joseph School
16. Became Mother McAuley High School in 1956
17. West Side Chicago
18. West Side Chicago
19. West Side Chicago, became Siena High School
20. Became Saint Xavier University in 1992

Appendix B: Hospitals, Facilities, and Residences Owned and/or Sponsored by the Sisters of Mercy, Chicago Regional Community

1. Part of Mercy Hospital, Davenport
2. Part of Mercy Hospital, Davenport
3. Part of Provena Health Systems
4. Part of Provena Health Systems
5. Part of Provena Health Systems

Glossary

apostolate: Ministry or mission of a religious congregation or of the laity.

bands: Name given to a class of women who entered the novitiate in the same year.

bells (or call bells): Bells were rung to call sisters to a particular exercise or period of prayer during the day. Sisters were often assigned a call bell (the number of times and the manner in which the bell was rung) and were required to respond to it.

branch house: Often referred to as a *daughter house*. A convent in a new foundation, but still under the authority of the motherhouse.

charism: Spiritual foundation of a religious congregation, providing its distinct character and purpose.

cloister: An enclosed or removed space within a convent or religious house specifically set aside for religious seclusion of members of a religious community. Laity or clergy are barred from entering. In contemplative or cloistered communities, women religious traditionally were restricted from leaving their cloister. See *enclosure*.

convent: A building or structure where members of a congregation of women religious typically live.

Divine Office: The recitation of certain prayers throughout the day at specific times. Prayers come from the Breviary, or prayer book. Divine Office is also called the *Breviary* and *canonical hours*. The parts of the Divine Office are Lauds (prayer at dawn), Prime (early morning prayer), Terce (mid-morning prayer), Sext (midday prayer), None (mid-afternoon prayer), Vespers (evening prayer), Compline (night prayer), and Matins (prayer during the night, also known as *Vigils* or *Nocturns*).

enclosure: Synonymous with *cloister*, the rule enclosure restricts women religious from engaging in the secular society, restricting their movements within convents.

horarium: The daily schedule of a religious community. The horarium was set by a religious superior.

juniorate: A course or house of study as novice. A Sister of Mercy became a *Junior* after a temporary or first profession. The Sisters of Mercy created a House of Study in the 1950s when they extended the period of time before a novice entered ministerial work.

lay and choir nun or sister: A choir sister entered a religious congregation with a dowry, was normally better educated, and once professed was a full voting member of the community. She also recited the Divine Office in Latin and performed the ministries of the congregation, such as teaching and nursing. Lay sisters, on the other hand, came to a community without a dowry and with little formal education. They performed the domestic chores or duties of the community and did not engage in the congregation's ministries. There was a definite internal class distinction between choir and lay sisters, as lay sisters did not have a vote and could not hold office in the community. These distinctions were unpopular in the United States, as they were seen as undemocratic, and most religious congregations did away with them by the end of the twentieth century. The Sisters of Mercy, who rarely admitted anyone with these distinctions, officially did away with them by 1930.

local house: A convent under the direction of a motherhouse and in close proximity to it.

motherhouse/parent house: The principal house or convent of a religious congregation.

norms: An authoritative standard or model of religious life, guiding proper and acceptable behavior of a religious community. Norms were often articulated and explained in the Sisters of Mercy's *Customs and Guides*, which expounded upon the *Rule and Constitutions*.

novice: A woman in a period of probationary membership in a religious congregation. Sisters of Mercy became novices after a six-month period as postulants. They remained novices until the first, or temporary, profession after a year.

novitiate: The period of formation for women who entered the Sisters of Mercy. It is also the term applied to the building where formation occurred.

nun: A female member of a religious order who professes solemn vows, engages in a contemplative spirituality, and whose religious life is restricted by a cloister or enclosure.

postulant: A woman admitted to a religious congregation for a probation-ary period. The Sisters of Mercy had a six-month postulancy.

sister: A woman religious who professed simple vows within an active or apostolic congregation. Sisters, like the Sisters of Mercy, were not bound by rules of enclosure/cloister.

Bibliography

Manuscript Records

Archives of the Sisters of Mercy Chicago. Chicago, Ill. Record Groups: Community Life. Deceased Sisters Files. History. Ministry Hospitals. Ministry Other. Ministry Residences. Ministry Schools. Personnel Files. Religious Government. Special Collections Books.

———. Publications. *Agape*, 1964–67. *Dimensions*, 1979–86. *Exchange*, 1968–82. *Tidings*, 1995–2007.

Interviews

Anselme, June, RSM; Mary Ann Bergfeld, RSM; Lois Graver, RSM; and Elizabeth (Betty) Smith, RSM. Honore Street Focus Group with author. Audio recording. Regional Community Center, Chicago, Ill. June 30, 2008.

Barrett, Margaret (Peg), RSM; Madeleva Deegan, RSM; and Kathleen McClelland, RSM. Changes in Community Living and Purchase of Community-Owned Property Focus Group with author. Audio recording. Mercy Meeting Place, Chicago, Ill. July 3, 2008.

Benda, Ludmilla, RSM; Al Hathaway; Peg Hathaway; Ed Schloemer; and Helen Wunderam. Mercy Hospital Davenport Focus Group with author. Genesis West Health Center, Davenport, Iowa. June 13, 2007.

Betz, Laurette, RSM; Mary Ruth Broz, RSM; Cathleen Cahill, RSM; and Jane Schlosser, RSM. Pastoral Care Ministry Focus Group with author. Audio recording. Mercy Meeting Place, Chicago, Ill. July 29, 2008.

Blunk, Mary Clare, RSM; Renee Humble, RSM; and Lucia Lietsch, RSM. Iowa Focus Group with author. McAuley Convent, Aurora, Ill. June 7, 2007.

Bohmann, Jonella, RSM. Telephone interview with author. June 26, 2008.

Broz, Mary Ruth, RSM; Avis Clendenen; Emily Kemppi, RSM; Sharon Kerrigan, RSM; and Rita Specht, RSM. 80th and Wood Street Focus Group with author. Audio recording. Regional Community Center, Chicago, Ill. June 23, 2008.

Burns, Dorothy, RSM. Telephone interview with author. February 22, 2010.

Burns, Dorothy, RSM; Joella Cunnane, RSM; Conleth, Foley, RSM; Margaret Lyons, RSM; Judith Niemet, RSM. Community-Owned Homes Focus Group with author. Audio recording. Mercy Meeting Place, Chicago, Ill. July 23, 2008.

Clough, Joy, RSM. Conversation with author. March 13, 2011.

Condon, Brigid, RSM. Interview with author. McAuley Convent, Aurora, Ill. June 7, 2007.

Deegan, Madeleva, RSM. Interview with author. Mercy Convent, Chicago, Ill. January 9, 2007.

Fanning, Regine, RSM; Cora Finnane, RSM; Evangeline McSloy, RSM; and Marie Shefchik, RSM. St. Clotilde Convent Focus Group with author. Audio recording. Mercy Meeting Place, Chicago, Ill. July 2, 2008.

Flanagan, Ann, RSM. Telephone interview with author. February 25, 2010.

Flanagan, Ann, RSM; and Margaret Mary Hynes, RSM. Community-Owned Homes Focus Group with author. Audio recording. Mercy Meeting Place, Chicago, Ill. July 1, 2008.

Gannon, Laurus, RSM; Eleanora Holdgrafer, RSM; and Vernarda Lance, RSM. Iowa Focus Group with author. Chicago Regional Community Center, Chicago, Ill. June 4, 2007.

Heneghan, Barbara, RSM; Margaret Johnson, RSM; and Ruth Mutchler, RSM. Non-Traditional Ministry Focus Group with author. Audio recording. Mercy Meeting Place, Chicago, Ill. July 28, 2008.

Loftus, Mary, RSM. Interview with author. Audio recording. Mercy Meeting Place, Chicago, Ill. October 28, 2008.

McDonagh, Mary Catherine, RSM; Ann Sullivan, RSM; and Helen Weinfurter, RSM. Changes in Community Living Focus Group. Regional Community Center, Chicago, Ill. June 23, 2008.

McSloy, Evangeline, RSM. Telephone interview with author. October 15, 2006.

———. Interview with author. June 7, 2007.

———. Telephone interview with author. April 23, 2009, Chicago, Ill.

Murphy, Patricia M., RSM. Interview with author. Mercy Meeting Place, Chicago, Ill. December 4, 2008.

———. Interview with author. Audio recording. Mercy Meeting Place, Chicago, Ill. December 5, 2009.

Reed, Ronald R. Interview with author. Mercy Hospital, Iowa City, Iowa. June 14, 2007.

Sister of Mercy. Telephone interview with author. February 23, 2010.

Sister of Mercy. Telephone interview with author. June 8, 2011.

Sisters of Mercy. Focus group with author. Mercy Convent, Chicago, Ill. October 13, 2006.

———. Focus group with author. Provena McAuley Manor, Aurora, Ill. April 10, 2007.

———. Focus group with author. Regional Community Center, Chicago, Ill. April 17, 2007.

———. Focus group with author. Regional Community Center, Chicago, Ill. April 24, 2007.

———. Focus group with author. St. Catherine Residence, Milwaukee, Wis. May 16, 2007.

Smith, Elizabeth (Betty), RSM. Interview with the author. Regional Community Center, Chicago, Ill. June 19, 2007.

Thomas, Susan, RSM. Interview with author. Regional Community Center, Chicago, Ill. April 26, 2007.

Government Documents

1870 Federal Census, Fond du Lac, Wisconsin; and 1910 Federal Census, Milwaukee, Wisconsin.

List or Manifest of Alien Passengers for the United States, S.S. President Polk, from Queenstown, July 7, 1923. National Archives and Records Administration (NARA), Crew Lists of Vessels Arriving at Boston, Massachusetts, 1917–43; Microfilm Serial: T938; Microfilm Roll: 281. Ancestry.com. Boston Passenger and Crew Lists, 1820–1943 [database online]. Provo, Utah: Ancestry.com Operations, Inc., 2006.

List or Manifest of Alien Passengers for the United States, S.S. Albania, from Queenstown, Ireland, October 16, 1921. National Archives, Washington. Ancestry.com. New York, Passenger Lists, 1820–1957 [database online]. Provo, Utah: Ancestry.com Operations, Inc., 2010.

Published Sources

Amos, Helen, RSM. "A Moral Quandary for Sponsors: Like the Family and the State, Sponsorship Is an Institution." *Health Progress* (January–February 1996): 20–22, 42.

Amos, Helen, RSM; and Helen Marie Burns, RSM. "Restructuring the Sisters of Mercy." *Human Development* 12, no. 2 (Summer 1991): 16–20.

Annual Announcement of Rush Medical College of Chicago, Illinois, Session of 1849–50. Chicago: University of Chicago Press, 1849.

Andreas, Alfred Theodore. *History of Chicago from the Earliest Period to the Present Time, Volume 3.* Chicago: A.T. Andreas Company Publishers, 1886.

Apostolic Visitation of Institutes of Women Religious in the United States. http://www.apostolicvisitation.org/en/about/index.html.

Avella, Steven. *This Confident Church: Catholic Leadership and Life in Chicago, 1940–1965.* Notre Dame, Ind.: University of Notre Dame Press, 1993.

Blanchard, Charles. "Religion in Iowa—the Catholics." In *Annals of Iowa.* Des Moines: Iowa State Historical Department, 1962, 389–90.

Briggs, Kenneth. *Double Crossed: Uncovering the Catholic Church's Betrayal of American Nuns.* New York: Doubleday, 2006.

Burns, Helen Marie, RSM. "Reflections on Sponsorship: One Congregation's Perspective." In *Sponsorship in the US Context: Theory and Praxis,* edited by

Rosemary Smith, SC, Warren Brown, OMI, and Nancy Reynolds, SP, 1–16. Alexandria, Va.: Cannon Law Society of America, 2006.

Cabrol, Ferdinand. "Divine Office." *The Catholic Encyclopedia.* New York: Robert Appleton Company, 1911. From *New Advent,* http://www.newadvent.org/cathen/11219a.htm.

Cafferty, Margaret, PVBM. "The Think Tank on the Viability of Religious Institutes." In *LCWR, NATRI, and NRRO, A Critical Juncture: Assessing the Viability of Religious Institutes.* Silver Spring, Md.: LCWR, NATRI and NRRO, 1996, ii–iv.

Campbell, Debra. "The Heyday of Catholic Action and the Lay Apostolate." In *Transforming Parish Ministry: The Changing Roles of Catholic Clergy, Laity, and Women Religious,* edited by Jay P. Dolan, R. Scott Appleby, Patricia Byrne, and Debra Campbell, 222–52. New York: Crossroad Publishing Company, 1990.

Carney, Sheila, RSM. "The Constitutions: Our Corporate and Corporeal World," *The MAST Journal* 14, no. 1 (2004): 4–5.

"Catherine McAuley: Timeless Legacy." In *The MAST Journal, The Journal of the Mercy Association in Scripture and Theology* 6, no. 2 (Spring 1992).

"Catholic Action Program Chosen, Mar. 10, 11, 12 Dates Picked for Convention." *The Sketch* 1, no. 3 (February 1950): 1.

Chenu, R. P., OP. "Catholic Action and the Mystical Body." In *Restoring All Things: A Guide to Catholic Action,* edited by John Fitzsimons and Paul McGuire, 1–15. New York: Sheed & Ward, 1938.

Chinnici, Joseph P., OFM. "The Catholic Community at Prayer, 1926–1976." In *Habits of Devotion: Catholic Religious Practice in Twentieth-Century America,* edited by James M. O'Toole, 1–88. Ithaca: Cornell University Press, 2004).

"Catholic Women Chaplains: Yes and No." *Christian Century* 110, no. 17 (May 19–26, 1993): 547.

Clough, Joy, RSM. *First in Chicago: A History of Saint Xavier University.* Chicago: Saint Xavier University, 1997.

———. *In Service to Chicago: The History of Mercy Hospital.* Chicago: Mercy Hospital and Medical Center, 1979.

———. "Yesterday's City: Chicago's Sisters of Mercy." *Chicago History* 32, no. 1 (Summer 2003): 41–55.

Coburn, Carol and Martha J. Smith. *Spirited Lives: How Nuns Shaped Catholic Culture and American Life, 1836–1920.* Chapel Hill: University of North Carolina Press, 1999.

Cochran, Clarke E. "Sacramental and Solidarity: Catholic Social Thought and Health Care Reform Policy." *Journal of Church and State* 41, no. 3 (1999): 475–98.

Confrey, Burton. *Catholic Action: A Textbook for Colleges and Study Clubs.* New York: Benziger Brothers, 1935.

Condon, Mary Brigid, RSM. *For the Love of Humanity: a History of the Sisters of Mercy of Aurora, Illinois, 1910–1995*. Aurora, Ill: 1995

———. *From Obscurity to Distinction: The Story of Mercy Hospital, Iowa City, 1873–1993*. Iowa City: Mercy Hospital Iowa City, 1993.

———. *From Simplicity to Elegance: The Story of Mercy Hospital, Davenport, 1869–1994*. Davenport, Iowa: Genesis Health System Heart of Mercy Foundation, 1997.

Conon, William. *Nature's Metropolis: Chicago and the Great West*. New York: Norton, 1991.

Convey, Mary Fidelis, RSM. "Mother Agatha O'Brien and the Pioneers." Master's thesis, Loyola University, Chicago, 1929.

Coogan, M. Jane "The Redoubtable John Hennessy, First Archbishop of Dubuque." *Mid-America* 1, no. 1 (1980): 21–34.

Copp, Jay. "Residence Planned for Retired Religious; Housing Needed." *New World*. March 13, 1992.

Cott, Nancy F. *No Small Courage: A History of Women in the United States*. New York: Oxford University Press, 2000.

Cotter, Elizabeth M. *The General Chapter in a Religious Institute: With Particular Reference to IBVM Loreto Branch*. Bern: Peter Lang Ltd., 2008.

Coughlin, Roger J. and Cathryn A. Riplinger. *The Story of Charitable Care in the Archdiocese of Chicago, 1844–1959*. Chicago: Catholic Charities of Chicago, 1981.

Coyle, Sarah. "Progressive Nuns: Sisters of Mercy Break Free of Tradition to be CPA's, Chaplains in Business World." *Park Ridge Herald*. December 17, 1981, 17.

Cullen, Lisa Takeuchi and Tracy Schmidt. "Today's Nun has a Veil—And a Blog." *Time Magazine*. November 13, 2006. http://www.time.com/time/magazine/article/0,9171,1558292-4,00.html.

Cummings, Kathleen Sprows. *New Women of the Old Faith: Gender and American Catholicism in the Progressive Era*. Chapel Hill: University of North Carolina Press, 2009.

Dardick, Hal. "A Home of their Own: Joseph Corp. Gives People a Hand Up, Not a Handout." *Chicago Tribune*, July 17, 1994.

Delio, Ilia. "Confessions of a Modern Nun: Reflection on a Religious Divide." *America*. (October 12, 2009): 10–13.

Denis, Dionne. "Chicago School Desegregation and the Role of the State of Illinois, 1971–1979." *American Educational History Journal* 37, nos. 1 & 2 (2010): 55–73.

Deshon, George, CSP. *Guide for Catholic Young Women, Especially for Those Who Earn Their Own Living, Fourteenth Edition*. New York: The Catholic Publication Society, 1871.

Diner, Hasia R. *Erin's Daughters in America: Irish Immigrant Women in the Nineteenth Century*. Baltimore: Johns Hopkins University Press, 1983.

Dolan, Jay P. *The American Catholic Experience: A History from Colonial Times to the Present.* Notre Dame, Ind.: University of Notre Dame Press, 1992.

———. *The American Catholic Parish, A History from 1850 to the Present, Volume II, The Pacific, Intermountain West and Midwest States.* New York: Paulist Press, 1987.

———. *Catholic Revivalism: The American Experience 1830–1900.* Notre Dame, Ind.: University of Notre Dame Press, 1978.

———. *The Immigrant Church: New York's Irish and German Catholics, 1815–1865.* Notre Dame, Ind.: University of Notre Dame Press, 1975.

Dries, Angelyn, OSF. "The Americanization of Religious Life: Women Religious, 1872–1922." *U.S. Catholic Historian* 10, nos. 1 and 2 (1989): 13–24.

———. "Living in Ambiguity: A Paradigm Shift Experienced by the Sister Formation Movement." *Catholic Historical Review* 79, no. 3 (July 1993): 478–87.

Epiphany Association. http://www.epiphanyassociation.org/default.asp. November 19, 2007.

Ewens, Mary, OP. "Removing the Veil: The Liberated American Nun." In *Women of Spirit: Female Leadership in the Jewish and Christian Traditions,* edited by Rosemary Ruether and Eleanor McLaughlin, 256–78. New York: Simon and Schuster, 1979.

Fernand, Cabrol. "Divine Office." *The Catholic Encyclopedia,* vol. 11 (New York: Robert Appleton Company, 1911), http://www.newadvent.org/cathen/11219a .htm.

Fernandez, Lilia. *Brown in the Windy City: Mexican and Puerto Ricans in Postwar Chicago.* Chicago: University of Chicago Press, 2010.

Fisher, James T. *The Catholic Counterculture in America, 1933–1962.* Chapel Hill: University of North Carolina Press, 1989.

Fitzgerald, Maureen. *Habits of Compassion: Irish Catholic Nuns and the Origins of New York's Welfare System, 1830–1920.* Urbana: University of Chicago Press, 2006.

"Frequently Requested Statistics." *Center for Applied Research in the Apostolate.* http://cara.georgetown.edu/CARAServices/requestedchurchstats.html.

Froehle, Bryan T. and Dominic J. Perri. "Cara Report, Sisters of Mercy of the Americas Regional Community of Chicago: Pathways Toward the Future." March 1998. Washington: Center for Applied Research in the Apostolate, Georgetown University.

Getz, Lynne M. "'A Strong Man of Large Human Sympathy': Dr. Patrick L. Murphy and the Challenges of Nineteenth-Century Asylum Psychiatry in North Carolina." *North Carolina Historical Review* 86, no. 1 (January 2009): 32–58.

Ginzberg, Lori D. "'Moral Suasion Is Moral Balderdash': Women, Politics, and Social Activism in the 1850s." *The Journal of American History* 73, no. 3 (December 1986): 601–2.

———. *Women and the Work of Benevolence: Morality, Politics, and Class in the Nineteenth Century United States.* New Haven: Yale University Press, 1992.

Greeley, Andrew. *The Church and the Suburbs, Revised Edition.* New York: Paulist Press, 1963.

———. "The New Breed." *America*, May 23, 1964. http://www.americamagazine.org/content/article.cfm?article_id=11803.

Griffin, Jean Latz. "Nun Picked as City Health Chief." *Chicago Tribune*, February 8, 1991.

A Guide for the Religious Called Sisters of Mercy. Amplified by Quotations, Instructions, Etc. London: Robson and Son, 1886.

Hall, David D. ed. *Lived Religion in America: Toward a History of Practice.* Princeton: Princeton University Press, 1997.

Hansen, Karen. "End of the Line for 8 Catholic Schools." *Chicago Daily News*, June 28, 1968.

"Helping Milwaukee Working Girls." *Milwaukee Free Press*, June 11, 1916.

Henold, Mary J. *Catholic and Feminist: The Surprising History of the American Catholic Feminist Movement.* Chapel Hill: University of North Carolina Press, 2008.

Hilgers, Joseph. "Novena." *The Catholic Encyclopedia*, vol. 11. New York: Robert Appleton Company, 1911. http://www.newadvent.org/cathen/11141b.htm.

Hofbauer, Rita, GNSH, ed. *The Corporate Response: Why and How.* Silver Spring, Md.: Leadership Conference of Women Religious of the USA, 1988.

Hohn, Rev. H. *"Vocations": Conditions of Admission, Etc. into the Convents, Congregations, Societies, Religious Institutes, Etc., According to Authentical Information and the Latest Regulations.* Cincinnati: Benziger Bros., 1912.

Holbrook, Marj. "'Ordinary People' Called by God." *Beacon-News*, December 13, 1981.

"Horarium." *Oxford English Dictionary Online.* http://www.oed.com/.

Hoy, Suellen. *Good Hearts: Catholic Sisters in Chicago's Past.* Urbana: University of Illinois Press, 2006.

Illing, Patricia, RSM. *History of the Sisters of Mercy: Regional Community of Chicago.* Chicago: Sisters of Mercy of the Americas Regional Community of Chicago, 1994.

John XXIII. *Pacem in Terris.* http://www.vatican.va/holy_father/john_xxiii/encyclicals/documents/hf_j-xxiii_enc_11041963_pacem_en.html.

Julka, Christopher. "Top Need: Affordable Housing." *Beacon-News*, August 9, 1989.

Kantowicz, Edward R. "Cardinal Mundelein of Chicago and the Shaping of Twentieth-Century American Catholicism." In *Catholicism, Chicago Style*, edited by Ellen Skerrett, Edward R. Kantowicz, and Steven M. Avella, 63–78. Chicago: Loyola University Press, 1993.

Kauffman, Christopher. "Catholic Health Care in the United States: American Pluralism and Religious Meanings." *Christian Bioethics* 5, no. 1 (1999): 44–65.

Kaveny, M. Cathleen and James F. Keenan, SJ. "Ethical Issues in Health-Care Restructuring." *Theological Studies* 56, no. 1 (March 1995): 136–50.

Kennelly, Karen, CSJ. *Religious Formation Conference 1954–2004*. Silver Spring, Md.: Religious Formation Conference, 2009.

Koehlinger, Amy L. *The New Nuns: Racial Justice and Religious Reform in the 1960s*. Cambridge: Harvard University Press, 2007.

Koenig, Harry C. *A History of the Offices, Agencies, and Institutions of the Archdiocese of Chicago*. Chicago: Archdiocese of Chicago, 1981.

Kohler, Thomas C. "In Praise of Little Platoons, Quadragesimo Anno (1931)." In *Building the Free Society: Democracy, Capitalism, and Catholic Social Teaching*, edited by George Weigel and Robert Royal, 31–50. Grand Rapids, Mich.: William B. Eerdman Publishing Co., 1993.

Lantzer, Jason S. "Hoosier Episcopalians, the Coming of Women's Ordination and the 1979 Book of Common Prayer." *Anglican & Episcopal History* 72, no. 2 (2003): 229–54.

Layman-Roman, Maryangela. "St. Catherine Residence for Women: 'Home' and 'Family' to Thousands for 100 Years." *Catholic Herald*. January 12, 1995.

Lappetito, M. Michael, RSM. "Our Life Together in Mercy: Toward an Apostolic Spirituality." Federation of the Sisters of Mercy of the Americas, 1980.

Larkin, Emmet. *The Historical Dimensions of Irish Catholicism*. New York: Arno Press, 1984.

———. *The Pastoral Role of the Roman Catholic Church in Pre-Famine Ireland, 1750–1850*. Washington: The Catholic University of America Press, 2006.

Leo XIII, *Rerum Novarum (On Capital and Labor)*. May 15, 1891. http://www.vatican.va/holy_father/leo_xiii/encyclicals/documents/hf_l-xiii_enc_15051891_rerum-novarum_en.html.

Linstead, John. "Teacher Shortage: Nuns to Leave 10 Schools." *Chicago Daily News*. July 14, 1970.

Liptak, Dolores. *European Immigrants and the Catholic Church in Connecticut, 1870–1920*. New York: Center for Migration Studies, 1987.

———. *Immigrants and their Church*. New York: Macmillan, 1989.

———. "A US Sister of Mercy Dialogues with Tradition." *Mercy World*. http://www.mercyworld.org/_uploads/_ckpg/files/mirc/papers/liptakA4.pdf.

Maher, Mary Denis. *To Bind Up the Wounds: Catholic Sister Nurses in the U.S. Civil War*. New Orleans: Louisiana State University Press, 1999.

Magray, Mary Peckham. *The Transforming Power of the Nuns: Women, Religion, and Cultural Change in Ireland, 1750–1900*. New York: Oxford University Press, 1998.

Mangion, Carmen. *Contested Identities: Catholic Women Religious in Nineteenth-Century England and Wales*. Manchester, UK: Manchester University Press, 2008.

———. "Laying 'Good Strong Foundations': The Power of the Symbolic in the Formation of a Religious Sister." *Women's History Review* 16, no. 3 (September 2007): 403–15.

Mannard, Joseph. "Converts in Convents: Protestant Women and the Social Appeal of Catholic Religious Life in Antebellum America." *Records of the American Catholic Historical Society of Philadelphia* 104, no. 1 (1993): 79–90.

Marsden, George M. *Fundamentalism and American Culture, New Edition.* New York: Oxford University Press, 2006.

Massa, Mark S., SJ. *The American Catholic Revolution: How the 60s Changed the Church Forever.* New York: Oxford University Press, 2010.

McAuley, Catherine. *Familiar Instructions of Rev. Mother McAuley.* St. Louis: Vincentian Press, 1927.

McCarthy, Kathleen D. ed. *Lady Bountiful Revisited: Women, Philanthropy, and Power.* Newark: Rutgers University Press, 1990.

McDaniel, George William. "Catholic Action in Davenport: St. Ambrose College and the League for Social Justice." *Annals of Iowa* 55, no. 3 (Summer 1996): 239–72.

McDannell, Colleen. *The Christian Home in Victorian America, 1840–1900.* Bloomington: Indiana University Press, 1986.

———. *The Spirit of Vatican II: A History of Catholic Reform in America.* New York: Basic Books, 2011.

McDonald, John F. *Urban America: Growth, Crisis, and Rebirth.* New York: M.E. Sharpe, 2007.

McKenna, Mary Olga. "Paradigm Shift in a Women's Religious Institute: The Sisters of Charity, Halifax, 1950–1979." *Historical Studies* 61 (1995): 135–51.

Meagher, Timothy J. "Sweet Good Mothers and Young Women Out in the World: The Roles of Irish American Women in Late Nineteenth and Early Twentieth Century Worcester, Massachusetts." *US Catholic Historian* 5, no. 3/4 (June 1986): 325–44.

Melia, Susan Perschbacher. "Continuity in the Lives of Elder Catholic Women Religious." *The International Journal of Aging and Human Development* 48, no. 3 (April 1999): 175–89.

Melosh, Barbara. *The Physician's Hand: Work Culture and Conflict in American Nursing.* Philadelphia: Temple University Press, 1982.

Mercy Health Conference Task Force. *Dives in Misericordia (Rich in Mercy): A Guide to the Encyclical.* Farmington Hills, Mich.: Mercy Health Conference, 1983.

Meyerowitz, Joanne. *Women Adrift: Independent Wage Earners in Chicago, 1880–1930.* Chicago: University of Chicago Press, 1988.

Miller, Kerby A. *Emigrants and Exiles: Ireland and the Irish Exodus to North America.* New York: Oxford University Press, 1985.

"Misericordia Reconversion, Begin Care, Tests for Retarded Tots." *Brighton Park/McKinley Park Life*, January 20, 1955.

Monk, Maria. *The Awful Disclosures of Maria Monk, of, the Hidden Secrets of Nun's Life in a Convent Exposed.* Manchester: Milner, 1936.

Morneau, Rev. Robert. "'Aboutness': Religious Life Once-Removed." *Sisters Today* 45, no 3 (November 1973): 134–40.

"Most Precious Blood Parish Marks Golden Anniversary." *The New World*, November 29, 1957, 3.

Muckenhirn, Mary Charles Borromeo, CSC, ed. *The Changing Sister.* Notre Dame, Ind.: Fides Publisher, Inc., 1965.

Neuman, Mattias, OSB. "Religious Vows as a Pilgrim Stewardship." *Sisters Today* 45, no. 3 (November 1973): 123–33.

Nolan, Janet. *Ourselves Alone: Women's Emigration from Ireland, 1885–1920.* Lexington: University of Kentucky Press, 1989.

———. *Servants of the Poor: Teachers and Mobility in Ireland and Irish America.* Notre Dame, Ind.: University of Notre Dame Press, 2004.

Norbury, Frank B. "Dorothea Dix and the Founding of Illinois' First Mental Hospital." *Journal of the Illinois State Historical Society* 92, no. 1 (March 1999): 13–29.

Novak, Michael. "The New Nuns." *The Saturday Evening Post*, July 30, 1966, 22–25.

O'Brien, David J. *Public Catholicism.* Maryknoll, N.Y.: Orbis Books, 1996

O'Brien, Gabriel, RSM. *Reminiscences of seventy years (1846–1916): Sisters of Mercy, Saint Xavier's, Chicago.* Chicago: F. J. Ringley, 1916.

O'Connor, Isidore, RSM. *The Life of Mary Monholland, One of the Pioneer Sisters of the Order of Mercy in the West, by a Member of the Order.* Chicago: J. S. Hyland & Company, 1894.

O'Reilly, Bernard, SJ. *The Mirror of True Womanhood: A Book of Instruction for Women in the World.* New York: Collier, 1878.

"Ordination and Vocations." *Center for Applied Research in the Apostolate, 2008.* http://cara.georgetown.edu/ordvocation.pdf. July 18, 2011.

Orsi, Robert A. "Is the Study of Lived Religion Irrelevant to the World We Live In? Special Presidential Plenary Address, Society for the Scientific Study of Religion, Salt Lake City, November 2, 2002." *Journal for the Scientific Study of Religion* 42, no. 2 (June 2003): 169–74.

Orsi, Robert. *Madonna of the 115th Street: Faith and Community in Italian Harlem.* New Haven: Yale University Press, 1988.

O'Toole, James M. *The Faithful: A History of Catholics in America.* Cambridge, Mass.: Belknap Press, 2008.

Parisi, Tom. "Old Well House Foundation of Hope, City Trades Class, JoCo Join to Build a Home." *Beacon-News*, March 25, 1993.

Paul VI. *Lumen Gentium (Dogmatic Constitution of the Church).* (November 21, 1964), http://www.vatican.va/archive/hist_councils/ii_vatican_council/documents/vat-ii_const_19641121_lumen-gentium_en.html.

Peiss, Kathy. *Hope in a Jar: The Making of America's Beauty Culture.* New York: Henry Holt and Company, Inc., 1998.

Pius X. *Il Fermo Proposito (On Catholic Action in Italy to the Bishops of Italy)*. June 11, 1905. http://www.vatican.va/holy_father/pius_x/encyclicals/documents/hf_p-x_enc_11061905_il-fermo-proposito_en.html.

Pius XI. *Quadragesimo Anno (On the Reconstruction of the Social Order)*. May 15, 1931. http://www.vatican.va/holy_father/pius_xi/encyclicals/documents/hf_p-xi_enc_19310515_quadragesimo-anno_en.html.

Pride in Our Past; Faith in Our Future: 1869–1994. Davenport, Iowa: Mercy Hospital Davenport, 1994.

Reed, Rebecca. *Six Months in a Convent, or, the Narrative of Rebecca Theresa Reed, Who Was Under the Influence of the Roman Catholics About Two Years, and an Inmate of the Ursuline Convent on Mount Benedict, Charlestown, Mass., Nearly Six Months, in the Years 1831–2*. Boston: Russell, Odiorne & Metcalf, 1835.

Remigius Lafort, S.T.D., Censor. *The Catholic Church in the United States of America, Undertaken to Celebrate the Golden Jubilee of His Holiness, Pope Pius X, Volume II: The Religious Communities of Women*. New York: The Catholic Editing Company, 1914.

Rissing, Deborah. "A Healing Ministry after 10 Years of Crusading for Public Health, Sister Sheila Lyne Returns to Running a Hospital, the Job She Believes she was Called to Do." *Chicago Tribune*, January 3, 2001.

Robinson, James C. and Paul B. Ginsburg. "Consumer-Driven Health Care: Promise and Performance." *Health Affairs* 28, no. 2 (March/April 2009): W272–W281.

Rooeny, Miriam, OP. "The New Breed Enters the Convent." *Cross & Crown* 16 (December 1964): 396–405.

"Rosemary Welter." *Milwaukee Sentinel*. May 4, 2009. http://milwaukeeachiever.org/blog/2009/05/11/sister-rosemary-welter-rsm/.

Ruffing, Janet K., RSM. "The Burning of the Heart on Account of Creation." *The MAST Journal* 5 no. 2 (Spring 1995): 23–29.

———. "Enkindling the Embers: The Challenge of Current Research on Religious Life." *The MAST Journal* 4, no. 2 (Spring 1994): 7–14.

Ruffing, Janet and Theresa Moser. "An Option for Women?" *The Way* (Summer 1992): 89–100.

Ryan, Mary P. *Cradle of the Middle Class: The Family in Oneida County, New York, 1790–1865*. New York: Cambridge University Press, 1981.

Sabourin, Justine, RSM. *The Amalgamation: A History of the Union of the Religious Sisters of Mercy of the United States of America*. Saint Meinrad, Ind.: Abbey Press, 1976.

Sadlier, Mary Ann. *Bessy Conway, The Irish Girl in America*. New York: D. & J. Sadlier & Co., 1861.

———. *The Young Ladies Reader*. New York: D. & J. Sadlier & Co., 1875.

Schivelbusch, Wolfgang. *Railway Journey: The Industrialization of Time and Space in the 19th Century*. Berkeley: The University of California Press, 1986.

Schier, Tracy and Cynthia Russett, eds. *Catholic Women's Colleges in America*. Baltimore: The Johns Hopkins University Press, 2002.

Schlumpf, Heidi. "Call Waiting: The Stories of Five Women Who Want to Be Priests." *US Catholic* 66, no. 2 (February 2001), 12–17.

Shaw, Stephen J. "The Cities and the Plains, A Home for God's People: A History of the Catholic Parish in the Midwest." In *The American Catholic Parish, A History from 1850 to the Present, Volume II, The Pacific, Intermountain West and Midwest States*, edited by Jay P. Dolan, 304–56. New York: Paulist Press, 1987.

Sheehan, Lourdes, RSM; Mary Bender; and Stephen O'Brien. *A Study of Opinions and Attitudes of the Sisters of Mercy, Members of Mercy High Education Colloquium, Mercy Secondary Education Association, and Mercy Elementary Education Network*. Silver Spring, Md.: Sisters of Mercy of the Union, 1986.

Schulte, Lisa. "Six Regional Mercy Communities to Merge." *National Catholic Reporter*, February 23, 2007.

Shultz, Nancy Lusignan. *Fired & Roses: The Burning of the Charlestown Convent, 1834*. New York: The Free Press, 2000.

Siegfried, Regina, ASC. "Religious Formation Conference: 'Educating for Deepening Relationships: Theological/Communal/Societal/ Cultural/Ecological.'" *American Catholic Studies* 120, no. 1 (2009): 55–72.

"Sisters in Charge." *Chicago Tribune*, February 1920.

Sisters of Mercy. *The Customs and Minor Regulations of the Religious Called Sisters of Mercy in the Parent House, Baggot Street and Its Branch Houses*. Dublin: J. M. O'Toole, and Son, 1869.

———. *Customs and Regulations of the Sisters of Mercy, in the Dioceses of Providence, RI*. Providence, R.I.: J. A. & R. A. Reid, Printers, 1886.

———. *Rule and Constitutions of the Religious Called the Sisters of Mercy*. Pittsburgh: J. Porter, 1852.

———. *Rule and Constitutions of the Religious Called the Sisters of Mercy*. Philadelphia: H. L. Kilner & Co., 1890.

———. *Rule and Constitutions of the Religious Called the Sisters of Mercy*. Dublin: Browne and Littlefield, 1913.

Sisters of Mercy of the Union. *Constitutions of the Institute of the Religious Sisters of Mercy of the Union in the United States of America*. Bethesda/Washington: Sisters of Mercy General Motherhouse, 1941.

———. *Constitutions of the Sisters of Mercy of the Union*. Silver Spring, Md.: The Sisters of Mercy of the Union, 1986.

———. *Customs and Guide of the Institute of the Religious Sisters of Mercy of the Union in the United States of America*. Bethesda/Washington: Sisters of Mercy General House, 1957.

———. *Mercy Covenant, Special General Chapter Proceedings*. Washington: Sisters of Mercy Generalate, 1969.

———. *Mercy Covenant.* Bethesda, Md.: Sisters of Mercy of the Union/Sisters of Mercy Generalate, 1972.

Sisters of Mercy Chicago Regional Community. *Mercy.* Des Plaines, Ill: Mother of Mercy Novitiate, 1948.

Sivulka, Juliann. "From Domestic to Municipal Housekeeper: The Influence of the Sanitary Reform Movement on the Changing Women's Roles in America, 1860–1920." *Journal of American Culture* 22, no. 4 (December 1999): 1–7.

"The Sisters of Mercy—Contemporary Profiles." *The Defender—West, Chicago Defender.* March 21, 1981, 13.

Sklar, Kathryn Kish. *Florence Kelley and the Nation's Work.* New Haven: Yale University Press, 1995.

Smith-Rosenberg, Carroll. "Beauty, Beast, and the Militant Woman: A Case Study in Sex Roles and Social Stress in Jacksonian America." *American Quarterly* 23, no. 4 (October 1971): 562–84.

"State of the Sisters." *America* 204, no. 4 (February 14, 2011): 8.

Stewart, Jr., George C. *Marvels of Charity: History of American Sisters and Nuns.* Huntington, Ind.: Our Sunday Visitor Inc., 1994.

"The Structure and Meaning of the Mass." *United States Conference of Catholic Bishops, 2011.* http://www.usccb.org/prayer-and-worship/sacraments/eucharist/structure-and-meaning-of-the-mass-backgrounder.cfm.

Suenens, Leon Joseph. *The Nun in the World.* Translated by Geoffrey Stevens. Westminster, Md.: The Newman Press, 1963.

Sullivan, Mary C. *Catherine McAuley and the Tradition of Mercy.* Notre Dame, Ind.: University of Notre Dame Press, 1995.

———. "Catherine McAuley in the Nineteenth and Twenty-First Centuries." In Elizabeth Davis, Anne Hannon, Mary Lyons, Sophie McGrath, Mary Noel Menezes, Mary Sullivan, and Elaine Wainwright, eds. "'Fire Cast on the Earth-Kindling': Being Mercy in the Twenty-First Century." International Mercy Research Conference, November 9–12, 2007.

———. *The Correspondence of Catherine McAuley, 1818–1841.* Washington: The Catholic University of America Press, 2004.

Sunderman, Marilyn, RSM. "Dream Shaping/Dream Sharing: The Educational Vision of Catherine McAuley." *The MAST Journal* 6, no. 2 (Spring 1996): 52–56.

Szuda, Stephanie. "Ottawa Native Honored for Dedication to the Sick, Elderly, and Poor." *The Times,* April 19, 2010. http://www.mywebtimes.com/archives/ottawa/display.php?id=402260.

"Thank You for Your Service." *Catholic New World,* July 17, 2011.

Thompson, Margaret Susan. "Charism or Deep Story"? Toward a Clearer Understanding of the Growth of Women's Religious History in Nineteenth Century America." Review for Religious (May/June 1999): 230–50.

———. "Sisterhood and Power: Class, Culture, and Ethnicity in the American Convent." *Colby Quarterly* 25, no. 4 (September 1989): 149–75.

———. "To Serve the People of God: Nineteenth-Century Sisters and the Creation of an American Religious Life." Working Paper Series, Cushwa Center 18, no. 2 (Spring 1987).

———. "The Validation of Sisterhood: Canonical Status and Liberation, in the History of American Nuns." In *A Leaf from the Great Tree of God: Essays in Honour of Ritamary Bradley, SFCC*, edited by Margot H. King, 38–78. Toronto: Peregrina Publishing, 1994.

Tindall, George Brown and David E. Shi. *America: A Narrative History, Brief Sixth Edition*. New York: Norton, 2004.

Truesdell, Jeff and Sandra Sobieraj Westfall. "A Nun's Haven for the Disabled." *People* 73, no. 7 (February 22, 2010): 117.

Vermeersch, Arthur. "Cloister." *The Catholic Encyclopedia*. New York: Robert Appleton Company, 1908. *New Advent*. http://www.newadvent.org/cathen/04060a.htm.

"Vowed Members Invited to Contemplate Identity in Sacred Circles." *Vita* 15, no. 7 (July 2006): 12.

Wall, Barbara Mann. *American Catholic Hospitals: A Century of Changing Markets and Missions*. New Brunswick, N.J.: Rutgers University Press, 2011.

———. "Catholic Nursing Sisters and Brothers and Racial Justice in Mid-20th Century America." *ANS Adv Nurs Sci*. 32, no. 2 (2009): 81–93.

Ware, Susan. *Holding Their Own: American Women in the 1930s*. Boston: Twayne Publishers, 1982.

Werntz, Mary Regina, RSM. *Our Beloved Union: A History of the Sisters of Mercy of the Union*. Westminster, Md.: Christian Classics, Inc, 1989.

Wheeler, Carol Estelle, RSM. *Catherine: A Reflection on Values from the Mercy Tradition*. Baltimore: Mercy High School, 1991.

White, Deborah Gray. *Ar'n't I a Woman?: Female Slaves in the Plantation South*. Revised edition. New York: Norton, 1999.

Wittberg, Patricia, SC. *The Rise and Decline of Catholic Religious Orders: A Social Movement Perspective*. Albany: State University of New York Press, 1994.

Wolfe, Christopher. "Subsidiarity: The 'Other' Ground of Limited Government." In *Catholicism, Liberalism, and Communitarianism: The Catholic Intellectual Tradition and the Moral Foundation of Democracy*, edited by Kenneth L. Grasso, Gerard V. Bradley, and Robert P. Hunt, 81–96. London: Rowan and Littlefield Publishers, Inc., 1995.

"A Woman's Influence: Leo XII in Reply to a Deputation of Ladies." *Donohoe's Magazine* 1, no. 3 (March 1879): 224.

"You've Come a Long Way, Sister: The Editors Interview Sister Doris Gottemoeller, RSM." *U.S. Catholic* 65, no. 5 (May 2000): 18–22.

Zambrano, Mark. "School a Beacon of Hope in Austin." *Chicago Tribune*, May 27, 1985.

Index